WHERE LESS THE PATH IS WORN

The Eastern Continental Trail
Trail of the Ancients

by
M. J. Eberhart
Nimblewill Nomad

Thirsty Turtle Press™
Bloomingdale, Ohio

International Standard Book Number 978-1-64945-820-9
Library of Congress Control Number 1649458207

Published in Bloomingdale, Ohio, USA, by Thirsty Turtle Press™
4458 Andover Drive, Evans, Georgia 30909

Printed in the United States of America by Kindle Direct Publishing©
440 North Terry Avenue, North Seattle, WA 98109

Second Edition

Cover Photo by M. J. Eberhart – Entitled "God's Footprints"
Back Cover Photo by Wilfred E. Richard©
Cover Design by Dane Low, Ebook Launch©
Nomad Sketch by Lisa Harvey©
Book Scenes Sketched by Lena Auxier©
Edited by Sandra Friend
Formatted by Andrea Reider
Indexed by Index Busters©

To learn more about *Nimblewill Nomad*, to order copies of this book
or other books by this author, please visit nimblewillnomad.com.

TABLE OF CONTENTS

FOREWORD

It was the fall of 1999 and I had just finished my first long hike. I had found my way to Hanover, New Hampshire for the annual ALDHA Gathering, a seminar for hikers. I sat and listened as Eb *Nimblewill Nomad* Eberhart told of his remarkable journey from Key West to Cap Gaspé, Canada. That evening he guided the capacity crowd on a magical journey through life on the trail. He shared with us the hardships he had endured: the snow, ice and frigid temperatures of the north; the constant rain along the 1,000 miles of swampy Florida Trail; and the intense loneliness he felt as he welcomed new people into his life only to watch them leave—an hour, a day, or a week later. Each person, each place held a memory for him.

He also spoke of magic. He shared stories of the lives he had touched, and of those that had touched him. He talked about wanderlust, of that wind-in-your-hair kind of freedom, of fellowship and harmony. Of peace of mind. He taught his captivated audience many things that night, but the one lesson that stuck with me more than any other was his sincere conviction that we should all get busy working on our "one-of-these-days list" now, while we can.

Of all the hikers that venture to walk the entire 2,200-mile Appalachian Trail (AT), only about ten percent make it. It was thought to be unhikeable until Earl Shaffer accomplished the feat in 1948. Today somewhere between seven and ten thousand people have "thru-hiked" the AT.

The reason for such a high attrition rate is not the first hurdle, but most often the second. The first hurdle of any long walk is the physical part; the breaking in and toning up of the body. The second hurdle—the mental hurdle—is not so easily jumped however; unlike the physical hurdle, the mental hurdle seems to increase with the miles. Spending hours or days alone, walking mile after mile with only your thoughts and the sound of the wind to keep you company can wear on a weary hiker.

Imagine a journey more than twice as long as the AT, a journey not conveniently mapped out in data books and guide books. Imagine a journey that, on each end, loses the safety and simple comforts offered by the AT shelter system. Just a few short years ago that path did not exist, but today it is known as the Eastern Continental Trail (ECT).

Key West, Florida to Cap Gaspé, Canada. 5,000 miles. Ten million steps. Only a handful of people have accomplished the feat since John Brinda first hiked it in 1997. Only one person has done it twice. *One.*

Eb Eberhart is the kind of guy who would never be happy taking four balls and a walk from the pitcher. He would rather reach out and take a swing and run the bases, sliding into home plate as the ball arrives, spent from his run around the bases, jubilant with the experience he had just devoured. He is a firm believer that no land has yet been truly discovered. That, if we are willing, we can indeed go anywhere and make new discoveries.

Sure to brighten your day with his boyish grin and a bit of poetry, Eb was the second person to hike the ECT from end to end. He completed that adventure in November of 1998. That journey had such a dramatic impact on him that he had to return. In May of 2000 he returned to Cap Gaspé in Québec to discover North America's Appalachian Mountain range once again.

With more than 15,000 miles under his feet, Eb knows the struggle, the physical and mental pain that goes with long distance hiking. But his is not a story of pain. His story tells of so much more than blistered feet and the moan and groan of the next climb. Ah, this is a story of discovery, of jubilation. It is not a story of conquering, but of being conquered, and submitting oneself to the peace that comes with following a dream, to the peace that comes with having quiet time to think, to the peace that comes with living in harmony.

Friends, this is the first-hand account of the first southbound hike ever of the Eastern Continental Trail. It gives a taste of the daily experience of the people and places and the joys and heartache of more than eleven months on the trail and road, discovering a little more of North America with every step.

This book will fuel your wanderlust and may just restore your faith in humanity. Somewhere between Canada and Key West, you will find yourself laughing and crying with—and at—*Nimblewill*, rooting him on to the climax of this magnificent journey in Key West, Florida.

Just as clearly as I remember meeting him that first time in Hanover, I remember standing at the southernmost tip of North America, waiting with several other friends to see Eb complete this journey. I have been chasing my own dreams ever since.

Daniel *Sheltowee* Rogers
Author, *America, One Step at a Time*
sheltoweehikes.com

PROLOGUE

A REMARKABLE VISION

These are exciting times in the continuing evolution of hiking trails in eastern North America—for both the Eastern Continental Trail (ECT), which encompasses nearly the entire breadth of the eastern North American continent, and Trail of the Ancients (TA), which passes o'er the entire Appalachian Mountain range, from Flagg Mountain in central Alabama, to the far northern reaches of Newfoundland—Belle Isle, in "Iceberg Alley," the Labrador Sea. At the time of the first writing (2004), two new trail organizations were up and running, growing and prospering, the Alabama Hiking Trail Society, and the Newfoundland Labrador Chapter of the International Appalachian Trail (IAT).

As the remaining miles of footpath along the central Appalachians become protected on the venerable old Appalachian Trail, folks in Alabama are working diligently in the southern Appalachians to close the gap in a grand system of trails that will ultimately link to provide over 5,000 miles of uninterrupted treadway. And to the north, on the island of Newfoundland, enthusiastic trail builders are busy extending the trail system clear to the end of the Appalachian Mountains—as we know them to exist on the North American continent. No doubt, Benton MacKaye, the visionary who started the *vision*, would look on this with much favor.

And so, it is indeed humbling, what a great honor, and what a joy to know and to be associated with these great new trail pioneers, to be part of such a remarkable, continuing *vision*.

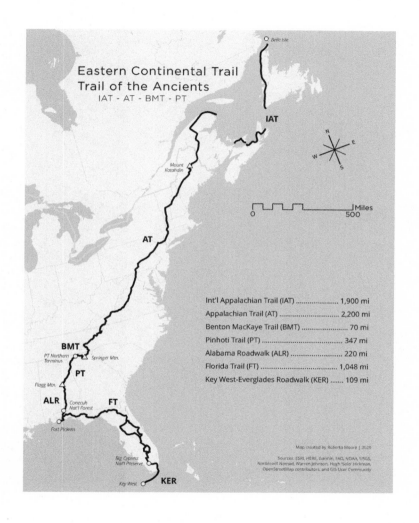

Eastern Continental Trail
Trail of the Ancients
IAT - AT - BMT - PT

Belle Isle

IAT

Mount
Katahdin

AT

Miles
0   500

AT

Int'l Appalachian Trail (IAT) .... 1,900 mi
Appalachian Trail (AT) .... 2,200 mi
Benton MacKaye Trail (BMT) .... 70 mi
Pinhoti Trail (PT) .... 347 mi
Alabama Roadwalk (ALR) .... 220 mi
Florida Trail (FT) .... 1,048 mi
Key West-Everglades Roadwalk (KER) .... 109 mi

BMT
PT Northern
Terminus   Springer Mtn.
PT
Flagg Mtn.
ALR   Conecuh
Nat'l Forest   FT
Fort Pickens

Big Cypress
Nat'l Preserve
Key West   KER

Map created by Roberta Moore | 2020

Sources: ESRI, HERE, Garmin, FAO, NOAA, USGS,
Nimblewill Nomad, Warren Johnson, Hugh 'Solo' Hickman,
OpenStreetMap contributors, and GIS User Community

INTRODUCTION

This is a true story about a 347-day trek by foot covering well over 5,000 miles, from the Cliffs of Forillon, Cap Gaspé, Québec Province, Canada, where the St. Lawrence meets the sea, to the southernmost point on the eastern North American continent in Key West, Florida. The journey doesn't end there, but returns north again, all the way to the island of Newfoundland, to continue among the Long Range Appalachian Mountains as they rise to meet the tundra, clear to the tip of the Great Northern Peninsula where the Vikings first landed over 1,000 years ago. Journey's end is on Belle Isle, the remaining mountaintop, the final bastion along the majestic Appalachians to hold its head above "Iceberg Alley" in the Labrador Sea.

As to this adventure, and as a distinction, this is the first known trek to cover the entire Appalachian Mountain range, at least as we know it to exist on the North American continent.

This odyssey is narrated in first person (journal entry) format, in hopes you might enjoy journeying along from day to day. Though vicarious your quest, be prepared to experience the joy, endure the pain, and test the loneliness and toil that only a trek of such magnitude could ever offer up. As it has been for *Nimblewill Nomad*, it is hoped this adventure will also prove a journey of inspiration and discovery for you. Indeed, the eastern North American continent is grand, such an expansive and magnificent place, with its natural beauty, its beautiful people.

But, dear friends, the delight of such discovery can be neither realized nor least understood by comfortably riding along in your air conditioned automobile. One must walk to truly *see* and understand. *Where Less the Path is Worn* will take you along that way. And so, a warning—this journey, unfortunately, will require that you also endure the doggedness of it, the seemingly countless miles, the countless days, the countless journal entries. You, too, must endure, as did *Nimblewill*. But your reward, your payoff is the magic of discovery; it's here among these pages.

He who rides and keeps the beaten track studies the fences chiefly.
(Thoreau)

CHAPTER 1

THE INTERNATIONAL APPALACHIAN TRAIL (IAT)

Wednesday—May 24, 2000
Trail Day—1
Trail Mile—5
Location—Cap Bon Ami overlook, Forillon National Park, Québec

This journey begins at the Cliffs of Forillon, Québec, Canada, the very tip of the Gaspé Peninsula—a place better known as "Land's End," where the St. Lawrence meets the north Atlantic. By the light-house, three hundred feet above the sea, two bronze plaques adorn their separate pedestals, marking the *beginning of the IAT. This footpath leads generally south and west through the provinces of Québec (and now Nova Scotia and Prince Edward Island), to New Brunswick, then into the state of Maine where it ends at Baxter State Park, a distance of some 730 miles. On Mount Katahdin, in Baxter

---

* *Since the first edition of this book was published in 2004, the IAT has greatly expanded its presence in the world. To read about these exciting developments, please visit wikipedia.org/wiki/International_Appalachian_Trail.*

State Park, I'll pick up the Appalachian National Scenic Trail, to follow it for over 2,100 miles, through the mountains and valleys of fourteen states, to Springer Mountain, Georgia. From there, I'll continue generally south on the Benton MacKaye Trail, the Georgia Pinhoti Trail, and the Alabama Pinhoti Trail. Then, by roadwalk, I'll connect with the Florida National Scenic Trail in the Florida Panhandle. These connector trails, plus the roadwalk, amount to some 550 miles. At Gulf Islands National Seashore, where the Florida Trail begins, I'll follow the Florida Trail east, then south, through the state of Florida for an additional 1,200 miles—all the way to the Everglades west of Miami. The final leg, God willing, will be a roadwalk of approximately 175 miles to the southernmost point on the eastern North American continent in Key West. This system of trails, with accompanying roadwalks, is becoming known as The Eastern Continental Trail (ECT), which covers a distance of approximately 4,800 miles. It will take some ten months to complete this journey along the ECT. I'm ready—if you're ready, let's get going!

I'm filled with both excitement and nervous anticipation, for I have been waiting so long for this adventure to begin. Arrangements have been made for Benoit "Ben" Gagnon, an interpretive warden here at Forillon National Park, to drive us to the cliffs at Cap Gaspé. John *John O* O'Mahoney, who will be hiking south with me, says goodbye to his son, Sean, who has driven us to Canada, and we're off to the Cliffs of Forillon. On the way, Ben talks about these aged and timeless Appalachians. He explains that the mountain we are approaching is one of the oldest of the old.

The IAT wastes little time getting right to our initiation. As Ben drops us off, the harsh winds are driving bitterly cold rain inland from the Sea of St. Lawrence. In my last conversation with Dick Anderson, President, IAT, he urged me to be careful descending the cliffs where the mountains meet the sea. The last 100 vertical feet are over rock and shale—a very treacherous beginning. Both *John O* and I, however, are determined to begin this odyssey in the surf, where the Appalachians plunge to the ocean floor, so down we go. We make the descent without incident to pluck some pebbles from Land's End, and at three in the afternoon we depart for Key West, Florida, the southernmost point on the eastern North American continent.

Though it is but by footsteps ye do it.
And hardships may hinder and stay,
Walk with faith, and be sure you'll get through it;
*For **where there's a will there's a way**.*
(Eliza Cook)

Thursday—May 25, 2000
Trail Day—2
Trail Mile—17
Location—Les Crêtes Trail near Le Portage Trail, Forillon National Park, Québec

The rain and wind continue as we break camp. The sea and mountains all around are in the shroud. As I pass, I pay little more than a nod to the observation tower atop Mont Saint-Alban. Had it been a clear day, we would have stood gazing from one of the most spectacular vistas I've ever witnessed in all my amblings along the entire Appalachian range. I try not to be disappointed. It is too early to deal with disappointment.

We climb to the ridge west of PQ-132. Here we get into bigtime snowpack. Our progress slows to a crawl. As the rain continues, the eggshell-thin snow crust becomes thinner and thinner. When I'm able to gain the snow crowns without breaking through, I have better luck. But as the afternoon wears on, the crust gives way with annoying and alarming regularity. *John O* is a big man. He's constantly post-holing, and is having a much tougher time of it.

> *Let me not follow the clamor of the world,*
> *But walk calmly in my path.*
> (Max Ehrmann)

Friday—May 26, 2000
Trail Day—3
Trail Mile—35
Location— Motel Flo Do, Rivière au Renard, Québec

The day dawns cold and rainy, the third straight. The hike today, through the western extent of the magnificent Forillon National Park, takes us quickly up to pass the delightful Lacs de Penouilles

4

(Pinwheel Lakes). This section of trail is the newest in the park, having been completed in 1998. It is a wonderful distinction and an honor to be the first to thru-hike the IAT in the Forillon, the first to see the striking view back down Rivière au Renard (Fox River) Valley, to the little village on the St. Lawrence Sea, and the first to witness the intimate lakes of the Pinwheels.

We haven't climbed far this morning before we're back in the snowpack. The rain works the snow crust to nearly a veil o'er the glistening whiteness. The depth of the drifts has increased, varying from two to nearly eight feet. There's moose sign everywhere, and there have been snowmobiles through sometime this past winter. We pass a snow depth-measuring field deep in the mountain interior. Apparently the Park Service monitors it at periodic intervals throughout the winter. We're able to follow the trail much easier as a result of the tracks, and the snow seems to be packed a little better. It is evident that *John O* and I are the first hikers through the Forillon this spring.

As the day passes, the snow becomes increasingly more difficult to negotiate. Our progress slows to nearly a standstill. When I interrupt my struggle to rest, and just look—in the presence of such total silence comes a very present uneasiness. The scenery is spellbinding. The ice on the little pinwheel lakes seems so forbidding, yet is there a unique and distinctive beauty. This is indeed a winter wonderland.

> *The winter! The brightness that blinds you,*
> *The white land locked tight as a drum,*
> *The cold fear that follows and finds you,*
> *The silence that bludgeons you dumb.*
> (Robert W. Service)

Saturday—May 27, 2000
Trail Day—4
Trail Mile—62
Location—Home of Ubaldine Dea, St-Yvon, Québec

Yesterday was a very long and tiring day. It was good to get out of the snowpack, off the mountain, and into Fox River to a warm room, a hot tub, and supper at Dixie Lees.

We're out early this morning, headed straight into the wind and rain to begin the roadwalk to Mont St-Pierre. Most folks don't care much for roadwalks, but I like them just fine, and this roadwalk is one of the finest in my book. But alas, this roadwalk certainly won't last, as trail building crews will be working all summer. Their goal: To move this IAT from the road to the ridge.

Currently, the trail follows PQ-132 along the St. Lawrence Sea for the better part of a hundred miles, past delightful French Canadian villages. To me it's like going back thirty to fifty years in time. The folks who live here take great pride in their homes, although most are very modest. The colors they choose to brighten the drear and cold of the harsh winter monochromes are a riot, an absolute jolt to the eye. White with fire engine red is predominant, but it isn't unusual to see orange, purple, and wild neon shades of blue, green and yellow mixed in. Clotheslines on pulleys are hooked to every house. Beside each are the universally staggering stacks of firewood. Up here, you can still run a tab at the local mom-n-pop grocery, and they'll deliver to your home if you can't get out—just like the little grocery store run by lifelong pal, Donnie, back in my sleepy little hometown deep in the Ozark Highlands of Missouri. Both up here and back home, people help each other. It's a way of life. And the payoff really shows, for these kind and generous folk are as happy and joy-filled as any I've ever met. Indeed, it is a beautiful thing.

Walking the road, one gets to meet and interact with the people; on the ridge, you don't have that opportunity. I like nature, and I like the mountains and woods about as much as anybody, but I like meeting the folks along the way just as much, if not more. Ahh, so now you know why the old *Nomad* dearly loves his roadwalks. This day is shaping to be remarkable, and for what better reason!

Toward evening, the rain intensifies as the wind keeps kicking hard and cold. I arrive at the little motel in St. Yvon where we'd hoped to stay, only to find weeds growing right up to the front door, and a "for sale" sign in the window. Up ahead, *John O* is drawn to the first house he comes to. He pulls off to inquire about accommodations further along the way. A frail little lady greets him at the door. She immediately invites him in. Arriving moments later I'm also invited in. Oh my, what a delightfully warm, cozy home. I meet Ubaldine Dea as she sets herself busy serving us grand slices of Gaspésian sugar pie along with cups of steaming hot coffee. After the second cup, my fingers start working again and I'm finally able to manage the fork to manage the pie...umm! Ubaldine speaks excellent English. We have a pleasant conversation over the pie and coffee. *John O* and I are both taken aback when she invites us to stay the night as her guests, and she is genuinely delighted when we accept her invitation. Ubaldine also insists on preparing breakfast for us in the morning. We do, however, manage to cut a deal on treating her to supper. So, after both *John O* and I enjoy the luxury of fifteen minutes each in Ubaldine's Jacuzzi, we are refreshed and ready to take her out to supper—in her car!

What had shaped up to be a hard, pound-it-out day turned into a remarkable and memorable one because of the generosity and kindness of this trusting and caring soul. We were but strangers along your way, Ubaldine Dea.

A trail goes by her way, the IAT.
And she, one rainswept day, befriended me.
Ubaldine Dea.

What joy has come my way, a mystery.
For miracles, they say, are history.
Ubaldine Dea.

*A debt I must repay, now filled with glee.
I search to find a way that pleases she.
Ubaldine Dea.

Alas, this dark-gloom day, what misery.
I find she's passed away...to Thee.
Ubaldine Dea.
(N. Nomad)

*I returned one year later bearing gifts for Ubaldine, to find her yard in weeds and the beautiful home that I had remembered in much disrepair. Her neighbors gave me the sad news of her death.

Sunday—May 28, 2000
Trail Day—5
Trail Mile—77
Location—Motel La Maree Haute, Grande-Vallée, Québec

After a welcome night's rest, *John O* and I are treated to a tank-stoking breakfast. We bid goodbye to our good friend Ubaldine Dea and are promptly greeted by another day of wind and cold, cold rain. Over the last two days, the road has climbed from the sea to the mountains, only to return again to the sea, and then to repeat the entire process again and again. I recall many delightful vistas along this way in '98, but the angry, swirling shroud will yield none of that beauty today.

Yet there is joy, as there always and inevitably seems to be, for it is as we are slogging along a vehicle pulls to the shoulder and stops. The driver emerges, dons his rain jacket and heads straight for *John O* and me. Oh my, it's Viateur DeChamplain from Matane, the Québec director for the IAT. Viateur has a bag of goodies for us, along with much-welcome upbeat conversation!

This day has been a long, bitter cold, soaking roadwalk. As we near Petite-Vallée we're both ready to call it a day, so into the little mom-n-pop grocery I go to look up my friend Jean "Jeff" François LeBreux, who befriended me in '98. Sure enough, he's still here. Jeff's face lights up in a beaming ear-to-ear grin as he exclaims, "*Nimblewill Nomad!*" Jeff had driven me to Grand-Vallée in '98 so I could find a place for the night. After a short while, Jeff loads us and we head once more for Grand-Vallée. Folks helping folks—ahh, 'tis indeed a beautiful thing!

> *Then come the wild weather,*
> *Come sleet or come snow,*
> *We will stand by each other,*
> *However it blow.*
> (Simon Dach)

Monday—May 29, 2000
Trail day—6
Trail Mile—94
Location— Motel du Rocher, Madeleine-Center, Québec

What a blessing to see the morning dawn to clear skies. Five constant and steady days of cold rain tend to wear on a fellow. Patience is a great virtue when one can muster enough of it!

The restaurant at La Marée Haute is a fine establishment. The place has been totally remodeled since I came through back in '98; all whiz bang new. I went over last night for spaghetti and was treated royally, so it's back again for breakfast this morning.

The plan today is to hike from the motel here at Grande-Vallée to Petite-Vallée, going south to north on the trail. Once there, we'll get a ride back again with Jeff to the motel here at Grande-Vallée. This plan works out just great, and Jeff has us back and on our way south again before eleven, Thanks, Jeff!

The road winds up and around through the mountains for the better part of the day to finally descend back to the sea and the little village of Rivière Madeleine, location of the fine restaurant Chez Mamie, Annie Langlois, proprietor. Her son Gilbert waits tables. As I enter I inquire about Gilbert. Annie calls her son, who comes right away—to swell up into that familiar broad-beaming Canadian smile as he sees the old *Nomad*! *John O* comes in and we enjoy a delicious spaghetti dinner served in grand fashion as we enjoy the evening searching the sea, looking for whales.

After a pleasant short nap in the comfortable living room, we head back out into the evening for a short roadwalk past the old lighthouse to Madeleine-Center and the Motel du Rocher. A delightful and enjoyable day.

> *I've also seen the storm clouds burst,*
> *And winds go rushing thro',*
> *But I always knew that once again*
> *I'd see my "Patch of Blue."*
> (Mary Newland Carson)

Tuesday—May 30, 2000
Trail Day—7
Trail Mile—106
Location—L'Anse-Pleureuse Gîte, L'Anse-Pleureuse, Québec

We are greeted by another fine day weather-wise as we continue our roadwalk west following PQ-123, a scenic, picturesque byway along the St. Lawrence Sea. We no sooner get the old jitneys warmed up good than we arrive beside a gravel drive leading to a lovely home beside the sea. The sign reads "Café Chez Diane, Repast Complet, Ouvert des 6hr. AM." Whipping out the little user-friendly and comprehensive *Bilingual Hiking Glossary,* with cross references for most-oft-used French and English words and terms (prepared for the IAT by Suzanne Bailey, Emma Jean Bailey, Jocelyne DeChamplain and Francis R. Wihbey), I'm able to determine that this lovely, well-kept home by the sea is actually a restaurant that serves all meals, and is open in the morning at six. In we go!

A pleasant, clean and tidy home it is, and indeed it is a home. We're seated in the dining room just off the kitchen. The bathroom is on the second floor across the hall from the bedroom. No his and hers, no exit signs, no emergency lighting, no fire extinguishers, no hood over the grill, no "no shoes, no shirt, no service" signs, just good wholesome food served up by the lady of the house with that rosy, broad-beaming French Canadian smile. Oh yes folks, we're going back at least half a century in time here as we enjoy these quaint, far away storybook lands along the St. Lawrence Sea—and the beautiful people living here.

As *John O* and I enjoy our breakfast, we see a fellow pass by on the road. He's heading west the same as us. It isn't until later when *John O* crosses paths with him again in a hardware store in Mont Louis that we realized he's the fellow we had been hearing about who's hiking the Gaspé Peninsula, collecting funds for "Dogs for the Blind." He's Andre Ducet, from Sainte-Foy, Québec, a gregarious and pleasant fellow. We first heard about him a couple of days ago. An auto speeding east screeched to a halt in the road, the passenger's hand came out, the kind lady quickly thrust five dollars into *John O's* hand, then just as quickly sped away. We looked at each other and shrugged. The best I could manage was, "John, I've told you about the people of Canada." In the hardware store *John O* finally gets the opportunity to deliver the lady's generous donation (plus a little extra) to where it rightfully belongs.

Today has been a totally pleasant hiking day along the sea and into the Gîte (B&B) at L'Anse-Pleureuse.

Beautiful faces are those that wear—
It matters little if dark or fair—
Whole-souled honesty printed there.
(Ellen P. Allerton)

Wednesday—May 31, 2000
Trail Day—8
Trail Mile—116
Location— Motel Mont St-Pierre, Mont Saint-Pierre, Québec.
Charlotte Auclair and Raymond Boily, proprietors.

Today will be our final, short day on the roadwalk west along the St. Lawrence. As I hike, enjoying the cool prevailing breeze from the sea, and the soul-calming scenic beauty of these timeless mountains as they meet the restless waves, I hearken back to a day not unlike this day, the day in '98 when I completed this very roadwalk at its eastern extent at Fox River. This time, it seems the time has passed so fast. Perhaps it's because then I had been on the trail so long by myself, and now I've had the luxury of pleasant company the whole way. Isn't it always more fun, and doesn't the time go faster, when one's joy is shared with others!

By early afternoon we arrive at the motel in Mont Saint-Pierre, to be greeted enthusiastically by my dear friends, Raymond and Charlotte. When they see me, that grand ear-to-ear Canadian smile lights both their faces. Raymond and I relax, catching up on events of the past two years. From the comfortable sitting room at the Motel Mont St-Pierre, Raymond points out a killer (orca) whale casually negotiating the harbor. As I sit here surrounded by this natural beauty, I wonder at the grandness of it all. The snowmelt is in full tilt, creating the most remarkable waterfall erupting from the very brink of the western bay escarpment. This tumultuous cataract must be in total free-fall for nearly 400 feet before careening from the angular rock face to plunge to the rocks and boulders below. The unparalleled grandeur, the joy-filled, beautiful Canadian people with their romantic and fascinating language; it is all so inspiring, making this little niche by the corner of the sea in Québec one of the most spellbinding places on earth.

Tomorrow we'll depart this place for Matapédia, Québec, to hike south from there on the IAT into New Brunswick. We will not be able to complete the grand traverse just ahead, over the tundra of Mont Jacques-Cartier, Mont Xalibu, Mont-Albert and Mont Logan, until the 24th of June. We will return then, once again, to this magic place by the sea to complete the traverse.

> *A smile is a light in the window of the soul*
> *indicating that the heart is home.*
> (Anonymous)

Thursday—June 1, 2000
Trail Day—9
Trail mile—116
Location— Motel Restigouche, Matapédia, Québec, Pete Dubé, proprietor.

Today will be a zero-mile trail day, a bus and train ride from Gaspé to Matapédia. *John O* and I are served a fine breakfast, prepared by Charlotte and brought to our table by Raymond. At Motel Mont St-Pierre, they have provided us the kindest Canadian hospitality. These generous folks would accept no payment for our room or for the services and fine meals provided us. They seemed content in their obvious pleasure of just having us as their guests. It's been such a joy sharing their company. Raymond and Charlotte, thank you for your generosity and kindness! You're Canada to the core, the finest example of your country's kind and generous people. I'll remain in your debt.

The bus ride back to Gaspé seems so short compared to the roadwalk. It's fun looking for little things again along the way, things one would only see while walking, like how the door is shaped and built on one of the neat little dwellings by the sea, or a narrow drive leading away to the mountains. Soon we reach Gaspé, and are immediately offered a ride to the train station way across the bridge.

Ever since I found out there was a passenger train still running up here, I've wanted to take a ride on it. There's something about trains. It's the old fashioned coming out in me I suppose, the nostalgia of it. Few passenger trains are still running in the states. Aside from Amtrak, those are little more than a novelty. Up here, there is an actual need for the train. There are folks who depend on this service.

And what a joy this ride turns out to be! As the train lurches, pitches, squeaks and moans out of Gaspé, sweet memories of my childhood come flooding back, of when Mother would take sis and me back east to visit our grandparents. Grandpa worked as a stationmaster for the Pennsylvania Railroad for as long as I could remember, and every summer or so he would send us tickets for the Missouri Pacific and the Pennsylvania Railroads, for the train ride to visit them. Those were grand times. Sitting in this old passenger car with my eyes closed, I can recall those times so vividly.

The trip takes us past Percé Rock, then along the bluffs of the Gaspé coast to pass through an impressive tunnel before finally arriving at Matapédia. Pete Dubé, owner of Motel Restigouche, kindly greets us and has our room all set. This has been a grand zero-mile day. Oh, but am I ever looking forward once more to the peace and solitude of the trail!

It seems to me I'd like to go
Where bells don't ring, nor whistles blow,
Nor clocks don't strike, nor gongs sound,
And I'd have stillness all around.
(Nixon Waterman)

Friday—June 2, 2000
Trail Day—10
Trail Mile—116
Location—Motel Restigouche, Matapédia, Québec

This day is spent in much-needed rest. We are late getting up and to the restaurant where Bruno Robert, one of my friends here in Matapédia, greets us. This is a day for working on journal entries and sorting equipment, organizing provisions, and preparing for our hike on to Squaw Cap and the canyon of the Restigouche.

Pete Dubé has been a member of the Life Extension Foundation for many years and is a strong proponent for a number of their natural health products. He and many of his friends have been taking them for years. Pete is sixty now and guides regularly for black bear and Atlantic salmon. A good friend of his (and now mine), Richard Adams, is in his nineties. Richard is a legend, for he has guided on the Matapédia, Kedgwick, and Restigouche Rivers for Atlantic salmon for over 75 years! One of the natural health products I take, provided by one of my sponsors, was first recommended to me by Pete. The The product is Osteo Bi-Flex, made by Sundown Corporation, a subsidiary of Rexall Drugs. This is a combination of Glucosamine HCL (1500 mg) and Chondroitin Sulfate (1200 mg). It promotes healthy joints and restores and rebuilds connective tissue—like in the knees! This product on its own, I truly believe, has kept me on the trail at near age 62.

In the evening, *John O* and I host the evening meal, a delightful get-together attended by Pete, Bruno and his girlfriend Carole, and David LeBlanc and his girlfriend Sally, with their new baby, India. Also present was David's brother Phil.

The journey not the arrival matters.
(T. S. Eliot)

Saturday—June 3, 2000
Trail Day—11
Trail Mile—138
Location—Glenwood Park near Dawsonville, New Brunswick

This day will be entirely a roadwalk as we cross the Restigouche River from Québec into New Brunswick, where we'll be hiking for the next couple of weeks. If plans work out, we should be somewhere near the US/Canada border in time to return to Mont Saint-Pierre, Québec, to complete the hike there across the tundra. Immediately ahead of us is an uninterrupted stretch of trail, the most demanding and technically difficult of any along the entire Appalachian range—the Restigouche Canyon. Then it's on to the two highest peaks in New Brunswick: Mount Carleton and Sagamook. From there we'll follow the Tobique River Valley to the St. John River, then around the Aroostook River to the border.

Before beginning our hike, we had stopped in to meet François Boulanger, Director, Parc National de la Gaspésie, at the Provincial Park offices in Saint-Anne-des-Monts. He requested that we delay our entry into the Chic Chocs until the 24th of June due to the ice conditions on the tundra and the caribou calving season; thus our plans at present and the reasoning.

Except for a few minutes walking through hail, the roadwalk today is uneventful, which is always nice for any roadwalk. In '98, part of this hike involved a climb over the third highest peak in New Brunswick, Squaw Cap. Due to continued timbering in the area, we were urged to take the alternate roadwalk route instead, so it has turned out to be a hammer-the-road day.

The friendly people of Canada have offered us many rides today. Their expressions are always humorous as the perplexed folks drive away after we politely decline their kindness. We are also offered much welcome and enjoyable conversation (plus water bottle refills) as we meet people out working in their yards on this beautiful Saturday.

By early evening we arrive at Glenwood Park. Glenwood was the first Provincial Park in New Brunswick but has been closed for a number of years. The entrance is barred, weeds and brush have taken over, and the whole place looks pretty well neglected. In the rear of the park remain a couple of buildings, one an old woodshed. I rearrange the place to make room for my bedroll while *John O* sets up under one of the old picnic table pavilions. This has been an enjoyable hiking day.

> *Afoot and lighthearted I take to the open road,*
> *Healthy, free, the world before me,*
> *The long brown path before me leading wherever I choose.*
> *Henceforth, I ask not good fortune, I myself am good fortune.*
> (Walt Whitman)

Sunday—June 4, 2000
Trail Day—12
Trail Mile—149
Location—Near the park bench, Restigouche Canyon overlook,
New Brunswick

The trail leads out of Glenwood Park to the mighty Restigouche Canyon. This day is a warm-up, with a few ups and down to get us prepared for the rollercoaster that will greet us the next few days as we hike south. The narrow, near-vertical cuts that interrupt the canyon rim are called gulches, and we are introduced to a few today. It is through these gulches that joyful brooks cascade to join the Restigouche, with the trail following along, straight down the gulch wall to the brook, across and just as abruptly straight up the next, to continue on interminably.

Today we manage 11 miles. *John O* and I are both exhausted, so, as we reach the main canyon overlook, complete with park bench, we decide to call it a day. Near the canyon but back from the wind, with the aid of birch bark, *John O* manages a fine warming and cooking fire. It will be "buckle the seatbelts" tomorrow.

> *The secrets of the Restigouche,*
> *Are known to only me.*
> *The first to hike this river trail,*
> *Along the IAT.*
> (N. Nomad)

Monday—June 5, 2000
Trail Day—13
Trail Mile—153
Location—Ridge above Upper Grindstone Brook, New Brunswick

We begin our hike through the canyon of the Restigouche, a remote, distant place, isolated except by boat to all except the most footloose and daring adventurer. This is indeed an enchanted land. For the next thirty miles, the IAT follows the broken and interrupted rim of the canyon of the Restigouche. The mountains here are not formidable by any standard, but the trail through this precipitous landscape follows the most rugged path that I have ever experienced. The strongest, fittest hiker cannot endure long without stopping to rest and wonder, to rest the spinning head from spinning free and to stop the pack-driven body from pitching straight off the next gulch wall. Then to wonder at the majesty, the rugged untamed beauty of it all. And finally, to wonder if there'll ever be an end.

Now begins the grand and indescribable challenge, for during the next three or four days we'll have scant moments of rest from the rigors of near-vertical ascents and descents. Interspersed, and just for variety, will be a mix of ice-cold fords and gulch wall side-slabbing. Each and every foot placement will be undertaken with total deliberation, for the risk of falling out of control to the gulch below remains a real and ever-present danger.

Bear scat and moose droppings appear all along the trail today, but we see neither animal. We've been blessed with beautiful weather, hiking from eight-thirty this morning until shortly after four this afternoon, with only a few brief breaks to rest and regain our strength. It will seem incredible but it is true that during this seven and one-half hours we have managed only 6,700 meters, a scant four miles. Through here today, as Bruce Otto, GAME '74 (Appalachian Trail, Georgia to Maine=GAME) would say, "A man can stand straight up and might-nigh bite the dirt."

All through these mountains there is cut,
A canyon long and deep.
And to its flank rush joyful brooks,
From gulches rough and steep.

And o'er this all the trail is laid,
Not for the faint at heart.
*Built by a chap they call *Maurice,*
A classic work of art.
(N. Nomad)

*Maurice Simon, IAT trail builder, New Brunswick

Tuesday—June 6, 2000
Trail Day—14
Trail Mile—161
Location—Woods road near Gilmore Brook, New Brunswick

We are greeted by gloom, but by mid-morning the mush burns away to reveal a beautiful warm day, plus blackflies and skeeters for real! The trail continues along the rim of the Restigouche Canyon. Over countless millions of years, this river has cut an amazing chasm all through these mountains. Where the mountains reach the canyon, they abruptly end, their ridgelines plunging to the canyon floor. Into each gulch goes the canyon wall, creating precipitous cuts. There goes the trail, up, down and through. Today the bone-numbing climbing continues, with some welcome interruption as the ridges widen some. But the gulches and ice-cold fords keep coming.

The old *Nomad* was the first to hike the canyon of the Restigouche. That was in the fall of '98. It appears that there have been very few travelers through here since. As I hike along I think of how this treadway must be much the same as was the treadway of another trail some fifty years ago. In *Walking With Spring*, Earl Shaffer's delightful book about his '48 thru-hike o'er the Appalachian Trail, Earl lamented as to having to literally walk on wildflowers growing directly in the trail! Much the same do we find this trail, as was the Appalachian Trail fifty years ago, for it is impossible to hike the treadway here without stepping on flowers and ferns, the beautiful and varicolored trillium and fiddleheads. So it's climb, climb, climb, trample, trample, trample; for it is impossible, as there is just no way to avoid stepping on Mother Nature's fragile, happy children.

The two days of rest at Pete's luxurious Restigouche Hotel have been a blessing to my shin splints. Oh yes, I've had problems. I was prepared for some very tough going through this section of trail, but the ankle swelling is settling down, and the shin pain has lessened.

It seems that today is the day to get lost. We are unable to follow the trail through Gilmore Brook. At first the treadway becomes very sketchy and difficult to follow, with many blowdowns and scant flagging. As we search ahead, following occasional blue and white survey taped trees, we arrive at what appears to be a worker's maintenance trail, which leads to a nearby access road. Here the flagging ends. Backtracking, we locate another flagged trail leading toward the gulch. After a little over a kilometer, climbing through countless blowdowns, then down and up another gulch, the flags end in an impenetrable wall of brush. So we backtrack again to the woods road for a long, circuitous hike around. After a mile or so we find a flat grassy spot and call it a day.

If in you there's some mountain goat,
Will serve you well indeed.
Sure-footedness on mountain walls,
A skill that you will need.

'Twill take you days to hike this through,
The miles you need not rush.
For it will take the strongest man,
And turn his limbs to mush.
(N. Nomad)

Wednesday—June 7, 2000
Trail Day—15
Trail Mile—169
Location—Woods road by Upper Thorn Point Brook, New Brunswick

We are greeted to an overcast morning, this one persistently stubborn. It is late morning before the sun manages to push some of the local clutter aside. We continue on the old logging road that tends to tack north-northwest. The river and its tributary brooks trend generally south-southwest, so we are hiking with the confidence that we will soon intersect the river and the trail again. We can see the open vastness and blue haze of the canyon off to our right, so this plan is working. Soon we pick up the familiar blue and white flagging, indicating we're once more on the IAT. I immediately recognize this spot; for it was here that I lost the trail in '98 and was unable to continue without taking the same detour around. Now I know why so much of the detour route looked familiar—I had hiked the same route, bumbling my way around, miraculously, the same way two years ago. It's just hard to remember a few steps out of ten million.

Since '98, the trail along the Restigouche has been marked to a great extent with the new metal blue and white IAT blazes. These are nailed to untreated dimensional eight-foot length, 2x4 spruce studs, the studs pointed and driven into the ground (as best can be driven) at strategic points along the trail. The original flagging in blue and white has survived amazingly well. Some sections have also been blazed with white paint blazes much like the venerable Appalachian Trail.

Do you ever have sort of a funk of a day? Oh yes, looks like this might be one of those days for me, for the cold and haze are hanging tight. Much as I hate to admit, I'm reverting to my old familiar thought patterns this morning—negative thought patterns. I'm thinking about the fact that this Restigouche section of trail now bypasses one of the most incredibly beautiful views anywhere along the trail in Canada, the view across and onto the sheer rock bluffs that form the Restigouche oxbow at Cross Point. In '98 it loomed forbidding and gray in the stark, mist-driven swirl of that morning, and I recall my thought being to forgive it this unwelcome gesture, as it would surely be a pleasant and grand place in the comforting rays of a warm, radiant sun. But alas, even as the sky is clearing and the day turns pleasant, this much anticipated vantage never comes, as I find this section has now been bypassed for the sake of saving a kilometer or two and eliminating one of the gulch pops. I don't understand this, I just don't understand.

So if you've got the yearn and bent,
I'd recommend to you,
To come and see what I have seen,
And plan to tough it through.
(N. Nomad)

Thursday—June 8, 2000
Trail Day—16
Trail Mile—184
Location—NB Trail km 243, near Saint-Jean-Baptiste-de-Resti-
gouche, New Brunswick

A good hiking day appears in order. The night was cold, but I kept warm and slept well. I like the luxury of the room in my Wanderlust Gear Nomad tent provided by another of my very kind sponsors, Kurt Russell from Myrtle Beach, South Carolina. The tent was designed and built by Kurt in order to fill a void in the lightweight gear market. At well under two pounds, it is by far the lightest and roomiest one-person backpacking tent on the market. Thanks, Kurt, for providing me your great product for Odyssey 2000, and thank you for your friendship!

We don't get far today before the trail wanders into a large clear-cut. There are no blazes and no flagging. We manage to beat around the brush in the clear-cut and find a couple of flags which seem to indicate the direction the trail once went. We check all along the clear-cut border for well over an hour, but are unable to locate where the trail goes back into the woods. Reluctantly, we finally turn to the logging road and follow it to the little village of Saint-Jean-Baptiste-de-Restigouche. From here, we pick up the NB Trail and head for Kedgwick, where there are many dear friends. The Restigouche hike is now history. There have been many memorable moments and we've made it through safely.

> *And now I bid thee, Restigouche,*
> *Enchanted land: "farewell."*
> *If you would know its secrets, come;*
> *For I will never tell.*
> (N. Nomad)

Friday—June 9, 2000
Trail Day—17
Trail Mile—193
Location—Home of Maurice Simon and Anne Marie Pallot, Kedgwick, New Brunswick

The NB Trail is an old rail-trail running across New Brunswick. We picked it up yesterday at Saint-Jean-Baptiste-de-Restigouche and followed it to Kedgwick, pitching for the evening by a little stream near a lovely meadow. We'll hike this very same NB Trail through part of the Tobique River Valley, as it is shared with the IAT.

We hike out with the rain this morning, but it isn't long until the wind and sun drive it away to reveal a delightfully pleasant day. The rail grade soon crosses NB-17 as it cuts the long side of a right triangle on a beeline to Kedgwick, so we stick right with it. At this crossing, however, there is a little homemade sign pointing to a building nearby. It reads "Mom's Bed & Breakfast." Oh yes, we'll make this little side trip. A SUV is parked in front with a New York tag and a big luggage bin on top, so it looks like Mom is open for business. Through the front window I see three hunters at the breakfast table. So far, so good! I open the door and one of the hunters motions me in. Mom hears the door open and comes from the kitchen to see me standing there with my pack still on. "Would you like some coffee?" is her hello! Looks like I'm in as I answer with an enthusiastic, "Yes ma'am." The hunters are from Buffalo. They come up every year black bear hunting. They've had great success this year. One more bear and they'll head home, each with his bear-shootin' story to tell. As Mom fills my cup for the second time, I'm asked if I'd like some breakfast. Well now, this is working fine! *John O* comes in and is also served a fine breakfast. Great conversation with Diana *Mom* Bolduc—and the bear hunters from Buffalo.

As we head for Kedgwick, Maurice Simon, New Brunswick IAT trail builder (and great friend from '98), comes hiking up the rail trail to greet us. What a joy seeing Maurice again! Of course

John O and I are immediately invited to stay at his home in Kedgwick. So off we go for a wonderful evening with Maurice, Anne Marie, and their children Fannie and Jerome.

Also living in Kedgwick are two other dear friends: Suzanne Bailey, coeditor of the neat little bilingual glossary, and Marc *Rainbow Bright* Mainville, GAME '99. I get to spend a few minutes with Suzanne but unfortunately, Marc is not home.

A shower, clean clothes, warm bed, hot meal—a great day!

Never miss a chance to rest your horse.
(Texas Bix Bender)

Saturday—June 10, 2000
Trail Day—18
Trail Mile—210
Location—Home of Bertin Allard, Superintendent, Mount Carleton Provincial Park, Saint-Quentin, New Brunswick

Today is a roadwalk as we head for Mount Carleton Provincial Park. We're out late as it is so easy to linger with dear friends. Before we know it, it's ten o'clock, and we've got at least seventeen miles to put behind us today. We're not far out of Kedgwick with the wind doing its best to discourage us, when an auto approaches slowly and a familiar, smiling face appears. I recognize Bertin Allard immediately. Bert is the Superintendent of Mount Carleton Provincial Park. What a delight seeing him again! He has messages for us from IAT President, Dick Anderson, also from NB IAT Coordinator, Mel Fitton. As he pulls away, I mention to *John O* that I bet this isn't the last we see of Bert today! *John O* says, "What do you mean?" "Just wait and see," I reply. At five, and with the seventeen miles behind us, we pull off by a spruce stand near a beaver pond. Few vehicles are passing now as I mention to *John O* that we should be watching for Bert. He gives me a funny look, but when we hear the next vehicle coming, he pops out to the road for a look. *John O* is no sooner around the corner than I hear, "There he goes!" I holler back, "Get him stopped." I head for the road now too, to find *John O* and Bert talking. He's come to pick us up and take us to his place in Saint-Quentin just as I had hoped, then anticipated, and finally pretty much expected. "*John O*, it's just that I know Bert and his predictable kindness!"

So it's off to Bert's we go, to his cozy, woodstove-warmed shop, for a tall longneck or two and the local delicacy, cipaille (meat pie). What a great day on the road, and what an equally great evening with Bert and his friends!

When the form of good operates invisibly, it produces happiness,
And when it operates visibly, it produces delight.
(Plato)

Sunday—June 11, 2000
Trail Day—19
Trail Mile—230
Location—Warden's bunkhouse, Mount Carleton Provincial Park,
New Brunswick

What a great night in the shop at Bert's place. More of Bert's friends come by to meet us this morning. After lots of coffee, cereal, and toast, we load up. Bert and his daughter Marie Eve run us back out to the road to continue our hike to Mount Carleton. Before leaving us, Bert offers *John O* and me the finest accommodations in the bunkhouse at Mount Carleton, so we'll hammer the road today to make it on in.

The freeze and thaw of the seasons play holy sam with the roads up here, and NB-180 has taken its licks. Some of the potholes are really scary—three to four feet long and nearly a foot deep. We watch vehicle after vehicle play the losing game today as they try dodging them, making for an entertaining show of it. Turning on gravel road NB-385, we haven't gone far before a Park Service vehicle pulls along and stops. What a grand smile from Warden Ralph Everett, a friend made during my '98 trek. Just as before, around here no news is big news. It seems everyone knows we're coming, so checking up on our progress is just part of the process. As we enter the park, another park vehicle greets us, with François and Sandra on board. François navigates while Sandra leans out the window with the park camcorder running!

The operation here at Carleton is first class even though the power and phone lines ended way, way back. A generator keeps things cranking, along with propane and cellular phones—it's sure not downtown, but *like* downtown! After a grand reception by all, we're ushered to the kitchen where Sandra has prepared a fine spaghetti dinner for us. Oh yes folks, we're way back in the north woods where roughin' it's the rule. But this ain't roughin' it!

Adventure awaits tomorrow—we'll climb Mount Carleton, then that spiritual summit, Sagamook. But for tonight, and in the waning mountain shadows, this very special place, it's a warm, soothing shower and color TV!

Adventure is worthwhile.
(Aesop)

Monday—June 12, 2000
Trail Day—20
Trail Mile—245
Location—Warden's bunkhouse, Mount Carleton Provincial Park,
New Brunswick

I sense this will be an excitement-filled day. The weather is cooperating with perfectly clear skies. Returning to Mount Carleton and Sagamook: this is a time I've been looking forward to with great anticipation.

Maurice Simon is supposed to climb with us today, but at nine-thirty he has still not arrived. *John O* and I decide to head out. Bert is like a little kid, wanting to go along, but it being Monday—and with new "casual" help to train—he must tend to the park and to his many responsibilities as park superintendent.

The climb begins as we ascend toward Mount Bailey. From here it's on to Bald Mountain Brook Trail. I have vivid memories from my climb up this brook two years ago, for it is one of the most magnificent climbs of all. Here is a singing and dancing brook so grand. To this place does Mother Nature send all her people of music and dance, for down this brook comes an absolute choreographed ensemble. I'm greeted immediately by the glad and happy children of the bounding waters as the brook cascades and free-falls past the boulders and rocks. The trail sticks tight to this delightful show, and I feel no effort in the near-vertical climb. The music and motion is so pure and sweet, not one false note, not one miscue, not one wrong step. Every note ever played through time is being played; every song ever sung is ringing forth, all in perfect harmony. Waterfall after waterfall form remarkable ballets of rhythmic motion, shimmering ballerinas dancing and pirouetting to perfect, pure sound. What a joy to be the audience for this performance. What a blessing to be alive on this day, here on this glad and happy trail!

As we gain the ridge, the trail turns to work its way up Mount Carleton. This being the highest point in the Maritimes, and in New Brunswick, it's a must climb, so up we go. But it is Sagamook that I'm anxious to visit again. No time is wasted retracing our steps to head for that sacred mountain. It is here that Maurice finally catches us, and we make the climb up Sagamook together. What perfect timing, and what a perfect day. What a memorable experience we share together. The earth, we are told, is ground, the physical medium of closure in the loop of energy as we know it. Should this be so, then the nodal point in this limitless sink of energy most certainly is Sagamook. This mountain is encased in boundless energy. This mountain emits boundless energy; this mountain *is* boundless energy!

In the evening we descend to Lake Nictau, much as, I'm certain, did the tribal chiefs over the eons descend after a day of council on Sagamook. Then it's a leisurely hike as we return to the warmth of the Warden's bunkhouse at Mount Carleton Provincial Park. A perfect ending to a perfect day.

The summit of ol' Sagamook isn't all that high,
But as I climb, I pass right through the bottom of the sky.
From here to turn and look—
and gaze, into the wild blue yonder,
And try and try, as best I can, to comprehend the wonder.

Now from this lofty firmament I let my spirit soar,
To mingle with the spirits of great Nations gone before.
And as I part this sanctity, a bit of me will stay,
To rest in God's eternal peace, that's present here—today.
(N. Nomad)

Tuesday—June 13, 2000
Trail Day—21
Trail Mile—271
Location—Bear's Lair, Riley Brook, New Brunswick. Don and Evelyn McAskill, proprietors.

Nadine and Louise, employees at the park, told us last evening they'd have fresh muffins from Tim Horton's for us first thing this morning. Sure enough, eight o'clock sharp, in they come with bags of muffins! This'll get the old jitney cranking.

We're up and out to another glorious day, with just the least bit of wind. Warden Ed Higgins told us about the old entrance to the park, which is now barricaded. We can hike that way, however, and save considerable distance by not going back out the park main entrance, so down the old road we go. The roadwalk today is one of those long, hammer-it-out roadwalks, the kind where it's possible to see the road for great distances ahead. There is hardly any traffic, an average of only two vehicles per hour, so we are able to walk an entirely friendly path along the road—even by the centerline. By late afternoon, we reach Riley Brook and Bear's Lair. This being bear-hunting season, the lodge is full, but Evelyn finds room for us in the loft. As we settle in, she prepares a fine evening meal for both *John O* and me. What a great and memorable time with all the friendly folks at Mount Carleton Provincial Park, but I'm glad to be heading on south.

> *Who is more happy, when, with heart content,*
> *Fatigued he sinks into some pleasant lair.*
> (John Keats)

Wednesday—June 14, 2000
Trail Day—22
Trail Mile—298
Location—Rogers Motel, Plaster Rock, New Brunswick. Wilfred Lagase, proprietor.

Evelyn has coffee ready soon as we head down this morning. The bear hunters are all in for breakfast. I enjoy talking with Bob from Pennsylvania and Rick, a medical doctor from Wisconsin. I know a little about the history of this very successful business from past discussions with Don and Evelyn, but this morning I sit in total captivation as Bob tells of his first visits here years ago, and how those hunts were organized from Don's dad's place up the road. It takes years to build a reputation in the guiding business, and the McAskills have one of the finest reputations for guiding hunters to bear anywhere.

The Tobique River Valley is such a special place. This is one of the most enjoyable roadwalks it has been my pleasure to experience anywhere, and I've done a few. The people here are so kind and friendly, the most hospitable, like William Miller III. I met Bill during my first hike through here in '98. Bill is a craftsman of wooden canoes, the very finest, a skill passed down from his father and grandfather. The canoe that Bill is currently creating is from the very mold designed and built by his grandfather seventy-five years ago. Thus, the canoe Bill is working on now will become the 75th anniversary Miller canoe, the first original Miller wooden canoe. What a proud tradition, what a remarkable heritage.

This valley is timeless; the moral values and passed-down skills of the people are timeless. And what a more fitting place than here in the most ancient of the ancient and timeless Appalachians. What a joy to be able to go back, to hike through it all once again, to be part of it all one more time! But alas, this roadwalk will certainly not endure, as plans are most assuredly underway to move the trail from the road to the ridge all along. It is truly a blessing to have experienced and enjoyed this spellbinding place.

While resting along the road and talking with *John O*, I mention that I wouldn't be surprised at all if we saw Mel Fitton soon. Mel is the driving force behind trail building in the province of New Brunswick. Sure enough, just as we pull into Plaster Rock to complete our roadwalk for today, who drives up but Mel Fitton, headed for a meeting up north. Mel invites us to dinner and we share a grand time with him and his assistant, Erin.

> *Blest, who can unconcern'dly find*
> *Hours, days, and years slide soft away;*
> *In health of body, peace of mind,*
> *Quiet by day.*
> (Alexander Pope)

Thursday—June 15, 2000
Trail Day—23
Trail Mile—325
Location—Gary Dimerchant's Boarding House, Perth-Andover,
New Brunswick

Good old Wilfred at Rogers Motel, he's always glad to see me, and indeed it's a pleasure seeing him again. He will never tell me how much he wants for a room, so I always have to try and figure what's fair, and as usual, Wilfred is pleased when we settle on the amount.

We've got a long hike today, a roadwalk of some eight miles. Then it's along the NB Trail, a multiuse rail-trail by the wide and grand Tobique, through the Tobique Narrows and into the St. John River Valley, a twenty-seven mile day. Since we're already south of town at Wilfred's and we want to head south, the decision is to continue on down the west side of the Tobique instead of going back into town to cross. We can reach the other side at the little village of Arthurette, pick up the NB Trail there and head on through the Narrows and on into Perth. It doesn't take long to realize that the decision to stay this side of the river is the right choice. We haven't gone far when a lady comes to her door and invites *John O* and me in for cookies and coffee. Here we meet more great folks who live here in the Tobique River Valley, Helen and Douglas Edgar and their grandson Brandon. They're getting set for a canoe trip with friends Phyllis and Len and Shirley and Victor. The cookies are great, and we're offered more as we talk about the valley—and about Bill Miller and his fine canoes! Helen gets her fiddle out for some grand old toe-tapping music, and before we depart and as we linger, both *John O* and I must sign their wall. Yes, that's right, we must *sign* their wall! Thousands of names, so it seems, grace every inch of wall space in the back alcove entrance, and with the aid of a good old Sharpie, we leave our mark.

By lunchtime we've reached the bridge at Arthurette, and oh my! Right decision again, as there's a fine little mom-n-pop restaurant on this side of the bridge. So it's in for lunch we go.

Across the bridge and just a short hike along the NB Trail we come to the Wagon Wheel Takeout, run by Cathy Sullivan and helper Cheryl. Time now for ice cream cones, compliments of Cathy—all kinds of neat flavors to choose from, even "Death by Chocolate." The treat tastes great, and we linger for the longest time in the warmth of the sun while relaxing at their picnic table right next the trail and the river. I finally shoulder my pack and head on south as *John O* remains behind for irresistible seconds!

This old railbed follows the beautiful Tobique for miles before it finally squeezes, as does the river, through the narrows. This timeless river has carved a path just wide enough for its own use, so man has had to blast and carve his own path from the vertical rock face that forms the Tobique Narrows. This has been a long day. I finally enter the little village of Perth. Here I head right for Pit-Stop Pizza, owned by Lloyd McLaughlin. Lloyd put me up in one of his boarding rooms above the Pit-Stop in '98, but alas, he is not here. Glenn, who is tending bar, gives me the bad news that all the rooms are rented now by the month, and all are full. As I relax and reward myself for a successful day with a couple of cool longneck frosties, Glenn makes some phone calls. He soon has Gary Dimerchant on the phone. Gary owns and operates the local taxi service and also runs a local boarding house, and he's soon right by the curb in front of the bar. He keeps a room or two open, to be provided as needed by the local ministerial association. After Glenn talks with Gary, the decision is to take me in. So I not only have a fine room for the evening, but Gary drives me to the local mom-n-pop where supper is provided to boot. Great folks, memorable evening, a fine hiking day. At ten *John O* still hasn't come in. I guess he's pitched somewhere out on the NB Trail for the night.

Trails are not dust and pebbles on a hill,
Nor even grass and wild buds by a lake;
Trails are adventure and a hand to still
The restless pulse of life when men would break...
(Helen Frazee-Bower)

Friday—June 16, 2000
Trail Day—24
Trail Mile—345
Location—Home of Dan Foster, City Administrator, Fort Fairfield,
Maine

Had a great night's rest at Gary's. Still no sign of *John O.* As I head out I go for my free breakfast at Bellevue Bed and Breakfast. Jeanne Hanson stopped to talk to us the other evening on the road to Plaster Rock and made us promise to have breakfast at the Bellevue in Andover, owned and operated by her mom, Shirley, so over I go. Here I find out that *John O* had been through a half-hour earlier but hadn't waited for breakfast, so I figure he's out ahead of me this morning, headed for US Customs at Fort Fairfield.

It's another blue-perfect hiking day as I thank Shirley for her kindness and step out to meet the day. The hike starts along the St. John River on the NB Trail, then joins the old Aroostook rail-spur to follow it around the Aroostook River to the international boundary at Tinker. On the walk along the Aroostook, I switch to the road for a little change of pace and to get a look at the front of some of the houses instead of the rear, as is commonly the view from the NB Trail. Back on the road, a pickup slows and stops. The driver asks the usual questions—those answered on the familiar hiker's T-shirt. Come to find out the two fellows in the truck work at the dam up at Tinker—yes folks, they work at Tinker('s) Dam(n)! How could I ever make this stuff up?

The road I'm walking abruptly ends at a barricade on the international boundary between the United States and Canada. Here I switch to the boundary cut, a swath about fifty feet wide that runs a beeline pretty much south. All along are monuments marking the exact line between our two countries. I know that I'm supposed to stay to the left of the monuments (in Canada) until I officially cross into the States at the border crossing in Fort Fairfield. But this is an impossible task, as the only way through the bogs and around the numerous beaver ponds is to follow the path that weaves from Canada to the States to get around them, just like everyone else does, including the Royal Canadian Mounted Police.

After a seven-hour day, the last hour being somewhat of a slog through the mud, I arrive at the border crossing by passing under a fellow's clothesline, first between his house and his side yard fence, then between his house and his car. The international boundary goes directly through his yard. To stay in Canada, I have to literally hug the south side of his house. This is way cool. The guy parks his car right next to his house in the United States, and then walks to his back door, which is in Canada. I didn't think to check what tag he's got on his vehicle, Maine or New Brunswick!

At US Customs I meet Lonnie Levesque. He asks if I'm a US citizen, and that's about it. Oh, then he says my hiking buddy got here about ten this morning and was picked up by Marsha Reed, the editor for the Fort Fairfield Review. Lonnie calls Marsha, and she and *John O* soon arrive to get me. Marsha wants a picture of us by the little flower garden welcome sign, the entrance to their fair city, then it's off to the newspaper office for the interview. Dick Anderson had asked me to get in touch with Marsha upon arrival at Fort Fairfield Customs, but turns out it was all set up and taken care of for me!

Over the remainder of the day I get bits and pieces of what has transpired with *John O* during the past two days. Seems his blisters were giving him fits during the roadwalk to Arthurette yesterday, so he ended his hike for the day at Cathy Sullivan's Wagon Wheel Takeout. The Sullivans had befriended Aaron DeLong during his IAT hike last year, taking him in for the evening. Yesterday, they took *John O* in. In the afternoon, Cathy drove him to the doctor in Perth, where he was given some medication to combat the bacteria and the blisters. He was then given a ride to Perth-Andover and then on to Customs at Fort Fairfield this morning.

We lounge the afternoon visiting with Marsha, having a grand time as she makes calls around to find a place for us for the evening and the night. Her very good friend Dan Foster comes by. Dan is the City Manager for the village of Fort Fairfield, a position to which he is apparently well suited and one that he likes very much. He is also a grand ambassador for this lovely little berg. We head for some supplies (and some cold ones), then it's out to Dan's place, a beautifully restored old farmhouse, complete with barn, machinery, fields of new-mown hay, a grand garden and a huge woodlot. Here we settle in for a relaxing evening as Dan entertains us, launders our cruddy clothes and prepares a grand evening meal. His parents John and Natalie and his brother and sister-in-law, John and Louise join us.

What a great hiking day, and what a memorable day, having made so many new and wonderful friends!

I learned early that the richness of life is found in adventure.
(William O. Douglas)

Saturday—June 17, 2000
Trail Day—25
Trail Mile—367
Location—Midtown Motel, Mars Hill, Maine. Steve and Rachel Burtt, proprietors; Dave Smith, manager.

Dan is full of excitement about golfing with his brother John this morning. I heard him make a promise to John that he'd pick him up at seven, so we're up and ready early. Dan gives *John O* a ride to Midtown Motel at Mars Hill. By the time he gets back he's running late, so he loans me his other car and sends me off to the border as he wheels off to get his brother. I'm given permission to park Dan's car (with keys in the ignition) at the US Customs office, and I'm headed south toward Mars Hill Mountain by seven.

Dan and Marsha, we've had a memorable time, dear friends. I'll long remember you and the delightful little village of Fort Fairfield, Maine!

The hike today continues south along the international boundary between the US and Canada. The only difference now is I'm supposed to stay to the right of the monuments—in the USA! But alas, the task is impossible, what with the numerous bogs and beaver ponds. Back and forth I go from country to country as I wend my way. I soon reach the shelter constructed on the US side by the Maine IAT Chapter. It is an elaborate and architecturally pleasing affair, fitted logs, picnic tables all around. Pinned to the shelter is a note from Dick Anderson. It reads, *"Nimblewill* and *John O*, Welcome to the United States."* I collect this precious little memento, take some pictures, and head on south through the ponds and bogs and the ups and downs.

In a while I arrive at another barricade, here to leave the boundary for good—to head for Mars Hill Mountain. I don't recall this section of trail being so strenuous in '98, but then I had just come down from Katahdin and from the rigors of hiking the grand old Appalachian Trail. Mars Hill Mountain was near the end of the '98 Odyssey, but now it is near the beginning of this one, and I'm two years older. I'm getting in shape again though. I'm eating like a horse, and I can feel the strength coming back into my arms and legs. This is truly a blessing at my age, and I'm both humbled by it and most thankful for it.

The views from Mars Hill Mountain are impressive. To the south lie Number Nine Mountain and the massif, Baxter Peak/ Mount Katahdin. To the north, so it seems, lies all of Canada.

There's another shelter here, constructed by the Maine Chapter IAT. From the flagpole in front of the shelter, where the sun first strikes the continental United States nearly every day of the year, the first 50-star US flag was unfurled at 4:33 a.m. on July 4, 1960.

This has been a long, hard 22-mile day, and it is approaching four as I reach the Midtown Motel in Mars Hill. We are lucky to get a room. *John O* has it all set up. I hit the tub, handwash a few things, then we head across the street to Al's for supper. A few phone calls in the evening, a few minutes on my neglected journals, and the sandman's call cannot go unheeded.

> *Nature reaches out to us with welcome arms,*
> *and bids us enjoy her beauty;*
> *but we dread her silence...*
> (Kahlil Gibran)

Sunday—June 18, 2000
Trail Day—26
Trail Mile—387
Location—Wilde Pines Campground, Monticello, Maine. Jack and Angela Wilde, proprietors.

I'm feeling good this morning despite the fatigue of yesterday. Today has dawned to yet another cloud-free wonder. *John O* has decided to head back to Arthurette, New Brunswick, to continue his hike to Mars Hill as I head for Shin Pond, some three days north of Katahdin. On Thursday evening, Dick Anderson and Will Richard will pick us up and drive us back to Mont-Saint-Pierre, Québec, to complete our hike over the majestic Chic Chocs and across the tundra. Thus there remain about three weeks of hiking to complete the IAT segment of our planned hike along the TA/ECT.

What a wonderful coincidence, what a grand opportunity, that this is Sunday. As *John O* heads back to Canada, I head for the Mars Hill Methodist Church and the Sunday morning service delivered by Reverend Elizabeth Vernon. I first met Elizabeth at the Blaine Truck Stop in '98 where I had stopped in for a bowl of soup and some hot coffee. Elizabeth came by my booth that morning, bringing some welcome and cheerful conversation. Upon departing, I found that my lunch had already been paid for. This was the first of many acts of kindness from this minister of God, and she has remained a bright star in my memory. Today I get to see Elizabeth again, to meet her kind and caring congregation, and to share the joy of the Lord with them. And what a blessing! I have been hoping with much anticipation, that I might see many dear friends again, and this odyssey is delivering, déja vu, in spades!

This is another hard, pound-it-out day. It's mostly a roadwalk down busy US-1, and this being Sunday, the crowds are out. There's a fully paved emergency lane all along US-1, yet this journey does not make for one of my favorites. What with church, then lingering to visit, I'm not on the trail until after noon, and today is another twenty-miler. I arrive at the Wilde Pines Campground by seven and pitch in a blanket of pine needles under the pine. I had stopped earlier at the Blue Moose for a bowl of chowder, so I roll in and am quickly lost in contented sleep.

But they that wait upon the Lord shall renew their strength;
They shall mount up with wings as eagles;
They shall run, and not be weary;
And they shall walk, and not faint.
(Isaiah 40:31)

Monday—June 19, 2000
Trail Day—27
Trail Mile—409
Location—Brookside Motel/Restaurant, Exit 61, I-95 at US-2
Ludlow, Maine. Carl and Carmel Watson, proprietors.

While I was working on my journal entries last evening, Jack Wilde
stopped by to chat. Jack is the owner and operator of Wilde Pines
Campground. He commented that had he known I was coming
through southbound, he would have given me directions to his
place, which would have brought me here quicker and with less
hassle—by coming down the old Aroostook railtrail, thus skipping
most of US-1. I didn't really mind the US-1 roadwalk yesterday, but
avoiding it would have been prudent.

When Jack noticed where I'd pitched under the pine he commented, "Wait till you catch the candle light in the morning sun."
He was speaking of the light green, almost transparent new growth
on the tips of all the pine boughs. I'd never heard this expression
before, and oh my, what a splendid show this morning as I rise to
be greeted by the first rays of the sun. For indeed the sun has set
every new pine bough tip ablaze with pure white light, like the little strings of white luminaries we all choose to grace our Christmas
scenes. Seems as though no matter what we create, Ma Nature has
already been there and done a much better job!

The trail zigs and zags along the ridges and by the little-used
secondary county roads. I no sooner get the old jitney up to normal
operating temperature than I get lost. I hike right by the first turn,
which dead ends in a farmer's front yard. With the farmer's kind
assistance, I'm soon back on track. The road I'm looking for is West
Ridge Road, but the sign where I should have turned reads Foster
Road. Heading down Foster Road and in a short while I pass this
grand, impressive farm, owned by guess who? Oh yes, the Fosters!
Maybe one of these days they'll get around to changing West Ridge
Road to Foster Road on the map. As I turn from Foster Road and

head for Haggerty Ridge Road, and by Dan Chase's beautiful home, I'm provided incredible views north to Mars Hill Mountain and then south to Mount Katahdin. For near Dan's house is the highest point in Aroostook County. What a grand photo op, and the day has turned perfect with bright sunshine, puff-cloud skies and just the gentlest breeze to boost me along. In just a while a truck pulls alongside and stops. It's Frank Burtt. He lives on the narrow little road leading to Wilde Pines. We'd exchanged greetings last evening. Come to find out he's cousin to Steve Burtt, proprietor of the Midtown Motel in Mars Hill. It's interesting and enjoyable how quickly I get to know the folks that are about (and all about their lives) as I pass through these little rural communities. If I ever need a rock mason, I know where to find a good one, because Frank Burtt has told me he's a good one!

A jog around Jordan Road, then it's a beeline west on Ludlow Road to Exit 61 where I-95 crosses US-2. Here I find the neat little mom-n-pop motel and restaurant, The Brookside, and I pull in for the evening. This has been a long day on the road, but there's been no lack of interesting diversion to break up the miles. The time has passed quickly. As I hike ever south, nearing the southern end of the IAT, I'm asked repeatedly, "Why—why are you doing this hike again?" Over the years many have tried to answer the question, "Why?" I attempted to find the answer all during my hike in '98. While writing my book, *Ten Million Steps*, I took another stab at it. In the foreword for that book, written by Larry Luxenberg, author of *Walking the Appalachian Trail*, he lamented over this dilemma. Not being one to let well enough alone, I've tried distilling this whole perplex down one more time. After over 400 miles this time out I've got it cooked down to this:

It's the people, the places,
The pain and the trials.
It's the joy and the blessings
That come with the miles.

It's a calling gone out
To a fortunate few,
To wander the fringes
Of God's hazy blue.
(N Nomad)

Tuesday—June 20, 2000
Trail Day—28
Trail Mile—431
Location—Dirty Dozen Hunt Camp, base of Mount Chase near
Patten, Maine

I had a fine time at the Brookside Motel and Restaurant, just as I
had anticipated. And what really made it special, I was able to get
in touch with Torrey Sylvester last evening. He has invited me for
breakfast this morning. Torrey lives just a short drive away in Houl-
ton. I first met Torrey in Key West, Florida, of all places. He had
flown down with Dick Anderson to be present to welcome Scott
River Otter Galloway as he finished his IAT southbound trek this
past January, and Torrey and I have since become good friends.

There's an interesting story about Torrey that I hope he won't
mind me telling. After the official establishment of the International
Appalachian Trail, trail building began moving along quite nicely in
the Canadian Provinces of New Brunswick and Québec. But to the
dismay of Dick Anderson, founding president of this fledgling organization, nothing at all was happening in his home state of Maine.
Until Torrey Sylvester came along. You see, Torrey has a cousin that
owns Mars Hill Mountain! As you know, Mars Hill Mountain is no
ordinary mountain, no-siree! Upon the summit of this mountain
the sun first strikes the good old USA nearly every day of the year.
It was from this summit the first 50 star US flag was flown. Well, as
it turned out, Torrey went to Dick with what he thought was "An
idea that might sell." And sell it did, for with permission granted to

build trail over Mars Hill Mountain, the IAT finally had a mountain to climb in Maine! Then shortly after, to nobody's surprise, the IAT Maine Chapter had a vice president. Oh yes, Torrey Sylvester! Thanks for breakfast, Torrey. Didn't we have a grand time! Oh, and please thank your cousin Marie Pierce and her husband Wendell for letting me hike over their mountain one more time.

I have decided to spend a night at Shin Pond Village. I stayed there during my northbound in '98 and have become friends with Craig and Terry Hill, owners of this fine establishment complex. Problem is, it's too far to hike in one day, so I've decided to take two days to get there from Brookside. This will make for two easy days and will also allow me the opportunity to take a look at another mountain that's held my interest ever since I heard Dick Anderson talk about it. "The IAT will go over Mount Chase," I remember hearing him say. This morning I've gotten encouragement from Torrey to give it a go.

It's another near-perfect hiking day (time for shades and cap) and I decide right away to take the detour and climb Mount Chase. I'm in good shape time-wise, and at three I make the turn onto the gravel two-track leading to Mount Chase. The DeLorme map I'm carrying shows the distance to be around three miles from the turn-off to the summit. But four hours later now and near exhaustion, I've yet to find the trail leading up the mountain. Numerous turns (none shown on the map) all end up a wild goose chase, petering out in jumbles of boulders and brush part way up. I've always had such good luck with DeLorme maps, and have often bragged about their accuracy and detail, but it seems the crew was out to lunch on this one! I remember passing an old cabin tucked away in the woods on the way in. With evening nigh, I backtrack there to prepare my evening meal and to rest before giving the mountain one more try in the morning. I arrive to find the cabin door unbolted. I enter the large main lodge room. Here I find a huge picnic table complete with lantern, candles and matches, and enough bunks all around to house "The Dirty Dozen" for which the place is so named. I find the main room clean and inviting and I move right in. Here I won't be hounded by the black flies for a while. Thank you, merciful Lord!

> *Walking brings out the true character of a man.*
> (John Burroughs)

Wednesday—June 21, 2000
Trail Day—29
Trail Mile—443
Location—Shin Pond Village, Shin Pond, Maine. Craig and Terry Hill, proprietors.

The day dawns a little iffy, but the goal today, no matter what, is to find the trail to Mount Chase, so I'm out and on my way early. I take the first road to my right this morning not expecting much, and sure enough after a few hundred yards it ends in a gravel pit.

As the two-track skirts the base of Mount Chase I try every side trail that leads up the mountain. I finally find one that looks promising as it keeps going up and up through the rocks and dense growth, but I encounter many old and recent blowdowns, and progress slows to a pitifully agonizing pace. But the trace of trail keeps going ever upward to finally gain one of the secondary spurs leading to Mount Chase. Here the path turns to little more than a game trail and as it winds along, first up and then down, I'm starting to have second thoughts about this whole ordeal. Wouldn't you think that getting lost in a place where you've got a compass and a map, and where going up would lead to the summit, and going down would logically lead back to civilization, that the concern about getting lost would be secondary? But believe me, there are places, like this place where there are many square miles and where up and down doesn't necessarily take a person either up or down.

I become very concerned as I enter another small drainage and the trail branches into a thicket of close-standing saplings. I start watching behind me as much or more than I'm watching my forward progress as I break saplings and branches to mark my path. Just when I'm hopelessly and utterly lost, and in fright-filled desperation, ready to quit and head back, I find a trail, a grand trail where even quad-tracks have passed. Well now, what a stroke of luck, and am I ever relieved!

To the left the trail seems to descend, and to the right it appears to go up, so I head to the right. In just a short distance this trail ends in a "T" as it joins another trail. Here there are signs. Great, now I should be able to figure out where I'm at and where I'm heading, but alas, the signs at the junction simply say "Trail A" and "Trail B." So, all I find out is that I've been on Trail B and that I must now choose to go left or right on Trail A or to backtrack back down Trail B. I head to the right and on up Trail A as it appears to be headed for the summit of Mount Chase.

In just a few moments I come to an old cabin, the ranger's cabin that once served the men who manned the fire tower on top of Mount Chase. Well, looks like I'm finally getting where I want to go, and sure enough, after another quarter-mile of near straight up scrambling, I'm standing on the summit of Mount Chase. What an ordeal, but what a reward—the remarkable vista o'er Upper and Lower Shin Ponds with the little village of Shin Pond below, set against the backdrop of Maine's own Sugarloaf Mountain. And to the southwest, one of the most striking views that I've ever seen of Mount Katahdin.

I have been afforded a grand reward for my effort, but I must hurry along, for as I descend, the clouds follow. The rain begins its no-nonsense presence as I hasten down the mountain on Trail A, heading for Shin Pond Village.

Arriving at Shin Pond Village, I'm greeted by Vicki and Megan and by the proprietor, Craig Hill. It's a joy seeing Craig again as the girls get me set to stay the night in the 100-year-old cabin, "Deer Run." As I settle in for the evening, and as the gentle rain on the old cabin roof makes me appreciate the snugness and charm of this rustic old dwelling, I peruse the cabin register. In the front of the old aged journal I find an entry dated July 18, 1996.

What a joy to read this, and what a joy to be part of this grand and glorious adventure, the creation of the International Appalachian Trail. The entry reads, "Bill Nichols, Don Hudson, Charlie Gilman and Dick Anderson spent a couple of days exploring trail locations for the International Appalachian Trail along the East Branch of the Penobscot River (Hunt Mountain) and Mount Chase." Folks, these men are the visionaries, the trail pioneers of our age, just as surely as the MacKayes and Averys were the dreamers and doers, the pioneers of the last century.

A grand trail to the end of the Appalachian Mountains, as we know them to exist, is an idea whose time has come. I find it strange, in this sort of thing, that a man has got be dead before he gets much (if any) recognition. So, all I can say to you, Dick, and to all of those laboring over this grand scheme with you—all I can say is I hope it's a long time before you get the recognition due! In the meantime it's a joy knowing you and calling you friend. What a time to be alive as a long distance hiker, to be part of a dream for a trail with no boundaries, indeed a dream of a trail through all of these mysterious and timeless Appalachians, and ultimately, the entire eastern North American Continent. Ahh yes, what a joy to be part of it all!

Two roads diverged in a wood, and I—
I took the one less traveled by...
(Robert Frost)

Thursday—June 22, 2000
Trail Day—30
Trail Mile—458
Location—Matagamon Store and Campground, near Matagamon
Entrance (north gate), Baxter State Park, Maine. Don and Diane
Dudley, proprietors.

What a great stay at Shin Pond. I'm much refreshed, out to a day of mixed clouds, but it appears set to turn fair. Before noon, as I hike toward Matagamon Lake—the north entrance to Baxter State Park—the day turns perfect.

The hike to Matagamon Campground goes well, and after a short five-hour day on the road, I'm in. This is a neat place, the kind of place you'd head for if you were really looking to get away. The power poles stop at Shin Pond; in fact, pretty much everything stops at Shin Pond. Don't think I saw half a dozen vehicles all day.

Matagamon Campground is located where the road to Baxter crosses the East Branch of the Penobscot River. No problem spending some time at this peaceful place, for here I'll while away the remainder of the day waiting for Dick Anderson, Will Richard and Barry Timson to come pick me up and carry me back to Mont-Saint-Pierre, on the sea in Québec, where I'll complete my hike across the tundra of the Chic Chocs, the Rockies of the East. They should be here around eleven tonight. Then we'll head for the border at Fort Fairfield, Maine, to pick up *John O.* He's a few days behind me on his hike because of down days he's had to take due to foot problems. On my pass through here in '98, I stopped to grab a sandwich and some ice cream at the campground, then was quickly on my way. Today I have the pleasure of spending some time with Don and Dianne. I learn a little about them, their family, and these special, far-off lands in the wilds of northern Maine.

Barry, Will and Dick are on time and I'm off, once more, for Canada.

Therefore am I still
A lover of the meadows and the woods,
And mountains; and of all that we behold...
(William Wordsworth)

Friday—June 23, 2000
Trail Day—31
Trail Mile—468
Location—Open ridge above Mont-Saint-Pierre near Parc National
de la Gaspésie, Québec

The trip back to the Peninsula takes all night. We stop for a few minutes at Pete's in Matapédia to pick up a few things from the box we've left there. Then it's on to arrive at Mont-Saint-Pierre around 9:00 a.m. I've had little sleep, but it's time to get organized and hit the trail. Raymond and Charlotte at Motel Mont St-Pierre are happy to see us again and to meet our friends. Raymond has talked many times in the past with Dick Anderson by phone but had never met him. We sort through our box left at Raymond's and are on the trail headed for Parc de la Gaspésie well before noon.

From a recent email received from François Boulanger, Director, Parc National de la Gaspésie, we know the snowmelt is well underway and that we're cleared to enter the high elevations above treeline on the 24th, which is tomorrow. We're right here, ready to get at it! We've got a day's climb to reach the Parc. We want to be in right on the 24th.

The climb goes well. *John O* and I manage to make it to an open ridge above the lovely little seaside village of Mont-Saint-Pierre. This has been a grand hiking day with numerous and varying vantages, plus much encouragement. But with no sleep for the past forty-eight hours, and with the strenuous climb today, I'm totally wore down. Little time is spent around the campfire before rolling in. Thanks, Dick, Will, Barry, for the ride back to Québec!

Live each day as you would climb a mountain.
An occasional glance towards the summit puts the goal in mind.
Many beautiful scenes can be observed from
each new vantage point.
(Joe Porcino)

Saturday—June 24, 2000
Trail Day—32
Trail Mile—480
Location—La Galène refuge (shelter) Parc National de la Gaspésie, Québec

We're up and out early to a cold, clear day. Temperatures got down in the low forties last night, but I slept very snug in my new Feathered Friends Rock Wren bag. It had been mailed to me here in Canada, and I picked it up on our stop in Matapédia. Feathered Friends is one of my sponsors for Odyssey 2000. Sure pleased to have your fine product folks—and your support, thanks!

The trail from Mont-Saint-Pierre to La Galène is all new treadway, just opened recently to get the seventeen miles of trail from the Parc to the sea off the road. This hike in '98 took a short day but now the distance is much longer, an estimated total of around twenty-two miles, and there is a fair amount of climbing. So, the journey to the Parc will now be two full days. This new treadway is marked with elaborate routered signs attached to 2x4s driven into the ground. Even though this trail has been here only a short time, the vandals have certainly been able to find it. Many of the signs have been ripped from their posts, or the posts have been broken off or pulled up and thrown into the woods. The trail along the Restigouche Canyon in New Brunswick was marked in similar fashion, with the bright blue and white IAT blazes nailed to 2x4 posts driven into the ground at strategic points along the trail. On our hike through there, we found most of that trail marking effort to have been in vain. Many of the posts had either been broken off or ripped up and tossed into the woods. Seems the IAT will be going through the same learning curve as did the Appalachian Trail Conference. The AT folks found out the hard way that the only lasting method of marking the trail is with paint. Vandals have a tough time with paint! It saddens me to see these signs destroyed. A lot of thought, preparation and time went into their construction and placement, all for naught.

We arrive at La Galène, a bunkhouse area in the Parc, before two-thirty. In the office, while we're talking with the caretaker, in comes Viateur DeChamplain from Matane. Viateur has just returned from the mountain (Mont Jacques-Cartier), where a special program has ushered in another grand season for Parc National de la Gaspésie. He spends time with me as we pour over the maps for the Parc and for the Matane Wildlife Reserve. Looks like we'll be in here around eight days. Dick Anderson has left a box of food, provided for *John O* and me by Dave Hennel, the Trail Gourmet, at le Gîte du Mont-Albert, so we should be good-to-go on food for our hike on through. François Boulanger also returns from the mountain, and I'm able to talk with him at length about his great work here in the Parc, and about my second grand traverse of the tundra o'er the majestic Chic Choc Mountains.

John O and I settle in the snug bunkhouse, complete with wood-burning stove. We've got the whole place to ourselves. It's been a fine day!

> *We are building in sorrow or joy*
> *A temple the world may not see,*
> *Which time cannot mar nor destroy;*
> *We build for eternity.*
> (N. B. Sargent)

Sunday—June 25, 2000
Trail Day—33
Trail Mile—493
Location—Le Gîte du Mont-Albert, Parc National de la Gaspésie,
Québec

This is the day for some of the most exciting hiking through some of
the most breathtaking and spectacular scenery and landscape imag-
inable—the climb over Mont Jacques-Cartier, the highest point
in southern Québec. We are greeted by yet another cool, clear day.
What a blessing. As we begin the climb from La Galène, it becomes
evident we'll have visibility for miles, with only the very least bit of
haze to limit our view. Yesterday, as we talked with François in the
parking lot at La Galène, he mentioned that the forecast was for
favorable weather the next few days.

The flanks of Mont Jacques-Cartier make for an awesome presentation this morning—pure rock and ice. The Chic Chocs and
the McGerrigle (Mont-Albert and its surrounding tundra) are
known to folks around (the few that even know about this area of
the Appalachians) as the "Rockies of the East," a descriptive and
accurate comparison. As we continue our ascent, *John O* and I stop
for many pictures of the snow, ice and rock. Here is displayed the
sheer might and startling majesty of this ancient and grand old
mountain. There is a bus parking area just above the bunkhouse—a
building described by the Parc wardens as a refuge—where tourists
are brought to begin their ascent. The first bus does not run until
10:00 a.m., so it appears we'll have the mountain to ourselves this
morning, all the better for the pleasure of it.

We reach the summit just after ten to find that we are indeed
the first to arrive. What a glorious sight! I described my feelings and
reaction to being here in a ballad written during the Odyssey of '98,
"The Ballad of the IAT." Here are two of the verses:

If climbing mountains to the blue
You'd rate a perfect day,
Then come traverse the Chic Choc range
And climb Jacques-Cartier.

You'll stand spellbound while 'round you'll see
Mont-Albert's skyland tundra,
And to the north, clear to the sea,
More of Gods boundless wonder.

Yes folks, the Chic Chocs are truly a magic and spiritual place. For those of us who love the mountains as our own, coming back to this place is likened to a pilgrimage, a return to the place of our ancestry, a place for fulfillment—fulfillment of that universal, deep down urge to be free, truly free, an undeniable natural instinct that lives and resides in all of us, in the depths of our very soul. Here I'm at peace with man, with myself and with the Lord.

In our climb over Mont Jacques-Cartier and across the barren tundra of these far-northern lands, as we stumble along, our concentration and vision glued to the jumble of boulders and rocks at our feet, I hear *John O* exclaim, "There, there, the caribou!" And indeed, just a scant hundred yards to our left are grazing twelve to fifteen woodland caribou. In the group, there's a dominant bull with his huge set of antlers, and a cluster of cows, also with their antlers (like all of Santa's reindeer). And wobbling, stick-legged and within the circle of security, one very young calf! I was so hoping to have the opportunity to see these rare and impressive animals (only 300 or so have survived south of the St. Lawrence), and here they are right before me. What an incredible day this is turning to be!

For here you're nearing Santa's land,
With reindeer roaming free.
You'll hike a wonderland of snow,
A Christmas fantasy.

As we work our way across to Mont Xalibu, to begin our descent to le Gîte Du Mont-Albert, we are confronted with a very large and expansive snow field, the trail leading directly onto it. Now is the time of challenge as mentioned by François yesterday, "The problem is not negotiating the snowpack, which is easy enough, for it will support your weight. The challenge is finding where the trail emerges from the snow field!"

This is a very large and barren area, sloping down to our left and off to our right, with the trail concealed under many feet of deeply packed snow. The trail could lead in either direction. Looking to the far side (in hopes of seeing a familiar and much-welcome rock cairn), brings only disappointment, as the distance is so deceptively great and the features far across and down are unrecognizable. So onto the snowpack we go to search the edge all along in hopes of finding the emerging trail. For some reason, as I pass around an island of huge boulders jutting from the snow field, I move toward the center of the snowpack. Here, just to the other side I see the very top four inches of one of the posts that mark the trail. What a stroke of blundering good luck! Sighting back to where the trail entered the snow field, I'm now able to get a much better fix on just where the trail is headed. In only moments, as we progress onward over the snowpack, and on the far side, I spy a small rock cairn just past the snow field. What a blessing to make the traverse successfully! We soon clear the snow field and are back on the trail to Mont Xalibu.

While we are stopped for lunch by a high-mountain shelter, from behind us come Simon Thibault, S-Iline Lavoie, and Simon's father. Simon and S-Iline are guides for Destination Chic Chocs and are under contract with the Parc. As we enjoy each other's company I quickly realize that they've been sent out by François to check on us and to help us across the snow field. We are obviously the first to do the grand traverse this year, as there are no other tracks ahead.

The remainder of the day is uneventful. As I descend from Mont Xalibu and emerge from the woods, I find *John O* waiting for me at the Gîte. A warm room, a full tub of hot, soothing bathwater, then to dine in absolute luxury (linen and silverware, the works) at the Gîte Restaurant. What a rewarding, adrenaline-pumped, memorable day!

> *The strong life that never knows harness;*
> *The wilds where the caribou call;*
> *The freshness, the freedom, the farness—*
> *O God! How I'm struck by it all.*
> (Robert W. Service)

Monday—June 26, 2000
Trail Day—34
Trail Mile—507
Location—Le Pluvier (cabin), Lac Cascapédia, Parc National de la Gaspésie, Québec

Looking out the hotel window this morning, the mountain looming above, puts sheer fright into me. To repeat a phrase, "I've climbed some mountains," offers not the least degree of comfort as to what this day is destined to bring; for here is a mountain with such overwhelming power and might, each vein-like gulch appearing to pulse with snow pack so deep, with such enormous energy that even the kind, many warm suns of June cannot overcome.

There are many things that must get done this morning before moving out—to be far from civilization and phones for the next seven days. But as (bad) luck would have it, as I'm talking with the kind officer at Baxter State Park, the pay phone goes dead. In fact, all the outside phones here at the Gîte have gone dead. Oh well, I know that I must make written reservations to stay in Baxter. I was getting the kindest assistance in setting up my accommodations. However, I do manage to get a letter off to Baxter, airmail, thanks to Chantal, the kind receptionist here at the Gîte, the same lady who secured my permit to enter the tundra of Mont Jacques-Cartier after the Parc closed in '98. Folks, I know I've already said this, but danged if "This isn't déja vu in spades." I'm getting to see so many great friends as I relive this dream once more!

The IAT seems to no longer officially climb Mont-Albert, choosing instead to follow a less strenuous partial climb around the mountain. That's fine, but I say the ECT goes up and over! So up and over I go, but not until after enduring nearly two indescribable hours of struggle as the mountain keeps me in its constant and relentless grip. What a climb, and in my humble opinion, is this climb the likes of any along the venerable old AT; and what a reward! For standing here at one of the observation points along the boulder-strewn treadway, I'm staring in awe at the expanse and majesty of the Canadian tundra.

On the summit now, one of the Parc's interpretive wardens/ rangers has a high-power scope set up. Once again I get to see the caribou, small white-gray objects dancing about in the blue at a distance of over four kilometers. I quickly realize how very fortunate I was yesterday, to have seen the caribou at such close range on the tundra of Mont Jacques-Cartier!

From here, by boardwalk and marked pathway, the trail crosses the tundra of the McGerrigle. The joy and smugness of this confident hike becomes quickly dashed as the trail plunges from the mountain, over the brink and into an enormous, head-whirling, and brutally steep chasm. In this place the landscape is like no other I've ever seen, forbidding, cold, and most unwelcome in its nature. The enormous boulders, the crags formed, are not the steel-gray familiar granite, but an eerie, mysterious shade of brown, much like the camouflage color of desert warfare. Oh no, this is definitely not the comfortable environment you'd seek when wanting to be "at one with nature."

Here in the gulch, the streams and waterfalls are roaring with resounding might, such as would demand and be given utmost respect. After descending a near-vertical drop-off, the trail turns to abruptly ascend another wall, directly into an enormous snow field. I cannot see the upper reaches of the snow-pack, nor can I see where the trail might again emerge. I quickly realize the only way is to climb the snow field in search of the trail.

Looking up never seems as scary and forbidding as looking down, and as I continue kicking toeholds in the heavily consolidated snow, I pause to rest for a minute—and look down. Holy hell! I'm halfway to the moon and can now see neither where I began nor where I'm headed, just a crescent of white to oblivion in all directions. These places are so deceivingly enormous. I think about returning, back-stepping my way down, but after a couple of these risky maneuvers I realize this is futile. This is scaring me to death, looking down into space.

So, it seems my fate is sealed. I must continue climbing, toward whatever is up there. I see more boulders above, jutting from the snow-pack, and I vary my course slightly and head toward them. As I continue up, a deceptively beautiful area of blue appears ahead and just above. Arriving, I find pure ice. "Oh Lord, now what; how will I ever get out of this predicament!" I finally decide to kick in a couple of good deep toeholds, then to rest and try leveling my head to this cockeyed place. I want to remove my pack, but rather, decide to just lean forward against the ice—and calm my fears. Finally, I convince myself I'm okay, and continue up, climbing, hacking the ice with my shortened sticks. It works remarkably well, but progress is agonizingly slow. In no time I again become very scared—horrified would better describe my plight, and I'm having much difficulty concentrating. I'm in constant fear of losing my footing, then to plunge clear off the side of this mountain. I muster patience, though, then to continue climbing. After a while, the ice and snow become less steep and I'm able to continue on up with positive footing by simply using my poles for stability.

Looking around, I see what appears to be a rock cairn just to my right, and I head straight for it. Glory be, I'm on trail again and free from harm's way! Thank you Lord, for guiding me through—one more time!

The old log cabin at Lac Cascapédia is all I remember it to be; not much. That suited me just fine in '98, and it'll suit me just fine this go 'round. Here, does a sense of peace and calm pervade. It comes from the past, from another time, when this old cabin first took its place here on the shore of this peaceful lake. It's nearly dark now and *John O* has yet to come in. Back at the last refuge, I had met some fellows from Montreal that are hiking around the Parc. That bunkhouse is about five miles back, on the other side of Mont Ells. *John O* must have pulled in there for the evening.

One thing I'll give the Canadians credit for is their ability to hook up wood stoves so they'll draft properly. All the stoves I've ever used up here work just fine with the door open. Try this little no-no on just about any stove that's been rigged up in the states and see what happens. You'll get smoke and plenty of it! But tonight at this quaint picture-book setting, the little cabin, le Pluvier on the lake, I'm able to get a fine fire going to quickly prepare my evening meal, over the fire, with the stove door open! This has been a hard hiking day. I'll likely never forget the pull up and over Mont-Albert and the frightening climb through the ice there.

> *Oh mountaineer of time, upon your dizzy height—*
> *What lies beyond the day? Beyond the night?*
> *You need not answer, for we're climbing too*
> *And soon enough—will come to share the view...*
> (Edward Abbey)

Tuesday—June 27, 2000
Trail Day—35
Trail Mile—525
Location—Lac Thibault outfall at beaver dam above Lac Gaudreau,
Parc National de la Gaspésie, Québec

I have decided to wait until at least ten this morning, in hopes *John O* might come in. I want our hike to continue, together. Our destination yesterday was set here, at this quaint little picturesque cabin on Lac Cascapédia, a hiking distance of only thirteen miles. But thirteen miles in these rugged Chic Chocs can be comparable to hiking eighteen to twenty miles almost anywhere along the trail in the states, and *John O* has been having difficulty with stamina and endurance on the killer uphills. This unfortunate circumstance is not due to how he's attacking this challenge, with either his heart or his head, for *John O* is 200% grit and go. His problem is due, unfortunately, to an energy-sapping condition for which he must take regular medication. He's talked about this, to me and with others, since we began hiking together. To this, he is neither bitter nor resigned. I'm positive, should our days lead us shorter distances, under less demanding circumstances, it would be no problem. Here, it is a problem.

The hold-up to go pays off, for just a little after nine *John O* pulls in. He had stayed at the last refuge (shelter) just as I'd hoped. I quickly find that he isn't a happy camper this morning, as he laments the extreme difficulty he has been having doing the miles. He comments with much dismay, "I'm out here to have a good time, but this is no fun and I can't keep it up; I just can't continue like this." Our planned destination this evening is a shelter at Lac Thibault, a distance by trail of only twelve miles. But this hike today will be a ball-buster with long and extremely steep pulls over Mont Ernest-Ménard, Pic du Brûlé, Mont du Blizzard and Mont Arthur-Allen. *John O's* decision is to take the roadwalk around and through the valley which is somewhat further but which also leads to Lac Thibault. Having already hiked five miles today, and as we part ways, he comments that he may not go the entire distance. In a somewhat unusual and formal tone of finality, he bids me goodbye.

The climb from Lac Cascapédia is extremely difficult, but what a payoff for having succeeded! For, from the precipice at the summit of Mont Ernest-Ménard and following all the way around to Pic du Brûlé, is there a trail laid down like no other trail I have ever hiked. To Mother Nature, sheer ruggedness has special meaning, I'm certain of it, for with the creation of extremely precipitous mountain features does she also bring out the most spectacular vistas in her remarkable and seemingly boundless and unlimited repertoire. These mountains are steep, near conical, and their impact on all the senses sends me reeling in total bewilderment. For here the trail follows the edge along near-vertical drop-offs, cliffs that plunge for thousands of feet. The view is totally unobstructed, into space and to the horizon for the better part of a mile, and this morning the wind is in a rage, trying to drive me over the edge. I've hiked many a mile in my time, but this is the most sensationally wicked, awesome mile I've ever hiked, anywhere!

Coming off Mont du Blizzard, the trail plunges nearly straight down, bringing a feeling, I suspect, not unlike being flung from a catapult. It is at this moment I lose that ever-critical edge of total concentration, which causes me to lose my footing, which causes me to be flung. Out of the catapult I go—the most incredible and sensational "Flying W" header I've ever taken, even including all the years of dirt bike racing. I get my hands out as I see the rocks coming up to greet me, and I'm somehow able to haul myself in, but only after I manage another job on my right hand. One brief look and my head starts spinning, my vision goes to tunnel and my legs turn to rubber.

I manage to drop my pack and crawl onto a half level boulder, here to spend many agonizing minutes pondering my predicament, and talking to myself and to the Lord, most of which time is spent asking his forgiveness for what I've just said to myself.

Well, I've done a fine job this time, much better than the two messed up hands I managed during Odyssey '98. This doesn't look good. My little finger is turned in flat against my palm and won't re-extend at all, and along with my ring finger, both are separated from my index and second finger in the most bizarre way. Looking at the back of my hand I notice my ring finger no longer has a knuckle! Now that my peripheral vision has returned and my head seems to have cleared the least, it takes little time deciding what must be done. A strong arching jerk to the little one pops it back into joint and it seems to work okay again. However, as I take a steady tug on my ring finger all I get is profound and excruciating pain. I go straight for the coated aspirin, 1000 mg to start. Seems what I've managed to do is break my right hand. All the daredevil years as a kid (guess this still makes me a kid!) I've watched all my buddies hobble around with broken legs and busted arms—even went through it with my older son, Jay. But somehow, all these years I've managed to avoid the unpleasantness of a broken body. Oh, but it looks like my time has finally come. What I'm looking at is a broken bone, the one between my ring finger knuckle and my wrist. There's another joint here that doesn't belong and I can articulate it freely, for the bone is completely in two, permitting the finger and knuckle to collapse toward my palm. No matter what I try, I can't straighten it. Harnessing my trekking pole I find, miraculously, that I'm able to grip it firmly with very little discomfort! Time to suck it up, grit it and go, old man! And that's what I do. Any medical remedy will likely take me from the trail. So, the hand will just have to heal in the Leki pole grip position, just as are my toes, all ten permanently sans toenails, now conforming to the shape of my cross trainer shoes.

It's late when I reach Lac Thibault. Somehow I manage to miss the shelter. I realize this after I've hiked clear to the lower end of the lake. But what a beautiful spot to pitch for the evening, looking over Lac Gaudreau. This has been a blockbuster day and I'm totally spent, physically and emotionally. I retire full with fear and doubt, but sleep is splendid.

Elvis is dead and I don't feel so good myself.
(Lewis Grizzard)

Wednesday—June 28, 2000
Trail Day—36
Trail Mile—536
Location—Refuge near Mont Louis-Marie-Lalonde, Parc National de la Gaspésie, Québec

I'm up and out to a beautiful day. First order is to backtrack to near the other end of Lac Thibault to pick up the trail. There are a number of climbs today, the major ones being Mont Jacqes-Ferron and Mont des-Loupes. I also pass many beautiful tarns, high-held glacial mountain lakes. Two of the most picturesque are Lac Chic and Lac Choc! The moose have pretty much taken over the treadway here, churning it to a bottomless quagmire in places. *John O* saw a moose a couple of days ago and was surprised at how dark it was, nearly black. The ones I see today are also almost pure black.

From the ridgelines and summits, the views to the north extend to the sea and beyond, perhaps for thirty to forty miles. From one vantage, I see a freighter plying the waters of the St. Lawrence. On the coast is Cap-Chat, the location of the famous eggbeater wind turbine. It sits on a high ridge facing the sea just above the village. There are also many other enormous traditional wind-driven turbines. High-tension lines run nearby and their large metal towers look toy-scale in comparison to the turbine blades. One turbine blade length on one of the three-bladed props is nearly three-quarters the height of one of the power line towers. All of this is visible, including the beautiful valleys of Cap-Chat and Sainte-Anne-de-Beaupré.

The hike today has not been as strenuous or demanding, and I'm in by three-thirty. The pain in my hand has been troublesome but tolerable. I've been able to grip and manipulate my trekking pole quite well. It's turning chilly this evening, so not only will a cooking but warming fire be in order.

Let me tell you about the shelters up here. They're grand affairs, more like dwellings, complete with bunks/mattresses for eight, tables and chairs (with arms and backs), airtight wood-burning stoves, and firewood provided. Many have enclosed porches; all are insulated and have double-pane windows. No disrespect, but you can have your Adirondack lean-tos with ball bat bunks. I'll take one of these five-star dandies anytime!

I keep looking expectantly all evening for *John O,* but he does not come in. There are some very difficult and strenuous climbs ahead in the Matane Wildlife Reserve, and I'll have to be pushing hard constantly. If I'm going to make Flagg Mountain, Alabama, the southernmost mountain above 1,000 feet, the symbolic end of the Appalachian Mountain range, and the Trail of the Ancients—if I'm going to get there by the end of the year, I've got to keep moving. So, perhaps this is the end of our hike together. It's been my pleasure hiking with you, and I wish you well, *John O.*

Up through the Whites and Presidents,
You touch the alpine zone.
But in the Chic Chocs,
You're above the trees for miles...alone.
(N. Nomad)

Thursday—June 29, 2000
Trail Day—37
Trail Mile—548
Location—Near Rivière Cap-Chat, first ridge on ascent to Mont
Nicole-Albert, Reserve Faunique de Matane, Québec

It's a chilly, clear morning as I head for Mont Logan. I soon pass the narrow two-track by which I ascended Mont Logan in '98. I was not permitted to hike any of the IAT in Matane Wildlife Reserve due to moose hunting season. In fact, I was initially refused entry to the Reserve until I spoke to an assistant director by phone. Only then, after much discussion, was I permitted to pass through, and only by road between the hours of 10:00 a.m. and 3:00 p.m. In addition, I was required to wear the orange hunter's vest that my good friend Bruno Robert from Matapédia had the good sense to lend me. So the hike from here to the Matane River at PQ-195 will be on tread-way I've not previously hiked.

One of the reasons I'm doing this IAT hike again is to see and experience the beauty of the rugged western end of the Chic Chocs. Everyone who I talked with after the '98 hike, who knew the Matane, expressed dismay and regret that I was unable to hike this section. So to all my dear friends in Matane, and all who know the Matane, I'm back to finish it, to experience it and to take it all in. So here goes!

It's pretty much a straight shot across from Mont Louis-Marie-Lalonde, and I soon see the summit of Mont Logan just ahead. And also just ahead, another small herd of caribou, possibly twelve to fifteen. Wow! The triple crown of caribou spotting in Parc National de la Gaspésie: Mont Jacques-Cartier, Mont-Albert and now, Mont Logan. I was hoping to have the opportunity to see these rare and remarkable animals at one of the known sites, but all three! What an incredible way to start this day!

The hike into the Matane Wildlife Reserve from Mont Logan to Mont Coleman will remain one of the most awe-inspiring natural wonders I experienced anywhere during Odyssey 2000. Folks, thanks for insisting I come back again! This hike follows a long and sometimes steep and scary razor-sharp ridgeline, the very brink of the escarpment. First, it goes over needlepoint Mont Fortin, then down the razor edge and up and around Mont Matawees, then to dive off to the next sharp saddle and to ascend Mont Collins. The hike through this section is definitely time-consuming, but part of what takes the time is taking it all in. There's just no way to believe that these are the Appalachian Mountains; you must come and witness this place for yourself. Oh, and it's another blue-perfect day, just me, the sky, and this indescribable corner of paradise, most surely home to the less lofty angels on high! As my old hiking buddy *Wolfhound* would say, "Life is good!"

One more good leg-sapping climb and I'm over Mont Coleman, headed down, down, down to Cap-Chat River. The trail map given me by Eric Chouinard and Jean-Pierre Harrison, both from Matane, shows this final leg today to follow a narrow valley down to the river. I'm hoping for an old settler's woods road, but instead get the most incredible jumble and tumble of rocks and roots, mostly side-slabbing, that I've ever had to traverse, mile after endless mile.

The mosquitoes try carrying me off where I'd planned pitching for the evening by the Cap-Chat River. Both they and an oncoming storm chase me up the mountain toward Mont Nicole-Albert. First it's across a suspension bridge with the centerboard missing. Why does the centerboard always have to be missing? Then it's into an absolute water wonderland. You can take all the waterslides in the world, hook and run them together, and you still wouldn't have anything to compare to Chutes Beaulieu, the cascading rapids and thundering waterfalls that I'm experiencing along Sentier Petit-Sault. The trail seems to run straight up, fall after fall, the trail leading right to the pools of thunder. The brook is of respectable size, and the sound is deafening. The rock on which I'm standing is literally vibrating. Up, up, up, the trail continues. Down, down, down, the falls roar and plunge through narrow-walled chasms, only to crash against buttressed granite walls, then to turn and leap, flying from another head-spinning brink. Gravity is certainly at work here. The trick is to figure which way it is actually tugging. "Disoriented" describes the feeling perfectly. I don't know what it takes to push your senses to total overload, but I'm tanked!

The storm starts to set in, politely announcing that I have about ten more minutes to find a place and get pitched for the night. I soon gain a narrow cove, clear out a flat spot and get set up. But the storm's jumped the gun; that's only seven minutes! I'm finally in, a little damp. Rain or sweat, what the hey; little difference out here. Folks, this hike is an absolute hoot! My poor raggedy hand has caused me little bother today. Oh the joy to find, then stand on the very tip-top edge of life every day. It's a wonder, it's a blessing. No, it's a miracle!

> *Miracles abound*
> *In this world of toil and sin.*
> *But we must keep an open heart,*
> *To take the blessings in.*
> (N. Nomad)

Friday—June 30, 2000
Trail Day—38
Trail Mile—560
Location—Refuge, Summit Mont Blanc, Reserve Faunique de Matane, Québec

The rain continued most of the night, but I slept well. With morning, the storm has subsided, but the sky remains overcast, with dark, gray clouds swirling above. With the chill and the wind, their presence tells of what this day will likely be—cold and wet. But as I continue the hike over Mont Nicole-Albert, the day attempts to turn fair, bringing views as breathtaking and grand as any awarded thus far.

"Terrifying shudder" are the only words I can gather to describe my feelings along the trail over Mont Nicole-Albert. At one point, the trail leads me through a canopied over-story, pretty normal treadway, much the same as the "green tunnel" we're all familiar with. Then, just up ahead on my right, I see a rope tied to the trees along the trail. "Guess they don't want anybody over there for some reason," I'm thinking. But as I get closer, standing in absolute shock, I see nothing but open space through a gaping crevasse right at trail-side. Gripping the rope and peering down through the narrow, vertical-walled chasm, I find it simply disappears into space, as if we're hanging from the sky, perhaps even as if in flight. There's nothing anywhere below for a thousand feet! Fright? If this won't strike fear into you, I'd sure like to know what it'd take. Oh yes, I'll be very careful when I step off the trail from now on.

How incredibly inspiring are these mountains, but how indescribably agonizing they are, for up here in the vastness of these far-off, untamed, and everlasting Appalachians does heaven and hell coexist in such close proximity, separated only by the short measure of one's height. Here, my eyes have free take of Nature's most heavenly treasures, riches so profound, limited not by man's narrow scope of possibilities, what he believes to be or even what he might believe *could* be! And below, below at my feet, the most brutal treadway, demanding all of my energy and resolve, demanding I climb and descend near-vertical grades through difficult obstacles of rock, brush, roots, and blowdowns. My head is literally in heaven and my feet in hell. Indeed, this trail through the Chic Chocs, the IAT, is like no other!

The heavy gray from the north finally rolls in and takes over for the remainder of the day. As the mist begins, the show shuts down. I must neither complain nor find fault, because I have been blessed with such glorious good fortune—clear, haze-free days that have allowed me fleeting glimpses all the way to the wide open gates of heaven.

The trail from Mont Nicole-Albert to Mont Bayfield is almost impossible to follow at times. The familiar IAT blazes peter out just across the suspension bridge. The fiddlehead ferns have grown to their full glory, nearly hip high in some areas. Flagging here, bits that remains from the time of trail construction, have been whipped and bleached to little nickel-size knots on the spruce boughs. Luck hands me a fragment of flag on the ground at times, and any chain-saw work is a dead giveaway. The whole exercise sounds easy enough, but where there's no treadway—the result of little or no traffic—and where blowdowns and brush are everywhere, staying on trail can be a tricky proposition. After much backtracking from helter-skelter moose trails and after many hours, I reach Lac Beaulieu. Here there's been traffic, and I'm able to follow the trail easily.

The climb from Lac Beaulieu to the cabin atop Mont Blanc is long and tiring. I stop often to look up, only to see more up. Straight up! As I finally crest the mountain, my energy totally spent, the wind and rain hit me with full force. Visibility is near zero, but I finally see the little cabin dancing in and out of the rain and clouds just ahead.

To be free of the bitter-cold wind and rain brings such a secure and comforting feeling. Oh, how we take most everything for granted anymore, especially the basic things we need to survive. Like shelter! I'll let this little snug dwelling shutter me; it will protect me from those wicked elements that would cause me harm. Some kind soul, perhaps one of my good friends from Matane (whose names I see here in the shelter register), has gathered and dried some old pine knots. With this lighter fuel I quickly get a warm, glowing fire going in the old wood-burning cook stove. The sheet metal oven box has long since rusted away, so the fire is now built right in the oven, the oven door working just as would the stove door.

My little den in the storm is soon warm and comfortable, and I settle in for a very enjoyable night. I have brought only a quart of water up the mountain. Taking a couple of frying pans from the cupboard and setting them under the roof drip line outside, I soon have plenty of water to prepare my evening meal, right over the coals, right in the oven—but not quite in the way this old cast iron relic was designed to be used!

Thank you Lord for guiding my footsteps today...

And as I stumble o'er the path,
I need to keep in mind.
That He has cleared a way for me,
That faith will help me find.
(N. Nomad)

Saturday—July 1, 2000
Trail Day—39
Trail Mile—580
Location—Refuge, Summit Mont Blanc, Reserve Faunique de Matane, Québec

The light of this new day wakens me and I rise to peer at an impenetrable slate of gray against the cabin window, its homogeneity broken and distorted only by the rivulets of water from the dismal, wind-driven rain. So the storm continues.

I was able to get out a while last evening and with the help of the bow saw, one of the fine and useful cabin tools, I was able to cut ample firewood for another day. I stacked it on top of the old stove where it remained all night. So now it is dry enough to get another fire going this morning, for I see no sense in fighting this storm or these mountains today. They're challenge enough in times of fair weather. This day will be spent resting and writing, two things I very much need to do.

The mind...in itself,
Can make a heav'n of hell,
A hell of heav'n.
(John Milton)

Sunday—July 2, 2000
Trail Day—40
Trail Mile—602
Location—End of built trail, west end, Reserve Faunique de Matane,
to home of Viateur and Jocelyne DeChamplain, Matane, Québec

Mont Blanc is still in the clouds as I descend this morning, as the swirling mist starts kicking anew. What a snug, relaxing and joy-filled two nights and a day spent in the little cabin. Folks dream all their lives of getting away—if for just a little while—to such a remote, cozy little place, but never get the chance to realize the pleasure of fulfilling that instinctive desire. I have lived it and have loved every minute of it. You absolutely cannot buy these simple pleasures with any amount of money. I know what a blessing this has been to me. I'm humbled by it and thankful for it. And thank you, all my dear friends in the Matane Chapter, Québec IAT!

The rain sets in, and the ferns block the trail. I have a slow, fretful time of it climbing Mont Craggy and Mont Pointu. From Lac du Gros Ruisseau I must climb a mountain comparable to almost anything in the Mahoosucs, and it doesn't even have a name. It was on this mountain today that I experienced a natural occurrence few ever live through. I was struck by lightning. Yup, I got a grand jolt of it! Oh, I can hear you doubters now: "There he goes again, he's so full of it; this guy has lost all sense of reality." Well folks, I've been a tinkerer all my life, played around with electricity, and as a result, got bit plenty of times by it, lots of 110 and a few 220 jolts. One-ten will set you straight for a long time, and a single run-in with voltage in the range of 220 and you're cured for life! I'd say today I got hit with voltage somewhere in or above the 440 range. The main bolt struck a tree nearby—KA-POW—a simultaneous flash and report. I got what bounced off! My trekking poles may have saved me. I was soaking wet, but the soles on my shoes are rubber and the grips on my poles are some sort of hard cork, both good insulators. The strike hit somewhere around the top of both my trekking poles, which were dug in hard above me as I pulled myself up the mountain. The current surged through the poles, setting them to quivering and vibrating as it sought ground through the carbide tips embedded in the rock and mud. My hands were drawn paralytically tight around the Leki grips, and I could feel the incredible surge of energy as it pulsed down the poles. The shock seemed interminable, and I recall waiting for the current to peg to infinity and take me with it. But just as it so unexpectedly happened, did it thus end, and I was left standing there, a hopeless bundle of wet mush. In a few moments I managed to gather my wits and my strength and continue on up no-name mountain.

While I sat and rested for a while at the picnic/camp area at Lac Matane, soon comes Jocelin, one of the Reserve wardens. Viateur and Jocelyne DeChamplain had inquired at John, the entrance to Matane Wildlife Reserve, as to my whereabouts. The wardens have been looking for me. In moments, Jocelin is in contact with Viateur, by way of radio to John, and arrangements are made for me to meet Viateur this evening when I complete the trail here in the Reserve. Oh my, this is great; I've been invited to return to Matane as their guest for the evening. What a blessing, as the rain has not relented and I'm getting very wet, cold, and tired.

The folks in Canada are such open, caring people. The DeChamplains are a wonderful example. It was at their luxurious home in Matane where I stayed in '98 after finishing my last day of hiking in Canada. They took great pleasure in sharing and enjoying my 60th birthday and the success of my hike. They have since become such great, dear friends.

I have misjudged the time necessary to negotiate this last section of trail, for there is one pull over an enormous mountain that

I had overlooked. It is getting very late and I'm bone-weary tired from fighting the fiddleheads and from the emotional drain of the lightning strike. But my friend Viateur is not impatient with me, nor is he concerned that he has spent much time preparing to greet me, and to take me to his home this day. Soon, just as I'm sure he has given up on my ever arriving, up the trail he comes, bringing a much-needed hug of friendship and encouragement and that ever-present grand Canadian smile!

Jocelyne has prepared a feast for me, and we enjoy such a memorable evening together. Thank you my dear friends, thanks from the bottom of my heart! What a day, what a day!

But I shall climb among hills of vanished lightning,
And stand knee deep in thunder with my head against the sky.
(Winifred Willes)

Monday—July 3, 2000
Trail Day—41
Trail Mile—617
Location—Les Camps Tamagodi, PQ-195 at Matane River Bridge,
Québec. Dennis Lord, proprietor.

Viateur prepares a fine breakfast, as Jocelyne is off to work. I'm clean and warm, and my gear and clothing are fresh and dry. Hiking like this may prove difficult!

We load up and head back to the Matane Wildlife Reserve where the IAT meets the road a few miles east of John. The entrance to Reserve Faunique de Matane is an hour and a half round trip from Viateur's home.

The hike today is a roadwalk, totally a roadwalk along the main Reserve road. The day is pleasant and the treadway such a welcome relief to my sorely complaining feet. By early afternoon I have reached John and am surprised to find Georgette on duty.

Georgette is the kind lady who speaks no English, but who aided me in getting a permit to enter the Reserve during moose hunting season in '98. By mid-afternoon I arrive at the point where my journey in Canada, during the Odyssey of '98, was completed—the Matane River Bridge at PQ-195. There were many folks from Matane present at that time, folks who have since become my very dear friends. They were here to share my joy in a successful journey, and to help celebrate my 60th birthday. I stand here now, the far-off whisper of glad music playing in the shadows of my thoughts as a slow-motion replay of those poignant moments is reenacted in my mind's eye. It is said, "You can never go back." But I have gone back. It is now, but it is also then. It is October 30, 1998. There's the old rail fence where, in my arms, I rested and cradled my teary-eyed head to thank the Lord for such an incredible miracle in my life, and for the sixty wonderful and rewarding years of my life. There is Lucy with her tripod and her camera, trying to capture the waning rays of light as we all pose, with broad-beaming Canadian smiles (I've got that smile down, too!). Just look at us there, what a happy bunch of hikers. Oh, it does this old heart such good to see all these folks again! But alas, the brightness of this day soon overshadows the dim shadows of that time-sealed space, and the spell is broken and gone. But for just a moment the time seal was also broken, and I found pleasure and joy in taking a journey back through time to the nostalgia of that grand, memorable occasion.

Across the highway and by the bridge is Les Camps Tamagodi, a row of old but well-maintained rooms coupled to a convenience store and restaurant. I check in, have some lunch, and settle in to do some writing. In a while, when I head for the pay phone to download my email, in rolls this big van. I recognize it right away. It's the same van Eric Chouinard drove here with the contingent of folks from Matane in '98. With him are Jean-Pierre from Matane, Dick Anderson and Will Richard from Maine, and Katia Galindo from Huixquilucan Estado de Mexico. All are here to hike sections of the Matane Reserve and to take Will to the many breathtaking sights for shots for the 2001 IAT Calendar. So much for the writing session this evening! Later comes Bob Melville. It's time to party and have another grand time with dear friends at the Matane River Bridge. Seems there's never a dull moment in this old hiker's life!

> *But all true things in the world seem truer,*
> *And the better things of earth seem best,*
> *And friends are dearer, as friends are fewer,*
> *And love is all as our sun dips west.*
> (Ella Wheeler Wilcox)

Tuesday—July 4, 2000
Trail Day—42
Trail Mile—638
Location—Shore of Lac Matapédia, Québec

After breakfast with the gang and a grand sendoff, I'm bound for the village of Matapédia, the last leg on this journey in Canada. Today I'm heading into "get lost" territory. I had a devil of a time staying on trail through certain sections here in '98, and, so it seems, there will be no difference today.

I manage just fine all the way to Saint-Vianney, but after this little village, the roadwalk turns are not marked. I first try following orange flagging, as the trail was marked with orange flags earlier in the day. After four or five miles of wandering every which way, I finally get directions to Lac Matapédia from a young fellow on a four-wheeler. "Just follow the snowmobile signs," he says. And so I do. Two hours into this hike I finally see a single, solitary IAT blue and white blaze nailed to a tree!

The zig-zags around Lac Matapédia lead to another wild goose chase. I finally follow the most direct route by compass, which seems to be leading toward the little town of Amqui. I've spent half my time hunting for the trail today rather than hiking it, which has sapped me both physically and mentally. I did manage to enjoy the half-mile long bog bridge and the view of Lac Matapédia from the neat summit shelter. I pitch near the lake for the evening, get a warming and cooking fire going, then try to calm down and relax a little before rolling in. No fireworks here on my 4th. God Bless America! I'm asleep in just a blink.

> *True happiness is seldom found,*
> *Among the polished stone.*
> *For on the path where most have trod,*
> *Scant faith has ever grown.*
> (N. Nomad)

Wednesday—July 5, 2000
Trail Day—43
Trail Mile—662
Location—Auberge La Coulée Douce, Causapscal, Québec

The rain comes hard during the night and is still thumping and hammering my tent this morning. It's a great convenience being able to get dressed and to have the ability to organize my pack while still in my shelter. These tasks were impossible in the little Slumberjack tent I carried in '98. Back then, on days like this, I was in for a good soaking right off the bat. Another grand feature with this tent, Kurt Russell's Nomad, is that it weighs less than the Slumberjack! The only problem that I've encountered so far is condensation. Not a nice thing when you're using a down bag. I think, for the next tent I have Kurt make, we'll do the whole thing except the pan in no-seeum netting, then cover it with a sil-nylon fly. I figure this arrangement shouldn't weigh over an ounce or two more. This may not eliminate the condensation problem, but at least it'll remove it from direct contact.

On this section from Amqui to Causapscal, I got big-time lost in '98. With what I've just been through, I'm concerned about the same problem again. So with the rain intensifying, the wind pushing near-bitter cold, I decide to make this day a roadwalk from Amqui to Causapscal. I'm saddened and disappointed that I must bypass this section of trail. However, this is not the day to be lost in the woods and I need to move along, so off I head on PQ-132. Shortly, a vehicle pulls alongside and an officer with that broad-beaming Canadian smile beckons me. I recognize him immediately. It's Luc Forest, Warden, Reserve Faunique de Matane. He had stopped to talk with me as I hiked the Reserve in '98 and he had heard from Jocelin that I was coming through again. What a pleasure and coincidence seeing Luc once more!

There is much traffic on PQ-132, but the wind and rain are at my back. Except for the torrential blasts accompanying the thundering eighteen-wheelers, the roadwalk is not all that unpleasant. I arrive in Causapscal a little after five.

I'm splurging and indulging myself much more this time around, for this may well be my last time around. I choose to stay the evening at the grand La Coulée Douce, a delightful old inn on the hill overlooking the confluence of the Causapscal and Matapédia Rivers. This is prime Atlantic salmon fishing territory. Fly fishermen, all decked out in their proper and impressive garb, parade about. On the dining room wall hangs a picture of Jimmy and Rosalynn Carter accompanied by Kurt Gowdy. George Washington didn't sleep here though, so it isn't quite that famous. I check in, a little out of place, but the kind Canadians look on my presence with no more than mild amusement. So I guess I kind of fit in.

We are, all of us, subject to crosses and disappointments,
but more especially, the traveller...
(William Bartram)

Thursday—July 6, 2000
Trail Day—44
Trail Mile—662
Location—Auberge La Coulée Douce, Causapscal, Québec

Oh, is this old inn a fine establishment! I decide to while away another day here as I rest and get caught up on my journal entries.

Man has indulged in the sport of fly fishing for Atlantic salmon as long as this spectacular species has been known to exist. The region within and surrounding the rivers Restigouche, Kedgwick, Matapédia, Causapscal, and Upsalquitch is *the* place to be for fly fishing. At Causapscal, it's a grand tradition. Here at La Coulée Douce, an historic inn for fishermen, I'm reading about the glorious history of this popular sport. I'm told that the outdoorsman in all of us has not truly lived until locked in the struggle of fighting an Atlantic salmon caught on a fly, as the fish explodes from the pure cold rushing waters of the Causapscal.

What a pleasantly rewarding and relaxing way to spend the day!

Men go fishing all their lives without knowing
that it is not fish they're after.
(Thoreau)

Friday—July 7, 2000
Trail Day—45
Trail Mile—680
Location—Meadow above Creux Brook crossing, Québec

The trail from Causapscal follows the old gravel road above town out and into the vast timberlands of Canada. Here are rolling hills and cold-rushing streams. The trail meanders, following old logging roads, to finally enter the narrow, rugged canyon of Creux Brook.

Here the trail tumbles and climbs as it squirms and wriggles its way along and beside this friendly, fast-rushing brook.

Rain has threatened on and off all day, and it finally comes, good and steady, to be my companion for the evening. I pitch on a small plateau-like meadow near where the trail fords Creux (deep) Brook. This has been a good mileage day. Except for getting sidetracked onto a new logging road for a couple of miles and finally having to backtrack, I have done well and am pleased with my success. The rain pattering my tent hastens the arrival of deep, contented sleep.

I saw God wash the world last night.
Ah, would He had washed me...
(William L. Stidger)

Saturday—July 8, 2000
Trail Day—46
Trail Mile—700
Location—Motel Restigouche, Matapédia, Québec. Pete Dubé,
proprietor.

The rain persists, more a moody mist than rain, as I break camp and prepare to cast off for the day. First order is to ford Creux Brook. Rather than wrestle with my gaiters and hiking boots, I opt for my camp shoes. To my joy, I find the ford much less an event this year, as the water level is much lower and the current is not so swift. I make the crossing in short order and decide to remain in my camp shoes until fording the Assemetquagan River. There are many fine vantages this morning as the trail seeks the high ground along the bluffs overlooking the canyons of Creux Brook and the Assemetquagan. Such a remarkable appearance are the canyons, shrouded in a swirling turbulence that opens here, then there, to reveal the breadth and depth of this enormous place. It's the mountains and me; we're literally above the clouds this morning. And this heavenly sight? To me, has there ever been such an appearance, such a grand and glorious affair!

I have decided to attempt two days of hiking in a single day, for I have gotten out to a very good start, and hiking in the rain with the thought of pitching, cold, wet, and tired on the cold, wet ground this evening provides the impetus to move along briskly. The ford at the Assemetquagan is a delightful experience. The river is breathtaking in its beauty and in its sheer width. But the depth is a shallow affair, remarkably uniform for nearly two-hundred feet, with the polished gleam from the millions of tumbled stones providing a colorful array of brilliance.

I'm moving south now, almost due south, as I follow the road into Saint-André-de-Restigouche. I soon arrive at the church. So very prominent is its presence on the very top of the ridge that is Saint-André, the trail follows beside the church's side-yard, then to pitch off again, right into the Canadian countryside.

The rain continues as I continue battling the fiddleheads that grope and cling as I pass, but there are less than fifteen kilometers to go to arrive at Pete Dubé's Motel Restigouche, and I'm on schedule to arrive there by early evening. I'm so pleased with my progress and with the great distance I have covered today. My reward will be a grand reception from Pete and from Gaby his girlfriend; a full tub of hot water in my own dry, cozy and comfortable room; and a great evening meal at Pete's beautiful restaurant.

Oh, aren't some things so predictable? For Pete and Gaby are right here to share in the excitement of my finishing the Canada segment of my hike at the very front steps of the fine Restigouche! It is so great to be back once again at Pete's place. And what a memorable evening with Pete, Gaby, Bruno and Carol, and David and Sally and their precious little baby girl, India. Memories that are good are blessings indeed, for one who is searching the fringes of beauty. But to relive such precious memories, memories that are part of God's hazy blue, bring joy beyond description. I'm in the very midst of such an intense and remarkably rewarding time. Thank you, dear Lord, for your boundless and merciful love.

> *It seems God always finds a way,*
> *To find a way for me.*
> *His guidance comes thru steadfast love,*
> *'tis there for all to see.*
> (N. Nomad)

Sunday—July 9, 2000
Trail Day—47
Trail Mile—700
Location—Motel Restigouche, Matapédia, Québec

The Motel Restigouche is such a comfortable, enjoyable establishment. I'm always totally exhausted, so much a physical wreck each and every time I arrive, it makes every stay so outstanding and memorable—if for no other reason than the sheer pleasure of recovering in this restful haven. I have so many dear friends here now, friends made during my previous and numerous sojourns.

One of the dearest is Bruno Robert. Bruno saw me the very first day, the very first moment I entered Matapédia on that cold, windy October day in '98. Shortly after arriving, Bruno came by the hotel to meet me and to introduce himself. At the time, he was a member of David LeBlanc's trail-building crew. I remember him saying, "I know right away when I see you on the highway with your hiking sticks that you are hiker and that you come a very long way." Ahh, yes, Bruno, I had come a very long way! Thanks for taking the time to meet me that day and for being such a positive influence, an influence that started this lasting love affair with your delightful village, Matapédia.

Bruno is always one of the first friends I see when I enter Matapédia, and he's usually one of the last, always spending much time with me while I'm here. This morning he comes by first thing to sit with me and to have coffee. Little do I know the plans he's made for this day, as he explains (much as a child filled with excitement and glee) "I want you to come with me and Carole. We will have breakfast together with David and Sally and their little baby, India. Paul and Georgette (David's parents) will come to join us too, just after church." Bruno continues, "Then we will spend a great day on the river. We will ride the river together!"

Bruno, my dear friend, you have planned this perfectly, on such a beautiful, warm day. Didn't we have such a fun time at breakfast! Paul LeBlanc is one of Pete's dear friends, and now also one of my dear friends in Matapédia. He is a medical doctor here. As soon as he arrives from church, Bruno insists he examine my broken and disfigured hand. After much time spent gently flexing and probing he concludes that I indeed have a broken hand. He says, "Your second metacarpal appears to be completely fractured. However, there remains good alignment and apposition. No reduction is necessary and instead of pinning the bone, if you have good hand movement and flexibility, you can choose to let it heal as is. But it will always be just a little crooked." Thanks Paul, what good news! Decision is, my hand shall always remain "...just a little crooked!"

After breakfast, we head for David's new business location on the river. David is a guide and runs his own canoe concession, Nature Aventure, a well-established service that provides enjoyment for pleasure-seekers and fishermen. He and Bruno, who is also a guide on the river, decide that we should use the two-seater kayak today. They have it quickly loaded on David's van. David drives us north to where we put in on the rolling, picturesque Restigouche. From here, we'll while and drift the day along as the current carries us back down in tumbling, brisk fashion, all the way to the little village of Matapédia.

The river is alive with excitement, a perfect day, a perfect Sunday for families of fun-seekers to converge upon this magic and picturesque place. The vantage from the river, o'er these placid but-often-rollicking waters, is an inspirational adventure. There are grand old fishing clubs and lodges all along, all that remain from the halcyon of yesteryear, and as a constant backdrop, the remarkable canyon walls looming, faces boulder-scarred, projecting to the heavens. And above, a blue-perfect sky flooding us with blinding brilliance. The diamond-studded rapids boil before us, and Bruno heads straight for the largest projecting boulder and the deepest sculpt, a whirling pool, and we glide and bounce right through! Oh my, what a day, Bruno, what an incredible day!

But this day is not yet over, for as evening arrives is there ushered in a grand affair. At Pete's fine restaurant I'm treated to a memorable evening as Pete's guest. At the table are Pete, Paul and Georgette LeBlanc, Bruno and David. And what great joy to have arrive and to have join us, the legendary guide of the Restigouche for over three-quarters of a century, my dear friend Richard Adams.

Time has flown by so fast. And comes the time when the good times must end, when the farewells and goodbyes must be said. This is, indeed, such a sad time for me, for I know not when or if I'll ever return—or see these dear friends again. Goodbye my happy, joy-filled, kind and generous Canadian friends, goodbye.

All our sweetest hours fly fastest.
(Virgil)

Monday—July 10, 2000
Trail Day—48
Trail Mile—700
Location—Matagamon Store and Campground, near Matagamon Entrance (north gate), Baxter State Park, Maine. Don and Diane Dudley, proprietors.

Much effort has gone into organizing a relay of rides to shuttle me from Québec through New Brunswick and back to the US.

Bob Melville comes first thing this morning to carry me to Kedgwick, New Brunswick. From Kedgwick, Maurice Simon then drives me to the border at Fort Fairfield, here to be picked up by Torrey Sylvester who delivers me to the campground at Matagamon. From this point tomorrow, I'll resume my hike on to Baxter State Park, the end of the IAT and the beginning of the AT.

The first leg in this incredible Odyssey 2000 is now history. I have completed the IAT in Canada. All that remains to finish the IAT is to climb Mount Katahdin, which I'll probably do Wednesday if weather is agreeable. I can send my compass home now.

> *If you can dream—and not make dreams your master;*
> *If you can think—and not make thoughts your aim;*
> *If you can meet with triumph and disaster*
> *And treat those two impostors just the same...*
> (Rudyard Kipling)

Tuesday—July 11, 2000
Trail Day—49
Trail Mile—720
Location—Russell Pond Campground, Baxter State Park, Maine

It's always a pleasure seeing Don and Diane Dudley again. Diane departs with friends today on a trip to Alaska, and she was bubbling over with excitement last evening. I pitched down by the Penobscot, and while setting up was greeted by Vinyl Pierce. I later joined him and his wife, Collene, at their camper for tea and an enjoyable evening of conversation.

First order today is a short roadwalk to the north entrance of Baxter State Park. I'm overjoyed when I see who is at the gate. It's Dana Miller, the same gatekeeper who greeted me on my way through in '98! He recognizes me immediately and we have a grand time talking about the park and the trail. I'm quickly up to speed on all the latest in Baxter. Ed Cunningham is no longer at South Branch, but Tom Lohnes is still at Russell Pond where I'll be staying tonight. And what a joy finding out that Brendan Curran is now the ranger at Russell Pond. I met Brendan, a roving ranger at the time, at Daicey Pond in '98. Dana gives Brendan a shout on the radio and lets him know I'm on my way.

The roadwalk continues though Matagamon Gate to South Branch Pond, then it's a cruise down to Russell Pond. I'm in by two-thirty, to be greeted enthusiastically by Brendan. We spend a relaxing afternoon in conversation beside placid, scenic Russell Pond, as cedar waxwings flit about among the spruce.

In the bunkhouse, just as the shadows of evening descend, I get a cooking and warming fire going. I'm thinking what a pleasure it has been, seeing these friends again. This has been a fine hiking day!

Bid good-by to your sweetheart, bid good-by to your friend;
The Lone Trail, the Lone Trail, follow to the end.
Tarry not, and fear not, chosen of the true;
Lover of the Lone Trail, the Lone Trail waits for you.
(Robert W. Service)

CHAPTER 2

THE APPALACHIAN NATIONAL SCENIC TRAIL (AT)

Wednesday—July 12, 2000
Trail Day—50/1
Trail Mile—731/8
Location—Daicey Pond to The Appalachian Trail Lodge,
Millinocket, Maine.
Don and Joan Cogswell, proprietors.

I arise at six to a totally cloud-free day and quickly decide to go for it, to summit Katahdin and complete my second thru-hike of the IAT. I'm on the trail for Roaring Brook Campground before seven and make very good time, arriving around ten. I look for Simone Rossignol, ranger at Roaring Brook, for I want to cancel my reservations at the bunkhouse for the evening. But she is out about the campground, so I head on up the Healon Taylor Trail for Pamola and Mount Katahdin.

This climb is a long and strenuous climb with few breaks, as the trail winds ever upward. Above treeline, large rocks and boulders

make the scamper especially difficult, requiring constant and total concentration lest I slip, instantly ending my hike. I claim the summit of Pamola before two to begin the traverse of the infamous Knife Edge. Aptly named, the Knife Edge is a glacier-honed (sharp as if razor-stropped) ridge, narrow and treacherous, with drop-offs, ledges, and slides plummeting thousands of feet on either side. On this "trail" it's time to be patient to a fault, to an all-encompassing, cover-all-bases kind of fault—with plenty of nimbleness thrown in, nimbleness for the old *Nimblewill*! The day remains pleasant with only a moderate, steady wind. I'm blessed to have this good fortune, this favorable weather. I make good progress for the short distance to the chimney. Here there is a bottleneck, a jam-up of folks that seem to be wishing they were anywhere but here right now. I must wait, as there is no way around. One by one, the dear ones must be assisted with foot placement and guidance over the blind, straight-down ledges that seem to pitch to oblivion. Once through this traffic, I do fine and I'm very pleased with my progress, for I'm negotiating this trapeze-like treadway with my sticks and a full pack.

By two o'clock I'm standing on the summit of Mount Katahdin, here to be greeted by an overwhelming flood of emotions, as memories of my '98 hike descend to engulf me. I go to the rocks beyond where I can be alone for a while, to compose myself and to clear and prepare my mind for this day's experience, an experience that will bring other grand memories anew, for the remainder of my life.

Clouds are banking to the west and north as I hurry down the Hunt Trail and off the mountain, the storm now sweeping toward the summit, enraged by the wind. On the ascent in '98, I don't recall this being such a great distance or such a technically difficult traverse. Time seems to pass so slowly as I continue descending, anticipating my arrival at Katahdin Stream Campground.

I'm anxious to get to the base of Katahdin, for here on a bronze plaque affixed to a large boulder are the words of a former Governor of Maine. He worked tirelessly and diligently the last thirty years of his life amassing the lands he would subsequently give to the people of Maine—over 200,000 acres, including Mount Katahdin; the lands now known as Baxter State Park:

Man is born to die, his works are short lived.
Buildings crumble, monuments decay, wealth vanishes.
But Katahdin in all its glory,
forever shall remain the mountain of the people of Maine.
— Percival Proctor Baxter, 1876-1969

The hike from Katahdin Stream Campground to Daicey Pond is a pleasant one along the park road and around the ponds. I arrive at Daicey to be greeted with grand smiles and the kindest welcome by Rangers Marcia and Gabriel Williamson. I have been so looking forward to seeing them both again, and as luck would have it they've just returned this day to Daicey Pond. I flop right down on the same chair I flopped down on in '98, and with much excitement, we exchange happenings since our last meeting.

My plans are to go on to Millinocket this evening. While we're catching up on past events, a radio message comes in from Togue Pond Gatehouse. A hiker is being brought to Daicey Pond, and the driver will be returning to Millinocket. Hot dang! Looks like I've got myself a ride, hopefully right to the steps of Don and Joan's Appalachian Trail Lodge. As I hike down the road to the thru-hiker shelters at Daicey and at the parking area, Dave Hopkins from Farmington Falls, Maine, greets me. He has brought a young hiker, trail name *Lurch*, to Daicey Pond. *Lurch* is flip-flopping. Having interrupted his northbound AT hike at Harpers Ferry, he'll be heading back there. Dave offers me a ride as he heads home through Millinocket. Oh my, how's that for a stroke of luck!

Soon I'm at The Appalachian Trail Lodge. Here I drop my pack on the front porch and head for The Appalachian Trail Café to make arrangements for a couple of days' stay and to get a good home-cooked meal. Here Joan and Don Cogswell, proprietors of the lodge and café, greet me. Looks like this is going to be a memorable stay in a neat little New England trail town.

A great supper, a luxurious hot soaking for my tired, aching bones, and I'm off to the Land of Nod.

There were times when the only thing that kept me going was the thought of standing there on top of Katahdin.
(Dorothy Hansen)

Thursday—July 13, 2000
Trail Day—51/2
Trail Mile—731/8
Location—The Appalachian Trail Lodge, Millinocket, Maine

What a great night's rest at the Lodge. The first order of the day is to head to the Appalachian Trail Café for breakfast, then back to work on my journal entries. In the afternoon, Don runs me out to the shopping center, then over to Baxter State Park Headquarters. I had hoped to meet Irvin C. *Buzz* Caverly, Director of the Park, but I just miss him. It's back to the Lodge for more time on journal entries. No hiking today.

> *I view the existence of this pathway and the*
> *opportunity to travel it, day after day without interruption,*
> *as a distinct aspect of our American life.*
> (Myron Avery)

Friday—July 14, 2000
Trail Day—52/3
Trail Mile—731/8
Location—The Appalachian Trail Lodge, Millinocket, Maine

If I'm going to do something about my broken hand—other than just let it heal as is, then that something has to be done pretty soon. The break is trying to glue, not popping and snapping like the first week following the mishap. So this morning I decide to head for the hospital here in Millinocket, get an x-ray, and see what the docs say.

Hospital reception sends me directly to emergency, from where I'm taken right in. All express much concern about my hand until I explain how long it's actually been busted. The x-rays confirm what I already knew, but it's good to see the break and to be able to make an assessment of what I'm dealing with. I'm pleased to find the break fairly clean, with little separation or deviation and only minor angular misalignment. One option that is suggested is to head for Portland to the hand specialist, spend a couple of days in the hospital there for surgery and have the bone straightened and pinned. The other option is to just let it heal crooked as is. I choose the latter. I'm given a removable cast and some Ace bandages to wrap the hand, and I'm sent on my way. Back at the Lodge, in my room, I try harnessing my trekking pole with the cast in place. This is not going to work. I wear the cast around for a short while and then relegate it to the circular file. If I can keep from wrenching or bumping my hand for the next week or so, I think I'll pretty much have this problem behind me.

After lunch at the Appalachian Trail Café, I borrow Don's bike and head back to Baxter State Park Headquarters. This time Director Caverly is in, and I have the opportunity to meet and talk with him. We discuss the directives and mandates set down decades ago by Percival Proctor Baxter and how the resources of the Park were to be and have been managed. Mr. Caverly has been entrusted with that responsibility for going on thirty years. We also talk about the IAT and my advocacy for that trail and for my interest and desire in seeing its successful construction/completion in Maine. Before departing, I compliment Mr. Caverly for his unwavering commitment to fulfilling Baxter's dream, a dream of seeing Katahdin remain in its wild and natural state. I extend my wishes for his continued success.

In the evening I relax, keep my feet up, talk with family and friends by phone, work on my journal entries, then tumble in. Onward tomorrow...

Rise, let us be going.
(Matthew 26:46)

Saturday—July 15, 2000
Trail Day—53/4
Trail Mile—750/27
Location—Rainbow Spring Campsite, Maine

While organizing my pack this morning, I decide to take it over to the scales and find out just how much I've been lugging the past few weeks. My dry pack weight on departing Forillon National Park in Québec was just under fourteen pounds, not counting food and water. Since then I have sent most of my winter gear plus some other items home, so I know my pack weight has gone down. Don told me yesterday about the dependability and accuracy of his scales, so I take my pack over and plunk it down. I'm pleasantly surprised to tell you I'm now carrying only nine and one-half pounds. Hot dang, this puts me in the ultra-lightweight category!

Early on, the folks at GORP.com, one of my generous and caring Odyssey 2000 sponsors, had expressed concern as to the adequacy of gear I planned to carry onto the tundra in Canada, and to the possible risk I might be taking by limiting my pack weight. I was asked to inform them at any time should I feel I had compromised my hike or myself as a result. I can tell you now and I'm pleased to report that I did not suffer for lack of needed gear. This does not mean there weren't times of discomfort due to adverse conditions, for the trek began in two to seven feet of snowpack and near-constant forty-degree rain for the first five days. But never was there a time when I feared for my safety or wellbeing, nor were there ever moments of fear as to my ability to effectively cope with the elements and conditions. I got wet, yes; I got cold, but in dealing with treadway flooded with snow melt up to my knees, at near-freezing temperatures through which I had to trudge at times, certainly little could have been done to improve the "comfort" level under those circumstances—no matter how much gear I might have chosen to lug!

And now, for you doubters who can't possibly believe I can be happy and comfortable on the trail with what little I'm carrying, I'll list all the items that make up my nine and one-half pounds. Please look this over, then try explaining to yourself what you must absolutely have that I'm doing without, keeping in mind all the while the pure joy I embrace by carrying perhaps 10-30 pounds less than you're lifting and lugging.

GVP G-4 backpack with hip belt
Wanderlust Gear Nomad Lite tent
Feathered Friends Rock Wren bag
Thermarest 3/4 Guidelite pad
Wanderlust Gear poncho
Pendleton long sleeve wool shirt
Patagonia long sleeve capilene shirt
Nylon pants
Lightweight wool socks
Asics racing flats
Hiker Trash painter's cap
Water bottle belt pouch
1-liter pop bottle
20 oz. pop bottle (2)
Aluminum cook pot
Aluminum bowl
Cookware stuff sack
Nylon ditty bag/w: stainless steel spoon/pot holder, First-Aid Kit in Ziploc, meds in Ziploc, medicated powder in Ziploc, Conquest in Ziploc, small vial of bleach, butane lighter, Photon Micro-Light, clothesline, tooth brush, floss, comb.
AT Data Book/ALDHA *AT Thru-Hikers' Companion* (select pages)
Nikon Nice Touch 4 35mm camera, extra 36x slide film

Sharp TM-20 PocketMail
Bread wrappers for stuff sacks
Large garbage bag

I carry no toilet paper and use no foliage (figure that one out). I can get by fine on a pound to a pound-and-a-half of food per day. I seldom carry more than a liter of water. I'm immune to *Giardia lamblia*, so I drink directly from select water sources. I'll occasionally use bleach to treat water from questionable sources. I cook on open fires and can get by fine on cold food on those days that I cannot build a fire. I have a six-ounce hobo "little dandy" wood burning stove I'll carry through those states where open fires are prohibited.

On my person, in-pocket, or otherwise not included in my pack weight are the following:

Nylon shorts
Short sleeve Polypro shirt
Homemade gaiters
Lightweight wool socks
Vasque cross-trainers
Watch
Medicine pouch with touchstone/talisman
Compass
Gerber 400 lockback knife
Smith & Wesson Magnum 3G sunglasses by Olympic Optical
Half-eye readers
Plastic wallet with cards/cash/change
Cotton headband
Ponytail band
Panasonic microcassette recorder
Data sheet for the day
Leki Super Makalu trekking poles

Don loads me up, and we're headed for Abol Campground in Baxter State Park. We'll drop Harold *Houdini* Richards off. He's flip-flopping and will continue his thru-hike south from Katahdin. Here at Abol I meet Ranger Darren Bishop. Kevin Donnell, who I met in '98 at Roaring Brook and who helped me north through Baxter and Matagamon that year—he's also now working out of Abol Campground. Alas, he is not here today, so I ask Darren to give Kevin my regards. On the way to Daicey Pond, Don hails a Park vehicle headed the other way. Here is Stewart Guay, one of the Rangers at Roaring Brook. Don has to show me off and tell Stewart all about my hike. I take pride in knowing so many of the great folks here on the staff at Baxter. And the reason? The reason is they're all very good at what they do and take pride in fulfilling Baxter's dream.

At Daicey, Don and I linger with friends, Rangers Gabriel and Marcia Williamson. We get some pictures, enjoy each other's company, and try putting off the goodbyes. But the time to shoulder my pack and head on down the trail soon comes, and I must turn and go. Thanks Don, Marcia, and Gabriel for your friendship and kindness!

In just a short while, I reach Abol Bridge Store and Campground. It is amazing, what with the thousands of hikers that have passed this way since '98, that Linda Belmont, proprietor at Abol Store, would recognize me. But as I enter she is at the counter. She looks up and a broad-beaming smile comes across her face! With this expression she remarks, "You've been here before, haven't you?" I reply, "Yes Linda, I've been here before!" Oh, what a joy seeing all these great folks again!

Linda is curious as to my route through Baxter State Park. She is very familiar with the IAT, and as I proceed to rid her shelves of food, we look over the maps of the Park. She is aware that the official starting point for the trail that leads to the end of the Appalachians in Canada begins right by her store at Abol Bridge, I explain however, that I have selected my own personal route, and that route begins/ends on Mount Katahdin.

I no sooner enter the Hundred Mile wilderness than comes the rain, but the sky soon clears, and from Rainbow Ledges am I blessed with one of the most profound and striking views of Katahdin, perhaps even more so than the view from the summit of Mount Chase—many miles and many days ago.

Hurd Brook Lean-to is filled with a group of youngsters from New York, so I move on to pitch for the evening at the lovely Rainbow Spring Campsite. There's a piped spring and plenty of firewood. This has been a grand day!

> *When we leave this world for eternity,*
> *We don't even get to carry 10 pounds.*
> (Glen Van Peski, GVP [now Gossamer] Gear)

> *Love is the only thing that we can carry with us when we go...*
> (Louisa May Alcott)

Sunday—July 16, 2000
Trail Day—54/5
Trail Mile—770/47
Location—Logging Road Mile 46.0 to White House Landing Wilderness Camp, Pemadumcook Lake, Maine. Bill and Linda Ware, proprietors.

I think it's just naturally supposed to be raining and cold in the Hundred Mile wilderness. It rained off and on throughout the night, and I'm out in the cold, swirling mist this morning, making the day appropriate and providing the opportunity to close this journal entry with my ditty about this mystifying place—the Hundred Mile wilderness.

You'll notice as I write this, the word "wilderness" is not capitalized. According to Dave Startzell, Appalachian Trail Conference Executive Director, the Hundred Mile wilderness now carries a small [w] designation as opposed to an upper-case [W]! This was said, tongue-in-cheek, when I talked with Dave at AT Headquarters during my northbound thru-hike in '98. But there is more than a little truth to this statement, as there are many roads crossing the trail now. And at places like the new logging road at mile 46 (southbound) customary services and other civilized trappings and amenities are available to the AT hiker only a short distance from the trail. That isn't necessarily bad and I'm certainly not complaining, 'cause I'm a trail town boy! This old codger certainly likes all the conveniences when they're available, and he'll usually track a beeline right there.

So today, after an easy pull over Nesuntabunt Mountain, and after meeting and talking with *Kiel*, a northbound thru-hiker, I head in to White House Landing Wilderness Camp located only a mile from the trail. Access is an easy half-mile roadwalk along a new logging road, then off into the woods for another half-mile on a neatly groomed trail, which ends at a floating dock on the shores of Pemadumcook Lake, the largest lake in Maine. Here a handmade sign reads, "Honk the horn (an aerosol foghorn hangs from the sign) and we'll come pick you up. Please be patient, we may be busy with other chores." I give the horn a couple of short blasts and in only moments I hear a motor crank and see a small outboard head out across the lake. As the launch approaches, I'm thinking, "This is really neat." Shortly, I'm greeted by Scott, who invites me aboard, and we're off to White House Landing.

Here is a picture-postcard setting, an old log lodge nestled in the tall-spired evergreen, up just a bit from the lake and situated in such a manner as to provide the most sweeping and panoramic view down and across the grand expanse of Pemadumcook Lake. On the ride over, Scott explained that the only access to White House Landing is by boat, a distance of some ten miles down the lake to the nearest road. So, the conveniences here are what they've made them. And the owners, Bill and Linda Ware, to whom I'm promptly introduced, have spared no effort or expense in making each guest feel right at home. The whole operation is pretty much powered by propane, with a generator and solar panels providing energy for some conveniences. Gas lights add to the spell created by the grand, old rustic lodge, and I find I have not the least difficulty relaxing in front of the broad picture windows (with a cold one in my hand) to enjoy the show—the pure white manes of a million galloping steeds (long ago described by Sigurd Olson), a fascinating illusion created by the wind lifting, then casting waves across magnificent Lake Pemadumcook.

After settling in the bunkhouse and after enjoying the luxury of a hot shower, I head back to the lodge where Scott and his girlfriend Debbie prepare my evening meal, a fully loaded pizza. Goodness, goodness, if this isn't roughing it!

> *A trail thru Maine's north wilderness,*
> *Past bogs and ponds of blue.*
> *Beckons the restless wanderlust*
> *Down deep in me and you.*
>
> *So, off in the swirling mist we go*
> *With our boots and raingear on,*
> *While friends at home and folks we love*
> *Try figurin' what went wrong.*
>
> *But, we'll rove these woods and mountainsides*
> *Awaitin' that bye-and-bye.*
> *A perfect dawn when packs take wing,*
> *And the treadway climbs the sky.*
> (N. Nomad)

Monday—July 17, 2000
Trail Day—55/6
Trail Mile—772/68
Location—East Branch Lean-to, Maine

Rain comes hard and steady during the night but by morning it has settled to a light, steady mist. I head over to the lodge where Bill is preparing a grand AYCE breakfast. He serves me a heaping plate, which promptly stokes me for today. Scott then gives *Backwards Bob*, a northbounder, and the old *Nomad* a boat ride back to the other shore. I'm on the AT again by eight-thirty.

I encounter many puncheons (long, low, log bridges) across numerous bogs this morning. The rain makes these wooden structures extremely dangerous, for they're covered with what I call, "slime of the time." Slow, patient progress is the only safe way to approach these structures.

By noon the drizzle has subsided, and the mush begins to burn off. The hike into the afternoon and for the remainder of the day is enjoyable. On a short pop up and over Little Boardman Mountain, I meet northbound thru-hikers *Acrobat, Captain,* and *Albatross*. By early evening I'm at East Branch Lean-to, where I get a fine cooking and warming fire going. There's a chill in the air toward nightfall, so I roll into my warm and roomy Feathered Friends Rock Wren and soon am comfy and snug.

> *I wish I could walk for a day and a night,*
> *And find me at dawn in a desolate place*
> *With never the rut of a road in sight,*
> *Nor the roof of a house, nor the eyes of a face.*
> (Edna St. Vincent Millay)

Tuesday—July 18, 2000
Trail Day—56/7
Trail Mile—793/89
Location—Chairback Gap Lean-to, Maine

Rain sets in again during the night and remains my steady companion for this day. The ever-present rocks and roots are a constant challenge when dry. When wet, the least off-angle or misstep will quickly pitch you right in. I take a couple of flying pack-slammers and a corkscrew elbow-banger today, along with numerous dipsy-doo slaloms and swaggering sashays, but I'm none the worse for wear, for which I'm thankful. My right hand is trying very hard to heal, and it doesn't need any more banging around right now.

This morning I was faced with the first respectable climb since scaling Katahdin—up and over White Cap Mountain. Northbounders I've met raved about the grand view from this summit. But alas, this morning I'm looking into the likes of Navy-bean soup the entire traverse.

In '98 I passed by Gulf Hagas, "Grand Canyon of the East," in the hammering rain. It isn't hammering today, but the shroud is again here, not the kind of day I'd want to spend climbing around in the Gulf. So, reluctantly, I pass this AT landmark once again. Perhaps, for me, the Gulf is not meant to be.

After fording the West Branch of Pleasant River, a rock hopper, I arrive early afternoon at Chairback Gap Lean-to. *Aunt Mable* has already pulled in for the evening, and we discuss our respective hikes as I attempt to build a fire in the rain. As I try harder to get the soaking wet tinder to ignite, the storm sets in more fiercely, to finally descend in buckets, accompanied by crashing audio and fully illuminated video, all for our evening enjoyment. *Big Ring* and *Granny Gear* come in, and just as the thunder turns to stereo, up come *Pfish* and Adrian. *Aunt Mable* and I scooch over a bit, and there's plenty of room for all. What a joy to be in the protection of this shelter and away from the slam of this raging storm!

Aunt Mable offers to boil some water to warm and hydrate my noodles. I decline her kind offer, but when she offers the second time I quickly accept. I have sardines, bread and cheese for just such occasion, but a warm meal is always a better choice. Thanks, *Aunt Mable*!

> *Consider this from one who's done*
> *Before you move on down the path*
> *For every three days in the sun*
> *You'll taste a day of nature's wrath...*
> (Don Hursohn)

Wednesday—July 19, 2000
Trail Day—57/8
Trail Mile—809/104
Location—Wilson Valley Lean-to, Maine

The day dawns to locally generated mush, which soon burns off. The trail through here is badly overgrown, with many blowdowns for the better part of the day. Looks like there's been no maintenance to speak of since perhaps early last summer. This sure brings a feeling of appreciation for the fine trail conditions along other sections. It seems strange to be pushing through the grass and trail-engulfing foliage without getting totally soaked for a change, as the day has turned pleasant, and the treadway is actually trying to dry out.

There are a number of ups and downs today as I move on through the Barren/Chairbacks. First it's up and over Columbus Mountain, then to Third Mountain, Fourth Mountain, and finally Barren Mountain.

Wilson Valley Lean-to is a very pleasant site, with a grand fire ring, seats all around, and water just a short stroll away. I arrive by early afternoon to find the shelter to myself. In moments I have a fine fire going in the fire ring, then it's over for water to bathe, then freshen some of my clothing. I'm able to string a clothesline near the fire, and I empty my entire pack, draping things everywhere to drive away their soggy dampness.

I have been hiking off and on the past two days with southbounders *Pfish* and his brother Adrian, who arrive in a while. Later in the evening, northbounders *Shaman, Pixie,* and *Shakedown* come in. *Pixie* hiked some last year with Scott *River Otter* Galloway, who was the first to hike southbound from Cap Gaspé to Key West. I flew to Miami, then rented a car and drove to Key West to greet and congratulate Scott when he arrived last January. *Pixie* and I have a grand time sharing stories about this mutual friend.

After preparing my meal, I build the fire back up to warm and brighten the evening, and we all have a very enjoyable time sitting around and talking trail.

> *O'er stone and root and knotty log,*
> *O'er faithless bits of reedy bog...*
> (Maurice Thompson)

Thursday—July 20, 2000
Trail Day—58/9
Trail Mile—819/115
Location—ME-15 to The Pie Lady's, Monson, Maine. Sydney "The Pie Lady" Pratt, proprietor.

I awaken at seven-thirty to a glorious, sunshiny morning and am out and on my way to Monson. Today I'll complete my hike through the Hundred Mile wilderness, but a rugged ten miles yet remain. The blowdowns and overgrown treadway continue to Big Wilson Stream. After fording the stream, trail conditions improve. The trail

rattles up and down through what seems endless rocks and roots to finally emerge beside one of the most picturesque little ponds to be found anywhere in the wilderness. Lily Pond is a strikingly rugged but intimate pool, framed against a backdrop of conifers with the most impressive and massive granite temple rising in its midst. I pause for pictures, and then just to gaze upon its serene beauty.

I arrive at ME-15 around one and get a ride almost immediately, right to The *Pie Lady's* front door. What a joy to be here and to see my dear friend Sydney again. She greets me with a grand smile, exclaiming, "I've been looking for you!" We talk, and talk some more, as we get caught up on all that has happened in the past two years. Sydney shows me to the same little private room in the back of her lovely home, where I'll be able to work on my book, *Ten Million Steps*. In the next two days I must brush through the entire manuscript. Charlene Patterson, my editor at Falcon Publishing, has sent it to me in book form, complete with dust cover and illustrations. I must review it, then return it to her, as we prepare the book for printing. It frustrates me to interrupt my hike, but Charlene tried to prepare me for this months ago. It is true though—I'm becoming more excited about the book with every passing day as it comes together and we get closer and closer to completion. So, I'll take the time, stay right with it and get it done, but I know I'll be anxious to return to the trail.

I get cleaned up and presentable again before digging into this pile of work. In the evening I'm treated to the finest dining experience I can recall, perhaps since here last. Sydney is an absolutely superb cook. Then it's back to the little room to recline in peaceful contentment. It's great to be back here again, Sydney—déja vu, oh yes!

> *In the woods, too, a man casts off his years,*
> *as the snake his slough,*
> *and at what period soever in life, is always a child.*
> (Ralph Waldo Emerson)

Friday—July 21, 2000
Trail Day—59/10
Trail Mile—819/115
Location—The Pie Lady's, Monson, Maine

What a great night's rest! After a fine breakfast prepared by Sydney, I'm ready to get at it. But oh what a stack I must get through! What's taken me two years to write I must completely review in just two days.

By late afternoon I'm only on page 140. Not very good progress. Time seems so fleeting. I need a break, though, so I head downtown to Mike's for a great BBQ sandwich. I return to work until supper, and after, late into the evening.

Big Ring, Granny Gear, Pfish and Adrian all arrive before supper to stay the night.

> *Time is a gift to each and each,*
> *That hastens through our life.*
> *Bringing love, contentment, peace,*
> *And a fair-measured bit of strife.*
> (N. Nomad)

Saturday—July 22, 2000
Trail Day—60/11
Trail Mile—819/115
Location—The Pie Lady's, Monson, Maine

I worked late, so I slept late, missing breakfast, but Sydney has saved some coffee and that helps me get cranking this morning.

It's back to the book with determination, but I soon realize there's just no way to get this review completed today. It slowly sinks in—I'll probably be here at least until Monday, for I've also a week of journal entries to complete. Folks, hiking is hard; writing is hard. Hiking and writing is really hard!

By mid-afternoon my vision starts blurring and the old noggin locks up, so I take a break and head over to Shaw's Boarding House to spend a little time with Keith and Pat Shaw. I find Pat in the kitchen getting supper prepared for the hungry horde of hikers. As she continues peeling potatoes, we talk about the grand tradition this old place has become. When Keith comes through, I'm given the extended tour of his large and expansive facility. Even though he's pushing 73, Keith's still quite the handyman, full of boundless energy. A typical day here at Shaw's begins at 4:00 a.m. and doesn't end until all the hikers' needs are met, which is usually late evening. Keith, Pat, it's been great seeing you again; I wish you 24 more memorable years at Shaws!

In the evening it's off to the Appalachian Station Restaurant with *Big Ring* and *Granny Gear*. We're heading for the Saturday night special—prime rib. And does this ever turn out to be the right thing to do! Great company and great prime rib prepared by Maureen Trefethen, proprietor and cook at Appalachian Station. What a fine evening with my new southbound hiking friends, *Big Ring* and *Granny Gear*!

I have stuffed myself, it seems, to the point of bursting, and I'm unable to sleep, so I work on the book and my journals until 4:00 a.m.

I spent the day in the most agreeable manner in the
society of this man of singular worth. He led me over
his extensive improvements, and we returned
in company with several of his neighbours.
(William Bartram)

Sunday—July 23, 2000
Trail Day—61/12
Trail Mile—819/115
Location—The Pie Lady's, Monson, Maine

I finally manage some sleep, about five hours, so I don't roll out until after nine. While Keith Shaw was showing me his other house across the way yesterday, Reverend Daryl E. Witmer of the Monson Community Church was passing by. Keith introduced us, and during the course of conversation Daryl invited me to attend services this morning.

Sydney has saved some coffee for me again. After spending a few minutes with her, I'm right on time for church. The sermon covers a very familiar subject, one that is always good to review—that to be a disciple of Christ, we must place our love for God above the love of family, the love of self, and the love of material things. I'm still working on all three.

I spend the remainder of the day finishing up the book review/ proofing, and journal entries. Toward evening, Sridhar *Spider* Ramasami comes in. *Spider* began his journey from Cap Gaspé and he, too, is bound for Key West. *Caveman, Spider,* and I enjoy a grand time over dinner, talking trail.

It's time to get things ready for the post office, organize my pack, and prepare to depart for Stratton, Maine. I'm definitely ready for the trail again!

And every one that hath forsaken houses, or brethren, or sisters,
or father, or mother, or wife, or children, or lands,
for my name's sake,
shall receive an hundredfold, and shall inherit everlasting life.
(Matthew 19:29)

Monday—July 24, 2000
Trail Day—62/13
Trail Mile—829/125
Location—West of Horseshoe Canyon Lean-to, Maine

I seldom sleep in while on the trail, but at Sydney's it's been such a simple task. When I finally stumble out to the kitchen around nine, there's a piping-hot cup of coffee waiting for me. It's hard to eat everything Sydney puts on the table. As usual, there are leftover potatoes and pancakes, which she warms for me. Talk about being pampered!

Pfish and his brother Adrian are still holed up in the little cabin in Sydney's back yard. Sydney had taken them, along with north-bounder *La Tortuga*, to the outfitters in Greenville the other day. There they bought some new cross trainers to get out of their heavy hiking boots. Adrian's been having a devil of a time with his feet and knees. I think *Pfish* is also glad to get a break. They're southbound from Katahdin and are just getting started. As usual, with most AT beginners, both are carrying heavy packs. At my urging, *Pfish* also picked up a pair of Leki trekking poles (I sold a set of sticks for you, Leki!). Some of their decisions were no doubt based on my comments and suggestions—sure hope I steered them right. It's really great to see brothers sharing such quality time and enjoying each other's company. I wish you both well!

Caveman, a lover of spelunking when not hiking, has been recruited by Sydney to put up another hummingbird feeder. She has one by the window in front of the dining room table. So, as we dine, hummingbirds are frequent guests. *Caveman* is a big, tall kid, so he's been given the job of reaching way up and attaching another feeder so Sydney can also enjoy the colorful little birds at her bedroom window. In real life, *Caveman* is involved with computers, and this morning he sets to updating Sydney's Netscape Navigator from 3.0 to a newer version. This computer stuff is all so new and intimidating to folks like Sydney and me, but we're trying to learn. Sydney is kind, sharing all she has, so it isn't surprising that she allows stinky hikers into her room to use her personal computer—to get online and send email.

Since Thursday evening, I've been trying to get in touch with Dick Anderson, the President of the IAT. No luck. But this morning I'm finally able to reach him. He is pleased to hear about my good progress and is delighted to find that *Spider* is also here with me at Sydney's. *Spider* departed right behind me this spring, also southbound on the ECT/TA. These trails follow along with, and are superimposed over the IAT, and now the AT. All emerge from the sea, by the Cliffs of Forillon, Cap Gaspé. Both of us are headed for the beginning of the Appalachian Mountains in Alabama, and ultimately, the southernmost point on the eastern North American continent in Key West. We have a grand talk with Dick, who's always excited to hear good tidings from hikers.

I've been working feverishly this morning, trying to get ready so I can return to the trail. The last three days have been spent in final proofing for my upcoming book, *Ten Million Steps*, a 400-page hardbound book about Odyssey '98. I'm trying to get two boxes ready to mail: one to send home and one to bounce on to Stratton, Maine, my next maildrop. On the way back from the post office, I stop again at Appalachian Station, where Maureen prepares a fine lunch for me. I'm finally organized. Sydney drops everything once more to shuttle me back to the trail at four. Everyone is out and on the trail except me!

The treadway is friendly, and I manage about ten miles, even with the late start. I pitch in the woods just past Horseshoe Canyon

Lean-to. Before drifting off to contented sleep, my mind wanders to explore the thought of growing old. I've lately realized that I'm quickly becoming an old man. My bones are drying out, turning brittle, and are starting to scrape together pretty hard. I'll likely not pass this way again. Sydney, I'll dearly miss you, my friend; you have been so kind and generous to me. I'll remember you always. Goodbye...

> But at my back I always hear
> Time's winged chariot hurrying near.
> (Andrew Marvell)

Tuesday—July 25, 2000
Trail Day—63/14
Trail Mile—856/152
Location—US-201, Caratunk House, Caratunk, Maine. Jenson "Aunt Bee" Steel and Paul "One Braid" Fuller, proprietors,

I'm out and on my way south by six-thirty this morning, greeted by a gloriously clear, nearly haze-free day. Shortly, I meet a northbounder. *Lady Leaper* is bound for Katahdin. She stops, and we exchange an enjoyable conversation. Seems most northbounders have such a wicked focus now—on Katahdin, their final destination. Few want to tarry and talk; their minds are fixed with the singular purpose of completing their quest. *Lady Leaper* has her sights set too, but is taking time to truly savor these remaining few days. Great talking with you, *Lady Leaper*—my best, and congratulations!

As I hike along this morning, I'm thinking of my enjoyable stay in Monson. While I was in the shower yesterday morning, there came a knock on the bathroom door. Sydney said I had a phone call waiting. "I'm in the shower, Sydney," I replied. "Get their name and number and I'll call them back." So, I was surprised (as I emerged from the bath nearly ten minutes later) to find Sydney still on the phone, with the happiest, grand-smiling expression on her face! Come to find out that on the line was not only my good friend, but also Sydney's good friend, David *Fanny Pack* Atkinson. It isn't easy keeping in touch with all my friends while on the trail, but I'm making an effort, and with my little PocketMail I'm able to mass email them. Of course *Fanny Pack* is on that list, so he knew I was in Monson. Word has it that another big celebration is being planned at Tiorati Circle this year. *Baltimore Jack* is in the vicinity, and the whole bash sort of coincides with his arrival. Jack is *the* "Trash" in the clan that's affectionately known as "Hiker Trash," being one of the most beloved of the original clan. Great hearing from you, *Fanny Pack*. Thanks for your friendship and encouragement. I'm looking forward to seeing you again as I enter your neck of the woods. Keep in touch, my friend!

The hike today up to Moxie Bald is spectacular. Mount Katahdin is to the north and the Bigelow Range to the south. There's just the least bit of haze, making the presentation of these remarkable mountains from this vantage point such a mystical sight for dream-seekers like me. Today these grand cathedrals are truly on the fringe of God's hazy blue, that elusive, far-away, mysterious hither, thither and yon, where the wanderlust in all of us leads. Here on Moxie I run into *Big Ring, Granny Gear, Spider* and *Black Forest*. I also have the pleasure meeting *Bombadil, Mushroom* and *Orion*, northbounders. *Bombadil* had corresponded with me before beginning his AT hike, expressing interest in also doing the IAT, and here today does there spill from this lad amazing excitement in our meeting.

The hike today proves long on the trail but I have done well, so arriving at three-thirty at the side trail to Pleasant Pond Lean-to, I decide to continue on to Caratunk. Northbounders have spoken of this wonderful new hiker B&B that just opened up the first of June, and how they'd had such a pleasant stay there. So off to the Caratunk House I go! And did this ever turn out to be the right decision. Even though this has made for a twenty-seven mile day, the last six miles prove pretty much a cruise and I arrive around six-thirty. The Caratunk House can't be more than two or three hundred yards off the trail, a grand old restored (but original appearing) two-story dwelling at 218 Main Street. Here I'm greeted by *Aunt Bee* and *One Braid* and taken right in. I'm shown to a delightful period-furnished bedroom upstairs, and just as I finish showering in the spacious boudoir-designed and appointed bath, my pizza arrives! *Aunt Bee* gave me a cold one to enjoy with my pizza while he drove the fifteen miles round-trip to the store to bring back more refreshing long-necks! And what timing, for also just as the pizza arrives, so does *Spider*. We share an exquisite dining experience, with subdued light and mood music no less, right here in the beautiful dining room at the Caratunk House. I was going to do some writing this evening, but the sandman somehow got the pillow under my tired, sleepy head, and that was it.

> *I'm lucky; I've found my path,*
> *and I'm going to keep on strolling down it.*
> (Sandra *Navigator* Friend)

Wednesday—July 26, 2000
Trail Day—64/15
Trail Mile—869/165
Location—West Carry Pond Lean-to, Maine

What a great time at the Caratunk House! The decision by all was to sleep in this morning, so *Aunt Bee* and *One Braid* obliged by holding off breakfast until eight-thirty. There's a full pot of fresh coffee when I awake at seven. There are three for breakfast: *Lurch*, who had come in earlier yesterday, *Spider,* and me.

Spider gets organized and on his way before noon, but *Lurch* and I tarry, not getting packed and ready until one. After a photo op with *Aunt Bee, Lurch* and I head for the Kennebec River. Steve *Ferryman* Longley is waiting patiently for us, as he's been waiting patiently for hikers for 14 years. We have a great reunion. You wouldn't think *Ferryman* could remember all the hikers he's shuttled across over the years, but he sure remembers me. The sun is warm, the day perfect, and we linger for the longest time enjoying grand conversation at the picnic table by the shores of the Kennebec. *Ferryman* is such an enthusiastic individual, such an interesting person. Says he, "When I speak, the rivers and the mountains are within me and they speak for me."

Lurch and I finally shoulder our packs and are on our way south again a little before two. The old boardwalk to Harrison's Pierce Pond Camps is just as I remember. And the old lodge is such a remarkable and friendly place to visit. I get to see Fran again. She and her husband Tim have been serving tank-stoking breakfasts to hikers for years. Great talking to you again, Fran; thanks for your kindness, and thanks, especially, for the memories!

Lurch and I enjoy the afternoon hiking together, arriving late at West Carry Pond Lean-to. Here we find family members *Houdini* and *Spider* already in residence. I soon get a cooking-turned-mosquito-taming fire going and we enjoy a very pleasant evening together. What a joy-filled, happy day!

> *To us the enjoyment of solitude, complete independence,*
> *and the beauty of undefiled panoramas is*
> *absolutely essential to happiness.*
> (Aldo Leopold)

Thursday—July 27, 2000
Trail Day—65/16
Trail Mile—892/188
Location—ME -27 to Widow's Walk B&B, Stratton, Maine. Jerry and Mary Hobson, proprietors.

The forecast is for rain today, with locally isolated thundershowers, and the day seems headed that direction with cool, gloomy overcast.

I'm moving by seven, with *Houdini* out ahead of me. *Spider* and *Lurch* won't be far behind.

Yesterday, *Lurch* and I hiked the ten miles from Pierce Pond Lean-to to West Carry Pond Lean-to in three hours and twenty minutes, an exact three-miles-per-hour average. The treadway there was some of the flattest and smoothest I can ever recall hiking along the AT. It's not difficult to maintain three miles per hour on the roadwalks that I have done and will be doing, but to crank out this kind of mileage in the woods presents considerably more of a challenge. So it is that the treadway out of West Carry Pond Lean-to this morning is much more in keeping with the AT's three "R's"—ruts, rocks, and roots. And to this mix must now be added a number of very respectable ups and downs as we enter the Bigelows, one of the most rugged and picturesque of all the ranges that make up the ancient and everlasting mountain chain known as the Appalachians.

In a while, *Houdini, Spider,* and I get together, and we hike the up-up-up climb to Little Bigelow Mountain. The overcast is still in place above us, but below, we are afforded splendid views down to Flagstaff Lake, to *Avery Peak, and beyond. I recall with the fondest memory standing at this very spot in late August of '98 with *Easy Rider*. We had made it out of Stratton that morning to arrive here at Little Bigelow, to witness one of the most stunning sunsets I can recall. The sun descended behind Avery Peak, setting the sky ablaze in crimson. *Spider* and *Houdini* stop here for lunch and I move on, first to Avery Peak, which is engulfed in frigid, wind-driven mist, then to West Peak, which I find in a like rage as I scurry up, over, and back down.

The treadway is long, very bumpy and difficult, as I push on to Stratton. There's a blue-blaze trail leading directly to the little village of Stratton, but I bail off the mountain, staying on the AT as it heads for ME-27.

There's little traffic on ME-27, but John, a Stratton local, stops to give me a ride right away, his handshake followed by a frosty tall one. John drops me off in front of Widow's Walk, a quaint turreted, two-story B&B right next to all the conveniences. In '98 I stayed at the White Wolf Inn and was treated kindly, but hikers I've met along the way recently told me about the Hobsons at Widow's Walk, so here I am. Entering, I'm greeted by *Green Giant*, a south-bounder reclined on the living room couch, watching TV. He explains that the owners are away but I'm welcome to stay. "Just pick a room," says *Green Giant*. Looking the place over, I decide on the front bedroom with an impressive three-window bay below the spire-topped turret. Widow's Walk was undoubtedly a very fashionable place in its heyday. It's being kept up and maintained now by Jerry and Mary Hobson, who themselves have hiked sections of the AT. They have opened their spacious home to hikers for over twenty years. I head right away to the old claw-foot cast-iron tub for a soothing-hot bone soaking.

Then it's to Stratton Diner, not a hundred yards away, for carryout pizza. Then to Northland Supply just across, for some cold, frosty longnecks. Oh yes, as my dear old hiking friend, *Wolfhound*, would surely say: "*Life is good!*"

I stand on Little Bigelow
In all its majesty.
While all around, vast wilderness
Is all that I can see.

Once lived a man who loved this more
Than anyone I know.
Tears cloud my view of Avery Peak,
From Little Bigelow.
(N. Nomad)

*The mountain is named in honor of Myron Halliburton Avery, who pretty much single-handedly built the AT. Avery was a founding member of the Potomac Appalachian Trail Club (1927), and served as chair of the Appalachian Trail Conference from 1931 until his death in 1952.

Friday—July 28, 2000
Trail Day—66/17
Trail Mile—905/201
Location—Spaulding Mountain Lean-to, Maine

I'm having a frustrating time today. My bounce box hasn't arrived from Millinocket. The Postmistress said it should have been here overnight, since it was sent Priority Mail. That was four days ago. I'm to check back again at eleven, but I don't hold much hope. Sure enough, eleven o'clock comes and no bounce box. This really upsets me but I try not to show my anger.

Spider came in this morning. He's picking up a few items before heading right back out. I don't get on trail until two but still manage thirteen tough, hard miles for the day. *Spider* and I pile in to an almost-full house of northbounders at Spaulding Mountain Lean-to. The rain has threatened all day, and although it's held off, the ups and downs have been a muddy mess, the bogs, boggy, the trail a pure slider. A safe hiking day, though; a true blessing!

> *And so my prayer; a path this day,*
> *From harm and travails be.*
> *Then lead me safely to'rd Thy way,*
> *Till pure the Light I see.*
> (N. Nomad)

Saturday—July 29, 2000
Trail Day—67/18
Trail Mile—924/220
Location—ME-4 to Gull Pond Lodge, Rangeley, Maine. Bob O'Brien, proprietor.

The northbounders are an intently focused bunch at this point. I hear stirring about early this morning and awaken to find one of the fellows grinding on his cereal. By four-thirty there are only three of us left in the shelter. Six of the Katahdin-bound are already out and headed north!

I'm able to sleep until seven and manage to get packed and headed on south by seven-thirty. This day doesn't look a bit better than yesterday. No rain, but threatening all the while. I've got some really tough pulls ahead, over Lone Mountain, Saddleback Junior, The Horn, and Saddleback Mountain. There are no views as I proceed, and the cold, mist-driven wind is bitter company on the summits. I scurry up and over them, glad to be down in the shelter of the stunted spruce below. This treadway is brutal, the path literally filled with rocks, boulders, roots and bogs. And as usual, the whole trail is pure soup. I can't remember so many large, off-camber rocks. Best just look at them though. These I've learned to avoid at all cost, for to step on one is an invitation to disaster, an abrupt, unscheduled close-up look at the whole underfoot scene. Progress is agonizingly slow and treacherous. I'm thankful to remain mostly upright as I skid along, but I do manage a couple of pack slappers.

Along about late morning, I hear voices as hikers approach from the south. In moments I hear, "*Nomad, Nimblewill Nomad,* is that you?" Oh, what a wonderful surprise to again cross paths with the *Blister Sisters*! They're Bev Shenton and Betty Sue Allen. They're being slacked through this section by *Pittsburgh*. They started their hike northbound from Springer in 1989 and plan to finish this year, their eighth trip to the trail in their quest for Katahdin. Coming off Saddleback I also meet a couple of northbounders with interesting trail names. I stop and chat a while with *I'm Satisfied* and *He's Getting There*!

There's little traffic on ME-4, but in just moments, as I hook out my thumb, the Coleman family comes along in their new Ford Excursion—to haul it in and pick up the old *Nomad*. I can't believe they've stopped for this dirty, smelly hiker. "Ma'am," I exclaim as I open the door, "I can't sit in that shiny new seat!" "Get in, get in, we're hikers too!" the lady exclaims. They're locals, and I enjoy hearing about how so many thru-hikers have come back to Rangeley to call this place home. They're a happy family and are obviously proud of their community. Indeed, it is a beautiful mountain town, what with Rangeley Lake, the scene set with a backdrop of heaven-bound spires. It's such a peaceful, tranquil setting. As we ride along, I'm thinking, "I could return to live here, too."

My bounce box, which never arrived at Stratton, has all my trail data for points south—so might you suspect that here in Rangeley, I have not a clue where to settle in for the evening. I'm told by the bartender at the little watering hole downtown to check the bulletin board at the post office, so off to the post office I go. Along the way I look across to a street-side café with folks lounging around outside. Here I spot someone I recognize immediately; it's *Yogi* of the *Yogi and BooBoo* brothers from '98. *Yogi* is doing an AT southbound now in preparation for a northbound on the ECT/TA next year. We have a fun time over pizza and beer then spend the evening together at Gull Pond Lodge. This has been a long, hard day, and I'm sure glad to be in with all the conveniences.

> *I see that nature has told me something, has spoken to me,*
> *And...I have put it down in shorthand.*
> (Vincent Van Gogh)

Sunday—July 30, 2000
Trail Day—68/19
Trail Mile—942/238
Location—Bemis Mountain Lean-to, Maine

At first I was very disappointed upon arriving in Rangeley, for I was unable to reach David Hopkinson. David is the kind gentleman who gave me a ride from Daicey Pond to The Appalachian Trail Lodge in Millinocket after the long day over Baxter Peak. I had seen David's seventeen-year-old son, Rob, again the day-before-yesterday in Stratton. He had said his father was looking forward to my arrival in Rangeley, and that I should give his folks a call and plan on staying with them. But alas, when I tried calling I got the "number no longer in service" message. I must have written it down wrong.

But my stay in Rangeley turned out just fine. Isn't it interesting how circumstances turn, for I got to see my good hiking friend *Yogi* again, and we spent a great evening together. Gull Pond Lodge was a very comfortable place, and Bob O'Brien a gracious host. It was also a pleasant surprise seeing *A Little Bit,* whom I had first met at Trail Days.

Stoneman, up from New York to do some hiking in Maine, gives *Yogi, Yogi's* friend *Cutter,* and me a ride back to the trailhead this morning. His little car is groaning as we pull out of Bob's driveway, loaded with four hikers and their packs, as we bounce along on ME-4.

There's a lovely campsite at Bemis Stream. *Yogi* and *Cutter* plan on stopping there. I have plans to hike on through to the Bemis Mountain Lean-to, so we bid farewell for now and I'm on my way. The hike today is pretty much a cruise. The forecast had called for rain, but it's held off. The overcast keeps the day cool, very mild. The trail pops up and down along low-lying ridges with the only significant pull coming late in the day as I climb Bemis Mountain. I arrive around six and get a cooking fire going after much huffing and puffing. Late comes *G-Force,* whom I'd met at Trail Days, and we spend a great evening together talking gear. Three of us here are wearing New Balance 803s, a lightweight cross-training shoe. New Balance is another of my very generous sponsors and will be providing me with all the shoes I need to complete Odyssey 2000. I switched to the 803s in Stratton after putting nine hundred miles on my tried and trusty Vasques. The 803s are a little lighter weight shoe, so I think I'm going to like them just fine.

The smoke always seems to head for the shelter. There is an eerie haze as the beams of light flash about at Bemis, hikers reading or composing their journals. Sorry 'bout that folks! We're all in with lights out at eight-thirty.

*Human beings are of such nature that they should have not only
material facilities but spiritual sustenance as well. Without spiritual
sustenance, it is difficult to get and maintain peace of mind.*
(Dalai Lama)

Monday—July 31, 2000
Trail Day—69/20
Trail Mile—951/247
Location—South Arm Road to The Cabin, East Andover, Maine.
Marge and Earl Towne, proprietors.

The hike today is tough and rugged, very slow and deliberate. The
day has cleared nicely, and the warm sun feels good; however, the
trail is soggy and the bogs are boggy, making the rock scampering
especially difficult. The Bemis Range consists of many peaks, beginning with West Peak and continuing through Old Blue. I've done
only nine miles for the day and it's already noon, but this will be it
as I head for Andover to see my good friends Marge *Honey* and Earl
Bear Towne at "The Cabin."

I'm fortunate to get a ride right away with the local mail carrier,
and he drops me off at the corner station. I give *Bear* a call, and he
sends *Raven* right away to fetch me.

The Cabin is a perfect place for tired and hungry hikers. Nothing has been spared to make our stay comfortable, to make us feel
welcome. *Honey* and *Bear* have built this place with their own hands.
As a result, these kind folks have established a place for *family*, a
place that radiates love and warmth in such a caring and compassionate way. As I enter, comes over me this warmth, this presence,
and I'm *home*. Oh, what a much-needed and satisfying blessing,
for their love not to be withheld from us lonely, homesick hikers!
Undeniably, this sincere caring is what makes The Cabin so special.

We sit the day, relaxing and talking, as if *Honey* and *Bear* had
nothing better to do. In the evening, *Honey* prepares heaping bowls

of spaghetti for me and the other guests—*Raven*, Laura, Greg, Cindy, and *Old Sam*.

Every time I've seen these dear friends (and I have seen them often over the last couple of years, for they attend all the hiker functions without fail), they've always invited me to come and spend time with them here at The Cabin. So, today is that day, and are they ever so glad to see me! What a wonderful feeling to know this old man can bring joy to the hearts of others as, indeed, that joy is so bountifully returned to me. It is truly humbling. Thanks, *Honey* and *Bear,* for your friendship, kindness and generosity—for truly caring!

> *That path cannot be so lonely,*
> *For someone has trod it before;*
> *The golden gates are the nearer,*
> *That someone stands at the door.*
> (Florence Smith)

Tuesday—August 1, 2000
Trail Day— 70/21
Trail Mile— 961/257
Location—East B Hill Road to The Cabin, East Andover Maine

I had a great night's rest, even managed to work some on my journal entries. The grand aroma of bacon in the skillet wakes me a little before six, so I head down for some coffee and a chat with *Bear*. In a while, he shows me a book, a yearbook. They've kept one for each "Class," and a grand one it is for the "Class of '98." I help drain the coffeepot while looking at letters, cards, and pictures *Honey* and *Bear* have received from all their (and my) dear friends.

The hike today is only ten miles to East B Hill Road, where *Bear* will come for me at one this afternoon. "Isn't it a bit early to end the day?" you might ask. Ahh, perhaps, but perhaps you do not know the Mahoosucs. For these mountains have gained notoriety among AT hikers as being the most rugged and difficult of all the near-countless ranges along the Appalachian Trail. At one in the afternoon I'm pooped.

And so it is, by the time the weary northbound thru-hiker reaches East Andover, it's time for a few of the things we all enjoy in life but miss out here on the trail—like home, family, some good food, a warm shower, a real bed, TV, a phone, and maybe a look at our email. And it's all here at The Cabin, especially the home and family. It's just great to be with loving, caring people! After a few short days and more time spent with folks at The Cabin, the hiker is ready to head out again, healthy, happy and content.

The mountains here in the Mahoosucs are not on the grand scale of the Whites and the Great Smoky Mountains, but they present a challenge not previously met anywhere along the AT. So after a hard, tiring morning, I'm ready for some more good old friendship and hospitality. *Bear* has arrived a little early at East B Hill, and he hikes in a ways to greet me. Together we enjoy the short hike back for another grand evening at The Cabin relaxing with family.

> *I'm in the habit of looking not so much to the nature of a gift*
> *as to the spirit in which it is offered.*
> (Robert Louis Stevenson)

Wednesday—August 2, 2000
Trail Day—71/22
Trail Mile—971/267
Location—East B Hill Road to The Cabin, East Andover, Maine

Today I'll hike ten miles, south to north, as it will be more convenient for the shuttle operation this evening. So, instead of hiking from East B Hill Road to Grafton Notch, I'll be going the opposite direction. *Punkin* and *Journey*, both northbounders thru-hiking the

AT from Springer Mountain to Baxter, will be hiking this section from Grafton Notch to East B Hill today. So I decide to join them. We enjoy a great day together with many fine views from the Baldpates. *Bear* again hikes in a short distance to greet us and we return to a wonderful evening of family fellowship at The Cabin.

And so, dear friends, you who have toiled over The Cabin, this is my final night with you. Being here these past short days, I have come to realize that you truly live your lives in such a special way. For you have given unselfishly. You make the words of that beautiful old poem ring true: *I Shall Not Pass This Way Again...*

> *Through this toilsome world, alas!*
> *Once and only once I pass,*
> *If a kindness I may show,*
> *If a good deed I may do*
> *To a suffering fellow man,*
> *Let me do it while I can...*
> (Anonymous)

Thursday—August 3, 2000
Trail Day—72/23
Trail Mile—990/286
Location—Near Gentian Pond Campsite, New Hampshire

Saying goodbye to dear friends is not easy, and I linger with *Honey* and *Bear* and all the new friends I've made these last three days here at The Cabin. There is *Momma C & Poppa C* and their son *Old Sam.* And there's *Raven* and Laura, her last name being Snickers; so, I've pegged her with the trail name *Why Wait.* I also met and hiked some with *Journey, Punkin, Wolf Man, Micah,* and his sister Jody. It's a long drive back to the trailhead at Grafton Notch. *Honey* and I have a great time talking about many things. Then it's another sad goodbye as I head on up the mountain.

Today is the day to do the Notch—Mahoosuc Notch. The hike off the Arm, followed by the rock scramble through the Notch, is one of the most difficult sections along the entire AT. But I have my sights set on Gorham, New Hampshire tomorrow, so I keep hammering through the ups and down and the incredible jumble of rocks and off-camber ledges. I manage one spectacular pack-slapper and bruise my leg. Somehow I'm able to cover nearly twenty miles for the day. This leaves me only twelve miles on into Gorham tomorrow.

I pitch in the rain, which has been my companion most of the afternoon, and no sooner do I roll in than the thunder also rolls in, to bring a grand light show and torrents. But I'm snug and warm in my neat little Nomad tent.

> *Whether you think that you can, or that you can't,*
> *you are usually right.*
> (Henry Ford)

Friday—August 4, 2000
Trail Day—73/24
Trail Mile—1002/298
Location—US-2 to Hiker's Paradise, Gorham, New Hampshire.
Bruno and Mary Ann Janicki, proprietors.

Subconsciously, something told me not to pull into Gentian Pond Campsite last night, so I found a flat spot to pitch, 100 yards or so off the trail above a little trickle about a mile or two north. And was this ever the right decision. For in the distance shortly after I get going this morning, for the better part of 15 minutes, I hear up ahead the shrill, piercing laughter and chatter of young girls, 20 or 30 of them. They've literally taken over the entire platform section at Gentian! And we wonder why wilderness and the hiking experience might not be quite like it used to be!

There are a couple of pops over some no-name summits and then the final pull for the day up and over Cascade Mountain. Shortly after, I bail off, down and down to the Androscoggin River and US-2, which leads to Gorham. On the front steps of a beautiful old, well-kept two-story home where the trail turns at US-2 is a telephone, placed especially for hikers to use to call Gorham for shuttle service.

I've never been able to figure what it's about, what happens when we shoulder our backpack—then to meet and interact with perfect strangers. But it's definitely for the good, totally predictable and undeniably real! As from a fount does there flow a degree of human kindness and generosity I've never before or otherwise experienced in my near-sixty-two years on this earth! This almost-continuous experience of dumbfounding joy while on the trail has become known to hikers as "Trail Magic," offered up by folks known as "Trail Angels." There's been much written on this subject and about this phenomenon, but to this day I have not ever truly been convinced what it could possibly be about, nor have I ever been entirely able to fathom or figure it out myself. The phone on the steps here is just a small example among countless examples of acts of kindness that are experienced almost daily by us trail-weary intrepid. It is humbling, truly humbling, and even though it brings pure happiness and joy, living and experiencing it is so perplexing!

The call to Hiker's Paradise brings the shuttle to fetch me. As I stoop to look across at the driver, I'm greeted in the most business-like and matter-of-fact manner. Here I meet Bruno Janicki, proprietor at Hiker's Paradise. On the way through town I get the canned, fully rehearsed long-ago guided tour pitch. Says Bruno, "There's the best café in town. That Oriental place is too expensive; try that one over there if you like Chinese food. There's the post office, and you can see the Pizza Hut, McDonalds and Burger King signs. And here's Hiker's Paradise, where you'll be staying. Let me show you around." Bruno then proceeds to explain, all the while continuing in his business-like fashion, what he has to offer and what he expects of me while I'm his guest. "You put your hiking shoes here or on the porch. Do not wear shoes upstairs; it is clean for you and we want it that way for others. We have full laundry, but do your wash before the motel guests start arriving." I keep repeating, "okay Bruno, okay Bruno, okay!"

Northbounders have told me about Bruno Janicki and his no-nonsense disposition. But in the same breath, I've also been told all about the great place for hikers that is Hiker's Paradise. Just as I chipped away ever so well at the porcelain facade around Sydney *The Pie Lady* Pratt a couple of years ago, it didn't take long to find the soft spot in Bruno's heart for us hikers. It really isn't hard to figure out, for you see, if all these folks that cater to us were interested in making some real money, they'd be doing something besides cleaning up after us and running us all over the place day in and day out! And it's true, with few and rare exceptions; all the hostel keepers have a deep and abiding love for us, a love they cannot hide, that just can't be concealed. And Bruno? Well, Bruno Janicki is probably the least likely of all to fit this mold. But fit it he does, even though he's an immigrant from Poland, his life and family having been crushed by the Russian Communist takeover of Poland. Bruno was just an infant then. I listen with astonishment as his wife Mary Ann tells the story about how Bruno's family was forced to leave their home at gunpoint with all their worldly possessions in a wheelbarrow.

Bruno gets me settled into one of his many bunkrooms, the quietest of the lot, so I can do some writing and get some much-needed rest. Please don't be angry with me for giving you away, Bruno! Regardless, it probably doesn't really matter, 'cause everybody's pretty much got you figured out anyway.

> *Wouldn't this world be better*
> *If the folks we met would say—*
> *"I know something good about you!"*
> *And treat us just that way?*
> (Louis C. Shimon)

Saturday—August 5, 2000
Trail Day—74/25
Trail Mile—1023/319
Location—NH-16 at Pinkham Notch to Hiker's Paradise, Gorham,
New Hampshire

What a wonderful surprise, the evening last. Came a knock on my door and I opened it to be greeted by *Jingle*, my dear hiking friend from '98. She's up here from Wisconsin to attend her sister's wedding and had heard from *Easy Rider* that I was at Hiker's Paradise in Gorham. We shared a delightful evening together, and this morning *Jingle* not only treats me to breakfast but also takes me back out to the trailhead to continue my hike south. Thanks, *Jingle*, for the wonderful surprise and for taking the time to see me!

I'm into the climb to Mount Moriah by eight-thirty. It sure doesn't take long to get the old jitney up to normal operating temperature, the pull being a nearly uninterrupted 4000-foot climb. I

have decided to go the full distance of twenty-one miles, all the way to NH-16 at Pinkham Notch, with the ups and downs adding to a total vertical change of over 13,000 feet. The treadway is brutal, but the scenery is breathtaking and the day is perfect, providing spectacular and near-constant views of the Presidential Range to the southwest, Mount Washington presiding.

Coming off Carter Dome, before arriving at Carter Notch Hut, a meeting that I've been looking forward to with such excitement and anticipation happens: The young man hiking north from Key West, Florida meets the old man hiking south from the Cliffs of Forillon, Québec Province. Here is *Jon *Class 5* Leuschel. What joy we share in this reunion. *Class 5*'s hiking companions, *Hopalong* and *Cutthroat,* stand in bewilderment as we hoot and holler and hug!

They departed Pinkham Notch around noon, and it is now a little after three, so I know that I can make it in today. I had been thinking of taking a day off tomorrow. I'll do that for sure now. We'll all meet in Gorham for a grand time.

The descent from Peak E off Wildcat Mountain is a free-fall, straight down, but I make it without incident to arrive at Pinkham Notch around six-thirty. Within minutes I'm given a ride directly to Hiker's Paradise. What an incredible, physically demanding and excitement-filled day! Thank you, Lord, for your blessings: good health and great friends...

> *Half this game is ninety percent mental.*
> (Yogi Berra)

*Jon *Class 5* Leuschel, and his brother, Dan *King Louie*, departed Key West, Florida on January 14th, 2000. Dan left the trail in New Hampshire, ending his hike. Jon continued on, reaching the Cliffs of Forillon, Cap Gaspé, Québec on September 26th, 2000, 255 days, 4,400 miles.

Sunday—August 6, 2000
Trail Day—75/26
Trail Mile—1023/319
Location—Hiker's Paradise, Gorham, New Hampshire

A day's rest will surely be welcome after the long, tiring hike yesterday. I'll have a chance to get caught up on my journal entries and spend some time with my great friend, *Class 5*, but first things first. It's time to head down to the dining room at Hiker's Paradise for breakfast. And what an interesting menu, created especially for thru-hikers—items like White Blaze, Blue Blaze, Flip-Flop, and my favorite, Yo-Yo. This one's a double helping of everything, starting with coffee, eggs and pancakes, to be followed up with a double helping of pancakes, eggs and coffee; yup, the Yo-Yo!

The trip to the post office shortly after I arrived Friday capped that day, for I finally got back together with my bounce box. This morning I sort through all its contents, rationing out more medication (coated aspirin, vitamins and Osteo Bi-Flex), then to look through the ALDHA *Companion* and *AT Data Book* for the pages I'll need next.

The evening is spent with *Class 5* and his good friends (and now mine): *Hopalong, Cutthroat, Cutthroat's* mom, JoAnn, his girlfriend, Carrie, and her sister, Jennifer. I join them as their guest for dinner. It's a joy to be taken in so freely, to be accepted as *friend*. Later in the evening, *Class 5* and I go over the details/itinerary that will involve his hike past Katahdin and on north into Canada.

> *When you're traveling, you are what you are*
> *right there and then.*
> *People don't have your past to hold against you.*
> *No yesterdays on the road.*
> (William Least Heat Moon)

Monday—August 7, 2000
Trail Day—76/27
Trail Mile—1038/334
Location—Lakes of the Clouds Hut, New Hampshire

Down at the restaurant this morning I find the place packed and it's not yet seven. Bruce Pettingill, who helps Bruno and Mary Ann keep this hiker thing running smoothly at Hikers Paradise, is already shuttling his second load of northbound thru-hikers back to the mountain. I relax and go for a light start, coffee and toast. Ahead of me I have the climb from Pinkham Notch, over Mount Washington, and into Lakes of the Clouds Hut. Somehow, Mary Ann manages to break away from her busy duties in the kitchen to shuttle me to the trail. Back at the Notch, after saying goodbye to another great new friend, Mary Ann of Hiker's Paradise, I'm on the trail again, heading ever south at eight.

The climb ahead of me today is one of the more difficult, leading ever upward through the rocks and roots. I try not to look, not to see the seemingly never-ending jumble and maze as the white blazes climb toward the sky, and I labor and climb with them. I've got my wind and my legs, as good as I'll have them ever again in my life, and on I grind, up, up, up, without a break for the better part of an hour. Finally, with a grand feeling of accomplishment, I successfully gain the ridge and head toward Mount Madison.

The rain, which came in during the night, with the mush pervading all, persists today. As I climb and as I near Madison Springs Hut, the rain not only begins again but intensifies. With it comes a driving wind, turning the day uncomfortably cold and harsh. Totally unfriendly! I'm greatly relieved to reach the hut, and as I enter, I receive a warm welcome from the "Croo." The storm continues as the rain pelts the hut windows. I feel smug, a certain sense of joy, in the simple pleasure derived from being in the warmth and comfort afforded by this cozy little place in the shroud.

After drying off and getting my core temperature back up with a couple cups of piping hot coffee, I head over to the bookcase. Here, one of the books, *Joe Dodge*, catches my eye.

I'm soon entirely immersed in the history of the Presidential Range, the Hut system, and the life and humor that was Joe Dodge. This delightful book, written by William Lowell Putnam, describes Joe's life as he lived it here in the Whites. As I read on, I become intrigued with the wit, humor and the apparent boundless energy of this man.

"Joe Dodge was a doer, he built the AMC [Appalachian Mountain Club] Hut System: the chain of nine huts stretching by mountain trail almost sixty miles across the upper waist of New Hampshire. All but one are located on mountain trails. Each provides food, shelter, and sleeping quarters for hikes at modest fees. Staffed by young men [and more recently, also by young women] who clean, cook and pack supplies from road-head depots...also dispensing mountain wisdom and humor...these huts develop character. Pride, competence, self-reliance, and humor—these are the characteristics evident in hut crews..."

I'm sure Joe would be pleased to know this tradition of pride, self-reliance, and humor is alive and well to this day. I've just had a grand dose of it!

Within the hour the rain diminishes, and I steel myself to the task of climbing up and over Mount Washington. Although I have much fear and doubt, I try not visualizing what lies ahead, as I know not what harrowing experience awaits. The rain and wind have returned, making the rocks and boulders incredibly slippery and treacherous. I'm blown from side to side as I stumble from cairn to cairn. I tremble and am overcome with fear; I cannot concentrate. On the wall of the Summit House here above, and during my '98 trek, I recall standing in disbelief as I read the list of names (125 at that time) of those poor souls who'd perished on Mount Washington. Below those names were these solemn words: "This can be a dangerous place. No one on this list planned to die here."

The wind is cold. The rain is cold. The gray, ascending wall of boulders before me is cold. This whole God-forsaken place is cold. My head is reeling and spinning. My heart is pounding in my ears. Time, it seems, is the only thing standing still on this heap of rocks in the sky. Even the boulders appear to be moving as I try bracing against the slam of the wind-driven rain. The higher I ascend into the gloom, the more treacherous and difficult the climb becomes. The shroud engulfs me. I can neither see nor follow the blazes. I cling, falter and grope on up. Finally, gaining the summit, I'm in the full rage of the howling gale. The whole place is shut down. Not a soul anywhere. Over an hour ago, while still in my ascent, I heard the last Cog Railway engine, which rattles and clanks tourists to the top, go rattling and clanking back down the mountain. The sound was hollow, eerie. The loud wheezing and chugging seemed so out of place. As the vibrating grind came closer and closer, it completely encircled me, as though to pass on either side; yet as I gazed in stunned bewilderment, I saw nothing. I wondered then how anyone could muster the courage to climb aboard a railcar that clawed its way straight to the sky, while being shoved and humped along by one of those ridiculous looking contraptions.

Let me share with you what Joe Dodge had to say about the Cog Railway. It is both humorous and sobering:

"Other than that business with Peppersass [one of the old engines that got away and blew up], the only problem I ever heard about on that railroad was with a baggage car. They used to take a little car on behind the engine, first train of the day, to take baggage and supplies up to the summit. During the day the crew would jack it up and set it off to one side of the tracks at the level area behind the Summit House. One day the crew uncoupled it then went for lunch...A little gust of wind came up while they were inside and started the damn thing rolling. Some lad came running in to tell the crew what had happened, but it was too late. The damned rattler was almost out of sight. So one of them called the guy at the Halfway Tank to tell him he better watch out for a loose car. 'Hell,' he said, 'that goddam thing went by here five minutes ago!'"

As soon as I'm off the summit, descending toward Lakes of the Clouds Hut, the wind relents, the sun breaks through, and I'm offered fast-shuttered snippets of the hut and the mountains below. As usual, the hut is packed with folks who had made their reservations months ago, guests that are going to be here no matter what—and with them, the swelling wave of northbound thru-hikers. I meet up with *Spider* again, and we wait to see how the evening plays out. After the paying guests are fed, we are invited to the kitchen to help ourselves to leftovers, and there's plenty to go around! When the dining room is cleared and the gaslights are nearly all extinguished, we are permitted to lay our bedrolls out for the night right on the dining room tables. Our tummies are full, and we are warm and comfortable. Sleep is a minor process! What a harrowing day.

I'll face my fear. I'll permit it to pass over me and through me.
And when it has gone past, I'll turn the inner eye to see its path.
(Frank Herbert)

Tuesday—August 8, 2000
Trail Day—77/28
Trail Mile—1049/345
Location—US-302 at Crawford Notch, to Johnson's Motel, Twin Mountain, New Hampshire. Mike Brady, proprietor.

The cook starts rattling around a little before six. I'm already awake, but I roll over for a few more winks, awaiting that drifting aroma of freshly brewed coffee.

I finally manage to get off the dining room table, get my pack organized, and have a cup of coffee. My morning duty done, I'm out to be greeted by a chilly gray-ghost morning. Perhaps for us thru-hikers the Whites might be better known as the Grays, for we haven't the luxury of watching the weather from our penthouse apartments in Boston or Hartford, waiting for that perfect weekend weather to go romping and climbing around in the Presidentials.

The hike today is steady and at times precipitous, as is the bail-off to Saco River. The wind along the ridge by Mount Franklin, Mount Eisenhower, and Mount Pierce is in a rage, driving the moisture-laden clouds straight across, forcing me to lean and brace against it. I'm relieved to get down to the comfort and shelter of Mizpah Spring Hut. Here in the library I find another copy of the book *Joe Dodge*, and I settle in with a cup of coffee as I await *Spider's* arrival. Joe Dodge apparently had a great deal of fun in life, and a great deal of fun with people. One hilarious story relates how he had dreamed up these imaginary mountain-goat-like creatures that supposedly inhabited the rocky areas of the Whites.

"They're all over the place up here, but they look just like the jeezly rocks, protective coloring, you know, so you don't see 'em much. They're of two distinct varieties, but you can't tell 'em apart by their color, and their hoof marks are identical, so you can only do it when you actually see one of 'em as they move around the mountain. There's the gauchers and the droiters, and they belong to the same species even though they can't breed. I've seen dozens, but mostly they've been the gauchers, the ones that go [around the mountain] to the left. The last few years, though, no one has seen many droiters [the ones that go around the mountain to the right]; they may have gone extinct. You see, because of the legs [gauchers—short right legs, droiters—short left legs], the gauchers can't breed with the droiters, and with the northwest wind so strong in these mountains, lately, the droiters have had a hard time getting around the hillsides."

The day has made an effort to clear, but Mount Jackson and Mount Webster are totally socked in by the cold, wind-driven mist.

Coming off Mount Webster, I'm pretty sure I saw a gaucher! He was crouched, aimed clockwise, looking like a rock, just like Joe Dodge said, but I could see his eyes as he blinked at me. At Webster Cliffs, overlooking the Saco River and Crawford Notch, the day finally brightens as the clouds lift.

At US-302, *Spider* and I hitch a ride into Twin Mountain. After a pizza and a few cold frosties, we're in for an enjoyable evening at Johnson's Motel.

> *Imagination grows by exercise, and contrary to common belief,*
> *is more powerful in the mature than in the young.*
> (W. Somerset Maugham)

Wednesday—August 9, 2000
Trail Day—78/29
Trail Mile—1065/361
Location—Campsite near Galehead Hut, New Hampshire

Mike Brady, proprietor of Johnson's Motel, offered to drive us to the local restaurant for breakfast, then back to the trailhead at Crawford Notch. And he's here right at seven, truck backed up, topper popped and the tailgate down, ready to load our gear. Looks to be the makings of another dreary day, with the rain coming steady as we load and head out. We've had a great stay, along with a fine, tank-stokin' breakfast. Enjoyed talking with you, Mike, thanks!

Today the treadway is an obstacle course through the rocks and roots, more-often nearly straight up or straight down. The level areas provide no relief, no break from it, being mostly bogs filled with ankle-deep mud. At times the rain comes in driving waves, and I slump into a bone-soaked, boulder-stumbling, mudboggin' funk. I try to remember and apply my positive attitude and philosophy: "There are no bad days on the trail, some just better than others." This day is sorely testing that positive attitude, that resolve.

Two bright spots light the otherwise darkened-over day, however. One comes in meeting Warren Doyle, Jr., his son Forrest, and all their intact "Expedition 2000" members as they head for Katahdin. I had gone up to Three Forks to greet them at the completion of their first day on the AT way back in May, and to take them a case of Snickers bars given me by M&M Mars. I didn't recognize Warren as he approached, being trim of body and untrimmed of beard, but as he nears, I hear, "*Nomad*, it's the *Nimblewill Nomad*," I realize who it is and we hug and hoot and have a grand trail reunion.

The second of the little trail delights began a few days ago and has steadily increased to a fair number today, for it is that many northbound thru-hikers are recognizing me and calling my name. These are folks that were at Trail Days in Damascus this spring and who attended my presentation at Rock School Auditorium. I'm now receiving such a gracious reception from them, such kind comments and warm greetings. My hat size is certainly changing. I must keep in mind the virtue of humility these grand old mountains have taught me, and I must not fail to thank the Lord for all these blessings, and to remain humble.

So it seems, days like this day, days that test our resolve, indeed, they bring us heightened resolve, along with a deeper appreciation as we continue searching for true patience and understanding.

Galehead Hut does not cater to thru-hikers as does Lakes of the Clouds Hut. Two thru-hikers have already been selected for work/stay, and they need no more help today. We are neither permitted to hang around for leftovers nor sleep on the dining hall tables after lights out—and we're ushered along.

So *Spider* and I head on south in the swirling soup to pitch far off the trail in the moss and spruce. As I pitch in this peaceful place tonight, I'm thanking the "Croo" at Galehead Hut for sending us on, for comes to me now, drifting across these lofty mountains, the soft lilt of a forgotten melody, a beautiful song of long, long ago. It comes as if a whisper through the quiet of this place—and now into the quiet of my mind. It's from The Eagles "...I got a peaceful, easy feelin'..."

> *Humility is strong, not bold; quiet, not speechless;*
> *sure, not arrogant.*
> (Estelle Smith)

Thursday—August 10, 2000
Trail Day—79/30
Trail Mile—1077/373
Location—US-3 at Franconia Notch to Cascade Lodge, North Wood-
stock, New Hampshire. Bill and Betty Robinson, proprietors.

The day dawns cold and dreary once again at my camp in the clouds. I'm up and out by seven-fifteen, after much coaxing and talking to myself. The treadway seems worse this morning, if that is possible, and it's hard to get the old jitney cranking and up to normal operating temperature in the damp chill. The rains of yesterday have brought even more mud and treachery, and there has been heavy foot traffic through this section. I truly don't believe you could bring in a sheepsfoot roller from an interstate highway project and beat this treadway down more thoroughly or any harder. Over time, the heavily-booted army that passes is a force to be reckoned with, slowly and methodically hammering the trail and taking its toll. For a short time, I come to a section where the trail has been moved, with new treadway cut. Here the spongy duff and humus underfoot feels so strange and unusual. The pounding and packing has already begun, however; it won't be long until this new pathway is "hardened in," where the only thing remaining will be a rut of rocks and roots, like the channel of a deep-cut creek bed.

There are no views from Mount Garfield or Mount Lincoln. Winds in excess of fifty miles per hour (and at times gusting to over sixty) persist across the entire traverse of Garfield Ridge and Liberty Ridge. My hands turn numb and my fingers quit working as I brace with my sticks against the mist-driven rage. The funk continues as I think of Jacob *Gatorboy* Cram, a young lad who died on Mount Lincoln while thru-hiking the AT in '97. The sadness I shared with his family during my '98 trek descends on me now. We met at Long Trail Inn. The Crams had returned to scatter Jacob's ashes along the trail here on Garfield Ridge.

Below Liberty Spring Tentsite, the day finally turns mild and the sun makes a rare appearance. The rocks and roots remain wet, however, and the descent to Franconia Notch is slow and scary.

I feel very relieved to complete this hiking day without incident. Though it adds up to only twelve miles, I'm tired, my energy totally spent, both emotionally and physically. A kind gentleman gives me a ride into North Woodstock, directly to Cascade Lodge. Betty, the proprietor, smiles as she sees me once again. She hands me the key to room #8. I go upstairs—and collapse. This has been one *hell* of a day.

If you are going through hell, keep going.
(Sir Winston Churchill)

Friday—August 11, 2000
Trail Day—80/31
Trail Mile—1080/375
Location—Gordon Pond, south of Mount Wolf, New Hampshire

Bill hauls me back to the trailhead at Liberty Parking. The only problem is that since I-93 came through, it's pretty hard to get to where the trail originally crossed US-3. So I've got a half-mile road-walk along the interstate exit back to where the trail now goes under the interstate.

The day looks to be setting up for clear and fair, but it doesn't take long for the mist and drear to return, again making its cold, dismal presence. This treadway is neither friendly nor kind. I try to set my mind to thinking of days that will come, days of sun, days of dry, wide open trail. But today I must satisfy myself with these thoughts as the ruggedness of the Whites deals me a rough, hard road. Here the trail is either up or down through endless boulders and roots. Or, should the trail flatten the least bit, then it's mudboggin' time.

North and South Kinsman are both hard pulls, and I'm glad to be up and over them. More miles of mud, rocks and roots, and I'm through the climb over Mount Wolf. With thunder building in the distance, I've had enough of this for today. So, I take the blue-blaze trail over to Gordon Pond for the evening.

I pitch by the pond, look around for the resident moose (with no luck), and manage a respectable cooking fire with wet birch bark. As soon as I put my cookpot on, the sky opens and I must dive for my tent. It's cheese sandwiches and sardines tonight as the rain comes hard, the full light and percussion show lasting the better part of two hours.

Sleeping dry and snug, in such basic shelter as a gossamer-thin tent in the driving rain, is pure contentment, and I'm indeed content in my little Nomad.

> *And he breathes a blessing on the rain...*
> (Henry Wadsworth Longfellow)

Saturday—August 12, 2000
Trail Day—81/32
Trail Mile—1092/387
Location—Sanitary Road to Glencliff Hiker Hostel, Glencliff, New Hampshire. John "Packrat" Roblee and Jonathan "Big John" McCue, proprietors.

Nature Boy came in last night and got pitched just before the rain began, but *Spider* didn't make it. The trees are still dripping this morning with more rain threatening, so I roll over and give it another hour. *Nature Boy* leaves long before I break camp. As soon as I hit the trail, the drizzle begins again.

The last of the sky-high summits that are the Whites looms before me today, Mount Moosilauke. From Kinsman Notch the trail climbs continually for nearly four miles, gaining 4,000 feet in the process. Near the summit of Blue Mountain, a short distance from Moosilauke, I come upon a gentleman looking at his maps. Here I meet Pavel Litvinov. We exchange pleasantries, and as I continue up Moosilauke, to my surprise, he not only stays right with me, but also talks of his interesting life without the least huffing. Pavel is a native of Russia. He was born in Moscow in 1940 and immigrated to the USA in 1974. He teaches now at a private school in New York. As we reach the summit of Moosilauke, waiting is Mark, the father of one of Pavel's students. Soon, I'm invited to celebrate, for I have arrived in time to join in congratulating Pavel in his ascent of Moosilauke, his last of the forty-eight 4,000 footers in New Hampshire. Mark uncorks a liter of hard cider and we drink cheers, sharing the joy of Pavel's proud accomplishment!

As Pavel and Mark start down, I linger on Moosilauke along with dozens of day hikers, waiting for the mush to blow on through as we are teased with glimpses of the vast expanse below. Folks come by where I'm sitting, bringing food and drink, wishing me well on the remainder of my odyssey. Just as I prepare to descend and as I'm hoisting my pack I hear, "*Nomad, Nomad,* it's so good to see you again!" I turn and am immediately embraced with a big hug from *Just Playin' Jane*. We hiked together in '98, enjoying each other's company, and we meet again today on Mount Moosilauke. We spend a short while together again, and as the sky finally clears we can see forever—from here on top of the world.

I hasten down the mountain. As I arrive at Sanitary Road, one of the routes leading to Glencliff, here are Pavel and Mark, and their friend Peter, who's been waiting to take them home. I'm offered a ride into Glencliff to Hikers Welcome Hostel, where they drop me off right at the front door. Here I meet Ian *Drifter* Moss, GAME 94 & 97, who is helping around for the day. In a while, after the lawn-mower is shut down, I meet one of the new proprietors, John *Pack-rat* Roblee. *Spider* soon arrives, and *Drifter* gives us a ride to town to load up on pizza and a few tall frosties. The Hikers Welcome Hostel is a quaint, homey-type place and we are made to feel right at home. A fine time with great friends, *Nature Boy, Spider, Drifter, Packrat, Harriet Tubman,* and *X-Man.*

> *And as you seek your fortune,*
> *And near your lifelong quest.*
> *There'll still be countless peaks to climb,*
> *Before your final rest.*
> (N. Nomad)

Sunday—August 13, 2000
Trail Day—82/33
Trail Mile—1113/408
Location—Firewarden's cabin, Smarts Mountain, New Hampshire

Drifter drives me back up Sanitary Road to the trailhead, and I'm out and moving south again by eight-thirty. The terrain and the forest have changed dramatically since the trail came down from Moosilauke. I have seen the last of the above-treeline tundra and the first pastureland since departing Katahdin. Comparatively speaking, the treadway is remarkably level and smooth, making for fast, easy hiking. The final summits of any significance that make up the Whites, Mount Cube and Smarts Mountain, pass easily beneath my feet. I had planned on calling it a day upon reaching Hexacube Shelter, but I arrive at three. I decide to hike on to the Firewarden's Cabin, making for a grand twenty-two mile day. This sets up the possibility of reaching Hanover tomorrow, a two-day hike instead of three, and I decide to go for it, to give it a shot.

The Firewarden's Cabin has survived. It's a remarkable old place now used by hikers. And it certainly is a cabin in the traditional sense, complete with windows, a door that closes snugly, and even a front porch. I get a cooking fire going quite nicely and settle in for a very comfortable evening.

Being on the tightrope is living; everything else is waiting.
(Karl Wallenda)

Monday—August 14, 2000
Trail Day—83/34
Trail Mile—1136/431
Location—Panarchy Fraternity House, Phi Sigma Phi, Dartmouth College, Hanover, New Hampshire

This will be a long, hard hiking day, the rain definitely setting it up for *hard*. The treadway, which has been so delightfully kind, becomes bumpy again, with increasing mud, up-se-downs, and rocks. The pulls aren't of the magnitude or difficulty of those in the Whites, but they're a challenge nonetheless. For some reason, my intent is to maintain an average today of three miles per hour, a task which I find just the least tiring as this old AT continues dishing it out.

Rolling off Smarts Mountain, it's a downshift into low gear for the pull up and over Holts Ledge; the same again for what seems the endless peaks of Moose Mountain. "*Nomad's* Neutral" is really kicking today (a downhill technique perfected during "Odyssey '98). It involves going into a slight crouch, much as sitting on a bicycle seat, with leg motion similar to rapid pedaling, all the while keeping the upper torso and backpack straight and steady, much as the straight, steadiness of sitting astride the bike. Downhill speeds in excess of four miles per hour are not uncommon, legs and trekking poles little more than a blur. Slipping and sliding decreases, and the stress and tension exerted on the knees during normal downhill descent are greatly reduced. The trick, however, is to maintain total concentration all the while, to avoid the unpleasantness of stumbling, which would thus lead to the not so entertaining prospect of a full launch—down and into the next county.

The final pull for the day comes as I approach Velvet Rocks, then it's "*Nomad's* Neutral" all the way down to Hanover.

I'm pleased with my hike today, having maintained two miles per hour on the ups, three miles per hour on the ridges, and four miles per hour on the downs, thus accomplishing my goal of averaging three miles per for the day. This allowed me to cover the twenty-three miles in less than eight hours. I arrive in Hanover in time to get my maildrop a little after four.

Friendly northbounders at the post office suggest I head for Panarchy House, as it will probably be my best bet for peace and quiet while trying to write. So over I go. The rain comes in buckets as I enter the grand room at Panarchy. Here I'm greeted kindly by one of the fraternity brothers. I learn to my dismay that they're full to capacity with AT thru-hikers, but the kind lad doesn't have the heart to turn me away and send me back out in the storm, so I'm shown around and given a place to sleep in the basement.

After a soothing hot shower, time to return to the storm, for pizza and a few tall frosties at one of the local watering holes. Back at Panarchy, I settle in comfortably in the lounge to write. But soon, hikers start dropping by, and I make many new friends as I spend the evening with Travis *Shepherd* Hall and the charmingly delightful Letcher sisters, Lucy *Isis* and Susan *Jackrabbit*, who are hiking the AT barefoot—uhh, yup, BAREFOOT!

I try writing later in the evening but fall asleep, so I head for my little corner in the basement. In my soft, down-filled Feathered Friends, I sleep soundly as the incessant rain continues.

*If everything seems under control,
you're just not going fast enough.*
(Mario Andretti)

Tuesday—August 15, 2000
Trail Day—84/35
Trail Mile—1146/441
Location—VT-14 at White River, Vermont, to the home of Steve and
Terrie Purcell, Canaan, New Hampshire

I really need to spend a day on correspondence and journal entries,
but having taken three days off in Monson for the final review of
my book, I'm now a day behind my planned schedule, an itinerary
designed to put me on Flagg Mountain, Alabama, before the end of
this year—to accomplish the first recorded southbound thru-hike
covering the entire Appalachian Mountain range, o'er a trail becoming known as Trail of the Ancients. So I'm intent on returning to
the trail today.

A call to my publisher before departing Hanover, and this day
is shaping great. We're ready to go to press! So the great new 400
page book, *Ten Million Steps*, should be available sometime in the
next six weeks.

A few days ago I had the pleasure of meeting Austin Bagley on
the trail. Austin had been in Damascus, Virginia, during Trail Days.
While there he attended my presentation at Rock School Auditorium. He's in New Hampshire now on his AT thru-hike, bound for
Katahdin. During our conversation, I mentioned that he looked too
clean, definitely way too neat and fresh, to have been on the trail so
long. That's when he explained that he and his hiking companion
Oopsadaisey had just returned to the trail after being entirely rejuve-
nated, the result of a recent stay with his aunt and uncle, Terrie and
Steve Purcell of Canaan, New Hampshire. Before heading our separate ways again, Austin handed me a piece of paper with his uncle's
phone number, urging me to call when a little further south. Said
Austin, "I know Steve and Terrie would enjoy meeting you and having you as their guest." So, after arriving here in Hanover yesterday,

and after some hesitancy, I gave Steve a call. Austin had obviously told his aunt and uncle about me, and Steve sounded pleased as he invited me to his home. Arrangements were made for Steve to pick me up after my hike today, so I'm anxious to get on my way.

By mid-afternoon, with my journal entries pretty much up-to-date and most of my correspondence completed, I head across the Connecticut River and into Vermont. Another state behind me; two down, fourteen to go!

The day remains warm and pleasant, the treadway very kind, and the hike goes quickly as I pass some interesting places, like Podunk. Do people actually live in Podunk?

Just before six, as I near the post office in West Hartford, a van pulls over; it's Steve. I'm greeted with a kind "Hello" and a glad smile. Austin was right. Steve and Terrie are indeed happy to meet me. And oh, is the feeling mutual. No wonder Austin and *Oopsadaisey* looked so fresh and ready-to-go again. Isn't it remarkable what a little time with family and friends can do for a tired, run-down soul!

The Purcells have a warm and comfortable home, deep in the New Hampshire woods. It's pure joy to be here, to be their guest. In the evening, after my clothes are all clean, after we partake a wonderful meal prepared just for me, do we then spend a happy time together! The Purcells are so proud of their children, four in all, three boys and a girl. I can sure see why, as I have the pleasure of meeting their daughter Symanie, who stops by for a visit.

In my room now, I log this entry for the day before retiring with the most contented feeling, a feeling that comes only from being with good, caring friends.

The mystic bond of brotherhood makes all men one.
(Thomas Carlyle)

Wednesday—August 16, 2000
Trail Day—85/36
Trail Mile—1159/454
Location—VT-12 to the home of Jim Johnston and Laura
Zantzinger, Woodstock, Vermont

Steve is up preparing breakfast as I wake. A thunderstorm is rumbling through, and I take a moment to give thanks for being with these new friends and for being out of it for a change. We enjoy breakfast together as Steve gets me stoked up for the day. Terrie then sets out for work, and Steve drives me back to the trail at the old steel bridge over White River.

Steve and Terrie, thanks for your kindness to me and for a grand time; I wish you the very best!

The storm has passed and the sky clears, but the treadway is a hopeless bog. I soon tire of sliding and slogging and decide to call it a day after only thirteen miles.

At VT-12 I stick my thumb out toward Woodstock. In only moments this Mercedes passes, stops and turns around. The driver is smiling as he wheels around again to pick me up. Here I meet Jim Johnston, Laura Zantzinger, and their delightful, bright-eyed children, Leverett and Mary. On the ride to Woodstock, Jim explains that I might not be pleased with the overnight accommodations there, not that I wouldn't be treated and cared for in a fashionable manner, but that I might not delight in spending upwards of $1,500 for the night! It's then that he and Laura invite me to come with them to their home and to be their guest for the evening. Says Jim, "As soon as we saw you by the road, when we saw your face, we decided to turn around and get you. You are welcome to stay with us in our home and have dinner with us this evening." After forcing a short degree of hesitancy, I quickly accept!

We stroll the streets of Woodstock for a while, and after a stop at the little general store on the way, we head for their place in the high valley. "We get a lot of snow up here in the winter; it snows almost every day," Jim says, as we climb through the valley. "Lots more than they get over on the ski slopes. We bundle the kids and spend a lot of time outdoors. We love the snow." I can tell we're getting close—the kids are becoming rambunctious.

We're soon at their home, a well-kept, renovated nineteenth century dwelling on ten acres of manicured lawns and lovely natural gardens. As soon as the car stops, the kids are out and romping barefoot all around. Oh, does seeing them running and playing bring such a flood of childhood memories. I didn't know how blessed I was as a child to have wide-open spaces to run and play. As Jim shows me his grounds and we pick our fill of luscious raspberries, I comment on how great it is to have such a place as this for Laura and the children. Leverett comes running and takes my hand, so full of glee, "Let's go see the Jeep!" he says, "Come on, come on!" and so—we go see the Jeep.

What a memorable evening with these kind and gentle people. The children are so trusting and innocent. They all take pleasure in having me as their guest, especially, so it seems, the children. It's such a blessing and such a joy to me.

So many gods, so many creeds;
So many paths that wind and wind,
While just the art of being kind
Is all this sad world needs.
(Ella Wheeler Wilcox)

Thursday—August 17, 2000
Trail Day—86/37
Trail Mile—1182/477
Location—US-4 at Sherburne Pass to the Inn at Long Trail, Killington, Vermont

The evening quickly slipped away last, and I got precious little work done on my journal entries, but just as well. This morning Jim prepares coffee, French toast, sausage, and cereal for me. Then we load in his car again, Mary, kids and all, as we head back to the trailhead at VT-12. Thanks Jim, Laura, Leverett, and Mary—you know you've saved me fifteen hundred bucks! Seriously, your kindness and generosity will remain in my memory.

The day begins bright, clear and cool, but the gloom and darkness brought by the overcast soon returns. My goal is to hike the twenty-three miles into Sherburne Pass, to The Inn at Long Trail. The treadway has had no opportunity to dry, so mudboggin' is the way of the day. The trail is not content to be up, and so down we go, and when down, it's time to immediately climb back up again.

Most all the northbounders recognize me today, one of them in particular, my good friend Jack *Baltimore Jack* Tarlin. He's on his sixth consecutive AT thru-hike. We hoot and holler and spend much time in excited conversation. Great seeing you again, *Baltimore Jack*! To all you intrepid bound for Katahdin, you, along with *Baltimore Jack*, will soon become *the* "Class of 2000." Congratulations!

The Trail through here has been relocated away from Sherburne Pass, and now crosses US-4 to the west before climbing to Pico Camp. This move was done in anticipation of development soon to occur on Killington. The old AT, the route I hiked my last time through, is still open to the Inn. It's marked with blue blazes now, so it's blue-blaze time as I head for The Inn at Long Trail. As I hike along, following blue blazes, I'm thinking about how this trail is constantly changing. Since I hiked the AT less than two years ago, countless changes have been made. In my many miles and many months on the AT, I've concluded that an attempt to hike past every white blaze, as some purists attempt, is futile. The reason is simple. Before one can make a scant five hundred miles, changes have already happening—more white blazes!

I believe there needs to be a broader vision now, and I believe I have that vision, as did Benton MacKaye, the father of the Appalachian Trail, have a vision during his time. With this vision comes a feeling in my heart. It's the feeling of pride in knowing that, in this evolutionary process, I can play a part. Oh, yes, I've taken flack, plenty of it, and I'll surely take more when *Ten Million Steps* comes out. There'll be comments like: "There's no such thing as Trail of the Ancients. There's no such thing as an Eastern Continental Trail. How dare you even suggest a *long trail* along the eastern reaches of North America, or along the entire Appalachian Mountain range! It takes an act of Congress to create trails like these. Did you get an act of Congress?" And so it goes. Words like these have already been hurled at me, along with the spittle from the hysteria that accompanies them.

Ahh yes, well folks, the Appalachian Trail does seem to be a long trail, such a grand institution. Granted, and there's no doubt, the AT is an institution, but it is not a *long trail*! Might I ask you this: Is there not a trail right here, right where I'm hiking this instant, that passed here before the AT was superimposed upon it, that was, and is to this day, called *The Long Trail*?

If you would, please come with me as I continue on from Cap Gaspé to Key West. I'm hiking the Trail of the Ancients, and I'm hiking the Eastern Continental Trail. I've hiked these trails before, and I'm hiking them again, and I'm having an absolute blast! And so, finally, you might rightfully ask, "How can this be? Indeed, how can this be, without an act of Congress!"

I'm concerned as to whether there'll be room for me at Long Trail Inn. At the reception desk, I'm told that the Inn is full, but as luck would have it, and to my good fortune, I immediately run into *Shepherd*, whom I'd met in Hanover. Seems as though *Shepherd* has a room with two beds, one of which he immediately offers me! So, after getting reasonably presentable, I head to the bar for dinner and a few tall ones. *Shepherd* joins me. We make many new friends, and are greeted by many old, including *Nomad '98*, and we all enjoy a great evening together at Long Trail Inn.

*Our ultimate aim is more than just a trail—it is a
whole system of them, a cobweb planned to cover
the mountains of the eastern country.*
(Benton MacKaye, Appalachia, 1922)

*The Long Trail, known as "Vermont's Footpath in the Wilderness," was built by the Green Mountain Club between 1910 and 1930. It is the oldest long-distance hiking trail in the United States. It extends for a distance of some 270 miles, from the Massachusetts/Vermont state line to the international border between United States and Canada. The Long Trail was the inspiration for the Appalachian Trail, which was later superimposed upon it for a distance of some one hundred miles.

Friday—August 18, 2000
Trail Day—87/38
Trail Mile—1200/495
*Location—VT-103 to the Country Squire Motel, North Clarendon,
Vermont. Elizabeth Anne "Bette" Mangels, proprietor.*

I've made a doozie of a blunder here at the Inn. I slept soundly last night, getting rest in concentrate. However, I woke around three and couldn't go back to sleep, so I headed down to the spacious, comfortable lobby to work my correspondence. While taking my shower last evening, I stomped out my socks, as I customarily do. But they weren't drying where I'd hung them in my room, so I got the bright idea of taking them down with me to the lobby where I draped them over one of the table lamps to dry. When I returned to my room well after four, I forgot to bring my socks with me. Oh yes, you guessed it, the kind lady whose responsibility it is to see that everything is kept tidy for all the guests, she finds my socks and pulls them down first thing this morning. When I finally remember and rush back down to the lobby, I discover that my socks are gone, and I realize that I'm going to catch holy sam from the housekeeper. Pondering, I seriously consider sacrificing the socks, since I have a spare pair, thus to avoid the scolding, plus the embarrassment. But better judgment prevails. I 'fess up and take my licks, plus the embarrassment. As the sweet lady hands back my (dry) socks, I manage meekly, with my head down, "Well ma'am, I did take my shoes off outside before I came in yesterday!" I'm sure you're all familiar with that one-eyebrow-up blank stare—oh, yes!

Funny thing happened in the bar last. I was enjoying the company of friends when a call came in from *Fanny Pack*. The barkeep called me over and handed me the phone, I wondered, "How does he knows I'm here?" "Hey, *Fanny Pack*, how's it goin'?" I barked into the phone. I was greeted by total silence; no answer for the longest time. Then, "Is that you, *Nomad*?" I replied, "Yes *Fanny Pack*, it's me, *Nomad*." More hesitation. Finally, "Is this the *Nimblewill Nomad*?" Finally, almost shouting, "Yes *Fanny Pack*, it's me, *Nomad*." It was then I realized what had happened. *Fanny Pack* and me, we're great friends, but he's also friends with my good friend, *Nomad '98*, who's hiking again this year, and who was sitting right there nest to me at the bar. Turns out, the call was not for *Nimblewill Nomad,* but for *Nomad '98*. Anyway, as always, it was great talking with *Fanny Pack*—hilariously funny coincidink!

Since I hiked through here two years ago, there have been major trail relocations around Sherburne. As previously mentioned, the trail no longer crosses US-4 by the Inn. It's been moved a considerable distance to the west. The old AT (coming and going past the Inn) still remains but is now a blue blazed trail. *Shepherd* and I decide to hike out on the blue blaze.

Though there are many ups and downs today, the treadway is reasonably friendly, and *Shepherd* and I make very good time with a pace of three per. We're in early at VT-103 to get a ride to Country Squire Motel in North Clarendon. This has been a very good hiking day!

God is a comedian playing to an audience too afraid to laugh.
(Voltaire)

Saturday—August 19, 2000
Trail Day—88/39
Trail Mile—1215/510
Location—FS-10 at Danby-Landgrove Road to Iroquois Landing
Campground, North Clarendon, Vermont

After juice, coffee and donuts, we load up. Elizabeth Anne drives us to the general store, then back to the trailhead at VT-103. We've had a very pleasant stay with you, Bette. Thanks!

What an amazing day this turns out to be, great for hiking and great for meeting old friends—and making new!

As *Shepherd* and I cross Wallingford Road we see a backpack leaning against the crash-rail. Soon comes the owner racing down the mountain toward us. Here we meet Dawn *Belcher* Stringer, a friend of Nina *Waterfall* Baxley. I have been so anxious to meet *Waterfall*. She's the other southbound AT correspondent for GORP.com. We'd exchanged email messages nearly a year ago while *Waterfall* was preparing to hike the Pinhoti Trail in Alabama. *Belcher*, who is northbound on the AT and who started the day at Wallingford Road, found out that *Waterfall*, her dear friend, had just passed through southbound, and she'd missed her. *Belcher* then set out to catch her—with no luck. So, today it looks like I'll finally get to meet *Waterfall*, if I can catch her!

We haven't gone another quarter-mile when hiking toward us comes Chuck *Swamp Eagle* Wilson. I had corresponded with him by email and talked with him by phone well over a year ago when he was hiking north from Key West on the Florida National Scenic Trail—and here our paths cross today. *Swamp Eagle* is headed for the Cliffs of Forillon at Cap Gaspé, the old *Nomad,* for Key West! As we meet, we hug and hoot with great excitement.

We discuss the unfortunate crossing of the ways between *Belcher* and *Waterfall*. The decision is for *Swamp Eagle* to catch *Belcher* and for me to catch *Waterfall*, hopefully, at FS-10. The plan is for *Swamp Eagle's* wife Betty (*Honeycomb*) to pick us up there so we can all spend the evening together.

Well, after some anxious moments, as the plan seems to be falling apart, glory-be, we're all finally together! Oh, and did I mention that *Waterfall* and *Swamp Eagle* are the best of friends? *Swamp Eagle* rescued *Waterfall* from a flash flood in Alabama earlier this year. Thus, from that incident, the origin of her interesting trail name, *Waterfall*!

In the evening, *Honeycomb* drives all of us to the Whistlestop Restaurant where she and *Swamp Eagle* treat us to dinner. Then it's back to the their motor home to work on strategy that will give *Swamp Eagle* his best shot at finishing the IAT in Canada before getting iced out.

What a remarkable day. We're supposed to believe that these circumstances are mere coincidence. But we all know there is some other power at play here.

The human heart feels things the eyes cannot see,
and knows what the mind cannot understand.
(Robert Vallett)

Sunday—August 20, 2000
Trail Day—89/40
Trail Mile—1232/527
Location—SR-11/SR-30 to Sutton's Place, Manchester Center,
Vermont. Frank Sutton, proprietor.

I tented last night at the campground, a beautifully manicured lawn with picnic table right next to it, everything dry for a change. I'm not used to sitting at a dry picnic table, let alone having a dry place to pitch! In the motor home this morning, *Swamp Eagle* and *Honeycomb* have piping hot coffee and breakfast prepared for all of us. We tarry to enjoy each other's company for just a while longer. Then it's time to load up. We see *Belcher* and *Swamp Eagle* off as they head on north at SR-103. Time for lots of hugs and hesitancy, followed by more hugs and pictures. Then *Honeycomb* turns *Waterfall* and me loose back at FS-10 as we head on south.

Swamp Eagle, I pray for your continued safe passage o'er the AT, then, as you continue on the IAT into Canada, I pray, also, for your successful completion of your ECT trek. You've got a long way to go north of Katahdin, but you've paid your dues. I'm confident that the strategy we've worked out will get you past the ice on the tundra in the Chic Chocs. I know the wicked intensity, the quest to reach the Cliffs of Forillon at Cap Gaspé, Québec. God Speed my dear friend!

Waterfall and I hike together for a while, but when she decides to take a break, I decide to move on. Aww, but aren't goodbyes so incredibly difficult? I must try with all my might not to let this day drift to a funky finish.

Oh, but I have plenty to keep me occupied as I continue pounding the miles south. There's Baker Peak, Peru Peak, Styles Peak, and finally Bromley Mountain.

At SR-11/SR-30 I get a ride just fine into Manchester Center. Along the way I see *Shepherd* and *Easy Rider* walking the road shoulder, and I get out to join them for the remaining short distance downtown. After pizza and a few frosty tall ones we head over to Sutton's Place to share a room.

It is good that I'm with friends here this evening, for leaving good friends behind often brings little more than solitary loneliness. Loneliness is always poor company.

But, oh the faith to pass this way,
The path few e'er have known.
For till we see God's face have we
Gone long and far...alone.
(N. Nomad)

*Chuck *Swamp Eagle* Wilson departed the southernmost point of the eastern North American continent in Key West, Florida, on November 14, 1999. On November 5, 2000, nearly a year later (and 4,614 miles later), he successfully completed his thru-hike o'er the Eastern Continental Trail, at the Cliffs of Forillon, where the Appalachians plunge to the sea at "Land's End," Cap Gaspé, Québec.

Monday—August 21, 2000
Trail Day—90/41
Trail Mile—1250/545
Location—Arlington-West Wardsboro Road to Sutton's Place, Manchester Center, Vermont

My very good hiking friends from '98, brothers Chris *Yogi* and Carl *BooBoo* Schmid, have moved from Arkansas to Arlington, Vermont. *Yogi*, who I ran into in Rangeley, Maine, and who's doing a southbound this year, made me promise to give his brother a call as soon as I reached Manchester Center. So last evening I called *BooBoo*. We made arrangements to meet for breakfast this morning, and since *BooBoo* has wheels, he shuttled the three of us around, first to the post office and then back to the trail. I was concerned that he might miss work. Oh yes, he's late for work. Thanks *BooBoo*, it's been great seeing you again!

I've been feeling strong, and since the treadway has opened up some, I'm really starting to move, cranking out the miles. On the uphills I'm able to maintain a two-mile-per pace, on flat terrain, three and with "*Nomad's* Neutral" kicking in on the downhills, I'm cruising right along at four. An eighteen-mile day takes just a little over six hours—not bad at all.

The trail today passes Stratton Pond, one of the most picturesque sites along the entire trail. The weather is fair and the pond puts on a show. The climb up Stratton is a long, steady pull, but I manage it without difficulty. Stratton Mountain is a special place in AT annals, for it was on this summit that Benton MacKaye first envisioned a trail o'er the backbone of the Appalachian Mountains. Myron Avery was inspired by that dream and ran with it, practically single-handedly building the trail in the process.

The trail off Stratton is a cruise, and I reach Kelly Stand Road before seven, immediately catching a ride back to Manchester Center and Sutton's Place. Frank welcomes me once more, and for supper I head to the Sirloin Saloon for a great steak. Indeed, as *Wolfhound* would say, "Life is good!"

> *Life is what we make it, always has been, always will be.*
> (Grandma Moses)

Tuesday—August 22, 2000
Trail Day—91/42
Trail Mile—1270/565
Location—By the Trail one mile north of Melville Nauheim Shelter,
Vermont

I called the Schmids again last evening and talked with *BooBoo's* mother. When she asked what they might do to help, I told her I'd need a ride back to the trail again in the morning. So, just a little after eight now here comes *BooBoo* with that carefree, broad-beaming smile of his! Seems *BooBoo* can pretty much set his own work schedule, so he takes time to shuttle *Shepherd* and me around. After breakfast together, he gets us loaded for the ride back to the trail. Thanks again, *BooBoo*!

The day is clear and cool, and the sun feels so warm and welcome. The treadway, which had been full of huge mud bogs, is even drying out. The wave of northbounders continues, and many who pass today recognize me and stop to talk. It's going to be hard finding a hat to fit this big head pretty soon!

With so many hikers on the trail, the shelters tend to be crowded. Anticipating a full house, I pull up short of Melville Nauheim Shelter to pitch just off the trail for the evening. It's been great seeing and spending time with old friends, but I'm beginning to miss the solitude.

> *I never found the companion that was*
> *so companionable as solitude.*
> (Thoreau)

Wednesday—August 23, 2000
Trail Day—92/43
Trail Mile—1297/592
Location—Bascom Lodge, Mount Greylock Summit Road, Massachusetts

I'm up and break camp to a glorious day, but no sooner am I on the trail than the sky darkens over and the rain begins anew. So much for the dry treadway. It doesn't take long for the mudboggin' to return as the trail once more becomes submerged. However, I'm bound and determined to make the miles today, twenty-seven, so I trudge on, my feet soaked from the ankle-deep sludge, my pack and me both soaked from rain and sweat. There are many long, hard pulls today, how many I fail to count. The last, Mount Greylock, the highest point in Massachusetts, is the hardest by far. As I gain the summit the wind is whipping, driving the rain in a rage. The Veterans Memorial Tower—I can see only the base of it in the swirling, wind-driven shroud.

Bascom Lodge is a welcome sight, fading in and out like a mirage in the surround of clouds and rain. What a joy to be out of it as Alex Steel, Assistant Manager, welcomes me. "Bring your pack and get dried off," he says, "You've made it in time for dinner."

Ahh, this is the way to end a long, hard day! I'm pleased with myself for having slogged on; I did the twenty-seven. Another state in my rearview now. Three down, thirteen to go. Thanks, *Magic*, for the tank-stoking meal and for the lunch to take along tomorrow!

> *It's the plugging away that will win you the day,*
> *So don't be a piker, old pard!*
> *Just draw on your grit; it's so easy to quit;*
> *It's the keeping-your-chin-up that's hard.*
> (Robert W. Service)

Thursday—August 24, 2000
Trail Day—93/44
Trail Mile—1313/609
Location—MA-8/9 to The Inn at Village Square, Dalton, Massachusetts. Lee Walton, proprietor.

The storm continued throughout the night, the wind making shrill and mournful sounds as it whistled and shook the Lodge. But I slept in sweet contentment in the warmth and shelter of Bascom, on this high point in Massachusetts. After a great breakfast prepared by *Magic*, I'm out into the gloom, on my way south to Dalton.

Today is a comparatively short day, only seventeen miles and mostly downhill. As I descend the mountain, the heavens brighten and the sun breaks through, making for a perfect hiking day. But for sure, this treadway will not be dry or the ankle-swallowing mud gone for a very long time.

Today there are fence stiles on the trail, and I must dodge the first cow patties on my journey south. Crossing the little valley near Cheshire, the trail passes right through the middle of a cornfield. Plenty of diversion today!

In Dalton lives my good friend (and many a hiker's good friend) Tom Levardi. I stop by his beautiful home to see him for a few minutes before heading on to the Inn. I camped in Tom's yard in '98, but this year I'm behind on my journal entries and correspondence so I must find a place to get my feet up where I can write. After a great meal at The Shamrock Restaurant and Pub, I settle in at the Inn at Village Square. The place is a bit pricey, but I've a nicely-furnished room. I even have my own telephone. What luxuries!

> *Give me the luxuries of life and I'll willingly*
> *do without the necessities.*
> (Frank Lloyd Wright)

Friday—August 25, 2000
Trail Day—94/45
Trail Mile—1334/630
Location—Upper Goose Pond Cabin, Massachusetts

I'm out and down the main drag to Duff and Dell's, Dalton's favorite hangout for morning coffee, plus great trail breakfasts. On the way out of town, I stop again at Tom Levardi's home to talk a while with members of the clan who are still milling about. As I leave Depot Street and cross the tracks to climb Grange Hill, I stop to tie on my sweatband and remove my shirt; it's going to be a glorious warm day. What a joy to be alive!

The forest has constantly changed since the trail descended Mount Greylock. Today, I take pleasure in walking in the beauty of such an old familiar friend again, so common to the understory all throughout the central and southern highlands, the lush, green mountain laurel. The spruce and fir, common all along the trail to the north, have retreated to occupy only the highest reaches. White pine and hemlock and hardwood take their place. The miles are accumulating, slowly adding up, finally meaning something. I'm actually getting somewhere, and the trail and all that surrounds it and gives it life is testimony to that success. The treadway is so kind in comparison to what I had to deal with further north. I can stretch my legs and move with confidence. Even the mud is not annoying, for again today the treadway is drying, requiring much less jumping and dodging about.

If you've followed along on my previous journeys, you'll know that I've yet to see a bear along the trail, not a single one. Today, a northbounder stops to chat and tell me about the bear he's just seen. "Ambled along the trail right in front of me, even got up and walked the puncheons," says he. And sure enough in just a while, right there on the log puncheons, and along for the greatest distance are there unmistakable wet bearpaw prints—no, I didn't see the bear! There'll be no bear picture for the cover of my book.

At Washington Mountain Road, I stop to see friends Roy and Marilyn Wiley. Roy is busy tending his blueberry patch. He has over 1,200 high-bush blueberry shrubs, and they're all full of cherry-size blueberries. Folks keep coming and going with buckets full of blueberries as Roy and I relax and talk. Marilyn has come to be known among hikers and on the trail as *The Cookie Lady*. Over the years, traditionally, all hikers stopping by the farm to fill their water bottles are treated to fresh-baked cookies, compliments of Marilyn. I don't get to see her today. Roy says she's working a regular job now. And her job? Well, *The Cookie Lady* is one of the cooks for the local school lunch program! It's been great seeing you again, Roy. Thanks, *Cookie Lady*, for the great cookies; Roy's been handin' 'em out!

Lots of ups and downs today—first Grange Hill, then Warner Hill, October Mountain, Bald Top Mountain, and finally Becket Mountain. But I'm pretty much able to hold three per for the day, to arrive early and in good shape at Upper Goose Pond Cabin. Here, I'm greeted by Dottie, caretaker for the week, and I quickly settle in for the evening. Yesterday I figured I had five twenty-mile days to knock down to reach Kent, Connecticut, by next Tuesday, my scheduled date of arrival there. Today, the first of those twenties was a breeze.

Anywhere is within walking distance.
(Anonymous)

Saturday—August 26, 2000
Trail Day—95/46
Trail Mile—1354/650
Location—Lake Buel Road to East Mountain Retreat Center, Great
Barrington, Massachusetts. Reverend Lois F. Rose, Director.

Hikers have lugged in bags of blueberries from Roy's blueberry patch. So what better use than for blueberry pancakes! Oh, and is Dottie a master at flippin'. Somehow she manages to keep the platters stacked high with blueberry pancakes this morning, as thirteen of us wolf and wash 'em down with pot after pot of freshly-brewed coffee. Yes indeedy, this day has started off in grand fashion. Thanks, Dottie, you're the star in this five-star operation!

I'm treated to another warm, sun-drenched day. What a remarkable and oh-so-welcome change. There are more ups and downs today, and lots more mud. But the mud is less troublesome as the treadway continues to dry. The climbs and bail-offs slow me down though, and it's after four when I arrive at Reverend Rose's East Mountain Retreat. She sees me and comes straight away to greet me. Ahh, these are the moments that are shaping Odyssey 2000 into such a memorable experience! Lois, what a joy seeing your warm smile and peaceful countenance again! It is from you that I have learned...

You must be the change you wish to see in the world.
(Mahatma Gandhi)

Sunday—August 27, 2000
Trail Day—96/47
Trail Mile—1378/674
Location—Brassie Brook Lean-to, Connecticut

I enjoyed a great evening at East Mountain Retreat Center. I ordered a large supreme pizza to be delivered, along with a liter of Mountain

Dew. As soon as I stepped out of the shower, the pizza arrived. They were out of Mountain Dew, so I ended up with a two-liter bottle of Coke as a bonus. Yup, I downed the whole thing. Oh yes, and I also put away the entire sixteen-inch supreme pizza!

I had only a moment to talk with Reverend Rose earlier as she was in haste to perform a wedding. But in the evening she came by, and we had the longest chat. We talked about many things, like how families can break up and drift apart, and how one can become lonely and heartbroken in the process. Ministers have their problems, too, so the conversation, the give and take of it, was equally shared. In '98, I was the first to pen an entry in Reverend Rose's thru-hiker register. And now, two years later, the book full, I'll make the last. Much has happened in both Reverend Rose's life and in mine during that span of time. On balance, it's been mostly for the better. Thanks, Lois, for being here for me. It's been such a joy seeing you again and to know that East Mountain Retreat has become all you've prayed for it to be.

The day is absolutely perfect for hiking—warm and sunny, with a refreshing and gentle cool breeze. I'm in the Berkshires now, no match for the mountainous hulks to the north in the Whites, the Mahoosucs, or the Chic Chocs, but I'm huffing and out of breath from the challenge of the many pulls. From high vantage, these mountains are such a graceful and peaceful lot, all standing proudly, as if patiently waiting for some grand show to begin. Their legions lift and crowd beyond the horizon.

I put another state behind me today as I finish Massachusetts. That's two Canadian provinces and four states down as I enter Connecticut. Seems every state has its Bear Mountain, and I'm faced with the climb up the one in Connecticut first thing. Toward evening I'm at Brassie Brook Lean-to, a lovely area with acres of lush mountain laurel and canopied overstory, with the happy, rollicking brook running straight through. I have the little shelter to myself, for it seems most northbounders are now north, southbounders, south. From reading the entries in the shelter register, I see that the Ridgerunner program has just shut down for the season.

This has been a fine hiking day, capped now by the solitude as I settle in to this quiet, peaceful place.

> *It is no use walking anywhere to preach unless*
> *our walking is our preaching.*
> (Saint Francis of Assisi)

Monday—August 28, 2000
Trail Day—97/48
Trail Mile—1401/697
Location—Trailside south of Carse Brook, Connecticut

The Berkshires are standing in full dress today, a day for inspection, and I'm the inspector! And what better high ground from which to see them at attention than Lion's Head, Billy's View, and Rand's View! I don't remember any of these places from '98 (it was no doubt raining and they were socked in), but I'll remember this day, and the beauty of the Berkshires.

The ridges now line up in such fashion that to continue south, the trail must cross them, making for near-continual ascents and descents. Between the ridges that run to the horizon, there are the valleys wherein lie all the quaint New England villages, with the trail running close to or through most of them. So, on the ridges I'm in the mountains I have come to know and love, but as I descend each ridge, the crush and grind of the highway can be heard. The far-off wilds of the North Woods are behind me now, and the din of man is becoming more the way of these days.

I pitch for the evening above Carse Brook, in the lingering warmth of the day. I'm alone now as I continue this journey, but I am *not* alone.

And by these temples where I rest,
The Lord takes care of me.
There is not one thing that I lack,
I've true serenity.
And so, you think that I am poor,
And want for sheltered home.
But here in God, I trust my fate
...For I am not alone.
(N. Nomad)

Tuesday—August 29, 2000
Trail Day—98/49
Trail Mile—1416/712
Location—SR-341 to the The Gibbs House, Kent, Connecticut.
Morette and Brian Orth, Innkeepers.

When I'm in the comforts of a dwelling, even a shelter, I'm seldom able to roust myself and get on the trail early. But when sleeping in my little Nomad tent, first light usually gets me stirring. It's quite the luxury on clear nights to just cast the tent fly back, exposing all the no-see-um netting full around, enabling me to enjoy the beauty and mystery of the night sky, the dark woods and hills without the constant annoyance of mosquitoes. Last night was one of those special nights in the dark of the wood, the kind of night one can only truly understand and appreciate by living the experience.

So this morning I'm up and cranking at a very respectable hour, respectable for getting in some miles early, that is. I'm anxious to get on into Kent, where I plan to stay for the evening. I have a short mileage day, only fifteen, having knocked out a couple of near twenty-fives from Dalton, and I would like to arrive by early afternoon.

The rollercoaster ride continues, but the treadway is open, and as I manage the pulls at a respectable pace, I'm cutting good time today. The din and clatter and the noon whistle from every little berg can be heard now, even from the ridge, as the populated areas become increasingly dense. By one I make the final descent over the stiles and across a pasture to SR-341 and Schaghticoke Road. There's little traffic this time of day, but a kind fellow in his old pickup finally hauls it down, and I load for the ride to Kent. Bouncing along, wedged between a mound of typical pickup bed junk and sitting on his grungy old spare, the wind and the warm New England sun working its charm on me, I reflect on the blessings of my health, my strength and resolve, and the remarkable success that is this journey. I give thanks for it all.

Kent is a touristy place, as are many of the little mountain villages, which are only a hundred miles or so from Gotham City. It's a tight-set little main drag of a downtown with shops all along. I head right for the post office, which is closed (from one to two). It seems to me that no matter when I hit the post office, it's closed; seem that way to you?

I'd planned on staying at the Fife and Drum, but the restaurant where the office is located is closed on Tuesdays, so I head for their gift shop. The lady seems totally noncommittal about whether I can rent a room. "I don't know if any rooms are available; I think they're all rented. I'll need to make a call," is her reply as she heads for the back room. I hear her dialing but there's no conversation. In a moment she returns. "I can't get anybody, but I think we're all full." That was her final comment as she turned away, abruptly ending the conversation, busying herself with other things. The screen door to the shop has an old fashioned return spring on it and as I leave, I push the door open wide and let it slam good and hard. Aww dang, old man; why'd you do that? I know it's my own fault. The lady simply had me pegged as a bum, because, to her, I looked like a bum!

Ed Garvey is rolling over in his grave right now, I know he is, bless his soul. Ed is a trail legend. He was known to admonish hikers for not being clean-shaven and neatly dressed. In his classic book, *Appalachian Hiker*, published originally in 1971, I can remember reading, "No one expects the Appalachian Trail hiker to wear shirt, tie, business suit, and shiny shoes. On the other hand, hikers...need not look like bums." Forgive me, Ed, I know you expected better, the trail deserves better. Sorry!

On up the street and in less than a block stands the beautiful Gibbs House, a lovely old two-story home. I no sooner ring the doorbell than I'm greeted with a great big smile by Morette Orth. She welcomes me and shows me to a lovely upstairs room with private bath directly across from their private bedroom. I'm in and soon settled—for considerably less than the other place would have charged had they liked my looks. I've my own phone right next to the bed, and I'm able to catch up on my journal entries, correspondence and phone calls. Things always do seem to work out for the better, don't they!

> *A man with a beard was always a little suspect anyway.*
> (John Steinbeck)

Wednesday—August 30, 2000
Trail Day—99/50
Trail Mile—1437/733
Location—West Dover Road to Sha Ra Du Bed and Breakfast, Pawling, New York. Lee Stevens, proprietor.

The post office opens at eight, and I'm right there ready to mail my bounce box along to Delaware Water Gap. Then it's over to where all the locals hang out for breakfast at the little mom-n-pop.

Today is a busy day for Morette Orth, as it is her daughter's first day at school. But she finds time to run me up to the trail, and I'm out and moving south again by ten-thirty. Thanks Brian and Morette, you've been very kind to me!

Today I put Connecticut in my rearview as I enter New York. Slowly but surely the mountains are flattening out, and the treadway is becoming much easier to manage. Save for a couple of section hikers (a local trail maintainer named *Walkie-Talkie,* and Richard, a southbounder, with whom I hike for a short while) I have the trail to myself today.

I have made good time for this twenty-one miler. No problem getting a hitch, for in just moments after arriving at the road crossing, I'm in downtown Pawling. I'd called Lee Stevens recently, and she'd given me directions to her B&B. I spot the place and head right over. Lee greets me at the door with a big smile. She hands me a key and directs me to my room on the second floor. What a grand old place, very spacious, with a large sitting room and a full kitchen. The shower is one of the neatest I've seen, an old claw-foot cast-iron tub with a curtain all the way around, and the shower head hooked to the ceiling!

In the evening I head for the Pawling Tavern for supper and a few tall ones. I have a fine pasta plate, and after my first longneck frosty, the locals pitch in, keeping a tall, cold one in front of me for the remainder of the evening.

I've really enjoyed this day, and the great folks of Pawling.

The invariable mark of a dream is to see it come true every day.
(Ralph Waldo Emerson)

Thursday—August 31, 2000
Trail Day—100/51
Trail Mile—1455/751
Location—RPH Shelter, New York

I'm up, surprisingly before seven, headed for the kitchen to brew a pot of coffee and fix myself some breakfast. When I'd talked to Lee by phone she said she'd haul me back to the trail, and at eight we're off. Thanks, Lee! I've had a great stay at Sha Ra Du B&B, and in your friendly little town of Pawling.

I've been thinking about a good old fashioned hotdog off and on for days, and after five miles of it this morning, at NY-55 I head east two-tenths of a mile to the Elite Dog, a mighty fine hiker-oasis of a motorhome-based hotdog stand. The place is called Bob's, and Bob Barrett, a disabled American veteran, runs it. He's just getting his little operation cranked up for the day but finds time to sit and chat while I down the two dogs he's prepared for me. After signing his register, I glance through, seeing many familiar names. *Spur* was number 61 in '99 and 161 this year. *Swamp Eagle* stopped by, and *Grandma Soule* was here, as were many others.

Bob and I are the same age, born within days of each other in '38. He went off to war and I went to the university. I got "educated," and he got shot-up. The heroes of this day are different from the heroes of our time. Most people today probably don't even know what DAV stands for. And so I must say, "Bob, you're my kind of hero; thanks for your sacrifice in keeping our country free. God bless you, my friend!"

Near Mount Egbert, I see hikers coming toward me. I've been on a not-so-enjoyable side-slab for the last while, all the while listening to the rasp and grind of the traffic below on I-84. First thing I do after the usual exchange of cordialities is to start griping about the treadway. I don't know why I'm acting like this; it's the first time. Oh, and am I embarrassed and ashamed about what I've just said, as I discover I'm talking to Karen Lutz, representative, regional office, Appalachian Trail Conference, and Ron Rosen, Duchess/Putnam Counties Appalachian Trail Conference volunteer. They're out to take a look at a recent relocation that has just been completed a little north of here. I'm obviously holding them up, but enjoy the conversation, which I've encouraged, as we talk trail. Their vehicles are parked at the RPH Shelter. I'll be spending the evening there, and Ron promises to bring me a Coke.

I arrive at RPH around three, take a bath by the pitcher pump, wash my sweaty clothes, and settle in for the evening. In a short while *Big John* comes in. He lives down the road and stops by almost every evening to check on the thru-hikers to see what they might need. "Would you like a pizza?" he asks. "Oh, yes!" is my reflex reply.

Karen and Ron are back with my Coke, and *Big John* is off to get my pizza. Life, indeed, is good. Thanks Ron and *Big John*!

In just a while, Walter comes in. He's going to be part of HATT, a weekend-long hike that will link hikers all up and down the Appalachian Trail. The plan is to create a link of hikers in contact with each other that will hike the entire AT over the Labor Day weekend, quite a project. A friend of *Spur's*, a young lady with whom I've been in touch by email, *Ready,* also comes in for the evening, and we have a grand time chatting before calling it a day.

> *...Take the power to walk in the forest and be part of nature.*
> *Take the power to control your own life...*
> *Take the power to make your life happy.*
> (Susan Polis Schutz)

Friday—September 1, 2000
Trail Day—101/52
Trail Mile—1476/770
Location—Old West Point Road to Graymoor Friary, Garrison, New York

I had been so hoping to meet the caretaker of RPH. I missed him during my stay in '98, and last night *Big John* said he doubted if Joe would be by, but first thing this morning comes Joe Hrouda, and we spend a grand time together. Joe, you've got such a grand place here, and the campsite south in the meadow by the AT is surely a dreamland to weary hikers.

The day is starting iffy with the weather, overcast and threatening, but as I climb Shenandoah Mountain the sun breaks through and the day turns sunny and quite hot. Most hikers have been complaining about these close, humid days, but I'm handling them just fine as I slug down plenty of water loaded with Conquest, an electrolyte replacement mix designed for use by ultra-marathoners, provided me by Gary *Bearbag* Buffington, MD, the developer of Conquest, one of my sponsors for Odyssey 2000. Thanks *Bearbag*!

More ups and downs today, but the treadway is basically open, permitting me to stride out and cover the miles. By one I've managed the fifteen to Canopus Hill Road. Here, as I climb the little pop before the road crossing, in half a daze from plodding, I look up to see two familiar faces. Both with such happy, broad-beaming smiles, both staring directly at me. I can't believe my eyes; I must be seeing things. These folks live clear down in Roanoke, Virginia. How can they be here in New York where the AT crosses this out-back county road, in what seems the middle of no place? Oh my, but here they are, my very dear hiking friends from '98, Scott *T-bone Walker* Baldwin and Tulie *Tulip* Kaschub. I'm so taken by their presence that I can't speak. Tears well up, filling my eyes, and I slump over my hiking poles. They stand in silence, continuing to beam at me. I finally manage to blurt, "Tulie, *Tulip*, is that you? And *T-bone, T-bone Walker*—oh, glory be, it really is you!" What a wonderful and unbelievable surprise! Says *T-Bone*, "We're up here for a friend's wedding. We've followed your progress, and knew you were in the area. After stopping at RPH Shelter and seeing your register entry, and after talking with Joe, and looking at the map, we knew we could catch you here at Canopus Hill Road!" After a couple of PBJs made by *Tulip* and near an hour of the greatest catching-up get-together, with tears welling and a lump in my throat I bid these dear young friends goodbye, and head on down the trail.

I can hardly wait for the completion of the hike today, for this day I reach Graymoor where my very dear friend, Father Fred Alvarez, is waiting to greet me. Father Fred is a friend to countless hikers, for he is the host for all the Friars, and for Graymoor, where the doors have been open to hikers for years. It has been Father Fred's chosen duty to welcome the intrepid as they arrive, a duty he has enjoyed with obvious satisfaction and joy. I first met Father Fred on my northbound odyssey in '98, and we became immediate good friends. As were the prayers of many, it was Father Fred's continued prayers that carried me through to the successful completion of that long and memorable journey. So now, with great anticipation and excitement, I enter the portals at Graymoor, and once again, just as before, Father Fred is here to greet me and to welcome me to Gray-moor. He then shows me to a spacious, private suite just for friends of the Friars. As we go, he too is bubbling with excitement, for he, too, is happy to see me! He insists on loaning me personal clothing while he takes all of mine to launder. "Get ready for dinner," he says, "I'll be back for you at five-thirty." And so I will, Father, and so I will. What a blessed day this has been!

And could I have one wish this year, this only would it be:
I'd like to be the sort of friend that you have been to me.
(Edgar A. Guest)

Saturday—September 2, 2000
Trail Day—102/53
Trail Mile—1493/787
Location—Seven Lakes Drive (second crossing) to the home of Joe Mercurio, Bear Mountain, New York

I had a restful stay at Graymoor, sleeping soundly. Rain began shortly after my arrival and continued into the night. Father Fred arrives at seven-thirty to take me to breakfast, where we enjoy a few short moments together. But as always, as it inevitably must, that time comes. Father Fred walks to the door with me, and after a prayer for my continued safe passage, we bid farewell. Father Fred, you have been so generous and kind to me. Thank you for caring, and for your prayers; there is no way I can ever repay you, but is it not such a wonderful debt!

Today is another day full with anticipation, for today I'll see my son's friend and my very dear friend, Joe Mercurio. Joe is a retired New York City police officer. After retirement he moved to Florida, taking

a job as bailiff with the Brevard County Sheriff's Department. Here he met my older son, Jay. I first met Joe when he accompanied my son on one of his visits to Georgia, and it was then that Joe and I became good friends. Joe lives above Bear Mountain Bridge now, and when he found out I'd be hiking right by his place, he invited me to give him a call, and to stay with him on my way through. I've made the call, and this morning I'll see Joe at Bear Mountain Inn. There we'll make plans for him to come take me from the trail this evening.

Departing Graymoor, I'm on the trail by eight to begin the climb up South Mountain. It's over seven miles to Bear Mountain Inn. Plans are to meet Joe there between ten and eleven, but the trail this morning is full of up-rocks and down-rocks, making progress agonizingly slow. I hasten along with much difficulty, stumbling all the while as I break in a new pair of New Balance 803s. New Balance is one of my kind sponsors, and they had sent a new pair of their great shoes to me in care of Father Fred at Graymoor. Most folks have a problem with their feet swelling, requiring larger boots as they go to new ones, but I've stepped down a half size. This is going to work much better, but my poor toenail-less doggies are barking as they take a pounding this morning. The treadway finally shows some mercy. As I hasten my pace, I'm able to arrive at the Inn by ten-thirty. Joe is waiting for me with hot coffee and a buttered roll. I sneak up on him from behind and he must turn as I surprise him by coming around the Inn the back way. We spend a few moments together, making plans for him to come for me at Seven Lakes Drive at three.

I have several hard pops left today, over Bear Mountain, Black Mountain, and Goshen Mountain. But the slower pace I've keyed into the schedule proves very doable, bringing me to Seven Lakes Road right on time. Joe comes to get me, and in only moments we're at his little hideaway overlooking Bear Mountain Bridge.

Joe has just purchased the old place, and he's smack in the middle of the labor of love fix-it-up phase. I estimate the project at a million bucks, but then the view down and across the Hudson to Anthony's Nose, along with the grand sweep of the river all the way to the magnificent Bear Mountain Bridge, is worth every bit of that. The thunderstorms return again. I'm so happy to be out of it. Joe prepares a great feast. In a while his brother John and sister-in-law Jean come by. What a grand time we have. I'm not lonely this day!

Inasmuch as anyone ushers you nearer to God,
he or she is your friend.
(Anonymous)

Sunday—September 3, 2000
Trail Day—103/54
Trail Mile—1509/813
Location—Lakes Road in Monroe, New York to the home of Pavel and Julia Litvinov, Tarrytown

The rain came hard again last evening, much thunder and lightning, with one strike hitting very close by. The scene kept changing constantly across Anthony's Nose and down to Bear Mountain Bridge. I watched, greatly relieved to be out of it, as twilight descended and the storm moved through. Joe, you're got such a special place here.

It's going to be a great hideaway. Thanks for sharing it with me, and thanks for your kindness and friendship!

Pavel Litvinov and I have made plans to hike together today. We met back on Mount Moosilauke. Pavel insisted we get together, and that I permit him to entertain me while passing through New York. With plans for the day made, Joe drops me back at Seven Lakes Drive, and I head south. In an hour or so, Pavel will begin hiking north from Lakes Road, on the other side of Mombasha High Point. If the timing is right, we should meet on or near Arden Mountain.

Oh, and isn't it great when a plan comes together, for just as I scamper over the last high boulders on Arden, up comes Pavel from the other side! Hiking with Pavel today is his running friend, Denis Daly. What better place to break for lunch, so we drop our packs to enjoy the view, the warm sun, and each other's company.

Both Pavel and Denis, also in their sixties, are in excellent physical condition, and we move along at a brisk pace. Hiking with these well-conditioned athletes is making for an absolutely enjoyable day. The afternoon passes quickly, and we are soon at Lakes Road and Pavel's car.

I had no idea it was such a great distance to Pavel's home in Tarrytown. We travel many miles, over many different roads and highways, finally crossing the Tappan Zee Bridge. The trip takes well over an hour before we arrive at the beautiful old Hackley School, where Pavel lives and teaches.

Here I meet Pavel's wife, Julia. In the evening she prepares a wonderful meal for Pavel, Denis and me. Umm, fried chicken and fresh corn on the cob. Thanks, folks, thanks so much for your kindness!

And who will walk a mile with me
Along life's weary way?
A friend who knows, and dares to say,
The brave, sweet words that cheer the way
And the quiet rest at the end of the day—
Where he walks a mile with me.
(Henry Van Dyke)

Monday—September 4, 2000
Trail Day—104/55
Trail Mile—1525/829
Location—Barrett Road in Waywayanda State Park, New Jersey to the home of Larry and Freida Luxenberg, New City, New York

We're up early, and after a fine breakfast, Pavel and I begin the long drive back to the trail. It is so good making and having new friends, but it is so difficult bidding them farewell, knowing you may never see them again. Goodbye Pavel. Your friendship will remain in my memory. Indeed, meeting you and sharing your company has been a most pleasant part of this odyssey!

I remember Cat Rock and the Pinnacles from '98, their high-flung boulders making such a rugged and picturesque presentation. Another beautiful day, and the views are spectacular.

Yet another state passes beneath my feet as I depart New York to enter New Jersey. At the Wawayanda Shelter I find an entry in the register with a note from Dan *Sheltowee* Rogers. *Sheltowee* hiked the AT in '99, and through correspondence and numerous visits, we have become good friends. *Sheltowee* lives in New Jersey now, and he has invited me to spend some time with him while hiking through. I'll give him a call later today.

I'll be at Larry Luxenberg's this evening. I met Larry at Trail Days a couple of years ago. More recently, he has taken me under his wing and has provided guidance and advice for my upcoming book. Larry is the author of *Walking the Appalachian Trail*. He has written the foreword for *Ten Million Steps*.

I have allowed eight hours for the hike today, more than ample time to hike the sixteen miles, for I don't want to keep Larry waiting at Barrett Road, the planned pickup point. As the time and the miles pass, it appears I'll arrive over an hour early, giving me time to relax and work my journal entries and correspondence. But as I near Barrett Road, the day has other plans for me. The sky darks over and the rain begins. I hasten to don my poncho as the sky opens, and as I reach Barrett Road I end up sitting hunched in retreat under my poncho as the rain comes steady and hard. Larry arrives early, and I'm relieved to get out of it. Along for the ride are Larry's sister, Deborah, and his two sons, Eli and Seth.

The trip back is another long one, over many roads and highways to reach Larry's home in New City, New York. But the time passes quickly as we're all full of chatter, enjoying each other's company. Waiting for us at Larry's are his wife, Freida, their daughter, Adina, and Deb's husband, Steve. I no sooner shower than the table is set. Larry has prepared burgers and steaks. He thru-hiked the AT in 1980, so Larry knows all about a hiker's appetite. What a feast they've prepared. I am fed well!

In the evening I call *Sheltowee* and we make arrangements to spend time together tomorrow. What a great day this has been!

> *You give but little when you give of your possessions.*
> *It is when you give of yourself that you truly give.*
> (Kahlil Gibran)

Tuesday—September 5, 2000
Trail Day—105/56
Trail Mile—1543/847
Location—Goldsmith Road (past Unionville Road) in Wantage, New Jersey to Jim Murray's "Secret Shelter"

This will be a very long day for Larry. He's suited up for work, but first he must drive me all the way to Barrett Road before heading off to New York on his two-hour commute. On the drive back we talk of many things. Larry has been such a help to me, my mentor if you will, giving of his time freely, guiding and directing me as I work through the throes of writing a book. His advice has been invaluable. Thanks Larry, and thanks all the Luxenberg family! You have all been so very kind to me.

New Jersey is still smooth going, but as the day progresses, the ride starts getting a little bumpy, not the notorious rocks that lie ahead, but an introduction!

I had planned on going into Unionville, but *Sheltowee* suggested I spend the evening at Jim's "Secret Shelter." And what a great place this turns out to be. I arrive to find a beautiful high meadow right next to the trail, old fruit trees and lush grass all around. A short way up, set perfectly against the mountain, two small cabins, one just for hikers, with running water, hot shower, lights, and a cozy, warm loft for sleeping. I arrive a little after three, make myself at home, and retire to the shade of an old walnut tree to do a little reading and to work some correspondence. In just a while comes Jim Murray, the proud owner. He is just returning from an afternoon hike. We spend enjoyable time together, talking trail and gear.

I can't resist the loft and a late afternoon snooze, and I'm quickly in hiker's dreamland. Shortly comes a knock on the little cabin door. It's *Sheltowee* with pizza and some cold frosties. Another great friend, another great time, another great day!

A candle loses nothing by lighting another candle.
(Erin Majors)

Wednesday—September 6, 2000
Trail Day—106/57
Trail Mile—1564/868
Location—US-206 at Culvers Gap to Forest Motel, Branchville,
New Jersey.

As I'm sitting, tending to my daily duty this morning, the privy door open, and as I look to the high meadow above the little cabins, I see three fawns cavorting under the old fruit trees there. And by the far upper meadow, where the field gives back to the wood, a dozen turkeys slowly forage along. The day has dawned clear but with a chill in the air, no better time for a hike!

Climbing to High Point, the rocks come on. This is the beginning of what a well-worn phrase describes as the "rocky road." Get used to it, dear feet. After the next two weeks of this brutality coming at us hard and steady, you'll think you've been planted here!

By three I've done twenty-one miles. "Enough of this rocky ricochet!" my weary feet exclaim, so I break and head for Worthington's Bakery. They were closed when I came through in '98, so I'm really looking forward to finally sampling some of their fine confections. But alas, a cardboard sign taped to the door reads, "Closed Wednesday, September 6th. Open again Thursday." I just can't win with these folks. Looks like they've closed especially for me. The sign should have read, "Closed today, because *Nimblewill's* comin' through." Ahh, but I'll hit 'em in the morning.

Right next door is Gyp's Tavern. I head there. Oh my, what joy, Yuengling Premium on tap; maybe the rocks aren't going to be all that bad! I get a ride right away to the Forest Motel a ways down the road. This has been a long, hard day. My feet are sore. I'm very, very tired. Sleep comes soon.

> *If you can force your heart and nerve and sinew*
> *To serve your turn long after they're gone,*
> *And so hold on when there is nothing in you*
> *Except the Will which says to them: "Hold on."*
> (Rudyard Kipling)

Thursday—September 7, 2000
Trail Day—107/58
Trail Mile—1582/886
Location—AMC Mohican Outdoor Center, Camp Mohican Road,
Blairstown, New Jersey. Dave Simpson, Resident Manager.

Five bucks to a family member of the motel proprietor gets me the two-mile shuttle back to Worthington's Bakery, and the trail.

Worthington's Bakery is open, and I finally meet Carl Worthington. Carl's grandparents opened the bakery in 1932. His father, George, ran it from 1952 until recently, when failing health forced his retirement. Carl runs it now. We talk as customers come and go, and as I manage to put the dwindle on his coffee, jelly rolls, and cookies.

I'm back on the trail at nine-thirty to yet another clear, sun-drenched hiking day, crispy cool. I've on not only my long-sleeve capilene, but my wool shirt as well. The hike today starts off with a bumpy pull up Rattlesnake Mountain, then levels to a smooth cruise along the ridge. As the climb and the sun both warm me, I stop in the glow of a sun-drenched boulder to remove both shirts. I sit and relax, enjoying the fresh scent of the forest, the calm quiet of the morning, and the gentle sun on my face. Sitting here now, it finally happens again, the inspiration to compose. I quickly get my little PocketMail out and open it to the memo pad.

In '98, during that Odyssey, I experienced countless moments of inspiration as poem after poem found birth within my heart, to flow effortlessly from pen to paper. But this year, many friends have asked why I've not shared new ditties with them. And I've had to explain that there's hardly been any. So what a joyful moment, and what a remarkably spiritual occurrence, for as I sit, contemplating the blessings that are mine this day, and as I reach for my water bottle, I glance down at the satin-green moss-covered rock beside me. And there, in the sun's shining whiteness and the moss's glistening greenness, lying in this little cameo-like depression, a remarkable little cross, formed of simple twigs, perfectly configured and perfectly aligned. At that moment came the inspiration that took only moments to record. It's entitled "Spirit of the Mountains." It will close my journal entry for this day.

The trail stays atop the ridge now, over old abandoned roads where once stood dwellings, the faint remnants of driveways, and cut-off utility poles—all that remain of a time long past when this ridge bustled with activity.

From Catfish Fire Tower, I descend the trail to Camp Mohican Road and the AMC Mohican Outdoor Center. As I enter, I'm greeted with a smile and a cheerful "hello" from Tiffany Charleson, naturalist-turned-receptionist. Here also this evening are southbounders *Greenjeans* and *Hymettus*. The bunkhouse is a jam-up affair. Plenty of room; hot, shove-you-back showers; full kitchen, refrigerator, stove, microwave, the works! *Hymettus* and I prepare a large pot of veggie and corn-beef soup from odds and ends left in the refrigerator. *Greenjeans* joins us for supper, and we have a grand time of it. A shower, shampoo and a braid job for my unruly hair by Tiffany, and this day is done. What a glad and happy heart hath I!

The mountains stand majestically,
For all of man's enjoyment.
And each the clan, engaged are we,
Full time in that employment.

We trek the good trek past these hills,
In search for answers to—
A journ' of faith our Father wills,
O'er pathways right and true.

Set to this task, we faithful home,
To'rd lasting, blessed peace;
Unto that Light, no more to roam,
Till God our souls release.
(N. Nomad)

Friday—September 8, 2000
Trail Day—108/59
Trail Mile—1592/896
Location—Church of the Mountain Hostel, Delaware Water Gap,
Pennsylvania. Karen Nickels, Pastor.

I roll out a little after six, boil water for coffee, and then try getting things together so I can be on the trail at a decent hour for a change. But it's seven-thirty before I shoulder my pack to go.

The trail again claims the ridge, providing many fine views to the valley below. As I near Delaware Water Gap, the ridge gradually drops to Sunfish Pond. I put another state behind me today as I pass through the Gap to enter Pennsylvania. Two provinces and seven states behind me, nine states to go to reach Key West.

The roadwalk along I-80 remains vivid in my memory from two years ago. Though made of concrete and steel, this mile-long bridge still shudders and vibrates as the army of eighteen-wheelers roars through, with each passing rig creating its own little tornado. I'm glad to get this roadwalk behind me, to enter the little village of Delaware Water Gap.

I head to the post office for my bounce box, then it's over to Trail's End Café for lunch. The nearby tavern burned down a couple of years ago, so Yuengling Premium on tap may not be an option this evening.

The Church of the Mountain Hostel is a grand hiker's haven, and I settle in, get cleaned up, and work on correspondence.

> *Who walks with Beauty has no need of fear;*
> *The sun and moon and stars keep pace with him;*
> *Invisible hands restore the ruined year,*
> *And time itself grows beautifully dim.*
> (David Morton)

Saturday—September 9, 2000
Trail Day—109/60
Trail Mile—1607/911
Location—SR-33 at Wind Gap, Pennsylvania to Gateway Motel.
Peter Patel, proprietor.

Everyone's up and out ahead of me. I tarry, getting my pack ready. What great timing, as Pastor Karen drops by. It's quiet, and we have a chance to spend some time together. I'd missed meeting her on my northbound hike in '98, even stopped on my way back south, but she was away for the day. So, it's a joy to finally meet and personally thank her for her long-term caring and genuine hospitality.

The trail leading south from the Gap is a special place, the climb well worth the effort, the reward being the remarkable vistas. Council Rock and Lookout Rock offer breathtaking views across and down into the Gap. Past Mount Minsi, on an old woods road, I see a vehicle approaching. It pulls alongside and stops. Here I meet Brian McDonnell and Gregg Tinkham, rangers with the National Park Service. As we talk about Delaware Water Gap National Recreation Area and about my hike, I notice that both of these kind officers are wearing Kevlar vests under their uniforms. I'm thinking, "Here before me is the reality of it, there's just no place that's safe anymore, even out here in the woods and the wilds."

Today has been a short-distance day, but by no means an easy day, as the rocks of old Blue Mountain really dish it out. Reaching Wind Gap, I turn up the road and head for Pete's Gateway Motel. I remember Pete and his little place from '98. I'm tired and anxious to return to such comforts. It's a short walk, and as I arrive, Pete greets me.

This hike is turning out to be an incredible joy-filled journey, even more so than Odyssey '98, if that is possible. In '98 I shared a room with Rob *100-Pound Stormcloud* Peterman, a retired Navy Seal Commander. Pete ran out and brought us back some great Yuengling Premium, then later took us to Sol's for supper. That was a memorable evening. Seems a rerun is definitely the order of the day, as tonight I share a room yet again with a retired Navy officer—John *Hymettus* Hutchins. Pete runs for the Yuengling longnecks again, then takes us to Sol's for supper! Thanks Pete for being here, and thanks for your kindness and friendship! Another grand day on the trail.

> *The rocks of old Blue Mountain*
> *Strike brutal and relentless...*
> *As we intrepid plod along*
> *Totally defenseless.*
> (N. Nomad)

Sunday—September 10, 2000
Trail Day—110/61
Trail Mile—1628/932
Location—SR-873 at Palmerton, Pennsylvania to Palmerton Hotel. Ana Maria DeMelo, proprietor.

I manage to get out on the trail by seven-thirty. The hike today into Palmerton is long, but mostly a cruise over abandoned woods roads atop Old Blue. The hiking days recently have been nothing short of perfect, with today being no exception. As I gain the ridge, I kick up more turkey, and white tail flags seem to be bounding and flying everywhere.

I had been dreading the rocks of Pennsylvania—memories of my '98 hike. Back then I was carrying entirely too much "stuff," and wearing heavy boots, and I hadn't yet perfected the technique of using trekking poles. This year things are different, much different, and even though I'm two years older, I'm handling the rocks with relative ease, even enjoying them!

In the afternoon, I enter the ridge above Palmerton, the area devastated by decades of zinc smelting in the valley below. Zinc is a very toxic element, and after decades of fallout from the smelters, the trees and all other plants began thinning, then finally disappeared entirely, leaving only barren rock and dead snags everywhere. The day is remarkably clear, but even with such glowing brilliance, the place looks incredibly forbidding and spooky. Water is non-existent here on the ridge, and I've run out. My throat is parched, adding to the unpleasantness. The treadway is visible for a great distance ahead as it winds around and through the barren landscape.

Looking up from plodding through and dodging the rocks, I see a hiker approaching. I know that I know this man, but I'm confused to see him here, heading north. I stop, and as he passes I ask, "Jamie, is that you?" He interrupts his smooth, effortless stride to answer, "Yes, it is I." So here I finally meet *Mr. Clean*! *Honey* and *Bear*, at The Cabin in Maine, had told me that I would meet *Mr. Clean*, but I doubted that happening. For you see, *Mr. Clean* departed on the AT from Abol Bridge on New Year's Day, headed for Springer Mountain. What I didn't know was his plan, a plan to take over a year to complete his hike. So, here today, in no-man's land above Palmerton, we finally meet, just as *Honey* and *Bear* had predicted, as *Mr. Clean* returns to his last campsite to retrieve an article left behind. It's been great seeing you, *Mr. Clean*! I know *Honey* and *Bear* will be pleased to know our paths have crossed.

I distinctly remember the climb up from Lehigh Gap in '98. I had to encourage and reassure myself during that ordeal. I remember looking up at the white blazes as they ascended to the sky, and I was mortified. I recall saying to myself, "You can make it fine over all those straight-up boulders, *Nomad*. The trail crew got up there with a paint brush and a bucket of paint, and you'll get up there too!" Now I'm looking down with the same hesitancy and fear. The trail pitches near straight off down and through the boulders. All I see is haze and the gaping chasm that is Lehigh Gap far below. Time for more encouragement, more reassurance, another pep talk: "Easy as she goes—don't look past the next few knee-breaking bail-offs, and you'll get down through it just fine." And so I do. Thank you, Lord, for the hand!

At the traffic light by the bridge, working the traffic coming off the bridge, I get a ride right away, straight to the front door of the grand old Palmerton Hotel. In the bar, as I adjust my eyes to the dimness, I'm greeted once more by Ana Maria. "Take your pack off and have a seat. What would you like?" I sigh that contented sigh of relief as I belly-up, "How's about a cool glass of that Yuengling draft!"

Ana Maria prepares a room and a wonderful meal for me. Full and contented, I end this hiking day! *Mr. Clean* calls it "happiness."

> *Not all chemicals are bad.*
> *Without hydrogen or oxygen, for example,*
> *there would be no way to make water,*
> *a vital ingredient in beer.*
> (Dave Barry)

Monday—September 11, 2000
Trail Day—111/62
Trail Mile—1653/957
Location—Hawk Mountain Road, Pennsylvania to Eckville Shelter.
Mick "Lazee" Charowsky, caretaker.

I enjoyed sharing a room again last night with *Hymettus*. The upstairs was hot, so we had to open the windows. A carnival was going full-tilt across the street, with all the associated commotion and racket, but just about the time I thought it was going to bother me—it's morning!

Bert's Restaurant opens at six, and I'm right there. Pancakes and eggs and lots of hot coffee, and my tank's stoked for the day. Brothers *Apollo* and *Man-in-the-moon*, southbounders, are being paid a visit by their parents, and I'm offered a ride back to the trailhead. This is a great favor, as the hitch out of Palmerton is really tough. I'm back on trail a little before eight. Thanks, folks, and good luck on your thru-hike, fellows!

At the first shelter up from Palmerton, I run into *EZ-E*. He plans on hiking to Hawk Mountain Road, twenty-five miles for the day. I look at the *Data Book* and the *Companion,* and decide to do the same, as there's a bunkhouse just down the road with shower, toilet, lights, and a refrigerator stocked with pop, juice and ice cream. What convinces me to go? The ice cream. I can pull the twenty-five easy with ice cream waiting for me!

The hike today is mostly a cruise, but in some places the ridge is shimmed up with haphazard piles of wicked, wild-angled boulders. Rock hopping is the way through these varied assortments of monuments and headstones, and I'm slowed very little. In fact, the challenge today is to just whack out the miles. No sense taking the numerous short-hop blue blazed side trails for the overlook views. There are no views today. They've gone to blazes, as the day settles into a mushy sort of hazy overcast.

I'm surprised to reach Hawk Mountain Road by four—an eight-hour hiking day. For the twenty-five miles, that's better than three miles per, not bad through the Pennsylvania rocks!

It seems less than two-tenths down to the little house and outbuildings, property of the Park Service, managed by thru-hiker *Lazee.* I'm there pronto, to shower and settle in. After, I hit the refrigerator a pretty good lick. *Lazee* comes from work, bringing me fried chicken, ice for my pop, and a chocolate ice cream cup for dessert. Then *Diggs* stops by, looking for *EZ-E*, and returns later with a case of Yuengling. Take your time *EZ-E*! Aww, here he comes.

What a satisfying day. I'm very pleased with myself. Thanks for boosting me along, *EZ-E*, and thanks, *Lazee* and *Diggs*!

These beautiful days must enrich all my life.
They do not exist as mere pictures...
but they saturate themselves into every part
of my body and live always.
(John Muir)

Tuesday—September 12, 2000
Trail Day—112/63
Trail Mile—1668/972
Location—SR-61 at Port Clinton, Pennsylvania to Port Clinton
Hotel. Billie Ann Russell and Paul Engle, proprietors.

The little outbuilding that's been converted to a shelter here at Hawk Mountain Road is very comfortable. There are bunks for six, a table, a library, lights, and a lounge chair. I was the only guest. *EZ-E* went off with *Diggs. Lazee* came over again last evening with this year's album, a well-organized and quite comprehensive collection of photos. I was surprised to find the number of folks I recognized, almost all "Class of 2000" northbounders.

Lazee had mentioned there were showers in the forecast, and sure enough toward morning I heard the rain, first gentle, then hard on the shelter roof. The morning dawns in a fog. *Lazee* is up and out to his day job, and I finally manage to get out and back on the trail.

It would be easy to be disappointed with this day, as the fog and mist hold, making for wet everything, especially the rocks. There are no views. I must admit some dismay, as I was looking forward to seeing the raptor migration at Hawk Mountain. It's peak season right now for the southern migration of more than 17,000 raptors along the Kittatinny Ridge, especially the broadwing, bald eagle, osprey, and kestrel; but alas, it's not to be.

Another old familiar friend has begun gracing the trail the past few days—the lush, broad-leafed rhododendron. I know that I'm making progress now in my journey south, the mountain laurel and rhododendron being the proof of it. The forests of spruce and fir provided a scenic landscape, and the trails up there certainly fulfilled all of my expectations, but the southern Appalachians are my mountains and I'm encouraged now by the changing vegetation and terrain—I'm heading home!

The sky continually threatens, but the rain holds, leaving the mist, fog and mush. Progress is slowed by the accompanying treachery the wetness brings to the rocks, but by one I arrive safely at Port Clinton. The little town hasn't changed much. The Port Clinton Hotel remains the same, much as during my previous hike. Paul and Billie Ann are excited to see me again, and I'm welcomed with open arms. That makes for a good day, one that would otherwise have been labeled just another get-on-south day.

> *There's some end...for the man who follows a path:*
> *mere rambling is interminable.*
> (Seneca)

Wednesday—September 13, 2000
Trail Day—113/64
Trail Mile—1692/996
Location—501 Shelter, Pennsylvania. George and Joan Shollenberger, caretakers.

After a few Yuengling premiums and a grand meal at the Port Clinton Hotel last evening, I headed back to my room to work my daily journal entries. I got the pillows stacked and my little PocketMail open and that was it. I fell promptly asleep. No sooner did a knock come on my door. It was a young lad with a large bowl of soup, compliments of Billie Ann. Putting that away, I quickly returned to dreamland. I had fully intended to spend more time with my dear friends in Port Clinton, but the old *Nomad* was just too pooped! Thanks Billie Ann, Paul, and Chunky. I had a great stay!

The hike today is pretty much a cruise, just a long day. I've got the Pennsylvania rocks almost knocked down now as I continue moving south. I've perfected a technique that works through the nearly constant jumble of smaller rocks, enabling me to stride out and maintain my three-mile per hour pace. Only the larger monuments and headstones tend to slow me. All care must be taken through these boulder fields, for they can be treacherous. I surely don't want to bust it now.

I arrive in good order and good time at the 501 Shelter to be promptly greeted by George Shollenberger, caretaker. He has placed the phone on his front porch for me to call the local pizzeria, which I promptly do. I go for the medium stromboli, a great quantity of food, way too much. So too, the two liter bottle of Mountain Dew. Hiking long distances every day requires incredible amounts of energy, the consumption of huge volumes of food. I'm trying to maintain my body weight, but I know I'm losing.

In just a short while, Jerry *Kodak* Brubaker from Bernville, Pennsylvania stops by. He'd hiked some with *EZ-E* this year before completing his AT thru-hike. He's come to fetch *EZ-E* from the trail. In a while *EZ-E* comes in, and he and *Kodak* are on their way. So, tonight I have the bunkhouse all to myself, a luxury in which I indulge by spreading my stuff all over the place. The large skylight here at 501 is perfect for watching the moonrise, which illuminates the entire room to a chalky, cold brightness.

If I were northbound, and in Virginia, I think I'd be suffering now from the "Ginnie Blues." I know the Pennsylvania rocks can bring on the blues. Certainly, being alone on the trail is part of it. Though the trail is my home now, the days are setting in on me— and I have such a long distance yet to go. I'm just tired. I need to sleep...

Learn to get in touch with the silence within yourself
and know that everything in life has a purpose.
(Elisabeth Kübler-Ross)

Thursday—September 14, 2000
Trail Day—114/65
Trail Mile—1713/1017
Location—Trailside near branch, north of Yellow Springs Village
Site, Pennsylvania

I had planned on hiking to Rausch Gap Shelter, an eighteen-mile day, but checking my planned itinerary again, I find to my dismay that I have only two days to reach Duncannon, not three. So I must hike on for another four miles, which will leave a long, tough twenty-five mile day tomorrow.

The rocks, boulders, ascents and descents, all are less troublesome, and I make good time, arriving in good order a little after four at a pleasant and happy brook just past Cold Spring Trail. I pitch for the evening, and get a fine warming and cooking fire going. In short order, I'm once again "home." The joyful little brook proves to be the friendliest companion. I no sooner roll in than Nature's light and percussion show begins, providing the evening entertainment. It is a gentle storm, bringing a rhythmic, comforting patter on the "roof" of my little Nomad tent. The show continues, with only occasional interruption, right through to the conclusion of Act III. As the lights dim and the closing curtain drops, I'm lifted and winged away to the land of Nod.

I'm never gonna' stop the rain by complainin',
Because I'm free, nothin's worryin' me.
(B. J. Thomas)

Friday—September 15, 2000
Trail Day—115/66
Trail Mile—1738/1042
Location—The Doyle Hotel, Duncannon, Pennsylvania. Kirk and
Shannon Nace, proprietors.

The trail glides along quite well for a while this morning. Then "Old Blue" (Blue Mountain), gets its hackles up to slam me around pretty good as I stumble through (as Joe Dodge would say) "the jeezly rocks." Patience and concentration, both in short supply now, must be called on lest I trip and fall, busting vital moving parts. I know my reflexes and balance aren't what they used to be, and I no longer bounce off things very well. But I do manage, and I do get through.

I'm blessed yet again with a perfect hiking day—cool, a gentle breeze, not a cloud in the sky. The views across the ridges and into the valley from Shikellimy Overlook and Table Rock bring reason for pause, offering peaceful repose, encouraging praise to a higher order.

At SR-225 this pleasant, warm feeling comes over me, for as I set foot here again I'm stepping onto familiar trail. In the past, and for many years, I worked hard at piecing together what I hoped would someday become a 2000-mile AT section-hike. But the farthest I ever got was a little past the halfway point here at SR-225. From this place, over fifteen years ago, and for the last few miles into Duncannon, I had the pleasure of hiking with my sister, Salle Anne. We talked of many things that day. It was a happy and joyful time. Our family's past is here, our past is here—over ten generations. Pennsylvania was in its infancy then, the times of William Bartram and Benjamin Franklin. Coming from Philadelphia, our forefathers would have known them and would have done barter with them. What a grand and proud heritage! Generations of our family are buried in the shadow of Peters Mountain, the mountain from which I'm now descending.

I can hear the grinding din of traffic and the growling rumble of the diesel locomotives as they pass the great gap cut by the Susquehanna and Juniata Rivers. I cross the Norfolk Southern tracks, then pass under US-22 and US-322, reaching Clarks Ferry Bridge.

Soon, I'm in Duncannon, location of the grand Doyle Hotel. The Doyle is such a remarkable and historic place, a highlight in any thru-hiker's journey. The Naces, who purchased the old darling from the Doyles in March of this year, have begun extensive renovation to the bar, known as "The Beer Hunter's Tavern" and to both the large and small ballrooms on the second floor. This once proud and stately establishment has stood as a landmark in Duncannon for the past 100 years. Anheuser Busch built it during the halcyon days of the late 19th and early 20th centuries. Through luck (and the good graces of time) it has survived adoption by many different owners. And so, the Naces have it now, and what a job they're faced with. Kirk and Shannon, it's good to be back again. I wish you great success with the grand old Doyle!

In the evening, as I lie resting, a knock comes on my door. Glory be, it's *Sheltowee*! He has come to spend a couple of days hiking with me as I head south to Boiling Springs. Oh my, prayers do get answered! It will be such a joy having someone to hike with for a while. "Shannon—a couple of tall Yuenglings, please, *Sheltowee* and me, we want to celebrate" Great times, great friends!

The melody is pure and sweet,
So gentle on my mind.
I hearken back to home and friends
...A far off place and time.
(N. Nomad)

Saturday—September 16, 2000
Trail Day—116/67
Trail Mile—1749/1053
Location—Darlington Shelter, Pennsylvania

I've managed to survive another night at the Doyle, none the worse for wear. After a stop at the post office to get my bounce box off to Harpers Ferry, *Sheltowee* drives us to the AYCE breakfast buffet at the truck stop across the Juniata. What a meal! We're stoked for this hiking day. By the time we're back to the Doyle, where *Sheltowee* has made arrangements to leave his truck, it's almost noon. Not to worry, we've planned only an eleven-mile day into Darlington Shelter.

The climb out of Duncannon is rocky and abrupt, but we're soon at Hawk Rock for a grand view back to the river and the little village sprawled all along. What begins as a cool, clear day for hiking soon turns rainy and cold. We stop to don our raingear, but we're no sooner going again than the sky clears, the gentle wind warms and dries us, and the day turns blue-perfect once again. The hike goes quickly, and we're soon at Darlington Shelter. *Sheltowee* goes for water and I get a cooking fire going. *Citrus, Sheltowee's* friend and hiking companion from '99 comes rolling in toward evening. This is a grand surprise for *Sheltowee,* and we share a great time together. As nightfall descends and the chill arrives, we crank the cooking fire on up to a warming fire. So now there is not only the glow from the fire, but that of the evening light, softly radiating the faces of friends. Ahh, and, too, is there that glow from the light that radiates and illuminates the heart—recalling the thoughts of a perfect day.

> *For I have good friends who can sit and chat*
> *Or simply sit, when it comes to that,*
> *By the fireside where the fir logs blaze*
> *And the smoke rolls up in a weaving haze.*
> (Don Blanding)

Sunday—September 17, 2000
Trail Day—117/68
Trail Mile—1763/1067
Location—SR-174 at Boiling Springs, Pennsylvania to the home of
Geneva "Mother Hen" Politzer

The day dawns clear and cold, and we all roll over for a few more winks, hoping for a warming trend in the meantime. We're finally up by nine, but sticking tight by our sleeping bags. At ten, *Citrus* heads back to his vehicle, so he can pick *Sheltowee* up later this evening at Boiling Springs. *Sheltowee* gets cranking at quarter-after. I don't move out until almost ten-thirty.

Sheltowee pulls up in a while to wait for me. Then together we descend what's left of old Blue Mountain, to begin crossing the wide, lush valley of the Cumberland. Once a quiet pastoral setting, the valley is now buzzing with traffic and commerce. The trail tries to avoid this hustle by zig-zagging through fields, but the distracting grind is never far away. First it's PA-944, then I-81, then US-11, then the Pennsy Pike, then SR-641, SR-74, and finally SR-174. *Sheltowee* and I detour at US-11 to the Middlesex Diner for lunch. The waitress says they have sweet tea, but it isn't sweet tea. Oh, am I so looking for that Mason-Dixon Line! After lunch it's on to Boiling Springs. We arrive at the ATC Regional Office to find *Citrus* waiting. It's now suppertime, so off to Anile's we go for pizza. *Citrus* then drives me to *Mother Hen's* for the evening.

Goodbyes are always so tough, but I'm uplifted when my good friend, Frank Buckowski, comes driving up on his way from New York to Florida. This has been a fun-filled and friend-filled day, and I'm just a little further south. Good old southern sweet tea, here I come!

Come look o'er this Eden, the Cumberland,
Come walk through this valley of time.
On a crisp, clear Sunday morning,
Hear the peal of the church bell's chime.
(N. Nomad)

Monday—September 18, 2000
Trail Day—118/69
Trail Mile—1782/1086
Location—Ironmasters Mansion Hostel, Pine Grove Furnace State
Park, Pennsylvania. Shawn Magness, caretaker.

What a great evening last at *Mother Hen's*. I had the whole lower level to myself, a comfortable couch, and plenty of light to write. Got caught up on my journal entries and much correspondence.

This morning *Mother Hen* prepares a heaping breakfast, then shuttles me back to the trail. Thanks *Mother Hen*; your caring is special, and I have made a new friend!

There is little of the valley left today, which I cross quickly. It has turned warm with a slight breeze, shaping yet another glorious hiking day. The climbs are becoming easier and I move with great confidence through what remains of the Pennsylvania rocks. I arrive early at Pine Grove Furnace State Park and must await the caretaker's arrival for the evening. I sit on the porch enjoying the afternoon. Heading into Pennsylvania I had much anxiety, the hangover from past memories, but as are most demons, the problems never came to pass. It's a very good feeling having the Pennsylvania rocks behind me. No half-gallon challenge this year, as the little store where the ice cream binge contest takes place closes for the season on Labor Day.

The old mansion is all I remember it to be—large, spacious rooms with high ceilings, all neat and tidy. Shawn, the caretaker, has an ear-to-ear grin as he recognizes me. We chat as he shows me all around, then sets me up in the back bunkroom where I have run of the place.

In the kitchen I throw together all the fridge leftovers for one large, tasty pot of veggie soup. Shawn joins me and we enjoy the slumgullion together—no more leftovers!

Trekking is a remarkably rewarding and worthwhile "occupation." I'm very satisfied with this day...

> *Never let your memories be greater than your dreams.*
> (Douglas Ivester)

Tuesday—September 19, 2000
Trail Day—119/70
Trail Mile—1805/1109
Location—Rocky Mountain Shelters, Pennsylvania

I'm awakened early this morning by the wind and rain pelting the windows. I get dressed and stumble to the kitchen to prepare coffee. Shawn comes down, and we have a chat about our respective modes of transportation, mine hiking, his biking. I linger, hoping the storm will clear, but the longer I wait the more it appears the day has set to steady rain.

Shawn takes my picture by the Ironmaster's sign, and then I'm out and into it. More ups and downs today, with plenty of rocks and mud mixed in. The rain stays steady, occasionally switching to hard and steady. By late afternoon, at Caledonia State Park, I decide to call it a day. I try hitching to the motel in Fayetteville to get cleaned up and dried off, but no luck. I can't blame any of the hundreds of motorists that pass me by in the next forty-five minutes. I wouldn't want a wet, smelly hiker messing up my upholstery either. Here I stand, feeling the early stages of hypothermia descending, as the eighteen-wheelers blast away at me.

I finally give it up and hike the three miles on to Rocky Mountain Shelter. Here I meet southbounders *Frog, Old Sam, Condemn,* and *Little Debby.* They make room for me, and I scoot in just before dusk. The rain is still pounding. I manage to change into reasonably dry clothes, and am thankful to finally be out of it. Great upbeat conversation turns the day.

> *This is my quest, to follow that star—*
> *No matter how hopeless, no matter how far.*
> (Joe Darion)

Wednesday—September 20, 2000
Trail Day—120/71
Trail Mile—1829/1133
Location—Ensign Cowall Shelter, Maryland

The miles keep clicking away, and today I put another state behind me. Pennsylvania has been a bumpy ride but much less of a challenge than I'd anticipated. I cross the Mason-Dixon Line a little after two. Maryland isn't really the south, but I'm getting close. Sweet tea, grits, hush puppies and good ol' suthn' fried chicken—not far now!

Old Blue Mountain has run its course, and I'm now on South Mountain. The Pennsylvania rocks have become the Maryland rocks, and in the manner and tradition of Blue, South Mountain has lots of ups and downs to dish out with plenty to spare, the day providing a steady dosage. I arrive early evening at Ensign Cowall Shelter and quickly get a cooking fire going. *Old Sam* comes rolling in just as last light dims the mountain.

Cooking and chores all done, we relax and enjoy the last glow of the day—and the warming embers. At around ten, in comes *Frog,* headlight on. He's doing the "Maryland Challenge," a hike that will take him from the PenMar line, clear across Maryland to Harpers Ferry, hopefully within twenty-four hours. Jeez, I'm out here pounding the miles, trying to stay healthy and in one piece (which to most sane individuals seems mad enough) while these kids are concocting games of it!

Frog wants to get back out at three, but around two, comes up this incredible wind-driven storm. No lightning or thunder, just wave after wave of rain, hammering the shelter from all sides. *Frog* sticks tight, and we all try sleeping through it. Finally around six the wind relents, the storm passes, the day breaks bright—and *Frog* is up and out to Harpers Ferry. He'll make it in twenty-four if he doesn't tarry. I need another hour of sleep!

> *The only difference between me and a mad man*
> *is that I am not mad.*
> (Salvador Dali)

Thursday—September 21, 2000
Trail Day—121/72
Trail Mile—1849/1153
Location—Crampton Gap Shelter, Maryland

The water source for Ensign Cowall Shelter is a classic little spring just south on the AT, crystal clear, ice-cold. But there's also a little trickle just below the shelter, which I sought out and cleaned out last evening. I can remember momma scolding me for playing in the mud. I would say, "Ahh, but momma, I have so much fun playing in the mud!" It's been a great time at Ensign Cowall.

The storm of last night has moved on, chased by the gusty wind. As I head toward Black Rock Cliffs, the day warms but the unmistakable hint of fall is in the air. Far across the ridges, with the sun playing its angular light against these ancient mountainsides, the subtle beginnings of autumn can be detected, the muted shades of red and umber emerging. Fall is a magical time of year, and I'm walking into it, the season of harvest and of joy. It is time to give thanks, another season of bounty, and I stop to give thanks to my maker, the creator of it all.

The I's are passing beneath my feet, another sure sign of progress. And what are the I's? They're the interstate highways. I started with I-95 shortly after crossing into Maine from the Canadian border at Fort Fairfield, and now I cross I-70. I'll eventually work my way all the way down the eastern North American continent as I continue on the TA, and finally the remainder of the ECT, crossing many more interstate highways in the process—to finally cross I-75 at Alligator Alley in the Everglades. I'll also see my old friends, US-1 and I-95 again, where they begin their northern paths deep in southern Florida.

I stand and I chuckle again at the Washington Monument. It was the first erected in Washington's honor and in his memory, by the patriots of Boonsboro, Maryland. Years ago, rumor has it, a hiker was overheard saying as he turned to depart the monument, "What a crock." Folks, it's a beautiful overlook, and a great tribute to George Washington. But danged if it ain't shaped kinda funny, like a huge crock!

Crampton Gap Shelter is my destination today, requiring a good pitch off the mountain. By the time I arrive, I'm closer to the highway than I am to the top of the ridge, what with the whirring lawnmowers, bellowing cows, and the near-constant grind on the traffic below. The shelter has been left a mess, lots of paper and trash scattered about, which I put to immediate good use in preparing a cooking and warming fire in the pedestal-shaped fireplace. *Old Sam* rolls in, again with the fading shadows of evening. We spend a grand time talking and enjoying the last of it before turning in. Near sleep, at that time of day that crosses between twilight and the pitch of night, I hearken back to childhood, to those endless, carefree summer days, when in the cool of dusk, momma would call me from the dust (or the mud), into her arms, and home.

It was a childish ignorance.
But now 'tis little joy
To know I'm farther off from heaven
Than when I was a boy.
(Thomas Hood)

Friday—September 22, 2000
Trail Day—122/73
Trail Mile—1860/1164
Location—Hilltop House Hotel, Harpers Ferry, West Virginia

I manage to get up and on the trail before eight, for I'm hoping to have lunch with Laurie *Mountain Laurel* Potteiger, Information Services Coordinator for the Appalachian Trail Conference in Harpers Ferry.

I'm making good time, so I take the blue-blaze trail to Weaverton Cliffs for the one-of-a-kind view down the Potomac. It's remarkable how the river has cut through South Mountain over the eons. All that remain are the mountain's backbone (sheer cliffs) and a few ribs (river rapids). From the cliffs I descend to the C&O Canal Towpath. This hike goes quickly, and I'm soon on the pedestrian bridge over the Potomac.

I'm at the ATC Center before noon. Laurie greets me and we're off to lunch. It's great seeing this dear friend again as we enjoy each other's company!

In the evening, I check into the Hilltop House Hotel, have a fine supper, and then retire to my room. Ed *Tric* Talone has come to hike a few days with me, and we sit and chat till late. I'm going to try getting back on the trail again tomorrow—easier said than done!

The passage of the Patowmac through the Blue Ridge
is perhaps one of the most stupendous scenes in Nature.
(Thomas Jefferson)

Saturday—September 23, 2000
Trail Day—123/74
Trail Mile—1872/1176
Location—Blackburn Trail Center, Virginia

I make it to the post office just before they close at noon to send my bounce box along to Waynesboro, Virginia. Then it's back to the ATC Center to sign the register and bid my friends farewell. I'm southbounder #65 to check in.

Tric has gone out well ahead of me, for I'm not back on the trail until twelve-thirty. West Virginia is behind me now as I cross Loudoun Heights into Virginia. Ten states and two Canadian provinces down, six states to go, four on the AT, five on the TA, and six to finish the ECT. I've got my wind; I've got my legs; I think I've got this trail. Ahh, but this trail, it's sure got me, and the wanderlust, she's got me—by the bones.

Tric took a detour for a sandwich at Key's Gap, and we meet up just as I'm crossing the road. I pose as he snaps my picture by the "Welcome to Virginia" sign.

My friend *Mogo*, who thru-hiked the AT in '98, is one of the assistant directors at Blackburn Trail Center. I was hoping to spend some time with her again, but she is away for the day. In fact, there's no one here, so I've got the place to myself. I'm settled in by the time *Tric* arrives in the evening. I've made myself at home in the bunkhouse. *Tric* chooses the porch. I build a warming fire in the little bunkhouse stove and enjoy the relaxing atmosphere of this peaceful, and serene high-mountain place.

The wanderlust has got me by the belly-aching fire
By the fever and the freezing and the pain;
By the darkness that just drowns you, by the wail of home desire,
I've tried to break the spell of it—in vain.
(Robert W. Service)

Sunday—September 24, 2000
Trail Day—124/75
Trail Mile—1890/1194
Location—Rod Hollow Shelter, Virginia

I manage to sleep in without the least difficulty, not rolling out until after seven-thirty. Tric is up and gone; there's no one else around.

Blackburn Center is owned and operated by the Potomac Appalachian Trail Club (PATC). It's an old cabin resting in a high cove south of Loudoun Valley. For years the job of restoring and modernizing the old place has been an ongoing PATC project. Each time I return, I'm amazed to see the additional work that's been done. At this visit I find an entirely new porch roof. The old one's been replaced with visually pleasing forest-green standing seam metal. It covers the entire place—and the project goes on. Scaffolding surrounds one of the stone fireplaces, with new rockwork almost complete. As I look around, taking in the whole scene, a pleasant warmth and contentment comes over me, a nostalgic feeling. Here

in this old cabin rests that mysterious, unexplainable ingredient that we all remember and long for, something to do with that secure, safe haven of our childhood, when we were kids without a care.

It's a short switchback climb to the ridge and the familiar white, rectangular AT blazes, and so a little after nine I'm back on the trail headed south. The endless jumble of boulders and rocks that have "graced" the trail for what's seemed countless miles to the north are petering out. And so, isn't it appropriate that they should have one last grand hurrah, an encore for the big finale, if you will! So does the trail this day pass Devils Racecourse, a place where demons surely hold their Olympics. Here is a narrow band of rocks coursing down the mountain in a manner so strange, straight as an arrow and rough as the proverbial "cob." Suffering nightmares, what a bizarre scene!

In just a while I'm at Bears Den Rocks and the blue-blaze trail to Bears Den Hostel. I look around for what surely must be the resident bear, but he is away. I'm not surprised, for there have been no bear on any of the Bear Mountains I have climbed, nor at any of the other places bearing the name "bear." I've trekked such a distance now on two separate odysseys, and have yet to see my first bear (save the one hanging at Bear's Lair in Riley Brook, New Brunswick). I've even been skunked twice while passing the bear compound at Bear Mountain Zoo. But no matter, it's a joy to return again to the old Bear Mountain Mansion. What a beautiful restoration by ATC!

Today is the day for the "rollercoaster," an up and down section of trail south of Blackburn. I haven't figured it up myself, but I've heard say that there are over 5,000 feet of elevation change through here, and I believe it. One ball-buster is no sooner over then it's bail off time to begin the whole rock-slam all over again, but I make it through in good order. Averaging three miles per hour brings me early at Rod Hollow Shelter. I'm surprised to not find *Tric* here, for this was our planned destination for the day. Instead, I'm greeted by Kathryn, a kind lady out for a section hike in preparation for an AT thru-hike *one of these days*. She has not seen *Tric*—strange! In fact, the other northbounders I met today had not seen *Tric*, so I'm thinking, "He'll come bounding in later," but dark descends and he never shows.

I spend the evening in enjoyable conversation with Kathryn as I prepare a fine fire and a warm supper. She's on the right track with her preparation, but like all of us as beginners, she's carrying entirely too much. I remember what Warren Doyle, Jr. said: "The more we carry for our comfort, the more uncomfortable we become." At least she hasn't brought a dog along.

With the dimming glow of the fire, and with my tummy full, I tumble in, tired and content.

> *There's a journ' that leads to happiness,*
> *Past the beaten path we know.*
> *It's on our list called "one of these days,"*
> *But we never stop...to go.*
> (N. Nomad)

Monday—September 25, 2000
Trail Day—125/76
Trail Mile—1914/1218
Location—US-522 at Front Royal, Virginia to Center City Motel

The cold rain comes during the early morning darkness, a few drops off and on for proper introduction. By first light it is steady, hammering. I linger in my warm and cozy Feathered Friends bag, not wanting to venture out, but by eight it's apparent that if I'm going to hike today, I'm going to hike in the rain. *Tric* must have headed back home—smart decision!

The "rollercoaster" is over and it's a cruise down to Ashby Gap. Here is another dangerous road crossing. I recall vividly almost meeting my Maker here during a section hike in the eighties. Today it's another time-it-and-run proposition, but I manage both double lanes safely.

My plans had been to spend the night at the delightful Jim and Molly Denton Shelter. But the rain has slammed me in hard waves all day, never completely letting up. I'm wet, cold and tired, and this little gingerbread-like shelter is not a welcome place today, dismally dark, cold and unfriendly—and I'm alone. So I decide to beat it on into Front Royal to a warm room where I can get dried out.

I make the twenty-four mile day in good order, though it has not been the most pleasant hike. A kind man slows, looks, then out of pity, stops for me, as I hunch over in the pounding rain. He delivers me straight to Center City Motel, where I Yogi a good room rate. I'm in and I'm out of it for the night. What a blessing! You've heard me say before, "There's no bad days on the trail." A bit idealistic, I suppose. This day sure put a dent in that philosophy. Thank you, Lord, for seeing me through!

Give me a mind that is not bound, that does not whimper, whine or sigh.
(Thomas H. B. Webb)

Tuesday—September 26, 2000
Trail Day—126/77
Trail Mile—1927/1231
Location—Gravel Springs Hut, Shenandoah National Park, Virginia

I had The Weather Channel on all last evening, watching as the storm tried moving east. It was having little success. It simply kept regenerating as it tussled with the mountains. I'm waiting it out this morning, still watching the weather radar. The forecast is for this gloom to break this afternoon, but it doesn't look too promising from the satellite view, or from my view. At ten-thirty I decide to go for it, managing to vacate the motel room by the eleven o'clock checkout.

From the motel it's a few blocks to US-522, which leads back to the trail. Along the way I pass an ATM and decide to get a little cash; bad decision! Oh, I get the "Quick Cash" alright, but while I'm counting my money, checking the receipt, and reaching for my card, the machine decides it wants my card back. Just as I'm reaching—slurp! The machine sucks it back in and it's gone. "Welcome to Wachovia," reads the message again (So long to you, buster!). In a moment or two, it dawns on me what has happened. This machine has my card and it has no intention of giving it back. I go straight into a dither, spinning around, thrusting my trekking poles to the sky. In a few moments, I manage some composure. I look around and decide to appeal to the kind folks in the Allstate Insurance office right by. The lady listens patiently as I explain my dilemma, then offers to call the bank's main office for me. The frown on her face is not what I want to see. She explains that the bank sees no urgency in the matter, that I'll have to come to the main office (over a mile away), and maybe, just maybe around four-ish, I can get my card back. Well now, are these bankers ever customer oriented!

I thank the lady at Allstate. She points me in the direction of the bank and as I head out, resigned to the whole mess, I glance back over at the ATM. There's a car parked there with nobody in it, and a big red and white sign that now blocks the entire ATM, which reads, "Out of Service." So over I go again. There's a door on the side of the machine. I hammer on the door, "Anybody in there?" No response. I hammer harder and holler louder, "This machine's got my card; I want my card back!" Finally from within comes this muffled voice, "You'll have to wait." So I wait, and wait, and wait. After five minutes the door opens and a lady from the bank steps out. She explains that indeed she has my card, but in order to get it back I'll have to go to the main office. I show her my transaction receipt and my driver's license—no go. After another five minutes of hassle and with all the constraint I can muster, I say "Okay, then just give me a ride to the bank." "Can't do that," she says, as she gets in her car and drives away! I raise my trekking poles to the sky again, gritting my teeth.

The bank is clear across town, a half-hour walk away. As I plod, I plot how I'm going to dismantle the entire bank, starting with the front door. Nearing the bank, better judgment prevails, as visions form as to how I'll be spending the next extended while in the local clink if I act on my plans. Entering the bank, a teller motions me right up. Clearing her throat nervously, and in the most business-like manner, she says, "I think I can help you; you want your card back, don't you?" Oh my, folks, will you ever be proud of me! I manage to keep my mouth shut, show my ID when she asks for it, and reach for my card courteously. Then, having spoken not a single word, I turn and leave! The front door has a closer, so I can't slam it.

In a total funk now, plodding the sidewalk back toward US-522 with my head down, I walk smack into a lamppost, cold-cocking myself good, Stars'n Stripes Forever, and the good old Liberty Bell—bong, bong, bong! On top of my gloom, the gloom of this day (which is supposed to leave) is showing no sign of leaving. The wind is now really beginning to kick, and it's turning downright cold. Yesterday in the cold rain my hands became chilled, and by the time I reached the road into Front Royal, my fingers had pretty much quit working. Passing a second-hand store, I head in to look for some gloves. The storekeeper is with a customer in the back, and after I stand in the doorway a while she turns and asks what I want. I explain that my hands are cold and it would be a blessing if I could get some gloves. She sizes me up a minute, then says, "We don't have any gloves," and turns back to her customer. I leave the store quietly, though I'm tempted to slam this door.

Up the street a half-dozen blocks now I round the corner, cutting through a gas station lot. As I pass the pumps, up pulls this minivan, down goes the window and I hear a lady's voice, "That woman in the thrift shop was mean to you." I turn; it's the lady customer from the store. I reply, "I'm used to that, Ma'am; people think I'm a bum." Without the least pause she says, "Get in, come with me; we'll get you some gloves." I manage, "Oh no Ma'am, thanks, I'll be alright, thanks anyway." She keeps insisting, finally getting out of her van. Relenting, I reply, "Okay Ma'am, okay, I'll come with you."

Isn't it strange indeed, how circumstances weave sometimes, directing our way, as if happenstance simply overrides any plan or notion we may have had—turning our day, and perhaps our life, completely upside down! It takes a lot of faith to ride this rail, and I'm trying with all my might to do better, especially when it comes to the virtue of patience, for with patience comes wisdom and understanding. "Go with the flow" is so very easy to say, but so very hard to do. I'm trying.

And so it is that I'm riding along now with this kind lady, Angela. Nearing the sporting goods store where she's taking me, I'm thinking, "The black lady who befriended me and helped me in Alabama during Odyssey '98, her name was Angela too!" The journeys then and now are so different, yet they're so much alike. It's the people, indeed it is the people that make the difference. Goodness and kindness abound in humankind. We need only be open to it, receptive to it, for it is there.

The store has an incredible selection of gloves and mittens. Angela's face absolutely beams as she sees me smile. In near tears I manage, "I like this pair, but they're terribly expensive." In a calm and reassuring voice, she replies, "Then they're the ones we'll get. I want you to have them."

Angela drives me back to the trail and we bid farewell. It's after two when I'm finally heading south again. Somehow I manage the thirteen miles into Gravel Springs Hut. The wind has come along, driving a bitter-cold mist, but in my beautiful new gloves my hands stay warm and my fingers keep working. I arrive at dusk to a full shelter, but everybody scoots over just a little, making room for one more.

What a bewildering, miraculous day. Ahh, but I'll not wonder about it or question why. Surely in its making, I know that I'm a better person.

Patience is the companion of wisdom.
(Saint Augustine)

Wednesday—September 27, 2000
Trail Day—127/78
Trail Mile—1940/1244
Location—Pass Mountain Hut, Shenandoah National Park,
Virginia

Nobody snored, and we all rolled over in unison, making for a pleasant night! The morning dawns clear and cold, and looks as though the blanket of mush that had the entire region in its grip has finally moved on through. Shenandoah National Park is a very special place, and I feel this will be a special day.

The trail this morning is full of hogbacks. First comes Little Hogback Mountain, then Little Hogback Overlook, then First Peak of Hogback, then Second Peak of Hogback, and finally Third Peak of Hogback. But they're all a cruise, for the trail has been built in such an incredible way! Hiking through, one gets little feel for the true ruggedness of these mountains, the Shenandoahs. Oh, the trail goes up and over all right, but much of the elevation change has been tamed with switchbacks and side-slabs that literally cling to the mountainside.

The AT through here is an absolutely brilliant piece of work, enduring the ravages of time and the tramping army since the thirties. Each year, thousands of hikers and backpackers enjoy the freedom of the backcountry and wilderness that is the Shenandoah. In 1964, the US Congress passed legislation now known as the Wilderness Act. This Act defines Wilderness as "...an area where earth and its community of life are untrammeled by man, where man himself is a visitor who does not remain." Shenandoah National Park contains nearly 80,000 acres of federally designated Wilderness.

It's hard to pass Elkwallow Gap without venturing the short distance to the Wayside, a store with all the things a hungry hiker is looking for, hamburgers, fries, shakes, and ice cream by the pint—the good local stuff, available at reasonable prices, not that overpriced brand we had to endure in New England. Oh yes, I'm in for all of the goodies listed above, plus some chips and candy bars for later.

The day is about as close to perfect as a hiking day could possibly get. The treadway is friendly and the views are absolutely splendid. Sharptop mountains are the most picturesque of all, and there are plenty of sharptops in the Shenandoahs.

My feet don't quite know what to think, what with the easy treadway and the short day, but they and I are happy for both! I've been hiking off and on the past two days with *Crazy Joe, Fairweather,* and *The Kid,* and tonight we share the shelter at Pass Mountain. Great warming fire, warm conversation, fine company!

> *You feel there's something calling you,*
> *You're wanting to return,*
> *To where the misty mountains rise and friendly fires burn.*
> (Geddy Lee)

Thursday—September 28, 2000
Trail Day—128/79
Trail Mile—1958/1262
Location—Big Meadows Lodge, Shenandoah National Park,
Virginia

The day is forecast to be clear and cool, but fog and low-flying clouds keep the day on the dark, cold side. No views from Marys Rock or Stony Man.

I hike the short side trail to the Skyland Camp Store for lunch and plenty of good hot coffee, which warms my hands before warming my innards.

Big Meadows is such a remarkable place, constructed and finished almost completely of pecky chestnut, milled from the dead and dying American chestnut trees struck down by the Asian blight during the early part of the twentieth century. Oh, but to have seen the beauty of that old forest. But alas, it is gone.

I had made reservations earlier in the day to stay at the lodge, so I take my time enjoying the magic of the Shenandoah, arriving late evening. I check in and have a relaxing, hot shower. Then to finish the day, it's prime rib and a few glasses of Big Meadows Pale Ale.

> *Therefore, of all the pictures*
> *That hang on Memory's wall,*
> *The one of the dim old forest*
> *Seemeth the best of all.*
> (Alice Cary)

Friday—September 29, 2000
Trail Day—129/80
Trail Mile—1978/1282
Location—Hightop Hut, Shenandoah National Park. Virginia

The trail weaves its way back and forth across Skyline Drive as I weave my way through the low-lying clouds. Another gloomy day, but the mush is burning off this morning. The day finally warms, and the views open to the east and west. The valley of the Shenandoah is a very broad, rich, and heavily settled region. From the ridgeline, the expanse of it is overwhelming, reaching to the horizon both north and south. Such a patchwork, such an impressive, remarkable, man-manipulated creation—a perfect example of the riches bestowed on this land, this blessed America!

I arrive early at Hightop Hut. What a grand place. Springs here in the Shenandoah are so impressive. Most are piped and running great volumes of pure, cold, and crystal clear water. Perhaps my ditty, "Sweet Shenandoah," will be appropriate to close out this day's journal.

I get a fine cooking and warming fire going, then settle in for the evening. Fall is starting to make a show, and I think of those wonderful days ahead as I drift into calm, contented sleep.

> *You can keep your wine and your bourbon and your beer,*
> *'n hang onto your scotch and gin and other forms of cheer.*
> *Don't offer me your sody pop, no coffee or no tea...*
> *For I'm high on Shenandoah's pure sweet majesty.*
> (N. Nomad)

Saturday—September 30, 2000
Trail Day—130/81
Trail Mile—1999/1303
Location—Blackrock Hut, Shenandoah National Park, Virginia

The day dawns cold but clear, and I'm out, feeling great, to a perfect day on the grand old AT in the spectacular Shenandoah National Park. There's no possible way the eye can absorb (let alone the mind comprehend) the heavenly glory of this presentation before me. Perhaps, just perhaps, Benton MacKaye could have tarried, to *see* it—then try. The trail weaves and twists its part of the braid with Skyline Drive. This over and back is hardly noticeable; certainly not an intrusion to the solitude sought by the intrepid on this trail. But the hum, rumble, din, and at times the outright roar of traffic along the parkway does tend to wear on one's nerves. I think I'm about ready for some other kind of trail.

I've been hiking off and on the last few days with *Blue Light, Fifth Wheel,* and *Banjo Bill,* and we all make it in good order into Blackrock Hut. At dusk, a bunch of weekend hikers come in to pitch in the tenting area below. We linger around the warming fire, sharing good company. This has been a divine day!

One day I will find the right words, and they will be simple.
(Jack Kerouac)

Sunday—October 1, 2000
Trail Day—131/82
Trail Mile—2019/1323
Location—US-250/I-64 at Rockfish Gap to Comfort Inn, Waynesboro, Virginia.

I'm anxious to get to Rockfish Gap, so I'm out and on the trail by eight. The sun comes early to burn the local mush away, and the day turns clear and warm. What a bright and dazzling fall day. Ma Nature's got her paint bush out!

Bear are everywhere in the Park; the trail is literally littered with bear scat. Care must be taken to avoid stepping in one of the huge piles of poop! But does the old *Nomad* get to see one of the poop ploppers? Oh no, no bear in his path!

There are a few more ups and downs today, and the treadway has become a little gnarly, but I make good time for the twenty miles to arrive at Rockfish Gap by two-thirty. I get a ride right away and settle into the Comfort Inn. In late afternoon *Blue Light, Fifth Wheel,* and *Banjo Bill* arrive, and I move them right in with me.

Downloading my email, I'm greeted with wonderful news from Falcon Press, my publisher. My book, *Ten Million Steps,* is finished and being boxed for shipping. Looks like a book signing at The Gathering will be a reality. What a great week ahead. I'm so blessed!

Well, we've seen the work of masters
Hanging in our galleries.
But none can match Ma Nature's hand,
When she paints autumn's trees.
(N. Nomad)

Monday—October 2, 2000
Trail Day—132/83
Trail Mile—2037/1341
Location—SR-624 at Reeds Gap, Virginia to Rusty's Hard Time Hollow

The motel offers a continental breakfast, so I head down for my fill of cold cereal, blueberry muffins, sweet rolls, apples—and coffee, lots of coffee!

I'd met Kirk Snell last evening. He offered me a ride back to Rockfish Gap this morning. "I pick up my mail at nine," he said, "If you're there at the post office, I'll give you a ride up." I don't want to bungle this good fortune, so I'm at the post office as soon as they open at eight-thirty. I hit the jackpot. My bounce box is waiting. And there's film from GORP.com, one of my faithful sponsors. The clerk also hands me a package containing my new custom constructed *Nomad* G-4 pack from Glen Van Peski, GVP Gear, another kind sponsor. This great pack, made by Glen, is the secret. It's what's enabled me to go ultra-lightweight. And he's sent me another, just in case. Not that the one he gave me to begin my southbound ECT trek in Canada wasn't doing just fine.

Kirk is right on cue, and he waits patiently as I rifle my bounce box, load all my gear in my new pack, and then get my bounce box back in the mail to Troutville. At nine-thirty, I'm finally squared away. *Banjo Bill* is also here for the ride. We load and head up the mountain. Kirk knows my friend, Ross Hersey, who also lives in Waynesboro. Ross was the editor of *The News-Virginian* (still the local paper) over fifty years ago. He'd interviewed Earl *Crazy One* Shaffer, when *Crazy One* came through on his historic AT thru-hike in 1948. As he shuttles *Banjo Bill* and me back to the trail at Rockfish Gap, I jot a short note for Kirk to give to Ross. We're heading south again a little after ten.

I was looking forward to the hike and climb up to Humpback Rocks, but the trail has been rerouted and no longer passes this scenic overlook. I absolutely do not understand why the trail is continually being routed away from these special places. It's almost as if the thru-hiker is not worthy of enjoying them without the added effort of hiking another four, six, or eight tenth's mile. I don't understand, I just don't understand. I wish someone would explain it to me.

When I hit the rocks coming onto Three Ridges, my forward progress slows considerably. Getting out late puts me in late at Rusty's Hard Time Hollow, but I arrive in plenty of time to be greeted warmly by Rusty. I get the grand tour. Oh, and getting my picture taken is a must. Every tenth hiker into Rusty's gets a free Rusty's T-shirt and yours truly is number ten. Thanks Rusty!

> *The girl at the post office handed me some letters,*
> *the first received on the trip, then said,*
> *"Mr. Hersey called and said to come right over."*
> *Says I to myself, "Why not?"*
> (Earl Shaffer)

Tuesday—October 3, 2000
Trail Day—133/84
Trail Mile—2059/1363
Location—Seeley-Woodworth Shelter, Virginia

What a great stay at Rusty's. He is a gentle, caring, and giving man who now devotes his life to hikers, taking us in, feeding us, sheltering us, and shuttling us back and forth. We spent the evening chatting, having a grand time. The little inspiration at the closing of this day pretty much sums up this man's life.

Rusty is up and has the grill hot when I climb down from the loft. He's a master at making pancakes—round like Frisbees, just as big and thick, and as fluffy as your first birthday cake. Three of these dandies and you've got a stack that'll take a while to get over. Stoked, oh yeah; this is high-octane hiker fuel! *Banjo Bill* came in late last evening, and he's at the table with me this morning. In a while, I get a picture of Rusty as Rusty gets a picture of *Banjo Bill*. Then we load up, and Rusty hauls us back to the trail at Reeds Gap.

It's another perfect hiking day with views to the far off hazy blue. I've got a fair warm-up before the trail lets me have it, as I bail off to Tye River. The climb up Priest is one of the remaining really long and arduous ascents, a continuous pull of three thousand feet in just over four miles. This up just seems to never end. Then it's lots of smaller pops, up and down—and up and down some more, into Seeley-Woodworth Shelter, a total of over a mile of vertical ascent today.

I arrive at the shelter to find I have it to myself. A sheltered little cove, the whole place clean and neat. A fine place to rest; even a delightful piped spring. I spend little time at the fire after dinner. I'm pooped. What a day!

What I kept, I lost; what I spent, I had; what I gave, I've got.
(Persian Proverb)

Wednesday—October 4, 2000
Trail Day—134/85
Trail Mile—2073/1377
Location—US-60 to Budget Motel, Buena Vista, Virginia.

I'm out and on the trail just as the sun peeks over the ridge. It's another glorious day in the Blue Ridge Mountains, and I'm counting my blessings as I get the old jitney up to normal operating temperature.

I have the trail to myself; no one else is about. All the overlooks and vistas are mine, all the little springs and brooks and the highland meadows and the snug little gaps with their hard apple trees—all this splendor, all this wonder, it's mine, all mine for this day. As I stand now in Hog Camp Gap, I vividly remember this magic little place from Odyssey '98. I pitched right there in the lush, green grass under the little apple tree. From here, in the quiet, still calm of the evening, one can hear the Pipes of Pan as they drift across the meadow. You too could come to this magic place; you too could hear them—that is, if you believe. These faint, melancholy whispers of sound are echoes from another time, echoes that lift the wanderlust within, beckoning, calling us to come, come to the edge, to the hazy blue horizon from whence they come, and from there to look and to venture beyond. I hear not the Pipes this day, only the restless wind, but should I linger, should I dream the dream of the mountain wanderers of times long past, the Pipes would surely come, and I would be caught up in their spell. In their presence time would have no meaning, no value.

The hike goes quickly today, and I arrive at US-60 right at noon. There is hardly any traffic this time of day, just the logging trucks rumbling up the ridge. But in just a while a kind man stops his pickup and offers me a lift. I'm soon at the Budget Motel in Buena Vista. A shower, a foot long sub, a few cold frosties, then a nap. This day goes into the book as a heavenly gift!

> *Here, in this wild, primeval dell*
> *Far from the haunts of man...*
> *May not one hear, who listens well,*
> *The mystic pipes of Pan?*
> (Elizabeth Akers)

Thursday—October 5, 2000
Trail Day—135/86
Trail Mile—2094/1398
Location—US-501/SR-130 at Glasgow, Virginia to Wildwood
Campground. Brian and Denise Hess, proprietors.

I walked downtown last evening to have supper at the Triangle Bar Café, to find it's now the Midway Café, the claim being that they're located halfway between Maine and Florida; well, by golly, I'm making progress south! The whole interior of the little triangle place has been ripped out. Now it's all fresh, clean and new, completely remodeled. That's okay, but I really liked the seedy old place better. It was fun mingling with the locals that came in to have a cold frosty along with their bacon and eggs for breakfast. On my walk back, I picked up some ice cream at the market (the good, hiker priced local brand), and hoofed it back to my room. I no sooner got the door open than the phone started ringing. It was my good friend Ed Williams, trail angel to thousands of hikers. I left a message for Ed earlier in the day. He and wife Mary Ann live nearby in Vesuvius, and I was hoping to see them on my way through.

I get a shuttle back to the trail by a local named William. On the way he tells me about his three-dozen-or-so grandchildren and great-grandchildren, and how he loves the mountains, being born and raised here and all, and about how (one of) his grandsons and he might just go bow hunting this weekend.

Waiting at the trailhead with a grand smile, a tall thermos of hot coffee and two slices of fresh homemade (Mary Ann's special) apple pie is, oh yes, Ed Williams! The trailside is a little wayside complete with picnic tables. Ed, William, and I spend a grand time chatting. Thanks, William, for the ride, and thank you, Ed, for coming out so early to see (and once more feed) the old *Nomad*!

Today will be a long, tough day, with pulls over Rice Mountain, Punchbowl Mountain, Bluff Mountain, and Big and Little Rocky Row. I first pass what little is left of Brown Mountain Creek Community. "Observe as you walk, be aware that history surrounds you. Keep your eyes and mind open to explore the secrets that are held by the land." These are the words that are cut into the sign by the little brook. Here lived freed slaves during the early part of the 20th century. The story continues, revealing the memories and insights into life on Brown Mountain Creek. According to a former resident, Taft Hughes, "The homes were small, the people hard working. The food was simple but nourishing." Mr. Hughes remembers his mother's ashcakes, which were cooked on an open hearth, covered with ashes and coals. "She would take them out of there and she had a special broom made from corn, broom corn. She'd sweep them off real good and then wash them. You didn't taste any ashes on them. They were much sweeter than if you baked them in a stove, much sweeter. We'd eat them right there, and lots of times for supper we'd have that and a glass of milk. I wished I had one now. It would be impossible to match that flavor." Dang, Taft, you're making me hungry; I can almost taste one myself! At Brown Mountain Creek Community, there's a few of the old summer cellar indents, smoothed and sculpted by time, some rock foundations, and the little two-track lane where the trail now passes. It's all that remains, along with the sweet unstinted spirit of the people who dwelt in this scornful old moldering place. Ahh, but does the spirit of those people still linger here, like the spirit of Taft Hughes, who welcomes me as I pass his door.

Oh, what a sad time it was in '98, standing where I stand now, on the very summit of Bluff Mountain. I cannot look directly at it, but finally, I *do* look at it again. I'd hoped that I hadn't rightly remembered, but I have remembered. I now gaze with much sadness upon this gray, stone-cold memorial for a dear little child. In granite are inscribed these words, "This is the exact spot little Ottie Cline Powell's body was found April 5th, 1891 after straying from Tower Hill School House November 9, 1890, a distance of seven miles. Age four years, eleven months." Someone has placed a little wooden red and blue toy pistol on the stone. Dear Lord, this is not a happy place, and once again, this is not a happy time.

Fall is in the air. There is snow forecast for Sunday. The mountains are ablaze with Ma Nature's paint. The leaves crunch beneath my feet, and though the season is glad, the mood is somber as I descend Bluff Mountain.

I manage a hitch right away to Wildwood Campground where Denise Hess greets me. She shows me to a neat little camper where I'll spend the night.

I'm so excited, yet I'm also very nervous about the morrow. For tomorrow, Larry Luxenberg will come to fetch me from the trail and take me to the Appalachian Long Distance Hikers Association (ALDHA) Gathering at Concord College in Athens, West Virginia. In the morning, Larry will hand me a copy of my new book, *Ten Million Steps*. My publisher has sent boxes of books to him, to bring along for the book signing scheduled for Saturday. I have not yet seen the book. Oh, and what an amazing circumstance, for Larry to be bringing my book to me. For it was Larry Luxenberg, author of *Walking The Appalachian Trail*, who provided such patient guidance. It was Larry's assistance and his wisdom that so shaped my book and made it what it is. And it was Larry Luxenberg, through his kindness to me, who penned the foreword.

Yes, I'm very anxious and excited about this special time. Ahh, seems no matter how hard I work on the virtue, patience, there's never quite enough of it! I'll sleep little this night.

Fall leaves are falling in showers,
Sun-drenched in crimson and gold.
And here in these lofty towers,
A ritual both solemn and old.

A mood-swing past joy to sadness,
Another autumn is cast.
Amid all this splendor and gladness,
I ponder...'haps this be my last.
(N. Nomad)

Friday—October 6, 2000
Trail Day—136/87
Trail Mile—2094/1398
Location—19th Annual ALDHA Gathering, Concord College,
Athens, West Virginia

A cheeseburger, a couple of frosties, and some chips at the little convenience store across the way, then back for a much needed shower at the campground bathhouse and that was it for the evening. I was full with anticipation but managed to fool myself by falling into deep sleep right away.

This morning I head back to the little store for a breakfast sandwich and some coffee, then to sit by the office at the picnic table working on correspondence and journal entries until Larry arrives to carry me to the ALDHA Gathering.

Larry comes along around ten, and after the warmest greeting I anxiously await his comments about the book. He says nothing but simply turns to open the hatch on his little van, and there they are, all the boxes still sealed. "Larry," I exclaim, "Haven't you looked at the book?" "No," he answers, "I wanted to wait, to see it with you for the first time!" And so, now the moment of truth. I hesitate, thinking of all the months that have gone into the making of this. Many people talk of writing a book someday, but few ever manage, for indeed it is an amazing undertaking, a task of the mind and of the heart. We're both filled with excitement as I tear at one of the boxes—and there it is! Oh, what a beautiful cover, what a beautiful book! I hand one to Larry, then clutch one to myself. This is the moment. This is the time I've been waiting for. What pleasure sharing it with the man who's had such a profound influence, both on me and on this work. We both laugh and are filled with glee!

The journey to Athens takes three hours. Time passes quickly, for we are giddy with excitement. Thanks, Larry, for sharing this time with me!

I had hoped for a new pair of New Balance 803s to wear at The Gathering. Larry takes me by the post office, but no luck. From here it's out to the Folk Life Center where we register, then to the bunkhouse, and that's it for an excitement packed day.

We do not remember days; we remember moments.
(Cesare Pavese)

Saturday—October 7, 2000
Trail Day—137/88
Trail Mile—2094/1398
Location—19th Annual ALDHA Gathering, Concord College, Athens, West Virginia

I had seen many dear friends last evening and again this morning as I head back to the Center for coffee.

Larry and I load and head for the college where all the Gathering functions will be held, and where my book signing will take place. A table has been saved for me right next the ATC folks, and friends help carry boxes of books up the stairs.

I no sooner get a few on the table than a long line forms. *Sheltowee*, later *Long Distance Man*, then *Jingle* help as my bookkeepers. I write note after note in book after book till my hand cramps up. I'm overwhelmed by the presence of so many folks, most whom I do not even know. Coming off the trail into this intensity after 136 days is making me reel with emotional overload. There is such profound energy in this Gathering group. I receive hugs and well-wishes from everyone! Box after box of books go out the door. This is so humbling, so incredible. What a weekend this is shaping to be!

I manage somehow to make it to Henry *Trickster* Edward's IAT slide presentation and in the evening, to hear Jim *Walkin' Jim* Stoltz play and sing. During all the confusion I miss *Sheltowee's* AT slide show, which I dearly regret. In between it all, I manage a bite to eat.

An hour before Steve *Worldwalker* Newman, the featured speaker, is due to go on, I'm informed by the Gathering organizers that he is caught in a traffic jam and probably won't make it. I'm asked to be prepared to go on in his stead. So Larry rushes me back to the Folk Life Center to dress and prepare to speak. As we return, and just as I'm finally set to go before the packed auditorium, Steve makes it in. Oh my, what an emotional slam-jam this turns out to be, but I'm so happy he has arrived and can go on as scheduled. Steve is a great storyteller. He relates his hike around the world. The show is great!

In the evening I'm so glad to return to the bunkhouse at the Folk Life Center where things are quiet. My dear friends Jan *Dutch Treat* and Lin *Hummingbird* Benschop come to the bunkhouse to toast my success and to prepare a delightful evening meal. *Paw Paw* comes by, and the four of us have a grand time as *Dutch Treat* plays and sings for us. What a day, what a day!

...With your smile dropped here, and a kind word there
From your gentle heart with your songs to share.
(Jim *Walkin' Jim* Stoltz)

Sunday—October 8, 2000
Trail Day—138/89
Trail Mile—2094/1398
Location—Trailside (soon-to-be relocation) near bluff across James River Foot Bridge, James River, Virginia

Another night in the bunkhouse last. This is the first time I've slept in the same place two nights in a row since leaving Monson months ago. I'm sure living up to the *Nomad* part of my trail name!

I'm up before dawn to attend sunrise service at the chapel here at the Folk Life Center. The chapel is right on the crest of the hill, which should make for a glorious sunrise. The morning dawns cold and clear, with frost over the vehicles and on the grass. I head to the Center for coffee, then on to the chapel. The service consists of testimonials to, recollection of, and blessings sent out for dearly departed intrepid. It proves to be both enjoyable and inspirational, and the sunrise is certainly one to remember.

Back to the college I attend the general membership meeting. Meetings such as this tend to be dry, but this group keeps it interesting. New officers are elected and other business is conducted. I'm able to get together with Dick Anderson and Will Richard from the IAT who have come down from Maine. Then it's back to the book-signing table for another day at it. Folks file by steady all day and by evening I've only four books left. Earl *Crazy One* Shaffer comes to the table and we have an enjoyable, uninterrupted chat. Thanks, Earl. What a joy seeing you again!

So it's time now to get ready for real, for my presentation before the full membership body this evening. I'm very tired, confused and weary after such a whirlwind weekend. I hope I'm able to get up in front of everyone, keep my enthusiasm and maintain my concentration for the entire hour, for you see, I use no slides, no prompt cards, relying totally on words to form the pictures. *Dutch Treat* has set two of my ditties to music and I'm excited about hearing him perform these musical creations tonight.

My goodness, the performance goes remarkably well! I forget and falter on a few lines as I recite a couple of my ditties, but no one seems to notice. *Dutch Treat* wows the audience, holding their rapt attention. To have this talented virtuoso on stage with me, a man who's performed with Peter, Paul and Mary, and John Denver, is a truly humbling experience. Concern was expressed earlier by a number of folks that The Gathering would be breaking up and people would be heading home, but all my dear friends are here, and we all have a great time. After my presentation, well-wishers file by, giving me more hugs and filling me with their remarkable energy. This has truly been one of the most amazing weekends in my memory, perhaps in my life, and I'll cherish it and keep it to my heart—forever.

It's such a joy when greeting old friends and such a sad time when it is time to depart. More hugs, more goodbyes, and more tears.

I get a ride back to the James River with Smith *Old Ridge Runner* Edwards and his wife, Jan. In all the excitement I have forgotten that I need provisions for at least two days on the trail, and I've only a candy bar in my pack. Jan saves the day by making me sandwiches and putting together a bag of other nourishing goodies for me to pack along. We're soon at the James River, right next to the new hiker bridge. The bridge superstructure is up and the decking is down the full 625 feet across, but the approach steps are not yet in place. "Keep Out" ribbons and signs cover the bridge, prominently displayed. But I had made my mind up on Friday morning I would cross the bridge (after finding out the relocated trail work has been done on the south side). I had met trail maintainers from the Natural Bridge Trail Club working the trail above the north side relocation last Thursday, and they had given me directions on how to hike the soon-to-be relocated section down to the new James Ridge Foot Bridge.

So, here we are, two o'clock in the morning, in the full moonlight. *Old Ridge Runner* boosts me up and onto the main structure. I thank him and whisper my goodbyes, then turn and cross, the moon casting long eerie shadows as the old *Nomad* becomes the first thruhiker to cross the James River Foot Bridge.

Once in a while you'll find a friend
Where the memories meet and the rainbows end.
(Jim *Walkin' Jim* Stoltz)

Monday—October 9, 2000
Trail Day—139/90
Trail Mile—2115/1419
Location—Cornelius Creek Shelter, Virginia

Trains pass during the night and rouse me momentarily, but I otherwise sleep soundly. I'm awakened by the sounds of workmen talking and making a racket on the bridge. After breaking camp, I go over near the southern end of the bridge where the men are preparing to move the steps structure into place and fix it to the main bridge framing. I venture to within ten yards of them on the newly constructed treadway, but they're all busy, consumed with their work, and none look around to see me standing here. I take a few pictures of the rusty red bridge, the rising sun setting it aglow, then I'm on my way south again. The day is cold and windy but it will be a fine hiking day nonetheless.

Climbing near Hickory Stand, I come upon a familiar figure also climbing the mountain. It's Bonita *Mother Goose* Helton, who I have hiked on and off with over the past week or so. She also attended the Gathering. We enjoy talking and exchanging stories about our weekend. Two fellows have been hiking with *Mother Goose*. In short time, I find *Ripshin* and *Rabbit* resting at a sunny spot along the trail. I stop and we chat. Most likely I'll not see these folks again, but then you never know.

I'm generating plenty of heat to combat the cold today as I climb up and over High Cock Knob, Thunder Ridge, and Apple Orchard Mountain. On this last ascent it has turned very cold and I'm hiking in a whirl of snow showers!

Near Black Rock I chance upon *Fair Weather* and *Crazy Joe*, and we spend the evening together at Cornelius Creek Shelter. The warming fire feels very good tonight.

Look up at the miracle of the falling snow, the air a dizzy maze of whirling, eddying flakes, noiselessly transforming the world...
(John Burroughs)

Tuesday—October 10, 2000
Trail Day—140/91
Trail Mile—2140/1444
Location—Wilson Creek Shelter, Virginia

I'm out on the trail by seven-thirty, my hands numb from the cold. With his wool hat on, *Crazy Joe* peeks one-eyed from his bag, giving me a nod as I depart, immediately tucking back in. Two days in a row I've bid farewell to newly made friends, friends I'll likely never see again. It's a fine feeling making good time, but certainly not a fine feeling leaving folks behind.

I've a hard pull first thing up and over Fork Mountain, which also brings the old jitney up to normal operating temperature. So I stop to remove my mittens and wool shirt. The wind is whipping, but the day is warming nicely. As I move along, I'm figuring that this cold, dry front is setting me up for some really beautifully clear hiking days.

I'm nearing the end of the ridge swaps the trail has had to make with the Blue Ridge Parkway. A few more zig-zag crossings up-and-over, and the ridge will be mine again. At the Peaks of Otter Overlook where the Parkway takes over and forces the stepchild AT down over the side into a pretty miserable no view, no fun side-slab, I stick with the Parkway. Yup, today I'm blue-blazing the Blue Ridge Parkway!

"How can this be?" you ask! Well folks, it's like this. I'm a member of the hiker-trash fratority (good little boys *and* girls), a probationary member that is. For until I've escaped the white (and pure) AT blazes for a while to blue-blaze (not so pure), preferably a section of the Parkway here or the Virginia Creeper near Damascus—until then, I'll really not be considered a full-fledged member. So today I'm up here on the Parkway, enjoying incredible vistas down both sides of the ridge all along. It's a glorious cool day with hardly any traffic; the mountains fully ablaze in autumn dress to the horizon. I've got my *official* hiker-trash painter's hat on, and I'm truckin'. All this fun, and I'm earning my lifetime membership in the hiker-trash fratority to boot. Oh yeah, I'm up here, *Sawman*; I'm up here, *Pirate* (two of the officers—I'm brownin' up)! What a deal, what a deal!

I arrive early to an empty shelter at Wilson Creek. Some previous kind sojourners have left plenty of kindling and firewood. With things drying out for a change, I'm able to get a fine warming fire going. I linger long into the twilight gazing into the flicker, then the embers, fixing this day to memory and reminiscing trail days past.

I'm nuthin' but blue-blazin' hobo HikerTrash from hell!
(Hiker Trash Pledge)

Wednesday—October 11, 2000
Trail Day—141/92
Trail Mile—2151/1455
Location—US-220 at Daleville/Cloverdale, Virginia to Best West-
ern/Coachman Inn

I was sleeping soundly when at two this morning I wake to footsteps approaching. I rise up to see a light bouncing up the shelter path. Soon comes *Gollum*, out for a night hike, bound for Troutville. We have a nice chat while he jots a message in the shelter register to his father, *Pilgrim*. Then he's out and gone. Back to sleep, but in just a while, I again hear footsteps approaching. I rise up again to see a light bouncing up the shelter path. This time it's *Pilgrim*. Turns out he's in no hurry to continue his night hike, so I invite him in. It takes only minutes as he gets his sleeping pad and bag out, and he's quickly down for the count.

With no further excitement I sleep soundly till dawn to awaken to a cool, clear day, perfect for hiking. *Pilgrim* is up too, and we're soon out and on the trail to Troutville. Along the way we discuss many topics—my retirement, his law practice, our hikes. I listen and I learn good things.

Have you ever noticed how time passes so quickly when you're hiking with a friend, enjoying their good company? We're soon at US-11 where *Pilgrim* heads for the post office. We bid farewell and I hike on to US-220 and the Coachman Inn.

It's a little early for check-in, being only one o'clock, so the first order of business is to put Western Sizzlin in the red for the day as over I go for the AYCE buffet bar. It takes the better part of an hour. I can hardly waddle back to the motel, enduring the pain of jogging across four lanes of flying eighteen-wheelers in the process. The desk clerk checks me in early and I'm in my room by two. It's been a good day on the trail, plus nearly a day off. Not bad *Nomad*, not bad at all!

In my walks, every man I meet is my superior in some way,
and in that I learn from him.
(Ralph Waldo Emerson)

Thursday—October 12, 2000
Trail Day—142/93
Trail Mile—2171/1475
Location—SR-311 at Catawba, Virginia to the home of Ron "Walrus" and Karen "Roots" Welles, GAME '98

Coachman Inn has a fine continental breakfast and I load up on a little (well, really a lot) of everything. I squirrel an apple and a blueberry muffin in my pack for later. I manage to make it back on the trail by seven-thirty. Miraculous!

I've got pulls today up to Hay Rock/Tinker Ridge, through Scorched Earth Gap to Tinker Cliffs, and finally up to McAfee Knob. In '98 I had the Knob to myself, but today, being the beautiful day that it is, I must share it. Just as well, for I want a picture, standing full pack right on the sky-high brink of it. A young lady obliges and I get the shot.

I remember Boy Scout Shelter from my last two hikes through. The place is run down, quite unkempt. I marveled then, and continue to marvel today, at how the old place has survived; the rusty tin roof, most sheets just thrown up helter-skelter. But there it remains, leaning precariously!

The trail and terrain are slowly changing, but they're changing, becoming the old familiar Blue Ridge of home, with the trail going straight up and over. Oh, there are still switchbacks, but the angle and position of the mountain spurs here in the southern Appalachians, the approach to them, make it easier for the trail builders to just head the trail right up, clear to the ridgeline or summit.

I made many friends from my '98 Odyssey, and two of them, Ron *Walrus* and Karen *Roots* Welles, live nearby in Christiansburg.

They long ago insisted that I contact them when passing through, so arrangements have been made for *Walrus* to pick me up this afternoon around three at SR-311. I've also called my good friend (and trail angel to thousands) Jeff *Southpaw* Williams, and they're both waiting at the trailhead to greet me. *Walrus* runs me all the way back to the Troutville post office for my bounce box, then we head for his home. I've been promised a grand pasta dinner and *Roots* is preparing it as we arrive. *Southpaw* and his wife Sue are also with us, and we spend a wonderful evening sharing many memorable trail experiences.

We carry memories, and unlike earthly things—they weigh nothing!

The best things in life aren't things.
(Art Buchwald)

Friday—October 13, 2000
Trail Day—143/94
Trail Mile—2192/1496
Location—VA-621 at Craig Creek Valley to Roanoke, Virginia,
home of Tulie "Tulip" Kaschub and Scott "T-Bone Walker" Baldwin,
GAME '98

What a great evening; such wonderful friends, the Welles and Williams. Thanks, folks, for your kindness, and thanks for having me as your guest!

We're up early. *Roots* gives me a goodbye hug and she's off to work. *Walrus* drives me back to the trailhead, and I'm again southward bound on another glorious hiking day—filled with the energy that comes not from the calories of nourishment (of which there's been bountiful plenty) but from the power of uplifting joy that comes from hearts plugged into hearts!

There are some tough climbs today, but each climb leads to great overlooks, wild rock formations, and grand ridge walks. Mother Nature is making her fall show in muted shyness this year, a shroud over her normally gay apparel. The woods stand in subdued shades of russet and umber with only occasional bright flashes of orange, yellow, and crimson. The hills have turned to rust. But in the bright noonday sun, there is a proud, silent-like mood, a celebration of greatness if you will, which brings to one who can *see* a feeling of everlasting peace. These ancient temples of time that thrust their glory to the sky are the most precious example of our Maker's love and steadfastness. Fall is truly filled with magic, a spell cast over all.

I have Rawies Rest and Dragons Tooth to myself. Though I've an ETA at Craig Creek Valley, there's time to tarry, time to take in these restful scenes, for these are special places. These are indeed the temples of the most high. If you have not made your presence in their calming shadow, you should come.

And the Audie Leon Murphy Memorial, on the high ground, such a fitting memorial to the man who fought fearlessly for the high ground, and though wounded, prevailed time after time. Audie was our most decorated World War II hero. It's just a simple stone placed in the woods at the end of a seldom-sought path. Audie, I don't know about the media idol-like heroes of today, but I do know this; you're my kind of hero. You stood up and fought for what this great nation was, hopefully still is, and forevermore shall be!

> *Show me the man you honor, and I'll know*
> *what kind of man you are.*
> (Thomas Carlyle)

I arrive at SR-621 in good time and am soon greeted by my dear hiking friend from Odyssey '98, Tulie *Tulip* Kaschub, and we're off to the bustle and dazzle of Roanoke. Just as we reach the drive, here comes Scott *T-Bone Walker* Baldwin, and we share the magic of a joyful reunion. *T-Bone* became well known all up and down the trail in '98 for his talented and polished guitar style, but I never had the fun and enjoyment of hearing him play. So after a great white pizza (yes, white!) at their favorite spot, I have the pleasure of hearing *T-Bone* and members of a group he performs with rehearse later in the evening.

Folks by the sidewalk and along the way complain of the cerebral effect that Friday the 13th, combined with a full moon, is having on their hemispheres. If there's any tug on mine, it is, and has been, nothing short of spiritually inspiring.

> *And on the grand horizon,*
> *There stand the mountains tall.*
> *True temples of God's boundless love,*
> *Triumphant...over all.*
> *And so, from sea to shining sea,*
> *Like from far heavens cloven,*
> *O'er all this vast majestic land,*
> *Her tapestry is woven.*

Ahh, yes! This grand creation,
Born on the loom of time.
For all to thrill, spellbinding still,
Ma Nature's gift...Divine.
(N. Nomad)

Saturday—October 14, 2000
Trail Day—144/95
Trail Mile—2211/1515
Location—War Spur Shelter, Virginia

Tulip and *T-Bone* grow basil in pots on their back porch. Along with a bag of these greens, I'm provided with enough goodies from their "hiker box" to keep me stoked for more than this day. They're both training for an upcoming marathon, and this being Saturday, what better opportunity to get in a little training along the quiet mountain back roads. We all load up for the drive up, me to my southbound trail through these eternal mountains, and they to their road training in the hills. Thanks, dear friends; the time spent with you once more during this journey, has been very special!

Tulip told me about a bunch of goats that live in the lofty crags of Sinking Creek Mountain. I thought she was just pulling my leg, but dang, after the long hard climb, here they are! There's a billy and a nanny, playing in the *jeezly* rocks. Well now, Joe Dodge, come look at this! The old black and white billy, a quite-proud old goat, one scraggly horn bent and near busted down, climbs to the uppermost boulder above me, then turns to present his good side to the sun, his whole pitiful scrawny little body framed in greenery on both sides, the infinite cloud-free blue, his backdrop. "Stay right there little buddy," I whisper, "I gotta get a picture, nobody will believe this." He cooperates, and I get the shot. Meanwhile, his girlfriend, the fawn-colored little nanny, has come up behind me. As I turn from taking billy's picture she licks up my arm, clean across my face! One taste of my salt and I can't get shed of her. She follows me everywhere. So I hasten along, whacking at her with my trekking poles. Next she tries taking a chunk out of my sweaty pack. So I move a little faster. Oh yeah, like I'm going to outrun a goat through these rocks! She finally tires of our little game and goes back to her charming boyfriend. Folks, I'm not making this stuff up. You gotta believe me; I'm not making it up. Hiking this old AT may get a little tiring, even a bit trying at times, but it's never dull. Nosiree-bob it's never dull!

As it sinks to Sinking Creek Valley, the trail passes through the most lush-green high meadow. Just over a little pop in the rolling field by an old post with the familiar white AT blaze, does there lie a hiker in contented sleep. I try passing to the far side, but the rustle of the new-mown hay wakes him. He opens one eye, then smiles the most contented smile! Here I meet fellow southbounder *Trashman*.

The sun is warm on my face and feels so good that I decide to rest and chat. It's interesting to read shelter register entries written by fellow intrepid who are ahead, entries they've made days earlier. You get to know a lot about them long before finally meeting. There's always anticipation and excitement in that moment. As I expected, *Trashman* is a happy, easy-going fellow, as his register entries suggested. It's a pleasure finally meeting this young man. He's also headed for War Spur Shelter, so we'll spend the evening together.

The mountains of Virginia are becoming more like the mountains that I know, that I love—the southern Blue Ridge. For they are worn in such a way, the trail more straight up and straight down, the laurel hells more the hells they can be, and the springs, ahh, the pure sweet water of the springs, right there in the gap, waiting for the weary, thirsty hiker!

War Spur Shelter is a lovely spot. Water is right by, and there's lots of firewood. I quickly settle in and get a good cooking and warming fire going. Soon comes *Trashman* and we enjoy the evening together. What an interesting day. Got my goat!

In the presence of eternity,
the mountains are as transient as the clouds.
(Robert Green Ingersoll)

Sunday—October 15, 2000
Trail Day—145/96
Trail Mile—2234/1538
Location—Campsite south of Symms Gap Meadow, Virginia

This will be a long day on the trail, so I need to get out and going. The days are becoming noticeably shorter now, sunrise not coming until nearly seven-thirty. I manage to get my pack on just before sunrise.

The trail lets me have it right away. The pulls of recent days have become nearly effortless, my pulse and respiration remaining steady all the while. This old jitney requires a fair amount of warm-up, and this morning the pull comes before I get cranking smoothly. "Slow down, slow down old man," I tell myself. "You're trying too hard. The blood needs to get to your legs." Ahh, and here's that old virtue *patience* again, for in just a while I'm climbing effortlessly once more! The first pull of the day takes me to over 4000 feet and the scenic Wind Rock Overlook. Folks have camped near here all night, and there is much commotion and activity about. I hasten on.

The trail seeks out the ridge nearly the entire day with a major bail-off to Stony Creek Valley. The *Companion* mentions a pond near Symms Gap Meadow, but it is little more than a mudhole with much animal activity all around. I had planned to camp here for the night, for the meadow is such a beautiful spot, with views to the horizon, the sunrises and sunsets spectacular. But I have precious little water, so I must journey on to the next water source, which I find in a small gap a fair distance beyond the meadow. There's level ground in the gap and an abundance of firewood, so I pitch for the evening. No one has camped here since the leaves began falling. The fire ring and ground are filled and covered with a dense blanket of leaves. I clear the ground a fair distance, pitch my little Nomad tent, and get a fine fire going. *Trashman* comes in just as I'm preparing my evening meal and finds a spot for his tarp.

A grand hiking day, but I'm very tired after such a distance of rocky treadway, making me wonder if I'm not back in Pennsylvania again. But I'm pleased with my progress, for I'm set now for a short hiking day, mostly downhill into Pearisburg, where I plan to spend tomorrow. Seems no matter how long one endures the trail, there's always that uneasiness, that subconscious feeling of doubt—will I be up to the challenge tomorrow?

> *The toil of the climb, heart pounding, the drum,*
> *A realm of the here and the now.*
> *Old memories past, sunrises to come,*
> *We falter to cradle our brow.*
>
> *We cling to a dream; we struggle and grope;*
> *We worry and trouble the trail.*
> *While all the time doubting, yet hoping on hope,*
> *While all the time fearing to fail.*
> (N. Nomad)

Monday—October 16, 2000
Trail Day—146/97
Trail Mile—2243/1547
Location—SR-634 at Pearisburg, Virginia to Plaza Motel

The night on the ridge was very pleasant, my best night's rest in quite a while. Sleeping in a different place every night takes some getting used to. I guess my tent seems the most familiar, though it's seldom parked twice in the same spot.

I'm anxious to get into Pearisburg this morning, so I'm up, break camp, and am on the trail before sunrise. Another glorious day is shaping. I'm above the clouds that lie in the valleys, and as the sunrise floods its brilliance across the sky, the world around and below appears set totally aflame. From Rice Field, a high meadow expanse on the ridge crown, this early morning show of glory is visible—a new dawn, a new day. I love this life!

The ridge soon breaks off, the trail with it, down to the clamor of Pearisburg. It always seems that the high-pitched whine of industrial machinery is the first to make its way up the ridge. Then it's the grind and drumming of the eighteen-wheelers as they charge and jake brake the winding ribbon below. I'm soon at Senator Shumate Bridge, where I must run the minefield gauntlet of broken glass from bottles and assorted junk that the highway scum have hurled from their vehicles. Across the bridge I head for Main Street and the not-so-pleasant walk to town. I'm able to settle in early at the Plaza Motel.

The remainder of the day I rest with my feet up to work correspondence and get caught up on journal entries.

> *You cannot stuff a great life into a small dream.*
> (Anonymous)

Tuesday—October 17, 2000
Trail Day—147/98
Trail Mile—2266/1570
Location—SR-606 at Bland, Virginia to Trent's Grocery and Campground. Jimmy and Sherry Miller, proprietors.

Sunrise comes later and later with each passing day. I'm up and out in what seems the dark of night. But it's already seven as I linger in the Dairy Queen finishing my biscuits and gravy (and my third cup of coffee). Looking out, the sky to the east turns to fire once again as the approaching sun ignites the horizon. It's seven-thirty now, but as I walk Cross Street back to the trail, cars still approach with their headlights on. The forecast is for rain today, but with the sunrise comes another beautiful, cloud-free morn. I'm on the trail by eight.

There's a tough pull right off, up Pearis Mountain to Angels Rest. Towns are seldom at the top of mountains, so almost always there's a bail-off to get to town. So too, for the hike out, seems there's always a long, hard pull to the ridgeline. Look for the highest point as you depart the village. Most assuredly that's where you're headed. Angels Rest is that point this morning, and there I'm headed, "Double-clutch, low-low, come on old jitney, let's go!"

It's been a couple of days since I've spotted a deer, but I have seen a couple of bow hunters; bow season is in now. There have been lots of turkey and grouse along the trail though. Every time I flush one of these birds it scares the holy-h right out of me, especially so the turkey. Up they come and crash they go, straight through whatever's there, like low-flying bombers. Sure doesn't take much to rattle me anymore, and the occasional explosion of a bird on the rise (which fractures my little dream capsule) will definitely do it!

Fall is in free-fall now. With each breeze, drift down now bushel after bushel of leaves to cover and conceal the trail. Their presence makes hiking the rock gardens increasingly more difficult and risky. All the little trail gremlins out to get me are in hiding now, camouflaged beneath a blanket of leaves and just waiting to trip me up, as if any more help were needed.

A couple more minor pops and I'm through the worst of it as the trail descends to Big Horse Gap, then to ramble along through the low-lying hills. The day passes very quickly, and I'm soon at VA-606 for the short roadwalk to Trent's Store. The pizza is even better than I remember. I talk the evening with the owner, Jimmy Miller, as the truck drivers come and go. Then I pitch again by the little bathhouse, through the gate and down the lane to the field past the horse pasture, just like before. It's great to relive these memories so lavished upon me like a gift. It's sheer joy—a blessing granted each day!

There's a trail way up yonder I'm fixin' to hike,
It has no beginnin' or end.
But awaitin' that journey, ol' AT—'n I'll be,
Chasin' rainbows 'round the next bend.
(N. Nomad)

Wednesday—October 18, 2000
Trail Day—148/99
Trail Mile—2285/1589
Location—US-21/US-52 at Bland, Virginia to the home of George
"Ziggy" and Reverend Murray Ann "AT Mama" Ziegenfuss

Rain on my tent rousts me around six. It's great being able to dress and ready my pack while still in my spacious Nomad tent. These tasks were impossible in the little Slumberjack bivy shelter I carried all during Odyssey '98. Breaking camp in the rain was an absolute ordeal, usually resulting in soaked pack, soaked me, soaked everything. But with the roomy Nomad, which actually weighs less than the claustrophobic Slumberjack, I'm able to remain dry; switching to race pit mode only at the last minute to collapse my tent, get my pack and poncho on, and get moving.

The campground is filled with a vagabond-like array of old propped-up pickup toppers and campers, every color (mostly double-drab), every description (mostly sagging with flat tires). A couple of hunters came rattling in late last night, right next to my tent, and they're up first thing, rattling around again this morning. I break camp, head to the bathhouse to do my daily duty, and stumble down the pitch-dark narrow drive to the store. The store opens at seven, and I'm right here for coffee, biscuits, and sausage gravy. I'm in the south now, and the folks down here know how to make biscuits and sausage gravy. By-the-by, I do believe I really am getting down the trail and closer to home!

How we spend our days is, of course, how we spend our lives.
(Annie Dillard)

Thursday—October 19, 2000
Trail Day—149/100
Trail Mile—2301/1605
Location—SR-623 at Burke's Garden, Virginia, to the home of Alex Chamberlain

What an enjoyable evening with Reverend Murray Ann *AT Momma* Ziegenfuss. I'd been hiking with southbounder *Rolling Stone*, and he had heard about *AT Momma's* kindness while at Woodshole Hostel. So after Yogi-ing a ride from a gentleman working at the Senior Center, once in Bland, we gave *AT Momma* a call; no luck, just her answerphone. But while *Stoney* and I sat having lunch at the downtown mom-n-pop, in came *AT Momma*! She had returned home, got our message, and hastened to find us.

Her home is a rental, a spacious old farmhouse in the country. She and husband, *Ziggy*, GAME '89, aren't yet settled in. Boxes of stuff were stacked in the hall waiting to be uncrated. But even as unsettled as they were, the place in disarray, none of this seemed to have any effect on their desire to be caring trail angel to weary thru-hikers. Yesterday and this morning, the lucky ones are *Rolling Stone* and *Nimblewill Nomad*. Thanks, *AT Momma* and *Ziggy*, for being number one trail angels!

AT Momma has ended up owner-by-default of a very nice dog. It had been left on the trail and was brought to her weeks ago. After much discussion and thought last night and this morning, the decision is for *Rolling Stone* to take the dog back on the trail with him. After an enormous breakfast of eggs and blueberry pancakes, we load in *AT Momma's* car and head back to the trail. *Rolling Stone* and the dog (Gabe) and me are back on the trail at eight-thirty. As *Stoney* and Gabe work at getting used to one another, I hasten on.

I have made arrangements for my friend Alex, who lives in Burke's Garden, to come up the mountain near his home and pluck me from the trail between two and three this afternoon.

The hike today is very enjoyable. I'm drifting along, my mind drifting in an aimless light-hearted flutter, until I reach the second trail crossing at Little Wolf Creek. Here, the memory of what happened on my last thru-hike jolts me out of it, for the memory of that day is so clear, so vivid. I stand now, looking at the stones that form the path across the creek. I can pick out the exact one that threw me, that pitched me headfirst into a total faceplant in the bottom of the creek. The result was a dislocated finger, two cracked ribs and a huge knot on my noggin. That day was a dismal, rainy day, and the creek was running in an angry fit. I'd tried jumping from one large rock to the next when it happened. My wet boot flew off and down I went. I emerged from the creek mad, wet, and cold—and with a deeper understanding of the word *adversity*. Today there's very little water flowing in Little Wolf Creek, the stones dry, to be safely and easily hopped. The lump on my head is gone, my ribs healed. But my poor twisted finger still hurts! Aww, enough of this whining and complaining old man; time to move on south.

This has been another glorious day for hiking, and before I know it, I'm at SR-623, the "back door" to Burke's Garden. Alex soon arrives. What a joy seeing this dear old friend again! We descend the mountain, gabbing all the way to his little home in the Garden.

Adversity is the diamond dust heaven polishes its jewels with.
(Robert Leighton)

Friday—October 20, 2000
Trail Day—150/101
Trail Mile—2331/1635
Location—SR-683/US-11/I-81 at Atkins/Rural Retreat, Virginia,
to the Village Motel and Restaurant

Alex and I shared a great time, but we also shared mixed emotions, for Alex's wife Carol passed away since we were together last. Carol was such a dear friend too. I really miss her.

It's cold in the Garden this morning, with frost everywhere. We load up, then sit and talk, as old friends often do, while the windshield defrosts. Then it's back up to the "back door." By eight-thirty I'm once again on the trail. Thanks, Alex, dear friend, see you in Florida!

I received an email yesterday from *Fanny Pack*, trail angel of trail angels. He's hosting a grand cookout this weekend at the five-star Mount Rogers NRA Headquarters Partnership Shelter. It's over forty miles by trail from the Garden to Partnership; will I make it? Oh yes, fear not, I wouldn't miss this for the world. I'll be there tomorrow afternoon with bells on!

This is my third time past the Garden, the first two times northbound, so things look a little different this go-round, this hike being southbound. There are some remarkable overlooks along the Garden rim, which the AT follows all the way to Chestnut Knob. I scamper up each rocky incline to take in the view. The day has turned perfect, cool and clear, and the views into the Garden, affectionately known as "God's Thumbprint," are magnificent. The Garden is such a lush, fertile place, a limestone dome that collapsed, forming a crater-like depression, a grand walled-up valley in the sky.

The high meadow at Chestnut Knob is so lush, so peaceful. Here is an old dwelling converted to a shelter, and from this place, the best view of all, down into the Garden. I pause for one last look before turning ever south.

I'm making remarkably good time today, reaching SR-610 before three-thirty. This had been my planned destination, but I'm still full of energy after doing twenty miles. It's only ten more miles to Atkins where there's a motel and restaurant right on the trail. So I head up and over Big Walker, then Little Brushy, arriving at I-81 at dusk, a thirty-mile day.

Oh my, has a good hot shower ever felt so relaxing, a heaping plate of spaghetti ever tasted so scrumptious!

> *Your friend is that man who knows all about you,*
> *and still likes you.*
> (Elbert Hubbard)

Saturday—October 21, 2000
Trail Day—151/102
Trail Mile—2343/1647
Location—Partnership Shelter, Mount Rogers NRA Headquarters, Virginia

The thirty-mile day that got me here yesterday has set me up for a short, casual hike on into Partnership Shelter today, so I sleep in until after eight. I take the most relaxed time enjoying breakfast at the Village Restaurant right next. It's after ten before I'm back on trail.

There are steady pulls today, over Glade, Locust, and Brushy Mountains, but I find it takes little effort to make these climbs anymore. The hike goes quickly, and a little after two I emerge from the woods at VA-16. As I reach the road, *Fanny Pack* is here to greet me with a broad smile and a grand "Hello!" Oh, it's so good to see this kind man again! We spend the entire afternoon at Partnership talking trail.

Later, toward evening, three weekend warriors come limping in with sore backs and tired feet. They're carrying enormous packs, wearing heavy boots. One of the poor chaps has a blister the size of a silver dollar on his heel. While he's dressing his wound, the other two take off and leave him. He also leaves shortly, but returns in so much pain he can hardly hobble. His hike is over, but there's a problem. His buddies have the tent they've all been using, but this guy's got the tent poles! After waiting for over an hour, the others failing to return, *Fanny Pack* gets his maps out and figures their next road crossing. Loading up a bag of cold pop, some snacks (and the tent poles), he's off. He's no sooner gone than the other two show back up here at Partnership. In a while *Fanny Pack* returns. The three are now together again, but their tent poles are lying out there on the trail at the next road crossing! In total frustration now, *Fanny Pack* exclaims, "Didn't you guys make any plans at all in case you got separated? What a Laurel and Hardy operation this has turned out to be!"

So it's late now and *Fanny Pack* has gone again, trying to get the three fellows and their tent poles back together, then to shuttle all of them to automobiles they've left parked, Lord knows where, while hungry hikers who've heard about the cookout *Fanny Pack* has planned come rolling in. Well, we wait, and we wait, and we wait some more—for *Fanny Pack* to return. No *Fanny Pack*! "Hungry" and "hiker" are synonymous. After waiting even longer, we can wait no more, so we fire up *Fanny's* grill under *Fanny's* neat portable pavilion and raid *Fanny's* score of coolers, helping ourselves to all the goodies *Fanny* had all set to prepare for us.

In the evening now and near dusk, *Fanny Pack* finally returns to a happy and joyful occasion! To help celebrate (and put away the grub) are *Rocks, The Rooster, Garbage Man, Bumpy, Leap* and *Frog, Manno* and dog Maverick, *Huckleberry, Big Guy, Earlybird,* Shannon, and yours truly. Later comes in *Ausable Mike*, with more bags and boxes full of goodies. *Ausable* is good friends with *Fanny,* having thru-hiked the AT this year. What a grand affair. Thanks, *Fanny Pack*, for your caring and for your giving! What an interesting and memorable day.

Love as much as you can, by all the means you can,
in all the ways you can, in all the places you can,
at all the times you can, to all the people you can,
as long as ever you can.
(Anonymous)

Sunday—October 22, 2000
Trail Day—152/103
Trail Mile—2374/1678
Location—Wise Shelter, Grayson Highlands State Park, Virginia

Well, it truly is: *"...the joy and the blessings that come with the miles."* But the anguish and sadness of leaving dear friends, friends I may never see again, makes for a funky beginning of this day. But the day has dawned crisp and clear, and I must contemplate what *Benton MacKaye said, as I begin preparing my eyes to see and my mind to comprehend the presentation the Lord has created for me tomorrow, Grayson Highlands State Park. And I must also prepare myself to receive the glory of that very special place, so that in humility, I might give thanks for once more experiencing the spiritual beauty of it. And so, I'm off, with this whirl of emotions, heading ever south.

I had first met *Rocks* at a small campsite just north of Atkins last Thursday evening. I immediately began shooting my mouth off about how I was wrapping up a thirty-mile day. After handing me a cool frosty, so we might celebrate such a profound accomplishment, that's when he mentioned that the hike from Partnership Shelter to Wise Shelter, also a thirty-mile hike, was a cruise. So today I'm on that train! There are some pulls up to High Point, over Iron, Pine, and Stone Mountains, then the beginning ascent to the Highlands, but these pulls are gradual and steady, the treadway very kind, allowing for long graceful strides. I maintain my goal, an average of three miles per, and I'm in, in good order by seven at Wise Shelter.

Here I'm greeted by *Leap* and *Frog*, who had hitched back to Partnership, as had *Rocks*, to enjoy *Fanny Pack's* hospitality yesterday evening. They've just completed a very enjoyable fifteen-mile day to arrive here at Wise. We get a warming fire going, then enjoy a fine evening of fellowship together. *Leap* and *Frog* are from Canada, and I just dearly love the kind, friendly folks of Canada.

> *Just journey on intrepid one,*
> *Come join this odyssey,*
> *'n we'll fix our head t'what *Benton said...*
> *To see what we truly see.*
> (N. Nomad)

*EMILE BENTON MacKAYE, 1879-1976—The father of the Appalachian National Scenic Trail, a 14-state National Park Greenway extending from Maine to Georgia.

"Let us tarry awhile till we *see* the things we look upon."

Monday—October 23, 2000
Trail Day—153/104
Trail Mile—2406/1710
Location—The Place, Damascus, Virginia

Winter comes early to high elevations, to these high places. Wise Shelter is situated at nearly 4,500 feet, so is there any wonder my fingers turn to sticks before I can get my gear packed and the old jitney geared up? Nearing Wilburn Ridge, from the exertion of the climb, and with the morning sun now on my back, I'm quickly warmed, and I'm comforted. Now I set my eyes and my mind to experiencing the calming solitude and to accept the spiritual warmth present here in the heavenly ether that surrounds and is present all throughout these high temples. Oh, what a bright, sun-drenched day to be

hiking through these lofty crags and pinnacles, these tabernacles of the Lord, that are the Grayson Highlands. Ah, and here again are the wild ponies!

What has been said about the Mount Rogers National Recreation Area, and in particular about Grayson Highlands is certainly true: "The Lord has dropped a little bit of Montana onto the rooftop of Virginia." The Highlands are indeed a rugged, grand, and majestic place, one of my favorite places along the entire Appalachian Mountain range. As I pass, I reflect on those not so fine past days of hiking, where, with all my energy and ability, I brought to bear my resources of patience and endurance. And for that effort and that resolve, am I now greatly rewarded, to overflowing, with this fine, remarkable day.

It has been said that, "Smart first time hikers take the Virginia Creeper Trail, and all second time hikers take the Creeper." I'm on my third hike through. On my northbound section hike in the 80s, I stayed on the AT out of Damascus, up and over Whitetop

Mountain. During Odyssey '98 I took the Creeper out of Damascus to a little above Creek Junction, then back to the AT and again up and over Whitetop Mountain. When mentioning this to folks, I'm constantly told that I should have stayed on the Creeper all the way to Whitetop Station. So today is the day to hike the Creeper all the way, and at Elk Garden, VA-600, I take the five-mile roadwalk to Whitetop Station, stopping, of course, at the little community of Whitetop for some orange juice and ice cream! But this is no short-cut and I must not tarry long, as my goal is to reach Damascus by evening, a distance of some thirty-two miles.

The location of the original Whitetop Station is an historic place. How fitting that a replica of the old train station has been constructed on the exact spot! The history is interesting. I quote from a brochure prepared by the Virginia Creeper Trail Club: "The Virginia Creeper Trail began as a Native American footpath. Later, the European pioneers, as well as early explorer Daniel Boone, used the trail. Shortly after 1900, W.B. Mingea constructed the Virginia-Carolina Railroad from Abingdon to Damascus. In 1905, the Hassinger Lumber Company extended the line to Konnarock and Elkland, North Carolina. Its nickname, Virginia Creeper, came from the early steam locomotives that struggled slowly up the railroad's steep grades."

As I hike down the gorge, staying to the Creeper Trail, I cross Whitetop Laurel Creek countless times. There are over one hundred trestles and bridges along the trail's path to Abingdon, with most of them in the gorge. Whitetop Laurel Creek tumbles and cascades in constant tumult throughout its journey in such a glad and happy way, that to hike along it brings the same gladness and happiness to he who passes. And this day do I pass this way to share in the constant revelry of this magic place.

It's dark as I complete the last mile along the Creeper, the lights and sounds of Damascus just ahead. I'm tired and weary and am so thankful to reach The Place, a hostel for tired and weary hikers. The little village of Damascus has opened its arms to take in those of us who trek along the AT, and their kindness and generosity have been lavished on us for years. Oh what a joy to be here again! It's stromboli and a few cold ones at Quincey's, then to The Place for a much-needed night of rest. This day is not in my debt!

None know how often the hand of God is seen in a wilderness but them that rove it for a man's life.
(John Muir)

Tuesday—October 24, 2000
Trail Day—154/105
Trail Mile—2406/1710
Location—The Place, Damascus, Virginia

Last night, while dining at Quincey's, comes in *Leap* and *Frog* and *Huckleberry's* family. They joined me at my table and we shared a grand evening. During the course of conversation, *Huckleberry's* father spoke up and said, "Meredith Johnson." I presumed to get my attention, for my first and middle names are Meredith and Johnson. I'm thinking, "This is strange; how does he know I'm Meredith Johnson?" Just then his daughter answers. Her first and middle names are also Meredith and Johnson! Folks, there's no way I can be making this stuff up. The sweet little girl's name is Meredith Johnson! I had recommended the calzone to *Leap* and *Frog*. Oh yes, that was the right recommendation.

It's amazing, the renovation at the hiker/biker hostel known as "The Place." I can't believe how beautiful the work has turned out, from top to bottom, inside and out. It's just remarkable. The property and the old two-story frame house belong to the Damascus United Methodist Church. Over the years they've opened their hearts and their facilities to hikers. It does my heart good to know that the hiking community cares and appreciates the goodness of the church and of its members, for it was hikers collectively that came together to help fund the improvements. Yes, I'm proud to have been and to be part of it all!

I have so much I must get done today. I would like to get back on the trail this afternoon, but I wonder. I'm behind on my journal entries. My bounce box is waiting at the post office, plus I want to get down to Mount Rogers Outfitters for a while.

Well, it's turned out about the way I figured. It's four o'clock now, the day's daylight nearly gone, and I've got very little of what I need to do done. So I'll be here for another night at The Place. Life sure could be a lot worse.

The gift of happiness belongs to those who unwrap it.
(Andrew Dunbar)

Wednesday—October 25, 2000
Trail Day—155/106
Trail Mile—2448/1752
Location—US-321 at Hampton, Tennessee to the Comfort Inn

I don't know what's turned me onto just haulin' today, good old heads-down, grind-it-out hiking. I got out early this morning; it's now noon and I've already done over thirteen miles. Passing Uncle Nick Grindstaff's grave puts me in a trance-like hypnotic funk—*lived alone, suffered alone, died alone.* My head goes down further, I stab the ground harder, and pound the miles faster. I put another state behind me today, Virginia. This one took a while. That's two provinces and eleven states down, five states to go.

There's no water at Iron Mountain Shelter, and somehow I miss the spring just the other side. The Vandeventer Shelter has no water either, so I keep on pounding. "Danged if I'll go halfway down the mountain for water," I grumble under my breath. I'm at thirty-three miles now; it's seven o'clock; it's getting dark. "I'll find water soon, then I'll pitch for the night," I try reassuring myself. Out comes my

little photon light and on into the dimming light of day I grind.
Stumbling through the rocks another three hours in the dark, the
trail and the old wizened-up *Nomad* finally bail off the mountain. I
find water, lots of water, Watauga Lake, but who wants to drink this
stuff! It's now ten-thirty. I've trudged forty-two miles on less than
a quart of water, and I'm bone tired, desert-dry, and dust-spittin'
thirsty—not quite your happy camper.

I'm at US-321 now, and like a reflex, out pops my thumb—in the
dark. Lo-and-behold, the next line of flying searchlights courses by,
and like a scheduled pit stop at Daytona, this guy dives for the shoulder apron, slams on his breaks, and hauls 'er down. I'm watching it,
but I can't believe it, what a stroke of luck! A young lad heading home
from his prison guard job has stopped to pick me up, in the pitch
black of night! Turns out the fellow's a hiker. He knows the trails all

around here. With a quizzical grin on his face as we exchange pleasant informalities, he replies, "You've walked from where, today?"

In just minutes I'm at the Comfort Inn in Hampton, feeding dollar bills into the pop machine. What a day. I remember Uncle Nick's grave, the dry, unending ridge walk, and—well, that's about it. Forty-two miles, holy cripes, I can't believe it! Oh, do these four twenty ounce Mountain Dews ever taste good!

> *Everything that slows us down and forces patience,*
> *everything that sets us back into the*
> *slow circles of nature, is a help.*
> (May Sarton)

Thursday—October 26, 2000
Trail Day—156/107
Trail Mile—2466/1770
Location—Woods road between Moreland Gap and Laurel Fork,
Tennessee to Laurel Creek Lodge and Hostel. Dennis and Mary
Hutchins, proprietors.

It's pretty amazing, but I'm able to get a hitch right away out of Hampton. It's dark and all the approaching vehicles have their headlights on, but this old rickety pickup slides to the side and shudders to a halt. I run to close the distance as the driver looks out the rear window over his shoulder.

And this fellow? Well folks, have you ever wondered why the innocence we see in the countenance of children always seems to disappear, not to be seen again until in the very elderly? To see this glow of peace and contentment in the faces of folks in their twenties, thirties, and forties is certainly unusual, and when it does occur, it's such a sparkling and enjoyably refreshing thing to witness! Such is my fortunate experience now as John Stonecypher welcomes me, for here is a man who has found peace in his life; one look tells the story. John's on his way home from his work shift. As we lurch along toward the trailhead he talks about his wife and children, how his life has been filled with pure joy and happiness. We're soon at US-321, where I was amazed to get a ride the evening last. John shuts the old clunker down, and we have the longest and most remarkable talk about—life! Thanks for your kindness, John!

The hike today takes me into Laurel Fork Gorge where the beautiful, breathtaking Laurel Falls tumble. In days long past, a railroad passed here. It's difficult to even imagine the possibility of a railroad ever having existed in this place, but the old railbed which enters straight into the awesome depths of the gorge, to cross sky-high trestles, bears witness to the fact that locomotives indeed once lumbered their way through. The AT follows this old railbed where it's been blasted from vertical walls of solid rock. What a train ride that must have been, a view of solid granite only inches away one moment, then gaping open space into the abyss, the next. Yes, it must have been quite a ride!

Laurel Falls is a natural wonder, rugged yet beautiful beyond description. The trail leads to the very base of the falls, where I pause to gaze with childlike amazement. In my passage through the gorge in '98, the sun presented in perfect alignment, casting its brilliance—to illuminate each water droplet propelled by the flood hurled from the lofty brink. The sun is away today, leaving only dark, monochromatic shadows, which give an eerie, forbidding relief to the sheer walls of granite. But in this starkness is there another form of beauty, for now, in this subdued light, do the steel-gray sentinels of rock loom, presenting such force and boldness. Indeed, it is a perplexing sight, offering such a different mood. We may continually question Mother Nature, yet does She ever answer with the least deliberation or in the least meaningful way? Yet, aren't the answers always found filled with truth and purity! While I stand here, gazing in awe and bewilderment, comes to my mind the words of Ivan Turgenev. Those words will close this journal entry.

Before lunch I arrive at Dennis Cove Road where I head for Kincora, a popular hiker hostel operated these many years by Bob and Pat Peoples. But alas, there is no one about. While sitting my table at The Gathering, signing books for the kind folks who sought me out, came *Sarg*, an old fellow now working with Dennis and Mary Hutchins here at Laurel Creek Lodge and Hostel. I recall him having invited me to stop by on my way south. Laurel Creek Lodge is right up the road, so I decide to look up old *Sarg*. Well, dang, *Sarg* is gone, too, but Mary Hutchins is here to greet me, and I'm soon enjoying a cheeseburger and an ice-cold bottle of Mountain Dew.

It's only a little past noon now, and I'm interested in getting in eight or ten more miles, but I'm also interested in spending the evening with Dennis and Mary here at Laurel Creek Lodge and Hostel. I'm thinking, "If I could hike on out, then be picked up later, that would be perfect." Soon comes Dennis. As I remark about wanting to hike on, and that I feel bad about missing a stay at this beautiful place, Dennis offers to shuttle me to where the trail crosses at a little-known woods road a few miles south. "I'll run you down there right now and you can hike back in, how's that?" he replies. "Oh yes," I exclaim, "Let's do it!" So off we go. This is great! And I know it will be just as great to spend the evening with the kind folks here at Laurel Creek Lodge and Hostel.

> *However much you knock at nature's door,*
> *she will never answer you in comprehensible words.*
> (Ivan Turgenev)

Friday—October 27, 2000
Trail Day—157/108
Trail Mile—2485/1789
Location—Overmountain Shelter, Yellow Mountain Gap, Tennessee

Mary and Dennis were awaiting my arrival as I hiked back north to Laurel Creek. In the evening, Mary prepared an absolute feast for Dennis and me. It was a peaceful, happy time.

After a great breakfast this morning, prepared by Mary, Dennis shuttles me back to the trail. I'm headed south by eight-thirty. Thanks, Mary and Dennis, for your hospitality; I've had a great stay at Laurel Creek Lodge and Hostel!

The trail today takes me over Doll Flats to the balds of Hump and Little Hump Mountains. These are the first of the southern balds over which the trail passes. The day is clear and fair and I linger, taking in the panoramic view from each. I thought I remembered the remarkable feeling of standing on these balds, but a refresher course always seems in order.

In my book *Ten Million Steps*, I talk about the Stanley A. Murray Memorial, (what was) a beautiful bronze plaque mounted on one of the large, jutting boulders near the summit of Hump Mountain. On the memorial is inscribed:

"Houston Ridge, in memory of Stanley A. Murray 1923-1990. Houston Ridge has been dedicated by the USFS and the Southern Appalachian Highlands Conservancy in the memory of Stanley A. Murray. As chair of the Trail Conference from 1961-1975 he was instrumental in bringing the Appalachian Trail to the Highlands of Roan. Because of his untiring effort as the founder and director of the Southern Appalachian Highlands Conservancy, thousands of acres in the Roan Highlands have been protected for the benefit of future generations."

I stand here before this memorial now, in dismay, much as I stood in dismay at this same spot over two years ago—because, you see, some thoughtless individual, hell-bent on destruction, has smashed and bent the memorial into the most disgusting appearance, and in that state does it still remain. It needs to be removed, cleaned, straightened and restored, then remounted in a more appropriate and secure location. The memory of this man deserves proper respect.

As I hike on, the trail leads down into Bradley Gap, then up and over Little Hump. I finish the day in a funk at the Overmountain Shelter, an old barn restored and converted for hikers' use. I manage a fine cooking fire and get my evening meal prepared just before a hard thunderstorm passes over the Overmountain.

> *As a result of this man [Stanley A. Murray],*
> *his unflagging dedication and effort, and the successful*
> *result thereof, the trail was moved onto Houston Ridge*
> *and the balds and Highlands of Roan.*
> (N. Nomad)

Saturday—October 28, 2000
Trail Day—158/109
Trail Mile—2506/1810
Location—Cherry Gap Shelter, Tennessee

The morn dawns cold and cloudy, and I hasten to get out and moving. As I climb toward Roan High Knob, the wind comes up, driving a cold, gray mist, and as I continue climbing, I realize I'm in the clouds. The trail soon turns to rocks, and the canopy above turns to boreal forest, not unlike much of the forest to the far north. The evergreen boughs filter the clouds, collecting the cloud-droplets, and the wind rains them down upon me. It is not raining, but I am in the rain. There are no sights to be seen from Roan Massif this day.

This hike I'm into now proves tough going, with the ol' AT letting me have it. It's a tough pull up and over Roan, followed by Little Rock Knob, Iron Mountain, and finally Little Bald Knob. It's late when I arrive at Cherry Gap Shelter. The cooking-turned-warming fire is both welcome and comforting. As is not unusual, I have the shelter to myself. Days like this, where one becomes encircled, engulfed, then embraced by the shroud, locked within the veil, does there seem to descend a feeling of such intimate security, womblike, near rapture with Nature. Here one's movement is reduced to only that space within the cloud-circle, an elusive past-the-mirror medium that binds you tightly. Yet, as you move to venture beyond the veil of it, does it move with you, constantly maintaining its distance and its bounds. From this ephemeral, wall-less room, there is no release, no escape. I remember the words of Robert Browning: "*...of what I call God, and fools call Nature.*" Ahh, these are the times I'm able to find peace, to think, to truly think—and as I ponder, am I able to *almost* plumb that restless driving that is the gut-fired lust within us all, the *lust* of the wander*lust*.

> *Here's to all hearts of that cold, lonesome track,*
> *To the life of the wanderlust, free.*
> *To all who have gone and have never come back,*
> *Here's a tribute to you and to me.*
>
> *With our feet in the dirt, we're the grit of the earth,*
> *Heads a-ridin' the heavens o'erhead.*
> *And they won't find a nickel of value or worth,*
> *When our fortunes are tallied and read.*
>
> *But no richer clan has there ever been known,*
> *Since the times of all ruin and wrack,*
> *Than those of us lost to the dust outward blown,*
> *Who have gone and have never come back.*
> (N. Nomad)

Sunday—October 29, 2000
Trail Day—159/110
Trail Mile—2522/1826
Location—Nolichucky Hostel, Erwin, Tennessee. John "Uncle Johnny" Shores, proprietor.

Another cold morning, but this one's clear. After bailing off and down (mostly a leaf slalom) into Low Gap, I slam into Unaka Mountain. Oh yes, the old jitney gets up to normal operating temperature in short order! Halfway up I stop and start peeling. Off come the mittens and gloves, then the wool shirt. Top down now, a slug of water for the radiator, and the old jitney shifts into second for the remainder of the pull.

After Low Gap, followed by the 4x4 low-low pull up Unaka, comes another low gap, only this one is called Deep Gap. Then it's a little pop-up and a cruise through Beauty Spot Gap to, you guessed it—Beauty Spot! And is this bald ever appropriately named. For from this "Spot" is one afforded a 360° vantage of the most spectacular of the southern Appalachians—to the horizon. It's still early morning. The local cloud clutter, which gathers in the lower coves and ravines, has not yet burned off, leaving the sharp-tops all around marooned in a sea of white. Above this cloud-ocean, yet below my lofty vantage, does a misty haze climb and roam each undulating ridgeline, creating in perfect relief full mountain regiments standing at proud, silent attention. I turn and spin in total awe. It's a mystery; it's all such an incredible mystery. Someday the veil will be lifted.

Over by the fire ring I see cans and bottles. On closer inspection I find them to be *full*, cold cans and bottles—of the finest beer! Below, in the parking area, two young folks are climbing into their vehicle. I hold up one of the cans and shout to get their attention. Shouting back, then climbing the fence, they return to the summit to greet me. Here I meet *Green Bean*, GAME '99, and his girlfriend. They're out to dispense a little trail magic, especially for their southbound friend, *Garbage Man*. After finding that *Garbage Man* is probably two days behind me, and that I'm headed for Erwin and the Nolichucky Hostel, and they're going right by the hostel, they decide to take the rest of the beer back to their vehicle, then to the hostel, and leave it for me. Well now, how's that for some well-timed trail magic!

Past Indian Grave and Curley Maple Gaps, the trail turns to side-slabbing, the kind that cuts the mountain hard, elbow-bumpin' to port, hazy-blue nothing to starboard. Daydreaming now as I cruise, the deep leaf carpet conceals a large off-camber root. When my right foot hits it, I heel violently to port. I slump to my left knee and when it hits the root, I'm propelled, as from a deck cannon, right over the side. Man overboard! Before I can shout "Bill Irwin" (the blind guy who hiked the AT and fell a lot), I'm blazing a new blue-blaze shortcut straight down to Erwin. Lucky for me there's rhododendron and greenbrier clinging to the mountainside, and between the two, they manage to grab hold of me and get me stopped. I remain in a daze for the longest time, fearing to move. I finally begin damage control, feet straight up and head straight down—looking straight down at Erwin. The devil's had little luck, for the Lord is certainly providing safe passage. The worst I suffer on this unscheduled detour is a skinned up knee, which still works fine. Oh, has this hike been charmed, and am I charmed!

Just this side of the Nolichucky, on one of the many little wooden foot bridges that span the smaller creeks, sits a chap with a box in his lap. As I approach, I'm greeted with an ear-to-ear grin from Ed *Not To Worry* Speer. Ed had been to The Gathering, had purchased one of my books, and remembered that tomorrow was my birthday, so here he is with a box of glazed donuts—to wish me "Happy Birthday!"

We hike on into Erwin together, reaching Nolichucky Hostel before two. After a soothing hot shower, there's another box of donuts waiting. Oh, and the cold beer the kids decided to bring is here, too!

While parked at the pay phone, downloading my email, I look over by the pop machines, catching a glimpse of a fellow passing by. As I hang up, I'm thinking, "That guy sure looked familiar." I give it no more thought until I'm around by the porch later in the afternoon. Then comes a voice from the little cottage across the way, "Is that you *Nimblewill*?" I turn, not believing my eyes, but sure as I look it's Pat *Garcia the Gray-Haired Guy* Jackson, the same fellow I'd seen in the little mom-n-pop store in the middle of nowhere in Alabama during Odyssey '98. "*Garcia*, is that you!" I exclaim. We both stand and stare at each other for the longest time, in total disbelief.

In the evening *Not To Worry* drives all of us, including Nick, a northbound section hiker, to the local Pizzeria. *Garcia* treats me to supper and we all have a grand time of it.

> *The veil that clouds your eyes shall be lifted*
> *by the hands that wove it.*
> (Kahlil Gibran)

Monday—October 30, 2000
Trail Day—160/111
Trail Mile—2533/1837
Location—US19W at Spivey Gap to Nolichucky Hostel, Erwin, Tennessee

After a few more donuts for breakfast, *Not To Worry* loads me up and we head for coffee downtown, then to Spivey Gap where I'll hike north, back to Nolichucky Hostel, a short eleven-mile day. *Uncle Johnny* wants to take me into Erwin for radio and newspaper interviews this afternoon, so I reluctantly consent to stay another day at Nolichucky—but I want to get in at least a few miles. As *Not To Worry* drops me off, we make plans to hike together some when I reach Florida. Thanks, *Not To Worry*, for your kindness and generosity. I'm glad you liked the book!

The hike is a cruise. I'm back to Nolichucky by noon to be greeted by *Uncle Johnny* sitting on the porch. Shortly after I arrive comes a southbound hiker across the highway. Well, glory be, it's *Batteries Included*, a happy young lad I'd been reading shelter register entries about for the past three or four weeks.

Uncle Johnny takes me to town for lunch and the interviews. Once back at the Hostel I try to catch up on some journal entries, with little success. Later in the evening *Batteries Included* and I order in a pizza and wash it down with the rest of *Green Beans* beer! Another interesting day, the beginning my 62nd year on this earth.

If you can't excel with talent, triumph with effort.
(Dave Weinbaum)

Tuesday—October 31, 2000
Trail Day—161/112
Trail Mile—2549/1853
Location—Hogback Ridge Shelter, North Carolina

I'm up at seven. *Batteries Included* and I finish off the rest of the birthday donuts that *Not To Worry* gave me. *Uncle Johnny* drives me back to the trail, and at eight-thirty I'm headed up the mountain from Spivey Gap in dense smoke from a nearby forest fire.

As I continue climbing, the wind drives the smoke up the ridge ahead of me, making breathing difficult. I'm anxious and very relieved to reach the ridgeline, for I feared the fire was climbing behind me. Hurrying along the ridge, I'm soon out of the dense smoke.

The pulls are long and hard, taking me above 5,500 feet at Big Bald. There are many viewpoints along the trail today, but visibility is limited due to the fires below. I can see billows of smoke rising from Spivey Gap as I stand on Little Bald. I pray the fire doesn't burn the trail, as many friends behind me still need to get through.

There is plenty of excitement every day now, things to look forward to and enjoy. Today I hasten along in order to keep an appointment at Little Creek Restaurant, down a ways from Rufus Sams Gap. Here I'll be having dinner with my good friends of many years, Chuck and Lenore Parham, who now live nearby in Mars Hill, North Carolina. I make it to the gap, get a hitch down, and they're right on time. What a great afternoon we spend together.

Rufus Sams Gap is really ripped up now, the trail hard to find. The interstate is coming through, so the whole place is busted wide open. Used to be, the trail came off the ridge, jumped the guard-rail, and passed this little old place that was slowly sliding down the mountain. Out front was an old pickup, windows busted, doors open, tires flat, the bed heaped full of beer cans and trash. Looks like that old pickup finally made one more trip. Seeing the gap now, the way it is, is a letdown. I'd been looking forward to seeing that familiar old homestead. The place was sort of symbolic, sort of the southern Appalachians as I know them, my home.

It's nearly dark now as I reach Hogback Ridge Shelter. I'm really exhausted. No fire tonight. I fetch a little water from the spring, then roll in for the night. It's unusually dark and I'm alone. The mice are scampering about, but their entertainment doesn't keep my attention for long.

> *The shelters belong to the mice family,*
> *We hikers, intruders of late.*
> *When they tire of us, fed up with our fuss,*
> *What will they be usin' fer bait?*
> (N. Nomad)

Wednesday—November 1, 2000
Trail Day—162/113
Trail Mile—2570/1874
Location—Little Laurel Shelter, North Carolina

The smoke came in during the night, not heavy, but it set a haze over the shelter. This morning I'm out at seven-thirty. We're off daylight saving time now. My body clock says I'm okay, but my watch says I'm an hour early. That doesn't help in adjusting to the changeover. It's important, however, to try and use these precious moments of early light, as the days are getting noticeably shorter, with dark coming now at six. I'm having my little headlamp sent back to me—gonna need it!

I'd hoped to make it to Spring Mountain Shelter this evening but the constant ups and downs really slowed me down. The smoke has given me a plugged head and a headache, and my energy level, which is usually very high, is noticeably off. So I end the day at Little Laurel Shelter, only twenty-one miles, where I'd hoped to do thirty. Doing thirty would have set me up for a short day into Hot Springs tomorrow.

I spend the evening with Denise and Belinda, northbound section hikers. They're out for a few days from their jobs with a river-rafting outfitter on the Gauley and New Rivers in West Virginia. Denise already has a fire going when I arrive, so hot coffee is the order right away, followed by my hot pot of gruel shortly after. We spend a relaxing evening chatting and listening to their radio.

Do not pray for easier lives, pray to be stronger men.
(Phillip Brooks)

Thursday—November 2, 2000
Trail Day—163/114
Trail Mile—2590/1894
Location—Sunnybank Inn, Hot Springs, North Carolina. Elmer Hall, proprietor.

I slept well, am up early, and anxious to get going, for today I'll reach Hot Springs, North Carolina, home of Sunnybank Inn and my good friend, Elmer Hall. It's a twenty-mile day, though, and I'm not on trail until seven. But if I can hold my average of three per I should arrive in Hot Springs before two. The ride is bumpy, but the pulls do not exceed 3,600 feet. No sense taking the side trail to Rich Mountain Fire Tower, as the sky is full of smoke and haze. This is just one of those hammer-it-out days.

The trail drops in rock-strewn switchbacks off Lovers Leap Rock to the French Broad River, and I'm standing at Elmer's backdoor a little before two.

It's a grand afternoon and evening in Hot Springs. Dang, Elmer, it's good to be back!

Reflect upon your present blessings—
of which every man has many...
(Charles Dickens)

Friday—November 3, 2000
Trail Day—164/115
Trail Mile—2605/1909
Location—Roaring Fork Shelter, North Carolina

Elmer Hall at Sunnybank Inn is such a great host. Don't know how many times I've stayed, doesn't matter as I never tire of the place, the neat old high-ceilinged rooms filled with not-so-fine antiques, the old porcelain bathtubs with the squeaky faucets that won't quite shut off, an incredible library—and the out-of-this-world veggie meals. Oh, it is so fine, so very fine! Thanks, Elmer, for your generosity and kindness, and for another memorable stay; I always seem to come away with a little of your wisdom!

Word is coming in about the forest fires. They're not only north of me, like the one that nearly smoked me out in Spivey Gap, but also south, clear into Great Smoky Mountains National Park (GSM). A stop at the United States Forest Service (USFS) office confirms the bad news. There's a wildfire in Davenport Gap. Mountain Moma's, the hostel at the northern end of GSM, was evacuated yesterday.

Kindness is more important than wisdom
and the recognition of this is the beginning of wisdom.
(Theodore Isaac Rubin)

Saturday—November 4, 2000
Trail Day—165/116
Trail Mile—2626/1930
Location—Davenport Gap (eastern boundary Great Smoky Mountains National Park) to Mountain Moma's. John and Carolyn Thigpen, proprietors.

It's difficult to determine if the day has dawned cloudy or if it's just the ubiquitous smoke-haze. I'm out at seven-thirty to be immediately greeted by the pull up Max Patch.

The Patch is such a remarkable place, a large, towering flattop mountain, cleared years ago to provide homesteads and fields for hay and pasture for grazing. It was part of a USFS purchase made back in 1982 in order to move the trail from a three-mile roadwalk that led to Lemon Gap. From the summit of Max Patch can be seen the highest and most spectacular of all the peaks and ranges of the Appalachians—to the south, the Great Smoky Mountains with Clingmans Dome, the highest point on the AT; to the east, Mount Mitchell, the highest mountain this side of the Mississippi. As I stand here now, a flood of emotions swells within me. I'm thinking of the first time I stood on Max Patch. That was 1985, over fifteen years ago. I was the first thru-hiker to climb the newly built trail o'er the summit of Max Patch, from there to gaze in spellbound wonder at the majesty that surrounded me. But alas, I see no towering, far-off mountains today. The smoke has filled the sky with a dooms-day-like haze, the meadows of Max Patch bathed in a sickening brownish-orange sheen, as the sun tries burning through. I'm struck with fear as I look toward Davenport Gap, the smoke lying there as if a cloud. I try to control my anguish and relax the knot in my gut as I turn to continue south.

The trail drops and bops through Brown Gap, then to a short climb followed by a bail-off into another Deep Gap, perhaps named after Mr. Deep, but perhaps not, as this gap is indeed very deep. As I crest Snowbird Mountain and descend to Spanish Oak

Gap, the smoke thickens, making breathing a conscious, laborious effort. I'm elated and very relieved to meet two northbound section hikers coming up from the gap, for from them I learn that I'll not only be able to get through to Davenport Gap, but that Mountain Moma's, my planned destination for the evening, is open again. At the Waterville Road crossing, I'm cautioned by USFS firefighters to be alert for falling snags and to watch carefully to stay on trail, the treadway having been crisscrossed by their fireline.

As I enter the blackened char, I'm pleasantly surprised to find the smoke less troublesome. The compacted treadway is all that has not burned, its brown ribbon remaining, winding through the horrid chamber of black. Hotspots with concentrated billows of smoke are everywhere. I can see and hear snags falling from the burned, smoldering overstory. Clouds arrive, and in a while, the rain begins. I can't remember ever being so overjoyed to hear the gentle patter of rain. Before I emerge from the darkened dungeon, I'm in a steady shower and I hear the sizzle as the hotspots explode with spatter and ash.

At Stateline Road, members of the fireline crew give me a ride all the way down to Mountain Moma's. The grill is open for another hour. I check in, dry off, then head back to the store, where I indulge myself, savoring one of Mountain Moma's huge and famous cheeseburgers.

The firefighters all sport full-faced grins as they mill around in the rain out front of Mountain Moma's. Ahh, and some good news: the fire has been contained here in Davenport Gap, so there are no fires south of me in GSM, and hopefully this welcome and needed rain will keep it that way.

Life is never dull on the trail. What an incredible day. Thank you, Lord, for providing such a wide, safe path!

Fear grows out of the things we think; it lives in our minds.
(Barbara Garrison)

Sunday—November 5, 2000
Trail Day—166/117
Trail Mile—2642/1946
Location—Tri-Corner Knob Shelter, Great Smoky Mountains
National Park

Mountain Moma's is on winter hours, which means they don't open until noon on Sunday. My good friend Caroline Thigpen will be taking me back to the trail as soon as she gets in, a little before twelve.

The rain of yesterday and last evening has cleared out, and it looks to be shaping into a fine hiking day. Carolyn arrives a little before noon and has me back on the trail before twelve. Thanks, John and Carolyn, for a great stay at Mountain Moma's! The fire is out, and we are all safe. It is a blessing.

Today will be a short hiking day as I've set a goal of only fifteen miles. I should reach Tri-Corner Knob well before dark. I soon realize, however, that I'll really need to push to get there by nightfall, for this hike today starts out very tough. I'm immediately faced with the pull up Mount Cammerer, over three thousand feet of vertical ascent in just over five miles. It seems the climb will never end. If this is any indication of what the trail has to offer today, there's no way I'll reach Tri-Corner. But after Cammerer the climbs ease off, and I make good time over Cosby Knob and up Mount Guyot. I arrive at the shelter well before dark. Three section hikers have already moved in, bringing lots of firewood. They soon have a fine fire going in the indoor fireplace and we enjoy the evening together. What a joy to be out of the smoke and fire. I've had a much happier time of it today.

Turn your face to the sun and the shadows fall behind you.
(Maori Proverb)

Monday—November 6, 2000
Trail Day—167/118
Trail Mile—2658/1962
Location—US-441 at Newfound Gap, Great Smoky Mountains
National Park, to Grand Prix Motel, Gatlinburg, Tennessee

The closer I got to Tri-Corner Knob last, the iffier the weather became, until finally the local mush took over. This morning, however, I'm greeted by a glorious, clear day, perfect for hiking through some of the most breathtaking scenery that the Smokies have to offer.

And what a day it is. I snap picture after picture from vantage after vantage. The Sawteeth and Charlies Bunion are perhaps two of the most remarkable places along this grand old AT, with raw, ruggedly majestic beauty beyond description. I linger in quiet, contented repose under the spell of this mystifying grandeur. If you have not been here, if you have not seen these high places, there are no words that I or anyone else could write that would help you understand. You must come here; that is the only way. You must witness for yourself—behold that which our Maker has lifted up.

I'm in early at Newfound Gap. The northbound section hikers I'd met heading for Mountain Moma's the other day told me that Gatlinburg was quiet, not the usual hectic mass of tourists, so I decide to go down. At the end of the parking lot I stick out my thumb, and in minutes I'm rolling along to Gatlinburg. I'd read and heard about The Happy Hiker, an outfitting store, so there I head for my first stop. Here I'm greeted by Randall, then by Howie, the manager of The Happy Hiker. Howie gets me lined up on where to stay and where to go for supper, then he snaps my picture to go on the overhead beam with all the other members of the Class of 2000. Thanks, Randall and Howie, for all your kindness! The Happy Hiker is a well-stocked outfitter.

I check into the Grand Prix Motel, get cleaned up, then head over to the Smoky Mountain Microbrewery for a stromboli and some of the finest (local) suds.

What a great hiking day, and what a great evening this trail-town boy is having tonight!

And in this mountain shall the hand of the Lord rest...
(Isaiah 25:10)

Tuesday—November 7, 2000
Trail Day—168/119
Trail Mile—2676/1980
Location—Derrick Knob Shelter, Great Smoky Mountains National Park

Well, the *Companion* mentions how easy it is to get a hitch into Gatlinburg, but doesn't discuss the difficulty of getting back out. What an ordeal! I'm standing at light #10, the last stoplight leaving Gatlinburg. It's seven-thirty. I've got eighteen rugged miles before me today, up and over Mount Collins, Mount Love, Clingmans Dome, Silers Bald, and Derrick Knob. I need to get back on trail; I need to get going. But at nine-thirty, a full two hours later, I'm still standing here at light #10, the last stoplight out of Gatlinburg. The only other time I've ever had to wait this long for a hitch was in New York, two years ago, while trying to reach the oral surgeon's office.

The forecast is for rain today. As I stand holding my cardboard sign, which reads "Newfound Gap," with my thumb still out, the rain begins. I seldom give up, but I finally do, to cross the street where I get under a service station canopy. Just as I reach the shelter of the pumps, a kind fellow tanking up his pickup sees my sign and motions me over. Oh yes, how about that saying "darkest before the dawn." And glory be, I've finally got a ride!

At ten I'm back on trail. Seems the rain has set in for the duration. Here in Indian Gap, and as I begin my ascent to Mount Collins, the day turns increasingly dark and cold, and the swirling, cloud-churned rain creates a gloom the likes of which severely tests the happy expression, "There are no bad days on the trail!" I'm heading now into what's obviously going to be another long, hard, grind-it-out day.

There's nothing to see up here in the shroud, save the morbid scene of dead and dying Fraser fir, victims of acid rain and the little bugs that keep sawing and gnawing away at them. All that's left of these once proud and majestic monarchs are their skeletons—cold gray snags, poking their deformed remains through the encircling gloom. Oh, does this present such a grotesque and pitiful sight. I'm on my third hike across Clingmans Dome, and this, my third time to witness such hell in this dreadful place. But should my eyes see all hereabouts in the brightest light, there would not be such a scene. At times does Mother Nature play what seems such senseless tricks? Ahh, but aided by the senseless acts of man, does she not play for keeps!

Me and my funky attitude (which I've easily managed to nurture today) arrive at Derrick Knob Shelter late afternoon. Matthew, a glad and happy section hiker from Augusta, Georgia, greets me. After much effort, Matthew manages a smoking, choking fire in the dilapidated, tumbledown fireplace. The wind and swirling rain have other ideas, though, and he finally gives up the notion of having an evening fire. I do manage to cook some angle-ninety noodles with gravy and am cheered by Matthew's positive attitude, glowing countenance, and upbeat conversation. The warm meal and good company succeed in driving away the funk.

The only disability in life is a bad attitude.
(Scott Hamilton)

Wednesday—November 8, 2000
Trail Day—169/120
Trail Mile—2697/2001
Location—Fontana Dam at Little Tennessee River to Fontana Inn,
Fontana Village, North Carolina

The rain came in pulsing waves during the night, accompanied by violent thunder and lightning. This morning I'm up, out, and in the dark and gloom of it by seven-thirty. A "great day in the morning" this is not!

As if possible, the treadway is even more treacherous now as I contend with a blanket of wet leaves. The ice-slick combination, a colloidal-like slime of mud and leaves, makes skating the way of the trail. Downhills are wild, with no run-away ramps, the going being pretty much either up or down. It seems there's little if ever any letup in the daily grind. I'll be trying to bang out twenty-one today.

My reward for huffing the pulls over the Thunderheads, Rocky-top, Devils Tater Patch, and Doe Knob is uplifting—uplifting wind-driven rain. Here comes the *attitude* again. The overlooks are here but I overlook all of them today. Just as well, for I must keep my eyes and my concentration totally on the trail. One false step, only one, and all the millions of steps before become meaningless. This is a crapshoot of the highest order, the odds impossible to calculate, a thought upon which I try not to dwell.

The grip of gloom (seemingly of doom) finally breaks as I make the ascent to Shuckstack, my final pull for the day. The shroud that's been engulfing this high-bound sky-trail finally and suddenly lifts, as if a curtain has been flung aside. I can see the far-off kin to all the lofty temples I've been laboring upon today. What a jolt to my dull and weary senses, like the crashing of cymbals abruptly ending a soft and gentle lullaby.

Fontana Lake is undergoing a periodic five-year drawdown, the reservoir way below its normal level. The dam, built in the early forties, was constructed of concrete only; no steel reinforcement was used, and the structure is now honeycombed with structure-weakening cracks. From the top of the dam I cling (white knuckles) to the railing as I gape at the barge nearly two-hundred feet below, where divers are preparing to plunge to the near-fathomless depths that remain at the inner wall to inspect the underwater structure. The shoreline both sides of the lake is a rock-barren, forbidding scene, both sad and shocking. Small islands, their uppermost sharp-tops the only visible aspect during normal water levels, now appear as bizarre, coned-shaped projectiles of earth, sporting oddly-festooned little topknots of green. What a weird and eerie place—very strange. This is not the placid, inviting lake where you'd want to spend a relaxing afternoon on the water!

At Fontana Dam Visitor Center I call the Village 800 number for a shuttle to the Inn. Soon comes Claude to take me to the reception office and then on to the Inn. Strange, but reception and the Inn are in different locations! On the ride down, I'm thinking, "Somewhere back there today I finally quit crisscrossing the line between Tennessee and North Carolina. Somewhere back there I put another state behind me, two provinces and twelve states down, four more states to go."

Fontana Village was originally constructed to house the workers while the dam was being built. It now serves as a resort on the west end of the National Park. It's a quiet, neat little trailside community, tucked away, way up here in the mountains. And the Inn? Ahh, to a weary hiker the Inn is five-star—special hiker rates, plush rooms, in-house sauna, and a grand restaurant right under roof. After a trip to the post office and the quaint little village store, I make myself presentable and head for the chow line.

This day really came around—finally. I'm clean, full, warm and dry, definitely a happy hiker!

A mind, like a home, is furnished by its owner,
so if one's life is cold and bare...
(Louis L'Amour)

Thursday—November 9, 2000
Trail Day—170/121
Trail Mile—2697/2001
Location—Fontana Inn, Fontana Village, North Carolina

I've been telling friends for the past number of weeks that I'd be thankful and very relieved to get over the high elevations in the Smokies, this being the time of year that weather conditions can become totally unpredictable. That goal now having been accomplished with relative ease (save getting past the fires near the east end of the park), here I sit this morning, looking out of my room at the pouring rain, then back to The Weather Channel showing the extent of this massive storm. My natural push and drive says, "Get up and go," while better judgment says, "Sit this one out." I decide to listen to better judgment. Smart move, as the day stays alarmingly dark, with the cold, steady rain coming in buckets. Tomorrow is another day, and the trail will still be there. I'll let the flood have run of the trail today.

Having decided to sit, I call the desk and arrange my stay-over, then it's down to the restaurant for breakfast. As I relax, enjoying yet another brimming hot cup of coffee, looking out the dining room window, I see the cloud-cloak lift momentarily, but in nearly the same instant the rain-driven shroud quickly returns, shutting down the mountains all around. I feel so fortunate not being out there in it for a change.

What a great day this will be. As the storm hammers on, I'll remain warm and dry, a much-welcome day of rest.

I got caught in enough storms without
going into one intentionally.
(Gene Espy)

Friday—November 10, 2000
Trail Day—171/122
Trail Mile—2710/2014
Location—Brown Fork Gap Shelter, North Carolina

I slept in this morning, then spent the most casual time over breakfast at the Peppercorn Restaurant here. It's after ten before I'm back on trail.

The forecast today is for cold and sunny. It's definitely cold, and ol' Sol is trying, but the local mush is very stubborn. It's noon before the sun finally makes it front and center. What a comfort, feeling its warmth and seeing blue sky!

Today is bump and bounce day. The first bump out of Fontana is a no-name dandy, then it's a bail-off bounce into Walker Gap. Follows then a bump and a bounce through Black Gum Gap, then a bump and a bounce through Cable Gap, then a bump and a bounce through Yellow Creek Gap, then a bump and a bounce through Cody Gap, then a bump and a bounce through Hogback Gap, then a bump and a bounce through Brown Fork Gap. Late afternoon I finally reach Brown Fork Gap Shelter.

This has been only a thirteen-mile day but I'm bumped and bounced completely out, a strenuous hike. These eight ups and downs have sure put a whuppin' on me!

It's dusk before I get a decent fire going and supper finally cooked. The temperature is plummeting and a steady breeze has come up. I hasten to finish my meal and get things in order for the night. Then to ball-up on my Thermarest Guidelite, in my cozy Feathered Friends 750-loft down bag—way back in the corner of Brown Fork Gap Shelter, all by myself. ZZZZ!

Fall seven times, stand up eight.
(Japanese Proverb)

Saturday—November 11, 2000
Trail Day—172/123
Trail Mile—2726/2030
Location—Basecamp at Nantahala Outdoor Center, US-19, Wesser,
North Carolina

I'm awake this morning at seven but linger in my warm little place for another half-hour, for it's crispy-crackin' cold! By the time I'm packed, have faithfully performed my daily duty and am prepared to depart, my fingers have become sticks. This never fails when it turns cold. The circulation in my hands is bad, so I invariably know this is going to happen; yet it always scares and frightens me. I can stand the blue-numbing cold and the pain that accompanies it, but the inability to make my fingers work, no matter how hard I concentrate or try, is really scary. Somehow I manage to get my gloves on and my fingers crimped around my trekking poles, and I'm out and going for the day.

Upon claiming the first bump above the shelter, and from the ridge, do I see a breathtaking, spectacular occurrence! Although the summits and ridgelines hereabout are covered in hardwood, the leaves have fallen now, the views for the most part unobstructed, and what a view is there before me now—more, I suppose, a phenomenon than a view. Everything is topsy-turvy. In the sky we call clouds, *clouds*. But on the ground clouds are not clouds; they're *fog*. But what I gaze upon now are no ordinary clouds—or fog, for below me and to the horizon in all directions stretch countless square miles of the most brilliantly white-glassed surface I have ever seen, perfectly flat, perfectly smooth, as if a sea. And projecting through this cloud/fog-sea are legions of islands stretching to the blue, islands that are formed by the heaven-high pinnacled sharptops that are these majestic southern Appalachians. This scene before me reminds me so much of, and do I reminisce now a similar scene from another place, another time. It was October 1998, and I was about to enter the rooftop tundra of the Chic Chocs in Québec Province, Canada.

On a cold, clear morning just as this, did I see such a scene so magnificent, a brilliant cloud-sea, like this before me now. I immediately
became captive to a spell, a spell over which I had no control that
transported me back in time. As I gazed in awe upon that mysterious, majestic sea, did I observe cloud-tufted masts and sails of tall
ships plying their way! Ahh, and am I captive yet again to such a
spell today. I search and search the sea, until the blinding brilliance
washes my visual sense to a dancing gray blankness; but alas, on this
sea there are no ships, only the shimmering cusp—to the horizon.

But wait, for it seems this eerie spell is not over. I'm descending now to Stecoah Gap, and suddenly do I realize that I'm on a
long, narrow peninsula, a peninsula that ends not at Stecoah Gap,
but at Stecoah Channel. For here the cloud-sea has cut the Gap, to
pass beyond, to form an enormous gulf. And beyond that gulf, yet
another brilliant pure-white sea, dotted with countless islands. As I
continue descending, reaching the very tip of the peninsula, I also
descend in another sense, submitting myself to the complete and
utter control of the spell, for it is now that I realize I'm about to
submerge in Stecoah Channel! But how can this be, I can't just walk
into the sea? But there is no other way, the trail does not veer off, but
plunges directly in, and as I submerge, holding my breath, does the
chilling-cold gloom engulf me, until I must finally breathe. With
the spell fully upon me, so very strange is it to breathe, to be taking
in huge gulps of the moist, cold sea—so very strange! An amphibian
now, I follow the path to the very depths of the channel through a
monochromatic frost-covered grayness of barren trees and plants.

On the far side, and climbing now, I finally emerge from the
channel's cold, dark depths and am again above the sea. The spellbound magic of it is broken as I hear the hammer-thump of an eigh-
teen-wheeler jake-braking the gap below, and I'm once again on the
grand old AT, heading ever south.

Would you believe all of this beauty and awe-inspiring mystery,
and I'm out of film! Yes, there's no film in my camera. My sponsor,
GORP.com, was to supply me with film for this journey, but there

never seems to be enough time to get the film to my next maildrop. If, as we are told, a picture is worth a thousand words, for this one, the thousand words will just have to do.

The day has turned blue-perfect, with the hazy blue of these timeless Blue Ridge Mountains showing forth in perfect light. From Cheoah Bald I witness the beautiful presence of these peaceful places. To the glory of God do these temples stand; to the glory of God do they proclaim His omnipotence. Indeed, the Appalachian Trail winds a magic, spirit-filled path, a path through time and space where man may find peace, true peace in life.

I arrive at Wesser by early afternoon, pick up my bounce box at NOC Outfitters, then head straight to River's End Restaurant for their hiker-stokin' platter of Sherpa rice heaped with ladles of chili and cheese. The kind lady at registration provides me a private room in one of the bunkhouses, where I settle in for the evening. Hey, the heater works!

What a special day, a day filled with magic (not intended to be photographed) and an inspirational, spirit-filled moment on the mountain. Thank you, Lord, for keeping me, and for teaching me.

In the mountains I see the peace of God.
(Kurt Russell, Wanderlust Gear)

Sunday—November 12, 2000
Trail Day—173/124
Trail Mile—2743/2047
Location—Campsite 0.4 mile north of Wayah Bald, North Carolina

I tend to get out late on short-mile days. I know the hike today, though only seventeen miles, is going to be tough, but I lounge and tarry anyway. It's eight-thirty before I drop my key in the box. The cold of the morning hits me as I reach the Nantahala River pedestrian bridge. There's frost a quarter-inch thick on the bridge planking, and kids are having a grand time running and sliding. One energetic young lad makes it nearly the whole way. I turn to see River's End Restaurant open, so I head in. The place is packed, but I wait anyway. I know better than to order up a big breakfast before hitting the trail. I've paid the price for that loony mistake before, so I tell the waitress I'd like a short stack. I hadn't looked at the menu. Apparently pancakes aren't on the menu, for the waitress responds with a blank stare, then manages, "A short stack of what?" I reply, "Buckwheat cakes!" The stare continues. I finally break it with, "Ma'am could you just bring me a couple-a pancakes?" That seems to work as she asks me what I'd like to drink. When the pancakes finally arrive they're cold, but they work just fine for soaking up the syrup, and the syrup is great. I manage to drain a whole thermos pitcher of coffee before I'm up and going again. It's ten before I skate across the pedestrian bridge, and return to the trail.

In the first four miles I have nearly a half-mile vertical pull to Jump-up Lookout. I'm sure glad I stayed away from the ham and potatoes! The pull continues to Wesser Bald, then it's a bail-off to Tellico Gap, followed by the pull to Copper Ridge Bald, one of the last of the remaining 5,000-footers. I'm pleasantly surprised to arrive at the campsite located below the final pull up Wayah before four-thirty.

The *Data Book* lists this spot as a campsite with water. It'll do, but it certainly isn't what I'd hoped for. The place is on a hillside, so there's no flat spot to pitch anywhere. I can hear the water, but it's ten minutes away through a blow-down and briar-entangled laurel hell.

The evening has turned cold, so I linger by the fire till after dark, alone as usual. As I stare into the dying embers, I'm set to pondering the interesting and utter difference between what, at times, we might embrace as near reverie, that oft sought-after thing called *solitude*, and what, at other times, we might look upon as no more than the hopelessly despairing pangs of *loneliness*. I've seen no thru-hikers since Erwin, and only two day hikers today. As expressed in my ditty, "Land of the Free," wanderlust can, indeed, deal us a "...cold, lonesome track."

> *Our language has wisely sensed the two sides of being alone.*
> *It has created the word "loneliness" to express the*
> *pain of being alone.*
> *And it has created the word "solitude" to express*
> *the glory of being alone.*
> (Paul Tillich)

Monday—November 13, 2000
Trail Day—174/125
Trail Mile—2757/2061
Location—Old US-64 at Wallace Gap to Franklin Motel, Franklin, North Carolina

The forecast is for rain today, but the day dawns cold and clear. I manage to break camp, get my gloves on, and get moving before my fingers turn numb.

The final short pop to Wayah Bald takes only minutes, and I'm soon standing on the uppermost platform of the old stone fire tower. From this vantage, to the north I see the high cathedrals of GSM dancing on horizon's hazy-blue. And to the south, to where the path will onward lead, I see Albert Mountain and Standing Indian, the last of the remaining 5,000-footers. As I look these grand and majestic mountains over, I'm comforted and strengthened in the knowledge that I'm in the presence of the Lord.

The hike today is mostly a cruise, and I finish another short mile day a little before one. My plans were to stay at Rainbow Springs Campground, owned and managed by Buddy and Jensine Crossman, but they have everything shut down and winterized. Their comfortable campground and the neat old bunkhouse for hikers are closed for the season. So, as I'm greeted by these kind folks, although they've just returned from Franklin some fifteen miles away, they offer to shuttle me to Franklin just the same, the offer of which I quickly accept. In just a short while I'm at the Franklin Motel. Thanks, Buddy and Jensine, for your kindness and for your time; you folks sure have a soft spot in your hearts for us hiker-trash! I know that it's been there for many, many years.

> *I'll lift mine eyes unto the hills, from whence cometh my help.*
> *My help cometh from the Lord...*
> (Psalms 121:1-2)

Tuesday—November 14, 2000
Trail Day—175/126
Trail Mile—2777/2081
Location—Standing Indian Shelter, North Carolina

I had a comfortable evening last at the Franklin Motel, managed by Edward Cagle. It's a very modest old place, but well cared for, clean and neat; thanks, Ed!

During the ride in with Buddy and Jensine yesterday, I had inquired about who to call in the area for a shuttle back to the trail. Without a moment's hesitation, Jensine responded, "That's easy; just go over to Prudential Realty and ask for Rich Bankston. They're just up the street from the motel. He'll not only shuttle you back to the trail, but I'll bet he also invites you to join him for breakfast in the morning. Be sure to mention your book."

So after Ed gets me settled in, I beat it over to Prudential Realty. I'm in luck; the receptionist ushers me right to Mr. Bankston's office. Jensine was right. Rich and me, we hit it right off! After a few minutes of upbeat conversation (and a mention of my book), Rich says, "Excuse me a moment," and picks up the phone, "Shelby, come down here. There's someone I want you to meet." So, in no time at all, I've met not only Rich Bankston, but also his wife, Shelby. Well now, these folks like hikers! Though it was an obviously very busy office, we spent the most casual half-hour talking trail—and about my book. As I'm leaving, Rich having offered to shuttle me back up this morning; oh yes, I'm invited to be his guest for breakfast in the morning!

At seven-thirty, right on cue as promised, Rich is at my door. I load my pack and we're off to the local mom-n-pop for breakfast. Here we share more great conversation. I know I've mentioned before how remarkable it is—the wonderful, lasting friendships made along the trail. Here's an example.

Plans were to have me back on the trail and hiking by eight-thirty, but we'll be a little late, as Rich has suggested a short side-trip to which I quickly and enthusiastically agree.

We're in Reverend A. Rufus Morgan country, and are near St. John's Church, Cartoogechaye (Cherokee for "the town over beyond) where Reverend Morgan conducted services for years. Rufus Morgan is a shining star in the annals of the Appalachian Trail. He was a AT Conference board member for thirty years and an avid hiker and trail maintainer. "...my principal joy has been hiking, with its associated wildflowers and wildlife interests. Mt. LeConte has been my favorite mountain." Although both blind and deaf, on October 14, 1977, Reverend Morgan celebrated his 92nd birthday by climbing Mount LeConte, his 172nd ascent.

Thanks Rich, for bringing me here. It's such a quiet, peaceful little church. I wish all who hike the AT could visit.

Although I've a twenty mile hike today, up and over the last two 5,000 footers the AT crosses in the southern Appalachians, Rich has assured me that it will be a pleasant, easy hike. And indeed, I find it to be just that. The ascent and short blue blaze to the summit of Standing Indian is the highlight of the day, with magnificent views, definitely a spiritual place. I arrive before dark at Standing Indian Shelter and manage a fire, but decide against cooking as the wind has come up and the evening has turned bitter cold. Instead, I settle for a couple of ham and cheese sandwiches with an apple and a bag of M&M's for dessert.

The scenes all along the AT are beautiful and awe-inspiring, but it's the people—indeed, it's the people that make the memories.

We are shaped and fashioned by what we love.
(Johann Wolfgang Von Goethe)

Wednesday—November 15, 2000
Trail Day—176/127
Trail Mile—2794/2098
Location—US-76 at Dicks Creek Gap to the Blueberry Patch Hostel, Hiawassee, Georgia. Gary and Lennie Poteat, proprietors.

It's bitter cold this morning, so I stay buried in my sleeping bag, not wanting to face the day. The sun is up, but so is the wind as I convince myself it's time to get going. The two water bottles left setting on the shelter floor are bricks. I'm unable to crack the ice in either one, so I just throw the frozen lumps in my pack. Time and again I pause to thrust my hands into my groin or under my armpits to keep my fingers working. I finally get everything tied, zipped, and snapped, and I'm out and on the trail south. I have hastened with all diligence these past weeks in an effort to avoid the very problems I've been dealt this morning, but winter's caught me anyway.

In spite of the cold, I'm able to get the old jitney up to operating temperature and humming remarkably well. The bail-off to Deep Gap goes quickly. Oh yes, another Deep Gap, named, no doubt, after the same family of Deeps from North Carolina and Tennessee! After the gap, it's straight up again, then straight down to Wateroak Gap, then up and down again to Sassafras Gap, then up and down yet again to Bly Gap. Ahh, and here is the long awaited state line between North Carolina and Georgia, and my dear old friend, the broken-down oak. I stop, drop my pack, and linger the longest time, enjoying the peace and serenity brought by the presence of this tenacious survivor. I celebrate with a rattling slug of ice water from one of my partially thawed water bottles. Two provinces, thirteen states down, three states to go!

The rollercoaster continues through Rich Cove Gap, Blue Ridge Gap, Plumorchard Gap, Bull Gap, Cowart Gap, and finally, Dicks Creek Gap.

Though this is a US highway at Dicks Creek Gap, there is little traffic. But as luck would have it, in less than five minutes (and no more than that many vehicles) I'm loaded and on my way to the Blueberry Patch. What a joy seeing Gary and Lennie again. They're great friends, members of the clan. I had called ahead, so Gary has made preparations for my visit. He's turned the water and the water heater back on in the washhouse and the heat back on in the bunkhouse. I'm the first southbounder to stay at the Patch this year, the last northbounder having gone through months ago. Gary's got the bunkhouse warm, and the shower house, ditto! I hurry to get cleaned up as I've been invited to be their guest for supper. What a grand time we have together. Lennie has prepared the finest pasta with sauce made from tomatoes grown and canned right here at the Patch. Aww, mother, I know you taught me as a child that it was impolite to go back for thirds when you're the guest in someone's home—and I remember that lesson well. But momma, please, I just couldn't help myself.

Oh, what a fine day. I'm clean, full, dry, and warm, and with the best of friends. What more could anyone ask!

Oh that it were my chief delight,
To do the things I ought!
Then let me try with all my might
To mind what I was taught.
(Jane Taylor)

Thursday—November 16, 2000
Trail Day—177/128
Trail Mile—2810/2114
Location—SR-75 at Unicoi Gap to Super 8 Motel, Helen, Georgia

The tradition goes on, and the joy of it. That grand occurrence being the AYCE pancakes-with-blueberry-syrup breakfast at the Blueberry Patch. I never expected everything to be so memorably special all over again, like during Odyssey '98. But the fact is, Odyssey 2000 is turning out to be absolutely pumped full of all those wonderful times, with all the great people, all over again. Thanks, Gary and Lennie, for being the special people you are to me, and thanks for your friendship, your kindness, and your generosity!

Gary shuttles me back to the trailhead at Dicks Creek Gap and a little after nine I'm headed south again on a cool, drizzly morning. Today is only a seventeen-miler, so I can cruise along at my leisure. Good thing, 'cause the trail roughs me up plenty. Lots of pops and drops as I start whittling away at the remaining 4,000-footers. Two down (Tray and Rocky), two to go (Blue and Blood).

As the day comes on, on comes the rain. By the time I reach Unicoi Gap, it has set itself into a persistent, no-nonsense steady and cold affair. But the rain bothers me not, for I'm full of that same excitement and enthusiasm experienced and shared by all intrepid about to complete an incredible journey, mine, a southbound thru-hike o'er this grand and venerable old Appalachian Trail. Although Springer Mountain is just another milestone for me to pass on this longer quest, the first southbound thru-hike encompassing the entire Appalachian Mountain range (an amalgam of trails that form what is becoming known as Trail of the Ancients), I'm taken and consumed by those same feelings and emotions. You can't be out here, enduring for month after month, and not feel the energy, the special power, the indescribable spiritual magnetism that make a journey on the AT such a memorable experience. Indeed, for all of us it is the journey of a lifetime. Springer Mountain is not visible;

its presence does not loom on the horizon for days, as does Mount Katahdin for those northbound intrepid about to fulfill their grand dream. But Springer is there—it is there just the same.

At Unicoi there's located a bit of AT history, for on a large boulder at the gap trailhead is affixed one of the three original bronze memorials cast in the late thirties to honor and commemorate the Appalachian Trail in Georgia. On it is lifted a likeness of Warner Hall, a backpacker and Georgia Appalachian Trail Club member of that time, along with these inscribed words: "A pathway for those who seek fellowship with the wilderness." Three of those plaques were made, and remarkably, each one survives to this day. What a miracle! There's one here at Unicoi, one at busy Neels Gap, and the other atop the monolith at Springer Mountain overlook.

As I stick out my thumb toward Helen, the trucks and autos whiz by, paying me not the least heed as I brace against their tagalong tornadoes. I can't blame them. Nobody wants to stop in this mess, let alone pick up a soaked, dirty hiker. As the cold starts digging into my bones, I begin pondering the futility of it. But my goodness, just as I'm about to realize that getting a hitch is going to be impossible, this van pulls over! Down goes the window, and two smiling faces greet me, it's Dave and Joe. Dave and Beverly Gale are the owners and operators of Wildwood Outfitters, located in both Hiawassee and Helen, and Joe is one of their employees. The two are on their way between stores. What a stroke of incredibly good luck! Folks, this is how this whole hike has been. One minute I'm standing in the dismal cold rain, the next I'm in a warm, dry van heading for a warm, dry room, this one in Helen, Georgia.

In a short while I'm checked into the hiker-friendly Super 8 Motel. It's amazing how the blessings keep on coming, keep rolling in—at just the right moment in time.

The successful hikers are the ones who find goodness and joy
even in the difficult times...
(Larry Luxenberg)

Friday—November 17, 2000
Trail Day—178/129
Trail Mile—2830/2134
Location—US-19/US-129 at Neels Gap, Georgia to Goose Creek
Cabins. Keith and Retter Bailey, proprietors.

Dave Gale, in his love for those of us consumed with wanderlust, and in his interest and desire to assist (me being one of those so consumed), offered yesterday to shuttle me back to the trailhead at Unicoi Gap this morning, the offer which I quickly accepted. At seven-thirty, just as promised, Dave is at my door. On the way up the mountain, we talk about many things, like our *one-of-these-days* list (and the WHY of this wanderlust thing). Dave is a contractor, not your ordinary stick-and-brick bungalow builder, but a real honest-to-gosh general contractor. He's on the cell phone now, ordering materials to finish up the dam he's building near Helen. Folks, certainly you can see by now what I mean when I say, "Life on the trail may prove trying and tiring at times, but never dull." Indeed, it's never boring. Thanks Dave, for your genuine caring and for your kindness, and thanks for ordering a bunch of my books for Wildwood Outfitters!

The forecast today is for windy and cold with a 30% chance of rain. Oh yes, the 70% not—is not! Up the mountain I go as I brace into it. I've a twenty-miler to bang out, with this day (so it appears) shaping to go in the journal as another of those grind-it-out days. The mountains in Georgia are not the high-looming towers as are those to the north, but one does not need tall mountains to have rugged trail, and the mountains along the southern Blue Ridge, especially in Georgia, have some rugged trail. My first pull this morning is in excess of 1,000 feet, steady, near straight up (another) old Blue Mountain, the next-to-last 4,000 footer. The mist is swirling and the wind is driving its sharp, bitter-cold teeth into me as I set my head and the old jitney to the task. And to make the task just the least bit more challenging—BANG, I hit the rocks, lots of rocks, big rocks! So stumble and grind and up I go, to finally prevail, one more mountaintop behind me, one more in the countless hundreds of mountaintops. Thank you, Lord, thank you for the energy, the will and the resolve. This practice, over all these months, over all these miles, has never become ordinary, for each accomplishment remains such a humbling experience. I think of all the many miles behind me now, the agony, the joy. I'll soon reach Springer Mountain, the southern terminus of this remarkable old Appalachian Trail. I've oft been asked the simple question, "Why?" I try to think about what it all means—then I try not.

As is often the case, just when it seems the trail has become impossible to endure, does it become the likes of the Yellow Brick Road! This morning the treadway cruises right onto such a path, an old woods road. What a marvelous work, this old roadway, for each little ravine has been filled with such handy care, each retaining wall built of rock blasted from the side of the mountain, each stone carefully placed to form true works of art, now covered with the algae-green patina that reveals all the many years it's been since the army of Civilian Conservation Corps (CCC) workers labored here. And the treadway; the treadway weaves along this delightful old road for miles and miles. What a fun hike!

The gaps leave no gap undone today. It's rockin' and boppin' time as the trail begins a rollercoaster ride along. Bop - Moreland Gap; bop - Hogpen Gap; bop - Whitley Gap; bop - Tesnatee Gap; bop - Baggs Creek Gap; bop - Bull Gap; and finally for the day, bop - Neels Gap!

In Neels Gap is the beautiful old stone CCC structure, Walasi-Yi, which houses the most complete outfitting establishment you'll find in such quarters anywhere. Jeff and Dorothy Hansen have been the proud outfitters/proprietors, the hikers' friends, helping beginners and old pros alike with their gear and other needs for over seventeen years. During that span of time, we have become the best of friends. I arrive to be greeted with a big smile and a grand hug from Bobby, one of the staff members, and then from Jeff. We share a great time together. Dorothy is out today, but I'll get to see her in the morning, for I'll be staying just down the road at Goose Creek Cabins and will return here tomorrow to continue on to Springer.

Jeff calls Goose Creek and soon Keith Bailey comes to fetch me. Goose Creek Cabins consists of a grand old lodge, a pond filled with ducks, and up the hill, the neatest bunch of old, well-kept cabins. At the lodge I meet Ken and *Lionheart*, GAME '00, and we chat while Keith checks me in and takes our order for dinner. I settle into a cozy, warm cabin as Keith runs to the BBQ place to bring back food for all of us.

Great friends, a great day!

If you ask the question [Why], you won't understand the answer.
You have to have a feeling for the trail.
Some of these things are hard to put into words.
(Robert *Sourdough Bob* Goss)

Saturday—November 18, 2000
Trail Day—179/130
Trail Mile—2845/2149
Location—FS-42 at Gooch Gap to the home of Lee and Carole Perry, Cumming

Ahh yes, *Sourdough Bob*, my dear friend—indeed "Some of these things are hard to put into words." But you know me, I'll keep on trying! It was such a blessing to be in (and out of it) last night, for it turned bitter cold. I relax and linger while Keith gets the fires going in the lodge, then we load up and he shuttles me back to the gap. Thanks Keith for another memorable stay at Goose Creek Cabins. Say hello to your dad, Claude, for me!

Oh, it's so good to see Dorothy Hansen again. Thru-hikers can form bonds that are strong and lasting, bonds no one else can understand. I've been up to the Center here many times, but it's different arriving with a backpack on, hiking through. I linger for the longest

time before heading up old Blood. Jeff, Dorothy, what a pleasure seeing you again! Don't forget *"A friend is here and waits for you."*

Just across the busy highway beside the trail is the second of the three old bronze memorials placed by the Georgia Appalachian Trail Club many years ago. And though it's affixed to a boulder right next the road, many pass here every day paying it not the least heed. In fact, I've been amazed at the number of hikers who are not even aware of it. To me, it's a special spot, a historic place. I stop to get a picture and to read its words, "A trail for those who seek fellowship with the wilderness." What a beautiful memorial.

Blood Mountain is the highest point on the Appalachian Trail in Georgia, standing at just over 4,400 feet. There are grand views from the summit near where the old CCC Blood Mountain Shelter is located. Here's another beautiful structure built of stone. It's more a cabin than a shelter, complete with fireplace and two separate rooms. But it isn't so comfy, as the fireplace has been blocked off and the window shutters and entrance door have been removed. I've come to this mountain many, many times, the last with Larry Duffy, my good friend from Dahlonega. He's hiker-trash. Larry is a professional photographer, and I'd talked him into lugging thirty pounds of camera gear up the mountain to get the photos that my editor wanted for the cover of *Ten Million Steps*. We spent the whole afternoon here while Larry took different shots in varied and different light.

Today I've a very enjoyable section of trail I've hiked many a time. I like the ridges and gaps in the southern Appalachians, especially here in Georgia, for they're nearly all filled with the towering and straight mature tulip poplar. Groves of these present in such grand and stately fashion.

The plan for this evening is to meet Carole *Goatskin* Perry at FS-42 in Gooch Gap, just this side of Gooch Gap Shelter. *Goatskin* hiked the AT southbound (MEGA), Class of '86. I met Carole and her husband, Lee while I was working at the Len Foote Hike Inn, where I'll be staying tomorrow evening. I'm to be their guest at their home in Cumming this evening.

It's a joy to be greeted by my dear friend, *Goatskin*, as I complete my hike for the day. She has food and some cold frosties for me. The warmth of the automobile heater, and the warmth of the company of a kind, dear friend: what a fine combination!

In the evening, after getting my tank stoked with pizza, the Perry's son, Brendan (who has thru-hiked the AT and is now into a hike on the Pacific Crest Trail) drops by to share some photos of his hike this past summer.

I'm clean, full, warm, and dry, and with wonderful friends. Crisp linen on the bed, covered with a down comforter. What a day, what a day!

A friend is here and waits for you,
The quiet, patient one.
Until all things with more to-do,
In life are finally done.

'tis then that you will realize,
The path you should have trod.
And to this friend most learned, wise,
You'll search the face of God.

Now on this path you chance to seek,
For you have learned thru life,
From those you love, who oft did speak,
The way to break from strife.

And who this friend? The trail, toward
Yourself! Free conscience know.
O'er mount and mead and brook to ford,
This journ' you'll finally go.

And searching now, life nearly spent,
In Nature's Bosom find,
Your answered prayers, aft deep repent,
True joy and peace of mind.
(N. Nomad)

Sunday—November 19, 2000
Trail Day—180/131
Trail Mile—2861/2160
Location—Springer Mountain, Georgia, to the Len Foote Hike Inn

From the Perry home in Cumming it's an hour's drive back to
Gooch Gap, so we're all up by seven. Before loading, Carole prepares a full-spread breakfast for me. The plan is for them to drop me
off at Gooch Gap, then for Lee to drive *Goatskin* on ahead to the

next road crossing so she can get in some hiking with me. But these plans start looking iffy as we begin climbing the mountain toward Suches. The rain came off and on all night, and this morning we no sooner get on the road than the rain begins again. As we continue climbing, the rain continues, slowly turning to snow. At first the snow isn't sticking, but as we near Suches, the road turns slushy. As we continue, the flurries intensify, finally turning to steady snow showers. Carole is driving and I beg her, "Please, Carole, don't take chances for me; we can hike another day." She responds by shifting into four-wheel drive! On we go, making it in good order to Gooch Gap. Here Carole and Lee drop me off, then head for the next gap. I watch as they disappear into the wall of white.

The snow begins blanketing the trail and the woods all around as I ascend from Gooch Gap. I'm thinking, "What a fitting way to end this second segment of my odyssey, in the snow, just as I began the first segment, the IAT, nearly six months ago, some 2800+ miles to the north." In just a while, I see a hiker coming toward me. It's *Goatskin*, sporting the happiest and broadest smile. Ahh yes, me too, two kids playing in the snow! It's really coming down now, and it's starting to pile up on the trail, making the slippery rocks and roots under the slippery leaves, under the slippery snow—kinda slippery! Out of necessity, in order to remain upright, our usually smooth, gliding strides turn to slow, cautious shuffles. But oh, are we having a grand time! We see Lee waiting patiently (and snugly) in their warm vehicle as we gain the gap. They've prepared sandwiches, and I'm offered one before they head out again, disappearing into the ever-intensifying wall of snow.

What a grand and exciting day this is turning out to be as *Goatskin* soon greets me again and we glide on together through the winter wonderland to Hightower Gap. By this time the snow has packed in my hair and on my beard, making me appear as so much a snowman. When Lee sees me, he loses it, guffawing with childish glee as he rolls down the window to get a better look. Another sandwich and a few pictures and I'm on my way again, bound for Cross Trails, just this side of Springer Mountain.

The snow slows me down considerably and I must crawl on all fours under the snow laden hemlock boughs in Stover Creek, but I do not mind. The hike today is a different hike, different than all the hundreds before, just as a southbound hike o'er this grand old AT is so different from a northbound hike. It's a joy to have the company of great friends today, for this hike's become mostly a solitary affair. I have seen many dear friends from Odyssey '98 and have made many new friends, some who have hiked along for a while with me. But for the most part I have been on this journey alone. So I have had much time to think, time to find out more about who I am and what I am. There have been times of struggle, both physical and mental, but just as was the case during Odyssey '98, I'm finding within a deep inner peace and joy as the days click away. I'm a better person, this I know. I'm stronger of will, more tolerant, with greater patience, and am slowly gaining of wisdom as I learn to trust in the ways of God and not in the ways of man—and of this world.

By the time I reach Cross Trails, the last short leg to Springer, I'm plowing along in nearly a half-foot of snow. What a glorious sight, what a glorious feeling! The Perrys are here waiting and they bundle up to hike the last mile on the AT with me. We're giddy and full of chatter as we head for the summit of Springer Mountain.

Just shy of the first white blaze, the blaze that marks the beginning (or the end of such a once-in-a-lifetime journey) begins another trail, the Benton MacKaye Trail (BMT). It is a trail so named in honor of the dreamer whose idea gave birth to the greatest of all trails, the trail now known as the Appalachian National Scenic Trail. *Goatskin* and I hike the short distance from where the BMT begins to the beautiful bronze monument that has been affixed to a large boulder here on Springer Mountain. This is such a special place, a spiritual place, a place where I experience the most intense feeling of pride. For it is humbling to have been chosen by fate and by time and circumstance, and by the will of the Almighty, to have been involved in initiating the idea and to have started the fund for the placement of this beautiful tribute to Benton MacKaye here on Springer. In the snow, this shrine

is so pure, so peaceful. No one has been here before us today; the blanket of snow is undisturbed. I hesitate, not wanting to invade the spell cast by such a wintry scene. *Goatskin* nudges me forward and I finally go to have my picture taken with Mr. MacKaye. There is just no way in words I can express how very special this moment is in my life.

We finally turn to hike the short distance to the summit where Lee is waiting to greet us. He sweeps the snow from the last of the three beautiful bronze plaques placed years ago by the Georgia Appalachian Trail Club, and it's picture-taking time again. I cannot see the last white blaze just beside the plaque, for it's covered with snow. But I know exactly where it's located, for I have cast my eyes down upon it many a time.

The snow has ended and the clouds have lifted for just a moment. Time to look, as Benton MacKaye would say, "...to truly see that which we look upon." Nearly 3,000 miles completed on this journey o'er Trail of the Ancients. Three hundred more to go to complete the first southbound thru-hike of the entire Appalachian Mountain range, then to continue on along the Eastern Continental Trail to Key West, Florida, a total distance of nearly 5000 miles, nearly a year on the trail.

The Len Foote Hike Inn is a beautiful facility. It's located on a trail that parallels the AT approach trail between Amicalola Falls State Park and Springer Mountain, requiring a hike the distance of some five miles for those who wish to enjoy its comforts. I had the pleasure of working here for over six months while I labored over the manuscript for my book, *Ten Million Steps*. I've been invited to be their guest this evening. So plans are for me to hike on in from Springer while Lee and Carole drive down, around, and up the service road to the Inn.

Just at dusk, to cap this perfect, memorable day, I'm greeted by the great folks at the Inn. There's Naomi, Josh, Shane and girlfriend, Kelly, Jeremy, and my great friend and fellow "Class of '98" thru-hiker, Dan *Cornbread* Briordy. Lee and Carole soon arrive, with a bottle of bubbly to celebrate the occasion, and Josh has prepared a hiker feast for me. The snow adds to the magic that is the Hike Inn, casting a spell of beauty and peaceful calm over this high-held place.

The second leg of this grand journey, Odyssey 2000, is now history, my southbound thru-hike o'er the AT, now history. So many memories, so many great people to thank for making the journey so special. And now a special thanks to my sponsors, most whom will continue on with me—Vasque, New Balance, GORP.com, Bottom Line Results, Conquest, Wanderlust Gear, GVP Gear, Cascade Designs, Cumming Foot and Leg Clinic, Leki, Rexall Sundown, Flash Photo, Appalachian Outfitters, and Feathered Friends.

> *...you will thank God for having the good health*
> *and great good fortune*
> *to be where you are enjoying some of Nature's best.*
> **This is the Appalachian Trail.**
> *Neither words nor pictures can adequately describe it.*
> (Ed Garvey)

THE GRAND CONNECTION BENTON MACKAYE TRAIL (BMT)

Monday/Tuesday—November 20/21, 2000
Trail Mile—2891 (adjusted)
Location—Home at Nimblewill Creek, Dahlonega, Georgia

The sunrise viewed from the Hike Inn is always special, no matter how many times one might have the pleasure of being here at just this moment. The Sunrise Room is appropriately named, for from this location there's an unobstructed view to the east, a view even more spectacular than from man's most heaven-bound tower or from the crow's nest of the tallest of the tall ships at sea. This morning, as dawn arrives so crisp and calm, does the sun set the eastern horizon afire. What a way to start this day, a fresh cup of steaming hot coffee warming my hands, and this magnificent sight—the sun igniting the mountain.

Cornbread is also up at dawn, at work in the kitchen, preparing a great breakfast for me. Carole and Lee soon come down, then the rest of the Hike Inn crew. Dear friends, what a great time—your taking this time to share with me. Thanks!

I've decided to rest a couple days at my little place down at Nimblewill Creek before tackling the Cohuttas. The Benton MacKaye Trail and the Georgia Pinhoti Trail are both tough hikes, especially the Pinhoti. For on that trail there remains much bushwhacking through sections not yet constructed, and I'll do the bushwhacks. I'm looking forward to the challenges just ahead, for I have prepared long and hard, but a little rest will be a great benefit.

Lee and Carole have offered to shuttle me off the mountain, and after lingering goodbyes with the Hike Inn crew, we're on our way to Nimblewill.

It's a feeling of great comfort to be home again, to return to my own little place. Thinking back, I believe I can count on one hand the times during the last 180 days that I've slept more than one night in the same place. It's the gypsy lore, isn't it? Ahh, it's the wanderlust, and I'm the *Nomad*, and I guess that just about sums it up.

It's time now to rest. There's no way I can get caught up on all the things I've neglected during the past six months, nor is there any way to get all my affairs in order for the next five. So I decide to just relax. That's the most beneficial way to spend this precious time, so that's what I do.

We never become truly spiritual by sitting down
and wishing to become so. You must undertake something
so great that you cannot accomplish it unaided.
(Phillips Brooks)

Wednesday—November 22, 2000
Trail Day—181/1
Trail Mile—2908/17
Location—The ridgeline north of Skeenah Gap, Georgia

I truly believe that Carole and Lee have found as much pleasure and joy as I have in the time we've spent together these past few days, for indeed it has been a joy. And what great help their time with me has been. This morning Carole is here to shuttle me back to the trail at Three Forks, where I'll begin the third leg of Odyssey 2000, the Georgia section of the BMT.

We're at Three Forks Trailhead by ten. I bid Carole farewell and I'm headed out on the frozen, ice-covered trail. The goal today is to reach and perhaps get just past Skeenah Gap, but with the miles, the tough ups and downs, and the ice, I decide not to push, to just see how the day works. There's been traffic on the trail, which surprises

me. Two sets of tracks, which I believe to be those of *Spur* and *Ready*, dear friends who have hiked north from Flagg Mountain, Alabama. *Spur* is on his way to completing a northbound thru-hike of the TA. Their footprints have compressed the snow. With the thawing and freezing conditions, the remaining packed snow has turned to ice, making the never-ending narrow, off-camber sidehills extremely treacherous. One slip and I'm quickly on my way, down and into the next county! I must set my trekking poles firmly and stomp in every foot placement to reduce the risk of slipping and falling. The uphills, of which there's no lack, are mostly on the north side of the crowns and ridges, the ice there adding another element of difficulty to the already tough, continual climbing. I'm able to move along without incident and am making good time, but this hike today is extremely tiring, and I'm becoming weary and fatigued. I try with much effort and fair success not to dwell on this labor, but rather to make my senses keen to the rare beauty here afforded me. For before me now is a true wonderland of brightness and purity. I must set my vision to the dazzle, my hearing to the void where is the usual din, my touch to the tingling sharpness of the air as I breathe, my body bound in the chilling spell—and that indescribable scent of the snow-covered woods in the grips of winter.

It is soon near dusk, and the miles have miraculously come to pass. Normally I would seek a campsite near a springhead or stream, but with the snow blanket all about I decide to stay the ridge tonight, for here are the driest twigs and firewood, and water is only a melted snowball away.

Oh, will this first day on the BMT add much flavor to all the days as it stirs into the blend.

The vision must be followed by the venture.
It is not enough to stare up the steps—we must step up the stairs.
(Vance Havner)

Thursday—November 23, 2000 Thanksgiving
Trail Day—182/2
Trail Mile—2932/41
Location—US-76/GA-5 at Cherrylog, Georgia to Lee and Carole
Perrys' cabin near Ellijay

While home I stopped by Appalachian Outfitters in Dahlonega for a good pair of gloves. They're one of my fine sponsors and I'm now sporting a luxurious pair of Marmot Primalofts. I'm now also toting a sleeping bag insert/liner that I've had for years. It's a Wiggys Wear synthetic weighing about a pound and adding another eight to ten degrees warmth to my three-season Rock Wren bag. Sure glad I had the gloves yesterday and the liner last night! These items have added to my pack weight, but they're needed and I'm very happy to have them along.

Today will be a long, difficult day with nearly continuous elevation changes. The ice is beginning to clear from the trail but there remains an additional challenge for the pulls over Wilscot, Tipton, and Brawley Mountains. It is noon by the time I reach Shallowford Bridge. The roadwalk up Stanley Creek Road takes a little over an hour, just enough time for the warming day to aid me in my 1,200-foot climb over Rocky Mountain. It's a great relief to have the ice gone, making the treadway much more friendly. From Scroggin Knob on into US-76 at Cherrylog, it's a downhill cruise and a roadwalk. I arrive at four, just as planned, where Carole is waiting to drive me to their cabin in the mountains near Ellijay. It's great to be with these friends again, to be warm and dry. Their son, Brendan, and his girlfriend, Susan, and their friends come in later, but I'm too tired to be very sociable. So after supper I make the final climb for the day—up the stairs to turn in.

> *I do not pray for a lighter load, but for a stronger back.*
> (Phillips Brooks)

Friday—November 24, 2000
Trail Day—183/3
Trail Mile—2950/59
Location—Beside small stream north of Holloway Gap, Georgia

Thanksgiving at the Perry cabin is planned for today, and I've been invited to stay over and partake of the feast. It's raining and cold out, and I'm tempted to accept their kind invitation, but I need to return to the trail and the task, so that is the decision. Brendan and Susan drive me back to Cherrylog, and I'm on my way by ten.

The day begins with a hike through Cherry Lakes Subdivision, created by Joe Sisson. The subdivision is expansive with much greenway area where the trail passes. There is also a chapel and shelter right on trail. Joe Sisson has been a friend of the Benton MacKaye Trail Association for years. The annual meeting of the BMTA is usually held at his fine meeting facility in Cherry Lakes. I had the honor of being their guest speaker last year.

This will be my final day on the BMT, another strenuous day with many ups and downs. This jumble of mountains known as the Cohuttas forms one of the most amazingly rugged areas of all the southern Appalachians, and with this raw ruggedness comes sheer beauty.

I find, however, on this cloudy, rainy day, that I'm dealing with a cloud of frustration. Today is the third day of it. But it isn't the rain, which continues and at times comes hard and cold, adding to the cause. What has brought this unsettled state is the fact that I've been hiking mostly north this whole time. The occasional day hiker or hunter I've seen along the trail who asks where I'm headed quickly points out that I'm going the wrong way. But I must make this loop up and around to reach the Georgia Pinhoti Trail that leads to Alabama.

The trail through much of this section follows the Tennessee Valley Divide, ranging every compass point. It's a wonder the runoff from the constant rain knows which way to go. But here goes the trail, and here I go toward my final destination on the BMT—Flat Top Mountain. As I reach a wildlife clearing, I'm almost back to North Carolina and Tennessee. I know the ribbons marking the turn-off, the beginning of the Georgia Pinhoti Trail bushwhack, I know they're nearby, but dusk is approaching. The cold rain has finally relented, and here is a small stream. Although I'd like to find the turn-off this evening, I decide to call it a day while I have a break. Right decision; I no more get camp set than the downpour begins anew. This has been a hard day—hard hiking, hard goodbyes.

I thank thee, memory, in the hour
When troubled thoughts are mine—
For thou, like suns in April's shower,
On shadowy scenes wilt shine.
(Branwell Brontë)

THE GRAND CONNECTION GEORGIA PINHOTI TRAIL (GPT)

Saturday—November 25, 2000
Trail Day—184/1
Trail Mile—2959/9
Location—Mountaintown Creek Trail to Ellijay Inn, Ellijay, Georgia

It's cloudy and cold, but the rain holds off as I hasten to break camp and get on my way. I become anxious as I pass the wildlife clearing and move on, for I know the cutoff to the new Georgia Pinhoti Trail should be nearby. I've talked recently with members of both the Benton MacKaye Trail Association and the Georgia Pinhoti Trail Association about where the GPT will begin, so I have a pretty good fix on where I should find it. But as I hike along, it seems I've gone much too far. As is most always the case, I'm not as far along as I think, and soon I see flagging and blue paint marks to my left.

This will be the beginning of the bushwhack. There is no trail, simply a marked line through the forest where the trail will ultimately be built. The flag and paint line moves along quite nicely for some distance before careening over the edge into an impenetrable maze of laurel, greenbrier and blow downs, on a long and seemingly never-ending side-slab. I must jam my hiking sticks into the sidehill, then place my feet in the uphill V created to keep from sliding hopelessly down through the thicket. Some places I must go to all fours and crawl. The going is agonizingly slow, but I'm making progress, getting through. Even where the line follows old logging tracks, the going is hindered, the way cluttered with blow downs and brush up through which grow saplings and blackberry briars.

I finally manage the worst of it to arrive at Mountaintown Creek Trail, a trail used by both hikers and bikers. The going here is pleasant and I move along at a brisk pace. The new Pinhoti Trail will break off to the right after a while. I keep looking closely as I proceed—for more than a while. Sure enough, I've gone too far as I arrive at the Mountaintown Creek trailhead. Backtracking, I soon find a single red flag just off the trail. "Ahh, here it is," I'm thinking, but after an hour of climbing around and whacking my way up the ravine all the way to the ridgeline I'm unable to find a paint mark or flagline. Back to the trail beside Crenshaw Creek, I spend another hour combing the side of the trail all along and up the main ravine but I'm unable to get back on track. Finally, totally dejected and fatigued, I head for the trailhead again, and the road out. I have failed this day.

I soon pass houses on the Forest Service road to reach a gated barricade at Gates Chapel Road. Here a fellow from one of the residences just passed picks me up and hauls me into Ellijay.

I check into the Ellijay Inn, and after a good hot shower and a warm meal, I call my good friend, Hillrie Quin. I'm in luck. Hillrie is the prime mover in trail construction for the Pinhoti here in the Cohuttas. Plans are for he and another dear friend, Cynthia Crotwell, to come and get me in the morning, take me back, and get me going in the right direction again. I feel much better now. I'll be able to rest. All is not lost, for I'll be able (with the help of these dear friends) to hike this trail, the grand Georgia Pinhoti, a trail, much of which is yet to be built.

> *Do not go where the path may lead,*
> *go instead where there is no path and leave a trail.*
> (Ralph Waldo Emerson)

Sunday—November 26, 2000
Trail Day—185/2
Trail Mile—2971/21
Location—Springhead near Mulberry Gap, Georgia

Just after dawn, up one vehicle comes to my door, and in a while another. My friends have arrived. First order is to get the old jitney fueled up. It's a great breakfast—waffles, eggs, grits, the works, compliments of Hillrie. Then we're off.

It's pretty amazing how these trail-building folks know their way around these mountains. In no time at all I have not a clue where we are. We pass through a locked Forest Service road gate, but not the one I came out of yesterday. From here we descend, to slide all over the side of the mountain as we zig-zag down and around and back again. We eventually arrive at a small clearing. After parking and hiking the faintest of an unmarked trail down a spur and into a gap, here is the paint/flagline!

Says Hillrie, "Okay now, here's how this is going to work. You hike down this line to Crenshaw Creek where you passed yesterday; it's about a mile. That's the only way you'll find where the trail breaks off there. The final 100 yards were left unmarked intentionally. Then you turn around and hike back up the line. We'll wait for you here."

Good plan, sounds easy enough as I plunge in. Aww, but dang, what kind of a torture gauntlet have I gotten into? Now I see why my friends have waited, choosing not to go with me. Penetrating this continual jumbled maze of laurel, briars and blow downs is near impossible with a pack on, but down and through I beat it. This ravine, which forms Heddy Creek, is a narrow near-vertical slot plummeting down the mountainside. As I descend, climbing over, crawling under, and wriggling around, the thought presents that I'm somehow going to have to bust my way back up through this stuff. The going seems to take forever, but Cynthia's little beagle has come along for company, waiting patiently as I drag and fumble my way. I finally break out at Mountaintown Creek Trail some distance above where I had been looking yesterday. Hillrie was right, I never would have found it. I rest a while then turn reluctantly around to beat my way back up. This has to be the most difficult two miles of hiking that I've ever done, save perhaps the night hike while lost in Big Cypress during Odyssey '98.

I'm finally back to the little clearing where my friends are waiting. The plan is for Cynthia to drive out to Bear Creek trailhead while Hillrie and I hike along together. We're on Little Bear Creek Trail now. Soon the Georgia Pinhoti paint/flagline takes off again through the boonies. Here I bid farewell to Hillrie, as he continues on down Bear Creek Trail and I return to my bushwhack. Thanks, dear friends, for your time and for your help. Your kindness will remain in my memory.

After a successful day of following the paint/flagline I arrive late at the springhead above Mulberry Gap. I'm soaked, filthy, and totally exhausted, but I believe I've got the worst of this bushwhack behind me. As I pitch in the only flat spot I can find, the dished out little hollow of a huge old oak, I set my resolve to finishing this bushwhack. That's my aspiration, that's what consumes me now.

What an incredible day—my, what an incredible day!

Far away, there in the sunshine, are my highest aspirations.
I may not reach them, but I can...try to follow
where they may lead.
(Louisa May Alcott

Monday—November 27, 2000
Trail Day—186/3
Trail Mile—2982/33
Location—Woods road above Rock Creek to ADCO Motel, Chats-
worth, Georgia

The wind came up during the night, but the rain held off. The wind has proved a blessing, though driving cold, for the brush and foliage along the paint/flagline this morning has nearly dried.

I soon reach Mulberry Gap. Here I walk the road a short distance, then pick up the Forest Service boundary line that runs up and along Turkey Mountain. This I follow to SR-52 at Cohutta Overlook. So far, so good!

The paint/flagline soon leaves the highway to return to the precipitous sidehills that are the mark of these rugged Cohuttas. In a while, my ankles totally mushed out, I reach Tatum Lead, the Forest Service road that runs the ridge down to Baker Creek Ravine.

From here it's bushwhack time again. But here, also, is a mature stand of oak and pine most of the way. Over-canopies such as this prevent the kind of jumbled understory I've been constantly dealing with, and the bushwhack now is very pleasant. The old hunter/game trail down and along this gleeful and playful little brook will prove a delightful section of the Georgia Pinhoti Trail.

As I continue along, I reach for my compass to better get my bearing, but to my horror, it is gone. Somehow, climbing around and through the wall of brush today, I've managed to lose my compass. Oh my, this is not good. These mountains stand, plunge and reach for the heavens with absolutely no rhyme or reason as to their glorious plan, and here I stand, lost in a disoriented whirl, trying to figure out where I'm at—without a compass. I'm on a not-much-used Forest Service road. There is no paint, no flagging. I know I'm in the Rock Creek section of the Cohuttas. That much I do know, for just a ways back I passed a sign for Rock Creek ATV Trail where nearby were parked two USFS vehicles. I've gone a considerable distance now, and instinctively I sense I'm headed the wrong way. The sun is setting in the wrong place. I turn and hike back. By the trucks I meet Ricky, one of the USFS personnel. Being evening, he's headed home. He cannot help get me back on track, but he does offer a ride into Chatsworth where the USFS offices are located. What a stroke of luck (more a stroke of God's plan)! "You'll need to talk with Larry Taylor," says Ricky. So the plan is for me to meet with Larry tomorrow morning. Larry is the ranger that's been marking the trail through the Rock Creek section. Hopefully, he'll be able to get me straightened out. I figure there's less than six miles of this bushwhack remaining until I break out at Dennis to begin the roadwalk across the Great Valley to Dalton. I've come so far, *too* far to give it up now. As we bounce along, I comfort myself with the thought that I'll finish this bushwhack through these rugged Cohuttas just fine—tomorrow. That, too, is instinctive.

With this reassuring feeling, I check into the ADCO Motel for a grand night of rest. The day has turned cold, very cold, as I walk to Mom's Restaurant for supper. Oh, it's so good to be in where it's warm.

Trust instinct to the end,
even though you can give no reason.
(Emerson)

Tuesday—November 28, 2000
Trail Day—187/4
Trail Mile—3009/60
Location—Dalton, Georgia, to the home of Reverend George Owen,
Rocky Face

The USFS office here in Chatsworth is about a mile from the motel, so I'm up early for breakfast and the walk to their office. I arrive just as they open, but alas, Larry Thomas is out of town today. All here are very helpful though. Ranger Keith Wooster gets the maps out, and after a brief review we are able to determine where I got off track. He then offers to drive me back up the mountain. He'll take me right to where I missed the turn. Folks, isn't this hike absolutely and totally charmed! Of course it's no fun getting lost, but just at the moment when it looked the darkest, the whole thing turned right back around! Again, and as always—thank you, Lord, what a blessing.

On the way up the mountain Keith and I have an opportunity to talk about my hike, and about his career as a wildlife biologist with the USFS. I quickly learn that when Keith enters the woods, things look totally different to him than they do when the rest of us venture there. He talks about fire and how throughout history it's played such a major role in the life of the forest, before man began his meddling, and how the lack of natural burns affect the ever-changing balance of nature. I did not know, for instance, that when the small pine trees burn, they die, but when the small oak trees burn they just send up another shoot from a stronger and healthier root system. Keith points out, and I now notice, how the small white pines have literally taken over the forest floor. "They're just waiting for their opportunity, for an opening in the canopy to take off to the sky," he says. "Without fire, the oak will eventually be totally driven out; there will be no more oak as we know today. It will not happen in our lifetime, but it will happen. Think about the loss of these hardwood trees, and the effect that will have on the wildlife that depend on mast for their survival." "But we can't have wildfires; they're destructive," I respond in a defensive manner. And so, it is true that the forest will change, and not for the better, and there is little that man will do to stop it, for we aren't about to let Mother Nature go around burning Her forests wherever and whenever She feels like it. Fires are destructive! Ahh, but we can fix it, with programs like "prescribed burns." Man just keeps on tinkering—and meddling.

Keith drives me to where I should have turned yesterday. I'd trekked way past, heading the wrong way. Ah yes, instinct! He hands me a compass, then tells me, "Stay on that old woods road over there, till you see the paint and flags again, four or five miles; turn there." I know I'll have no problem with the last six miles of bushwhacking the Cohuttas. I bid Keith goodbye, get out, and make the turn where I should have made the turn yesterday, go 'round the barricade, and head on south. Thanks, Ricky; thanks, Keith!

The last mile of the "bushwhack" is really the only bushwhack that remains, which I'm easily able to follow, the blue paint and pink flagging being prominent. I beat it right through—to the paved road at Dennis. I've done it, the unbelievably rugged and incredible Cohutta bushwhack is behind me. I'm so relieved, for now the hike will be much easier, the going more predictable, more routine. Yet, as I rest here by the road, I ponder, for I know that I'll miss the challenge, the mystery, and the unknown of it that evokes that vital, truly vital, feeling of really being alive, that gets the adrenalin pumping and your head spinning. That is all gone now, behind me. I'll miss it.

What a drastic change here, perhaps the most dramatic of any, ever, in all my vagabond ramblings. Here, I come out of the cold, dark woods, from the hell-tangled bushwhack of it, into this hot, shimmering environment of the tarmac, with noise and racket all about—to begin a bang-out-the-miles, wide open roadwalk.

First, I shed my gloves and wool shirt, then don my sunglasses. Next, I dig out my hiker-trash painter's hat. After much pause and much searching, and many thanks, my head bowed, I get up and get moving—on down the road toward Dalton.

It takes a while to set my gait after being in the slow-going tangle for so long. The remainder of this day will be a long haul as I try reaching Dalton before dark, nearly a thirty-mile day. The weather has turned cooperative, with only a slight breeze to my back. The bright, warm sun feels good as I get up to speed, rolling right along. By three I know I've got the hike in the bag, and I cruise on in.

This has been a pleasant roadwalk, passing through rural Georgia countryside, along old secondary roads with beautifully fenced horse farms. I remember this hike well from Odyssey '98, very pleasant. At dusk I pull into Kroger's on the west end of Dalton just this side of I-75. I've a good friend here who's invited me to spend some time with him as I hike on south. Reverend George Owen is a near lifelong member of the Georgia Appalachian Trail Club, and has been a member of the Benton MacKaye Trail Association, probably since its inception. He has invited me, through my friend Carole Perry, to stay several nights at his home. And he's offered to shuttle me to and from the trail. I call George right away from Kroger. In just a while he comes to fetch me and we're off to his lovely home, the Methodist parsonage in the little village of Rocky Face.

I get settled in and cleaned up. This has been a very long hiking day; yet it has been a successful and productive hiking day. I'm totally "bushed." George senses my weariness and urges me go up and right to bed. There is no argument.

'twas once a mystical brotherhood,
In the depths of the forest wild,
A code unspoken, yet understood,
Where each was to each a child.

And so this spiritual fellowship,
Unshakable, firm and strong,
Shaped all things within its grip,
Throughout the forest throng.

In glad refrain they'd meet the day,
As they hearkened to Nature's will.
Content in their work and in their play,
To Her call, to each task, fulfill.

'twas not the least disharmony,
'twixt all this sociable clan.
Least that's the way it used to be,
'fore the meddling of master, man.

And so came he to this magic place,
No matter he shouldn't or should.
Now all that's left is sad disgrace,
To that mystical brotherhood.
(N. Nomad)

Wednesday—November 29, 2000
Trail Day—188/5
Trail Mile—3027/78
Location—Trailhead at Snake Creek Gap to the home of Reverend
George Owen, Rocky Face, Georgia

What a grand night's sleep in such a comfortable home. I've got the whole upstairs suite to myself, a very large bedroom with sitting area and private bath. George is obviously delighted to have my company, and we share good conversation as he shuttles me back to Kroger. I'm out and going by nine.

From Kroger I continue west on Walnut Avenue, crossing I-75, then to climb Dug Mountain. Near the communication towers on the upper ridge, I see my first Pinhoti Trail marker. This is my fifth day on the Pinhoti Trail, and I'm just now seeing my first blaze. In my past ramblings, I've hiked many a long stretch between blazes, wondering if I were still on the trail. But five days, I believe, is about the longest stretch.

The Armuchees are totally different mountains, nothing like the Cohuttas, for here are there long, straight, orderly ridges running in near-parallel fashion for miles, not the jumble-upon-jumble as were the Cohuttas. Experts tell us they've got all this geology stuff figured out, but I don't know. To me, it's all just a mystery, a mystery that someday will be revealed to all of us. I'm on Rocky Face Mountain now, hiking effortlessly for miles along this long, level ridge. In a while the trail drops from Rocky Face to climb the next ridge and along I go again on Hurricane Mountain. Then it's off again and up and onto Middle Mountain, and yet another descent followed by another ascent, and along I go again on the ridge of Mill Creek Mountain. By early afternoon I'm at Swamp Creek Gap, where I'm soon greeted by George, who has come out to shuttle me back to his home in the little village of Rocky Face.

I'm not near as beat today and have really worked up an appetite, so after a hot, soothing shower, George and I are off to Shoney's for the AYCE buffet. Oh yes, I hurt myself, but then I have a great tolerance for pain. Another great hiking day. Another great evening. Thanks, George!

If we could push ajar the gates of life,
And stand within, and all God's workings see,
We could interpret all this doubt and strife,
And for each mystery could find a key.
(Mary Riley Smith)

Thursday—November 30, 2000
Trail Day—189/6
Trail Mile—3043/94
Location—East Armuchee Road to the home of Reverend George
Owen, Rocky Face, Georgia

I hear George moving about a little before seven, so I head down to join him for breakfast, a heaping bowl of corn flakes topped with blueberries and scoops of sugar, washed down with plenty of orange juice and coffee.

The hike today is a leisurely sixteen miles. With George getting me on trail by eight-thirty, I'll have no problem finishing by three. That'll give me time to rest and work on my email while I wait for George to retrieve me at four.

There's more ridge-walking today, along Horn and Johns Mountains, interrupted by a descent, then a steep climb beside the lovely Keown Falls. Here the Pinhoti follows an intricate system of rock steps, climbing and twisting to finally emerge at an observation deck right next the falls. From this vantage can be seen the far ridges and peaks all about. Nearby is The Pocket, a naturally protected cove. Looking down into The Pocket, I can see the last vestiges of fall. Here in these gentle hills, one will not find roaring waterfalls, gaping ravines, towering sharptops, or vast expansive vistas. Here the mountains can be embraced, much as holding someone dear. They're not awesome, aloof, or forbidding, as seems many of the mightiest mountain places are. Here, there is a feeling of gentle kindness, much as a familiar childhood feeling; like the bygone times with all one's family about; like being with Grandma and Grandpa. That's what these timeless mountains are all about to me—like being with dear family and friends. These are peaceful, gentle-loving, and graceful mountains; these are my mountains, my home, the Blue Ridge Mountains of Georgia. I sit, totally content. I'm not alone, for I have beside me this veil-like wisp of whispering, falling waters, such a happy and gentle little friend. It is my companion, just for a while, bringing deep inner warmth, much as the sun now warms me within. What an idyllic, peaceful place. Blessed is he who can hear, feel and see, and understand the majesty.

The trail works around and down Johns Mountain, through the pleasant pungency that is fall in the southern hardwood coves, to finally emerge at East Armuchee Road. From here there is a short roadwalk to Manning Mill Road, where George will come for me.

I find a spot where the sun has warmed the grassy road bank, to drop my pack and then to recline against it. Comes now time to reflect on the blessings sent my way this day. And does the sedative sun work so quickly, sending me away to the land of nod.

The crunch of gravel and the squeak of brakes bring me back to the corner of East Armuchee and Manning Mill Roads. George has come for me. As I journey further south, the ride back north to George's home becomes longer. But we have come to enjoy each other's company, for it seems we have much in common (not the least of which is our age) and we chatter our way along. George permits me to treat him to supper again, my choice—Pizza Hut! George goes for the salad bar and spaghetti dinner and I manage to put away a medium pan pizza. No yogurt or skimmed milk tonight, George. I've also been salting George's console drink holder with Nutrageous bars and peanut M&Ms, which continue to vanish. I think I'm a bad influence on the Reverend!

I live to hold communion
With all that is divine.
To feel there is a union
'twist Nature's heart and mine.
(George Linnæus Banks)

Friday—December 1, 2000
Trail Day—190/7
Trail Mile—3043/94
Location—Home of Reverend George Owen, Rocky Face, Georgia

I burn a day today. On the trail it's called a "zero-mile" day. And what a perfect place to rest, for is this place, this lovely home, such a peaceful, restful place. What a blessing to be warm and dry and clean! George is here for just a while this morning and then he's gone. I've never thought about folks that serve in the ministry as actually having "jobs." Indeed, for all who pursue that path, it is a faith-filled labor of love. But today, for Reverend George Owen, it would seem more one of labor, for this day I would not want this pastor's job. It all has to do with a member of his congregation, a member who has been deathly ill, who has been sent home to live out his remaining short time, aided by hospice—and by prayer. In forced words, Reverend Owen said to me yesterday, "I must be nearby, for I may be called at any time." The call has come, and he must go.

I'm hopelessly delinquent in my correspondence and way behind in my daily journal entries. I spend the entire day in a desperate attempt to regain some ground. By late afternoon I've nearly banged the keys off my little PocketMail, but I have managed to get nearly current and I'm feeling better about the whole ordeal.

George has been in and out. He has somehow found time to tend to my needs, first taking me by the post office to get my bounce box mailed, then later bringing me carryout for supper. Oh, and peach ice cream. Would you believe George has Breyers peach ice cream for me? George, you are a peach! What a glorious, restful day—just what the minister ordered.

> *Choose a job you love,*
> *and you will never have to work a day in your life.*
> (Confucius)

Saturday—December 2, 2000
Trail Day—191/8
Trail Mile—3060/111
Location—US-27 at Mack White Gap to Summerville Motel, Sum-
merville, Georgia. Mickey Patel, proprietor.

George's plans were to depart Dalton yesterday evening to spend time at his cabin near Blue Ridge, and perhaps, just perhaps, get in a little hiking. But those plans have long since been dashed, for now there are funeral preparations to tend to and members of his congregation with whom he must spend time and to whom he must now minister. We have a quick breakfast, and George has me back to the trail at Manning Mill Road by eight-thirty. It's such a joyful time making new friends, always a joyful time, but such a sad and agonizing time, it seems, when the time comes to say goodbye. And that time has come. We linger. For George, I recite the words to "Why Go" (shared in this book's epilogue). And for me, George says a prayer for my continued good health and safe passage. Goodbye, my friend and thanks, thanks for your kindness, for the giving of your precious time, for your generosity, and for your friendship, especially, and most of all, for your friendship.

I no sooner hit the trail than I hear gunfire. This is Saturday, a very fine Saturday, and the deer hunters are out in force. I don't believe I could intentionally dress to look more like a deer if I tried, with my fawn-colored pack and white headband with trailing tails. I did, however, have the good sense to listen to George's wise suggestion, to accept his offer to take along his orange vest. With more gunshots ringing out now, I stop and put on the vest!

The trail today follows dirt roads, paved secondary roads, grassy woods roads, and recently bulldozed sidehill trail. The hiking is all very pleasant, except for the recently bulldozed sidehill trail. I hike this bulldozed section totally and absolutely perplexed. I can't

understand how the Forest Service can be so concerned and so particular about what may be disturbed as a result of cutting new treadway, yet when the go-ahead is finally given, to bring in a bulldozer to
hack away what seems half the mountainside! The resulting new trail
here today is actually wide enough to drive my 4x4 pickup through
from one end to the other. Trees that have not been plowed away,
that are still standing beside the trail, are all bleeding from being
banged and skinned to death by the machinery. It's all an entirely
glorious mess, an abomination. That's what it is, an abomination! I
don't understand it; I just don't understand it. I know beauty is all
around, but it is difficult to see it here.

Two hunters come off the ridge and join me as I hike along.
They're calling it a day, heading back for their wheels. The forecast is
for rain to come in, turning to snow tonight. And until just a while
ago this day had been bright and sunshiny. But the sky has been
slowly a-darkin' over, a breeze is coming up, and it's turning cold.
As we hasten along, both fellows lament as to how great this area
used to be for deer hunting. That was until this road we're on now
was cut in and the area was timbered. Both seem to be in a funk, so I
reminded them that just because they didn't get a deer, that the day
wasn't *shot*.

As I near the end of my hiking day, a short distance remaining
to US-27, comes a fellow 'round the bend. I recognize him right
away; it's Reverend Owen! "I just had to get in a little hiking this
weekend—somehow!" he exclaims with the biggest, brightest smile.
Well, does the joy on this end of this hiking day make up for the
sadness on the other. "Come on George, let's hike!"

We soon reach the trailhead, and George loads me up and drives
me to the Summerville Motel a ways up the road. He no sooner
drops me off and I get checked in than the rain begins. I'm blessed
again to be out of this cold, wet mess. I've still a very long way to go,
and wet and cold can really get to wearing. In the evening, as I open
the door and take a gander, the snow begins. I retreat to the warmth

of my little room, count my blessings this day, say my prayers, and hit the hay.

> *God hides things by putting them all around us.*
> (Anonymous)

Sunday—December 3, 2000
Trail Day—192/9
Trail Mile—3093/144
Location—Creekside Inn, Cave Spring, Georgia

The snow continues throughout the night, but it has little luck sticking. This morning only the foliage and the vehicles out front are dressed in white. I head for the gas station deli down the road, where I put away three tenderloin/scrambled egg biscuits. I also knock a good dent in their coffee. Back in the room, I finally get all my gear in my pack and fret my way out and into it a little before eight.

As I cross to the northbound side of US-27, the snow begins again. The day remains dark from the low-swirling gloom, and vehicles fling their trailing little storms at me as they pass. Surprisingly, my third thumb-out is a hookup, as this fellow skids to the emergency lane. He's glad to have my company. The guy drives sixty miles to and from work every day, including Sundays, a 120-mile round trip. He seems happy and content, though. Hustles cars, whatever that job is—didn't ask him. He's an Ichabod Crane type, his Adam's apple moving up and down three inches every time he swallows. Would like to have spent more time with him, but we're soon to the gap and the trail. God bless you mister. Sure wouldn't want your life, not for love or money, no-siree-bob!

As I climb from Mack White Gap, ascending to Taylors Ridge, the magic begins. With each increase in elevation is there

an accompanying and ever-increasing blanket of snow, first a scattering here and there, then an inch or so, and finally near the ridge, a half-foot everywhere. I've never seen snow so fluffy yet so sticky. The fluff is sticking to everything, even the bark on the trees. Before me is an absolute wonderland of pure white. As the snow continues, the gloom of the day continues, but all around is there such an intense monochromatic brightness and beauty. Even the tangle of blowdowns and brush are sights to behold, their usual gnarly features transformed by the unmistakable qualities of provocation and beauty into nothing less than artistic masterpieces. My camera is flashing, the shutter clicking in every direction.

The trail rises before me, a pure ribbon of white, and as I glide along it seems to become the elusive and ever-sought pathway to Heaven. There are no burdens to pull me down this day, not mental, not physical. I'm free of pain, free of strife, free to fly untethered, unbound. Ahh, it's like "Sprouting Wing!"

An earthbound mystery...
The strangest thing;
Backpack up, the closer we
To sprouting wing.
(N. Nomad)

Down from the mountain now, down from the magic of the day, the trail continues along a rail trail section. The old railbed has been recently graded and from the rains of yesterday, patched with mud. As I try moving along, I grow taller with each step as the mud builds on my shoes. I finally give up, kick the mud, and move over to continue on a roadwalk along the busy highway shoulder.

As I progress I realize that I'm making remarkably good time today. Cave Spring is still eighteen miles south, but by continuing at my present pace, I can be there by evening. So continue the pace I do, and continue on I go. Temperatures are predicted to drop to the low twenties tonight, possibly more snow. I'll choose a warm bed over the cold, hard ground every time. Cave Spring, here I come!

The Georgia Pinhoti Trail goes through Rome, Georgia. Why, I have not a clue. There's an alternate blue-blazed route mapped out to the west that goes along and through rural countryside. I've come to the trail to escape the oppressive clash and grind of the city. I actually considered hiking in there but quickly concluded it was a dumb idea. Hiking through Rome would have involved an extra day of roadwalking through a dangerously congested area, for no apparent reason. I'll take the bypass, thank you very much!

I keep hammering the miles right into the twilight, finally arriving in the little trail town of Cave Spring by seven-thirty, a thirty-four mile day. I check into the Creekside Motel, totally bushed. Cave Spring has a number of restaurants, but they're all closed Sunday evening. So I run some hot tap water over my ramen noodles, fix a cheese sandwich, take a long, hot, bone-soothing shower, and hit the sack. This has been a tiring day but a great hiking day.

A people who climb the ridges and sleep under the stars
in high mountain meadows, who enter the forest and scale peaks,
who...walk ridges buried in...snow—these people will give their
country some of the indomitable spirit of the mountains.
(William O. Douglas)

Monday—December 4, 2000
Trail Day—193/10
Trail Mile—3093/144
Location—Creekside Inn, Cave Spring, Georgia

Cave Spring is a trail town lover's delight. If the post office were a little closer in, and if they kept other than banker's hours, the little berg would be darn near perfect! So I decide, after very little pondering, to burn a day and stay over. I need time to write, and a little rest will be a blessing.

It's still dark at seven, but the lights are on at Gray Horse and the klatch of locals are already at their usual table. I get a warm welcome from the waitress and a hot cup of coffee right away. Then it's a three-egg load-er-up omelet, a large bowl of grits, and a biscuit with a boat of gravy! Two more cups of coffee to wash it all down, and I'm set till lunch.

The local library is just off the square. I head over to get online—two computers and they're both available, how about that! Later, as I walk the old downtown, the day is warming nicely and the sun feels so good. Haven't been off the trail a day and I'm already missing it.

Back in my room, I have a long talk with myself about getting busy and being productive. The little pep talk works and I launch right in, writing up a storm, right through to bedtime. As the sandman comes along, it dawns on me—I'll put another state behind me tomorrow. This dream of a southbound TA/ECT thru-hike is coming true.

*All our dreams can come true—if we have
the courage to pursue them.*
(Walt Disney)

Tuesday—December 5, 2000
Trail Day—194/11
Trail Mile—3110/154
Location—US-278 to Lamont Motel, Piedmont, Alabama

At the Gray Horse, a full stack of pancakes and a side of grits are the order this morning, and of course, lots of coffee. I can hike very well on pancakes or waffles. Greasy foods like bacon or sausage give me a problem. Hitting the trail on a really full stomach doesn't work for me. It's kind of like going out running after a big meal, not good. And no, I don't run on the trail, although I have certainly been accused!

The last two miles of trail in Georgia are over private land belonging to Temple Inland. Negotiations are underway to secure sanctions to cross their land. I bushwhacked over Indian and Flagpole Mountains and then crossed their property during Odyssey '98. The real problem now is that these lands are leased for hunting, and it's deer hunting season! I dearly want to follow this same route, bushwhacking the last two miles into Alabama, but at the same time I don't want to compromise or muck up the relations and negotiations now underway between the Georgia Pinhoti Trail Association folks and Temple Inland. I've thought about just doing a roadwalk clear around, but that's out of the question. The temptation is just too great. I want to follow the planned and hopefully soon-to-be sanctioned and dedicated trail route. I know my way through, so it shouldn't take more than an hour or so to cover the two-mile bushwhack, so I finally decide to stealth my way. Maybe not a very sound or good idea, but that's my plan.

So I'm off this morning with a pretty unsettled, tentative feeling about the whole thing, hoping, this being Tuesday morning and a very cold one, that almost all the deer hunters are at work, and that I'll have the place to myself. In fact, that's just as it works out. When I arrive, there are no vehicles at the Temple Inland gate. When I enter to hike the old road a short distance to where the bushwhack begins, there is no one about! The bushwhack takes me fifty-seven minutes to reach the state line/time change cairn that I built in '98. Here I leave a little note for Marty Dominy and all his great trail building crew. Thank you folks (and thank you Lord). It was a risky, foolish, and potentially compromising move, but it worked.

The remainder of the day is literally downhill to US-278, with the exception of two "steep ascents" as described in the trail data, at which I chuckle.

The fourth thumb-out is a hookup, as a local stops to haul me to Lamont Motel in Piedmont. With the time change I'm in at two-thirty! I'm very tired, totally pooped, all from the emotional energy spent.

> *You are not a fool just because you have done something foolish,*
> *only if the folly of it escapes you.*
> (Jim Fiebig)

THE GRAND CONNECTION ALABAMA PINHOTI TRAIL (APT)

Wednesday—December 6, 2000
Trail Day—195/1
Trail Mile—3129/29
Location—Near Lookout Tower, Dugger Mountain, Alabama

I'm up and out by seven. Moving into Central Time is going to take some getting used to. It's still dark as I head for Waffle House about half a mile up the road. I count my blessings for being out of the cold for the night as I hasten along, stuffing my hands in my pockets and hunching my shoulders to block the cold. Two waffles set adrift in syrup and butter, a side of grits, and lots of coffee, and I'm stoked for the day. Last stop, the supermarket for provisions for two days, as I'll be pitching in the woods through the Dugger Mountain Wilderness.

There's little traffic passing the light where US-278 turns and heads for the mountains, but in less than half an hour I'm offered a ride all the way to the trailhead. I'm hiking south again by nine.

The Alabama Pinhoti lets me have it today with two good, hard, steady pulls, the first up Augusta Mine Ridge and the second up and around Dugger Mountain. Folks just look at me with puzzled expressions when I tell them about the rugged, remote mountains of Alabama. Oh yes, I'm in them today!

The day warms nicely. I'm finally able to remove my wool shirt and heavy gloves.

As the day comes to an end, the trail side-slabs around Dugger, then follows beside a jagged, rocky ridge. As twilight descends, I break from the trail and climb to the rocks. Here I find a calm, sheltered spot among the boulders and settle in for the evening. As night falls, the valleys below on either side come to life with thousands of flickering, twinkling dots of light—from Piedmont and far beyond. Above, the stars are there for the plucking. Winter skies can shine so clear and beautiful!

> *In winter the stars seem to have rekindled their fires,*
> *the moon achieves a fuller triumph,*
> *and the heavens wear a look of a more exalted simplicity.*
> (John Burroughs)

Thursday—December 7, 2000
Trail Day—196/2
Trail Mile—3145/45
Location—Laurel Trail Shelter, Alabama

I had hoped, by pitching on the very ridge, that in the morning should the sun be out and not blocked by clouds or the mountain, my tent would warm in its radiance. And so, as the sun comes to my little tent, its innards (and me), indeed are warmed, and I'm thankful for how this day begins. Though it is still very cold, my water bottle frozen nearly solid, I'm able to break camp and get my pack organized before my fingers poke like so many sticks.

Today the trail settles down as I hike into rolling, open woods roofed by a canopy of tall, mature, and majestic long-leaf pine. In some places these monarchs stand in groves so grand. How they've avoided being timbered I know not, but I know that I'm truly thankful for their stately presence.

It is late morning now and as I glide along, my sticks propelling me through the rustling leaves in a near-trance, I see another hiker approaching. I hesitate, falter, then nearly collapse in total glee; for here, coming toward me, is my very dear friend Mark Lee Van Horn. I'd sent him a hastily written email, inviting him to come out with me for a few days, but I held little hope he'd be able to make it on such short notice. But here he is. What a joy, what a true joy! After many moments of happy exchange, Mark Lee turns to hike along with me, and we continue on together through the grove of towering pine. Later in the day we enter, then pass a recent burn-over—very recent. There is much smoke and many burning and tumbling snags. An eerie, scary sight. It seems so strange to me at times that one moment Mother Nature can be so gentle and pleasant, the next so reckless and brutal!

We arrive at Laurel Shelter along with the cold of the evening, but I'm warmed by a delightful fire and the very best of company.

Life is short and we have never too much time for gladdening
the hearts of those who are traveling the...journey with us.
(Henri Frëdëric Amiel)

Friday—December 8, 2000
Trail Day—197/3
Trail Mile—3161/61
Location—FS-500 at Railroad Trailhead to Howard Johnson
Express Inn, Heflin, Alabama

In the shelter, the night didn't seem as cold, but the water bladder that Mark Lee left parked on the picnic table managed to accumulate plenty of ice. The day has dawned clear. Should we be fortunate enough to have a rerun of yesterday, it will warm up nicely by late morning.

The plan is for Mark Lee to hike back out to his car, a distance of about twelve miles, then to drive to the trailhead near Heflin and hike in to meet me. We wish each other good hiking and are off in opposite directions. The day indeed stays sunny, turning warm, and I'm soon able to shed my heavy gloves and wool shirt. As I near Lower Shoal Shelter I'm filled with anticipation. Meg and Rachel, two northbound hikers Lee and I had met yesterday, knew immediately who I was from messages left in the shelter register here. But they wouldn't tell me what the messages were. So I rush to drop my pack, hurrying to find out.

Oh yes, both entries are from great hiking friends! The first is from *Retread*, a kind gentlemen who I met and who also thru-hiked the AT in '98. He's been down here hiking the Pinhoti Trail in Alabama. Knowing I'd be coming through he's left words of encouragement for me. Thanks, *Retread*! The other great friend is *Spur*. I met him in Hot Springs, North Carolina, earlier this year. He was passing through on his second northbound AT thru-hike, and I was there as a guest speaker for Trailfest, a celebration for thru-hikers now in its third year. We shared a room at Elmer Hall's great place, Sunnybank Inn, and while we were together there, *Spur* was full of questions about the other trails north and south of the AT, trails that combine to form the TA. Turns out I poisoned him good! For when he reached Katahdin, successfully completing yet another AT thru-hike, he just kept on going—over the Knife Edge and Pamola, down into Roaring Brook and on north out of Baxter State Park, clear to the Cliffs of Forillon at Cap Gaspé, Québec Province, Canada. He then returned to complete his thru-hike o'er the Trail of the Ancients from Flagg Mountain just north of Montgomery, back to Springer, reaching there in the same half-foot of snow I tramped through coming from the north, becoming the fourth person to succeed in this unbelievable trek. So here is a great entry from *Spur*, discussing his happy time on the trail and thanking me for sending him along that path. Also written here are thoughtful words of encouragement, words to lift me up and propel me along as I near the completion of this, the first southbound thru-hike o'er such a remarkable trail, the Trail of the Ancients! I linger here for the longest time, in the warmth of the sun and in the warmth of the kind expressions left for me by these two dear friends. The blessings keep coming in so many ways, so many wonderful and remarkable ways. Thank you, dear friends, and thank you, Lord!

Rounding a bend, one of many this day, I find Mark Lee reclined on a soft carpet of pine needles at a grand overlook—sound asleep! He has hiked back from the trailhead to meet me, already completing a fifteen-mile day. What a fine place to pull up and wait my arrival.

It's a short hike back to Mark Lee's car at the Heflin trailhead, and we chatter and laugh, having a joyful time of it. Mark Lee then treats me to pizza before depositing me at the Howard Johnson Inn down by I-20. What a grand time with you, dear friend. Thanks for taking off from your busy schedule to come and hike with this lonely old man. I sure hope to see you and to have the pleasure of hiking with you again soon!

Three dear friends, *Retread, Spur,* and Mark Lee, all filled with wanderlust, and like the old *Nomad*, all of them "...lost, to the dust outward blow." We will all hike together. There will come that day.

But we'll rove these woods and mountainsides,
A-waitin' that by-and-by.
A perfect dawn, when packs take wing,
And the treadway climbs the sky.
(N. Nomad)

Saturday—December 9, 2000
Trail Day—198/4
Trail Mile—3176/76
Location—CR-24 south of Five Points to the home of Philip and
Margaret Wade, Waldo, Alabama

I wait patiently in my room this morning for the lady who is to pick me up and shuttle me back to the trail. I met her here at the motel last night. She said, "If I don't come to get you, my husband will; one of us will take you back." She even called my room this morning to tell me she was running about twenty minutes late. That was an hour ago. So here I sit now, trying with all diligence, trying to exercise patience, but patience isn't going to get it done this morning. The lady just isn't coming. So with this realization slowly sinking in, I turn to the labor of improving yet another virtue: tolerance. I find that by shifting from the reflexive thoughts that bring anger to more compassionate thoughts that bring genuine concern, that my level of tolerance rises sharply. Of concern now is the real possibility that some intervening emergency or other unfavorable circumstance has prevented her from coming for me.

I shoulder my pack, depart the motel, and head up the road. I'm now filled with the urgency of getting back to the trail, to my planned hike for today, a hike of fifteen miles, then to meet Maggie Wade, my good friend from Waldo who will be coming to pick me up at CR-24 at four.

I've my bounce box to mail ahead, and as I hike to the post office, the box under my arm, this van pulls to the side. The driver comes right around, greets me and places a folded bill in my hand. Before I'm able to respond, he says, "I'll give you a ride; where do you need to go?" I can't believe this. It's all happened so fast. I nearly break down as I respond to his kind offer, finally managing to blurt, "Yes, I can use a lift. I need to go to the post office, and then back to the Skyway overpass. But, oh please mister, I can't take your money."

He puts his hand on my arm to calm me. As his wife moves to the back with their children, he gently directs me toward his van. "We'll take you to the post office and then wherever you need to go," he says. Riding along and now here at the post office, I glance at the bill I'm clutching in my hand. There's a strange appearance about it. At the counter, and as the postal clerk weighs my box I open the folded bill part way to see revealed the number, 10. "That'll be four-sixty," he says. I pop the bill open to hand to him. That's when I realize, as the clerk looks at the bill, then at me, with puzzlement—that the kind man waiting patiently out front has given me a one-hundred dollar bill! The clerk continues his quizzical expression as I refold it, put it in my pocket, then to fumble for my wallet.

The family has waited patiently for me, like there was nothing more important for them to do this day than to cater to my needs. We're soon shimmying and shaking our way down the road. The old van is shot, the front end is gone, the springs are collapsed; it leans to one side. The windshield's cracked. The side window is flopping open. The seats are inside out. It needs new tires. It's burning oil. I plead with the man, his wife and children, "It's nearly Christmas. Please, folks, I'm so very grateful and thankful for what you have done. You are so kind. But, please, PLEASE keep this money for your family. You have so many needs." I shove the bill back toward him. He turns to look at me, and then gives a glance back at his wife and children. He looks back quickly to the road, then turns to once more look at me intently, "We want to share what we have with you, we will do just fine this Christmas." Another quick look to the road and he turns again to his wife and children, and together, all heads nod "yes" with him. I pull my hand back sheepishly and drop my head. I cannot think of what to say. Soon, we are at the trailhead. As I'm handed my pack and hiking sticks, I look on this beautiful family one last time. I'm at a loss for words. As they pull away, somehow I manage a feeble "thanks again."

This whole miraculous experience has taken less than twenty minutes, from the time I was stumbling along filled with worry about this day, till now, as I stand in total bewilderment, waving goodbye. I'm totally dumbstruck. My head and heart are spinning, in what I can best describe as free-fall. As I listen to the old van rattle away, I try composing and settling myself. But comes over me now an almost convulsive feeling, much as would be driven by a troubled and damning conscience. "Settle down, settle down," I try pathetically, attempting to reassure myself, "you have a very firm grasp on what is right and what is wrong. You were taught right and wrong early on by your parents, it's in you, it's your upbringing." But my gut tells me it was wrong to accept the money. That's when my heart butts in, telling me that "...it was not only good to accept the money, but it was *right*." My gut fires back, "Shame on you, shame, shame, you have fooled these gentle, caring people, how dare you do that!" My heart yells, "No, NO! The good was ever-so-much more the *giving* than the *receiving*; that is what really matters." But my conscience keeps struggling with it. "Why did you accept this money, you should have refused it. You don't need their money— that family *needed* their money!"

As I hike along, through the ups and downs of Horseblock Mountain, I continue frustrating the entire while. I finally decide to believe what my heart's been telling me, and to ignore the wrenching gut reaction that so overwhelmed me earlier. That's when conscience steps up to the plate to take one more swing at me; "You're just taking the easy way out, you jerk!" is what I hear from this not-so-wee-little voice. Aww, now I've got conscience siding with wrenching gut. "Okay, okay, time out here." I finally manage. "Listen to this." I come back, as I attempt to maintain a modicum of control over the moment. After finally settling down, one more time, I tell the two, "Listen, let me lay something out for you; if you don't buy it, then we'll back up and start over."

And so, as I hasten along now toward my appointed rendezvous at CR-24, I'll begin an attempt to make some sense out of (and perhaps begin to unravel) the elusive and puzzling mystery behind the question so oft asked—"Why Go?"

With conscience and wrenching gut's attention, I continue: "Can we all agree on something?" I ask. "Let me throw this out. This is really nothing more than a basic truism; can we all agree that it is indeed more blessed to give than to receive?" "Yes," is their reply. Okay, so far, so good. "This being true," I continue, "isn't it then a fact that, if giving is the way to go, there's got to be somebody out there on the receiving end?" Pause. No reply. I think we're getting somewhere. "Stay with me now." I go on. "How about, if perchance, there exists a mission for certain of us, that mission being the task of serving as vessels set about specifically to receive?" I've got their total attention now. This is sinking in. "Well, here's a thought," I offer. "This just might shed a little light on the whole age-old quandary (perhaps a partial answer at least) to that question we're constantly asked, that we don't want to be asked (because we don't have a clue to the answer), that question being—Why Go?" Another short pause. "Okay, now, think a minute. Is this not a pure purpose, an honorable calling, to go among the people as a receptive vessel for the good of giving, to be the means whereby humankind all about might gain insight into the joy that is the very act of giving, wherein, and in no small way, each instantly prospers by gaining the realization, the knowledge, that they're endowed with that true goodness that dwells down deep within each of us, that dwells within all of mankind!" Ahha, everybody's calm, everybody's quiet!

As I calculate my probable arrival time at CR-24, I'm relieved to find that I've plenty of time. In fact, there's enough time today for me to hike the half-mile along the highway from where the trail crosses US-431, to Five Points, and Spear's Store. Once there, I fill up on sweet rolls and hot coffee.

In '98, I got lost numerous times, having one heck of a go of it through this section, but the trail is now clearly blazed, the treadway well defined, and I'm making great progress. About a mile before CR-24 I see a hiker coming toward me. I recognize Maggie Wade immediately, and we share a grand time hiking back to her car.

Maggie and Philip have a lovely home, an old place that Philip has renovated and added to over the years. I no sooner get settled in than Maggie has the table set and our evening meal prepared and waiting. The Wades have offered to shuttle me for the next two days, bringing me back each evening to their cozy, warm home.

This has been a miraculous day, full of revelation and blessings, and now with the Wades, do the blessings continue...

> *Charity never humiliated him who profited from it,*
> *nor ever bound him by the chains of gratitude,*
> *since it was not to him but to God that the gift was made.*
> (Antoine de Saint-Exupery)

Sunday—December 10, 2000
Trail Day—199/5
Trail Mile—3189/89
Location—SR-281/Talladega Scenic Drive, Cheaha State Park,
Alabama, to the home of Philip and Margaret Wade, Waldo

This is going to be a short, enjoyable day, for I'll not be hiking alone but will be accompanied the entire way by Jay Hudson, a dear friend from Birmingham, and Maggie Wade, with whom I've been staying.

Maggie drives me to the trailhead at Cheaha State Park, where we meet Jay. We'll leave his vehicle here and drive around to where the trail crosses CR-24. They'll then join me in my hike as I continue south, and we'll have wheels at the trailhead when we end the hike this evening.

As we begin, things are pretty much socked in, the weather iffy. But the rain that has been forecast holds off and we're able to share a very enjoyable time together.

Both Maggie and Jay love the outdoors, both are strong hikers, and both are members of the Birmingham Sierra Club. Jay is the president of the Cahaba Chapter. Both are also very keen on conservation and the importance of hiking trails and how they fit into the scheme of things, especially as to their importance in accentuating the need for preserving not only trail corridors but also entire viewsheds. We talk much about all of this as we hike along, about the future of trails in Alabama, and especially about an "Alabama Thru-Trail," a trail connecting not only the Alabama Pinhoti to the AT, but a trail also extending south to the Conecuh National Forest on the border of Alabama and Florida, thus making possible a link-up with the Florida Trail, which runs for over a thousand miles.

We end the day in a shroud of clouds and mist at Cheaha, from here to enjoy a pleasant and memorable evening of dining at the beautiful Cheaha Lodge Restaurant. Then it's back to the Wade's home where Philip is waiting. Jay and I are treated to dessert as we continue the social aspect of the day, which lasts well into the evening.

Thanks, dear friends, for coming out and hiking with me today; and thanks Jay, for preparing maps to get me on through to Flagg Mountain!

Good company in a journey makes the way seem the shorter.
(Izaak Walton)

Monday—December 11, 2000
Trail Day—200/6
Trail Mile—3207/107
Location—FS-600/Skyway Motorway at Clairmont Gap, Alabama, to the home of Philip and Margaret Wade, Waldo

Another grand night with the Wades. They're such gracious and thoughtful hosts, treating me with kindness usually reserved for and extended only to family and the very dearest of friends. I have really enjoyed being with Philip. He recently completed a cross-country bike trek, and I've taken much enjoyment in listening as he tells of his remarkable adventure. As he relates his stories, I'm taken by the similarities between our respective odysseys: the experiences, the trail (road) angels and their magic, the day-to-day pain and fatigue, the ravenous appetites and accompanying weight loss, the loneliness, and the monotony—then exhilaration, which add spice to the mix. Philip has hung his bike up for now, literally; it's hanging by a hook on their porch, but he plans to get back into riding/training again soon. So, although our ways have been very different, taking us over dissimilar paths, there is much we have in common, much we can share and understand about the grand mystery of it all.

Maggie told me that Philip is not always the early riser, but he's up ahead of me this morning, preparing coffee and a great breakfast. Maggie is out and gone to teach the children at the Talladega School for the Deaf, lugging along maps and other data from which to make copies to help me along as I hike on past the southern terminus of the Alabama Pinhoti.

Philip has me back on Cheaha Mountain in good order at nine-thirty. The Wades have once again offered to shuttle me to their home this evening, so Maggie will come to get me around four at Clairmont Gap. It's such a joy not having to make and break camp in this cold, rainy, snowy weather. If not for the Wades, I would be sleeping on the hard, frozen ground and carrying a much heavier pack loaded with food. As I bid farewell to Philip, I insist that he and Maggie permit me the pleasure of treating them to supper out this evening.

The ridge south of Cheaha is rocky and rugged, a designated wilderness area, the trail following and meandering along with and at times within feet of precipitous cliffs. The weather is much as it was during my journey through in '98—near-freezing cold, cloudy, no visibility. My hopes of getting a view from McDill Point are quickly dashed. Also dashed is me, for I no sooner get in the boulder field than I take a terrible tumble in the rocks. A wet, leaf-covered, off-camber slickery sends me flying out of control. It happens so quickly, so it seems is the case with most off-loads. As I bump along and down I manage to keep my pack between me and the rocks for the first bouncing ricochet. Then I career off my right hip, striking my right leg with a thud against a sharply angled boulder, to finally come to rest. One of my trekking poles is wedged between the rocks, my arm now fiddle-string tight to the wrist sling. That's what actually stops me. After getting some slack and uncuffing my wrist, I cautiously and prayerfully run damage control. I'm relieved to find no blood spurting or anything broken. There is, however, a deep throbbing pain in my right leg just above my knee. Getting upright in this jumble of boulders is not easy, but I finally manage by shedding my pack and rolling over on one knee. I quickly conclude that I'm very fortunate not to have suffered serious injury, and I thank the Lord and count my blessings once more.

I manage to shoulder my pack, get my gloves back on, adjust my sticks and head on down the trail. I continue stumbling and lurching through the cold rain and gloom—and the incredible maze of boulders and rocks. My right leg begins stiffening up as I move along, the pain now very troubling. I'm having much difficulty concentrating and keeping my balance, and I stumble, tumbling forward and to each side many more times. I'm making pitiful progress today and must soon accept the fact that there's no way to reach Clairmont Gap by four, yet I hasten along as best I can.

In the afternoon, the treadway improves considerably, and somehow I manage a more rhythmic pace. I'm pleasantly surprised to find Maggie and her friend, Lynwood French from Lizard Scrape Mountain, hiking toward me only shortly after four.

During the day I'd doubled the dosage twice on my coated aspirin and Osteo Bi-Flex. In the evening now, after a long soothing shower, my leg begins unkinking and I feel much better. Bob Beadles, a friend of the Wades, comes by, and we share a fun-filled time together at the Outback Steakhouse.

If you want the rainbow, you have to put up with the rain.
(Anonymous)

Tuesday—December 12, 2000
Trail Day—201/7
Trail Mile—3216/116 (end of APT, SR-77 at Porter Gap); 3224/8
(ALR)
Location/Trail Mile— CR-7 to Hatchett Creek Trading Post, Coleta,
Alabama. Tom "Mountain Man" Hess, proprietor.

I've yet another grand stay with the Wades, in the warmth and comfort of their lovely home, and in the warmth that comes through
the friendship and from the love of such kind and gentle people.
I'm constantly asked, "Why, *Nomad*, why are you on this journey?"
And you know, by golly, I'm finally managing to figure it out. Oh
yes! It's becoming clearer to me each passing day. The answer? Ahh,
indeed it is the people, above all, the people, the outpouring of
kindness and generosity from the people met along the way. It is
their caring, their love; that's the reason, that's the answer! And why
should precious blessings such as these come to and be so generously
lavished upon someone just because he or she chooses to shoulder a
backpack and set out afoot? Well, perhaps there is a mission that we
may not really know, an intended interaction between those *giving*
and those *receiving*; I'm still working on that one. But I do know
this: I know that for all the reasons we might choose to pick up and
go, it is this outpouring of love, this sincere caring that comes from
the people we meet along the way, this is certainly the main and
driving force. These experiences make the pain and the drudgery,
the arduous part of it, no more than a passing concern in such a
grand and glorious scheme. Thanks, Maggie and Philip, thanks for
bringing the mystery of it into focus!

Philip is up early this morning to prepare a tank-stokin' breakfast, then to drive me the fair distance back to Clairmont Gap—
where I promptly head up the trail in the wrong direction! Even the
sign that shows the way to Dyer Gap slows me little, only setting
me to wondering why there are two Dyer Gaps so close together!

But in a short while, as I see other features now familiar to me from yesterday, I realize what has happened. Only then I turn, to return to Clairmont Gap, to continue my trek on south.

I remember little of the trail today, little about the ups and downs, the treadway that seems more kind. It's mostly a blur as I limp along to begin pondering the reality that I'm nearing the end of this trail, a seemingly endless trail through spiritually mystic mountains, a trail that surely begins and ends, as does this proud old Appalachian range begin and end. Today I cross the last brook, shimmy the last blowdown, climb the last switchback, dodge the last boulder, stand spellbound before the final breathtaking vista.

I'm descending to Porter Gap now. I can see the trailhead parking area below. Soon I reach the final blaze, the last foot of treadway. Two days of hiking yet remain to reach Flagg Mountain, the southernmost mountain of these grand Appalachian Mountains to stand above a thousand feet, but that is entirely a roadwalk. I stop now, to rest for a while as I try to collect my thoughts, to gain some composure as my feelings and emotions go running. I give thanks to God for bringing me on this journey, and for the bounty of joy-filled experiences—a gift through His grace and steadfast love. To me all this has been freely given, an old man in the waning years of his life. It is so humbling to be granted the health, stamina, and resolve, and indeed to be chosen to go, and then to have continued safe passage to complete such an incredible journey—the first southbound thru-hike o'er the entire Appalachian Mountain range.

Still trying to comprehend all of this, stumbling past the parking lot in a daze, I'm jolted back to the "real world" as a passing logging truck rattles and grinds its way. On the roadwalk I hearken back to the many times during this journey that I longed to be here. Those were the times when the going was particularly rough or agonizingly slow and trying. But now that I'm here, now that my journey along and with these beautiful friends (the Appalachians) is nearly over and done, I find that I'm leaving them behind with a feeling of sadness, a deep and forlorn sense of loss. These Appalachian Mountains; they're now a part of me, a part of my very being, no denying it, and I'm going to miss them, I'm dearly going to miss them.

In the evening, clouds gathering, storm brewing, and as the day darkens and the cold descends yet again, by the side of the road I come abreast of this welcome and familiar old place. Here resides a kind and dear old friend. The place is Hatchett Creek Trading Post and the dear old friend is Tom *Mountain Man* Hess. I cross the road to enter his yard. Just then the door opens and Tom comes to greet me, much as he greeted and welcomed me on another cold and stormy day back in '98. He invites me in, and as I enter, he introduces me to Carleton *Griz* Randolph. *Griz* extends both hands, one in greeting and the other to hand me a large mug of steaming hot coffee. Beaming now, he exclaims, "You'll like this coffee just fine, taste it!" Oh yes, hot coffee to turn a cold day, sweetened with a jigger of 'Bama's smoothest and finest! *Mountain Man* has a dandy fire glowing and dancing in the old hand-stacked creekstone fireplace, a fire to warm both hands and heart. He invites me to sit once again, as before, and to rest and chat. What a joy to return, to be here in the comfort of this old place and with this kind old friend. Ahh, life, indeed, is good!

Tom's is a gathering place. Folks come from miles around. His home is their home. "They're all just family," says Tom, as the glow from the warm fire complements and radiates the glow on Tom's you're-just-family-too smile. And so, after a fine supper prepared by *Griz* on the old wood-burning cook stove, "family" starts droppin' in. First there's Jerry and David and Jim and Russell and Ellen and Jason, and his wife Jackie (Tom and Ellen's daughter) and their kids Christian, Caleb and Cody. Then come Junior, Karen and son Jesse, Jonathan, Gary, Roger, Van and Sue, Hook, Tonya, Randy and Jamie, and Charlie Brown and Sonya, then Gerry. Whew, What a family! All greet and welcome me with gentle, sincere kindness.

Yes indeedy, folks, it's the people. It's their kindness, generosity and love. That's what makes the trail, that's what makes the trek, that's what makes the journey, which brings joy-filled, satisfying reward to this old man—to Odyssey 2000!

> *Be it ever so humble, there's no place like home.*
> (John Howard Payne)

THE GRAND CONNECTION ALABAMA ROADWALK (ALR)

Wednesday—December 13, 2000
Trail Day—202/1
Trail Mile—3245/29
Location—US-231 to Jackson's Trace Motel, Sylacauga, Alabama

Today is a continuation of the roadwalk from Porter Gap to Flagg Mountain. The morning dawns cold but clear. *Griz* is up before me, and he's prepared a full-spread breakfast, along with a lunch to send me on my way. Oh, and I've been invited back to spend some time (Thursday night, Friday, and Saturday) with everybody at Hatchett Creek Trading Post. There'll be much revelry and carrying-on in celebration of my completing the Trail of the Ancients. Tom and *Griz* have planned a pig butcherin' and barbecuin', along with plenty of cold refreshments for all! I'll have a ride back right to their door with Lee and Carole, who are coming over from Georgia to be with me as I climb Flagg Mountain, so I'm looking forward to all of it.

I've planned a twenty-one today, from here at Coleta, Tom's little community, to US-231 in Stewartville. I'll miss Goodwater this time around, the route taking me instead through the Hollins Wildlife Management Area, then the little berg of Hollins, and finally across Holman Crossroads to US-231. The traffic is no problem, as the wind helps me along. At Hollins I pull up at Country Cousins, a little mom-n-pop restaurant and general store. They've got everything here from grilled cheese sandwiches to nose rings for your hogs. I've a great lunch set before me, a huge platter of hamburger steak and a pile of mashed potatoes, with gravy over the whole heap. It's a fine meal. I show my appreciation and gratitude by getting up, shouldering my pack, and walking straight out the door without paying or leaving the least tip! I'm nearly a mile up the road before realizing what I'd done. Turning, I quickly beat a path straight back. Everybody has a smile when they see me returning; sure glad they didn't call the sheriff!

The hiking days have gotten shorter and shorter, and it's dusk when I finally reach US-231. As I poke my thumb out, the wind is really pushing. It's turning very cold, and the rain, which has been threatening all afternoon, finally arrives. The traffic is really whizzing, but to my delight I've got a hookup with the fourth passerby. Hot dang, this is great! Pulling to the side and rolling down the passenger window, as the cigarette smoke bellows out, the little old bony-faced geezer wheezes at me to come right up front. It's only five miles to Sylacauga, to the motel *Griz* had told me about, and in minutes the old fellow, hacking, coughing, and dragging incessantly on his cigarette, delivers me straight to the motel office.

What a blessing to be out of it tonight. From the office, heading to my room now, I follow the covered walkway all the way around to keep from the cold, pouring rain. Closing the door, I pull the drapes and crank the heat. Warm and content as I drop off, I'm thinking how long a time and how great a distance it's been from the Cliffs of Forillon to Flagg Mountain. Tomorrow will be a very exciting day.

*...all we need to make us really happy is something
to be enthusiastic about.*
(Charles Kingsley)

Thursday—-December 14, 2000
Trail Day—203/2
Trail Mile—3257/41
*Location—Flagg Mountain, Alabama, elevation 1152 ft. Southern
Terminus, Trail of the Ancients (TA), to Hatchett Creek Trading
Post, Coleta, Alabama.*

The folks here at the motel have been kind enough, but they insisted on a five-buck deposit before giving me the TV remote and room phone hookup. So I'm right back at the office first thing this morning to get my five bucks back.

I tell the owner he can keep the fiver if he'll give me a ride back to Stewartville. No luck, so out I head into the cold swirling mist. I've a short walk along the cross-town main drag to US-231. Turning the corner and hoofing it no more than two blocks, I've got my ride. Ricky Garrett greets me. As I toss my pack in the back and climb in he asks, "You're the hiker, aren't you? My boss, Pete Rodgers told me about you!" I answer, "Yes Ricky, I'm the hiker," as he reaches in the paper bag next to his seat and hands me an egg and bacon biscuit.

So now folks, let me tell you the interesting story about Flagg Mountain, and about Ricky Garrett's boss, Pete Rodgers.

After the Depression and during that era, a Civilian Conservation Corps camp was in operation on Flagg Mountain. There were a number of cabins, and on the summit, a one-room dwelling with a breezeway connecting it to a tall stone fire tower. The entire facility had been long-since abandoned and over the decades suffered the ravages of time, theft, and vandalism—until it became the interest of a group of local civic-minded individuals. As were many of the stone structures built by the CCC, the Flagg Mountain fire tower was a remarkable piece of work, an artistic expression if you will, representing countless man-hours of labor, and though suffering neglect and abuse, beautiful still!

And so, the ending to this story. Ahh, and a happy ending it is, folks! For you see, after many long and protracted rounds of negotiation with the powers that be, this local group, now operating as the CCC (Coosa County Cooperators—don't you just love it!) has managed to secure a lease covering the entire mountaintop, including the old CCC structures. The lease is for ten years at one dollar per year, with an option to renew the lease (costing one dollar) for ten additional years at the rate of one dollar per year. Since the Coosa County Cooperators took over the property, they have made extensive improvements and repairs to the fire tower and adjacent structures. The grounds are now landscaped, well-kept, and manicured. And Pete Rodgers? Well, Pete and his dad Joe, along with Roger and Randall Morris, Ollie Heath, Randy Snyder, Stan Messer, Asa and Dennis Farr, Charles Terrell, and Roger Moon, are the Coosa County Cooperators!

I thank Ricky and bid him farewell as he drops me at Stewartville crossroads, and I'm on my way to Flagg Mountain. The drizzle has let up, but the morning remains cold and overcast as I continue the roadwalk. The distance is twelve miles with a halfway break at the little crossroads of Weogufka. I've told folks I'd be on Flagg Mountain at three this afternoon, so I need to arrive at Weogufka no later than one. It's a little after twelve now, and I can see the Confederate States of America flag flying above Caperton's Old South Store at Weogufka just ahead, so I'm in good shape.

At the store I'm greeted and welcomed by the owner, Lloyd Caperton. Lloyd's just got the place up and running for the day and is busy putting on a pot of coffee and setting a fire in the old wood stove. I drop my pack and mosey, taking a look around. This old place is as much a museum as it is a store—pictures, memorabilia, gadgets, and guns adorning the walls all around. "The store's been in the family for close to a century, some eighty years now," Lloyd beams proudly. His granddad, Rufus Lloyd Ward, ran it; his mom Helen Lloyd Caperton ran it. Now Lloyd Allen is running it, has been since 1981. I linger, pick up some snacks and a cup of coffee, which is on the house, and Lloyd and I have a good chat. Kent Cooper comes by; he'd stopped to talk with me on the road. And in a while a fellow comes running in to look at one of Lloyd's used electric guitars.

Plans are for some friends to meet me here and hike the remaining six miles to Flagg Mountain. And sure enough, shortly arrive Maggie and Philip Wade and their friend Tina Cunningham, then Lee and Carole Perry from Georgia. What a joy having these friends along as I complete this hike o'er the Trail of the Ancients! They all get their hiking boots and daypacks on, and away we go.

Most folks cannot understand how anyone could possibly enjoy hiking great distances day after day, let alone hiking the highways and byways across this vast, expansive continent. But with me today are dear friends who do understand, and it is such a joy hiking along with them. Oh yes, the dogs bark and come to greet us at each passing farmhouse, and there is traffic whizzing by, but we are having such a giddy time of it that these minor distractions have little play.

At Unity, the road turns to dirt. We turn onto CR-55, and in just a short distance comes a vehicle from behind. The driver slows to greet us, and with such bright and beaming smiles we are hailed by Ed Rutledge and Mack Hall from Montgomery. They have come to share the joy of my triumph, the completion of the first southbound thru-hike hike o'er these grand Appalachian Mountains. I first met Ed and his wife Emily in Damascus, Virginia, at Trail Days this past spring. They were relaxing on the porch at the Maples Bed and Breakfast watching the parade festivities when Russ Shaw, who caretakes the Maples from time to time, invited me to come and stand at the rail and watch the parade from the very spot where Ed Garvey stood and watched for years. I was so proud; what a humbling, emotional experience. After chatting for a while, and after hearing the plans for my upcoming TA/ECT hike, both Ed and Emily insisted I give them a call upon reaching the Montgomery area. So call them I did, and here is Ed this morning! Great to see you again, dear friend, and yes Ed, I'm still hiking, have been pretty much every day shortly after we met in Damascus during Trail Days last May.

The road winds and climbs now, becoming rutty and rocky. The first view of Flagg Mountain came along the road to Unity, but clouds were hanging this morning and we were afforded little more than a glimpse of its ascending flanks. This mountain is the southernmost of the Appalachian Mountains to stand above 1,000 feet, rising to 1,152 feet. I have climbed countless mountains many times this high during the past six months, so I thought little of the ascent here this morning, but we're going up, up, and up some more! Soon, we all start huffing, so at the next sharp turn we stop to rest.

In moments we hear vehicles winding their way as they climb the mountain. Comes 'round the bend Jay Hudson from Birmingham and right behind, a TV news van from Alabama's ABC channels 33-40. Jay had called them and they were interested in capturing the moment of my arrival here at the summit of Flagg. I'm greeted with a hug from my kind and dear friend Jay, and with tears welling I'm introduced to Jerome Mabry, news photographer, and John Mangum, a reporter with ABC. John is interested in getting an interview right away, so Jerome sets his tripod and camera. I sure don't like having microphones shoved in my face, especially during such intense emotional times such as now. I gather my wits as best I can. John is gentle and kind with his questions and Jerome stays back with his camera, so we have a good time of it. Heading on up the mountain and as I continue my climb, Jerome runs along ahead taking snips as my trekking poles click the rocks.

At the summit now, with cameras flashing and grinding, I make my way, taking my last steps, to falter and collapse, trembling uncontrollably against the wall that forms the beautiful Flagg Mountain fire tower. Dear Lord, to you do I give thanks. Once again you have remained my constant and faithful companion, for more than 200 days, over 3,250 miles. Together we have completed this incredible journey. It's history now, the first southbound thru-hike o'er the entire Appalachian Mountain range. Thank you, Lord, for keeping me in Your pure light. For through Your grace has this fulfilling and remarkable experience come to pass.

Lee had driven to the summit. While we were hiking this way, he started a fine fire in the old CCC-built rock fireplace in the beautifully restored dwelling by the tower. It is here I'm ushered, to be greeted by all in the warmth of this charming old place, and in the warmth that is the love of such kind and gracious friends. I'm greeted and welcomed by Pete and Joe Rodgers, the proud folks with Coosa County Cooperators. And here, at this grand reception, are Philip and Maggie Wade and their friend (now my friend) Tina Cunningham. Also here are Lee and Carole Perry, Jay Hudson, Ed Rutledge, Mack Hall, and from ABC TV, Jerome Mabry and John Mangum. Oh my, how can these folks be happier and more filled with joy than this old intrepid! Ahh, but indeed, so it seems they are.

In a while Joe unlocks the door leading to the stairwell in the old stone fire tower. We all take the climb. The wooden steps, clinging to the rocks these many years, seem so precariously fixed. But neither do they shift nor sag as we climb. The old lookout is much as it was during the time when fire-spotter Kate Prater manned this old structure, the windows tight, the lofty little sky-perch flawlessly restored and maintained. The mist is still swirling, driven by the wind, but there's not the least draft. Thanks, Pete and Joe, thanks for welcoming us to your mountain! My regards, if you will please, to all with Coosa County Cooperators. And thanks, dear and faithful friends, thanks for coming and sharing the joy that has come to pass, this miracle, this day.

In the evening, as dusk descends, we descend Flagg Mountain. I'm with Lee and Carole now as we wend our way back to Hatchett Creek Trading Post. Soon we are at Tom's to be greeted yet again by many dear friends.

There has been seen and witnessed this day yet another miracle in this old man's life. And what a day it has been. What a joy, what a blessing...

Success is the sum of small efforts, repeated day in and day out.
(Robert Collier)

Friday—December 15, 2000
Trail Day—204/3
Trail Mile—3257/41
Location—Hatchett Creek Trading Post, Coleta, Alabama

Fresh air is generally not a problem here in Tom's place, especially when the wind is blowing the least bit. It just pretty much passes straight through. But that presents a problem when it's bitter cold as was this night. Jason, Tom's son-in-law, stayed over and kept the fire going and that helped ward off the chill, but the wind is whipping this morning, and until *Griz* gets the cook stove cranked in the kitchen, I'll camp in front of the fireplace—move over, Jason!

Toward noon, the day warms. So being outdoors is not the least unpleasant, and that's where I head to watch Gary and Roger kill and butcher the pig. A carefully placed twenty-two round behind the ear takes him down very humanely, then to be dragged from his wallow to the tall A-frame in the back yard. A rope to his hocks then up and over the A-frame to Tom's pickup tow ball, and he's soon hoisted and ready for skinning. You may not want to watch this part, especially when they cut off the head and open the gut cavity. It isn't all that enjoyable a show. I'd seen the operation countless times before on the farm near where I was raised, so I head back to the kitchen for a refill on my coffee and a couple more of *Griz's* woodstove-baked biscuits.

In a little while Gary, Roger, and Jason come in with the pig all dressed out to deposit the gleaming, dripping mass right on the kitchen table. It's *Griz's* job now to reduce this still-twitching heap to manageable size and into cookable pieces—then into the beer keg of marinade till tomorrow. *Griz* has obviously performed this task before, and with his honed and stropped knife (plus an old hand axe) he quickly and skillfully has big piggy in little pieces.

Yes, folks, I have nothing better to do today than to relax, lounge around, and toss down a few with the boys. That's the only plan. Folks around here know how to live. Hey-hey, and I fit in! Oh yes, "It's Friday night and I just got paid." Everybody shows, and it's party time at Hatchett Creek. Nine-ish, we're off the ground, wheels up, seatbelt sign off—this thing's flyin'. What a hoot! Tom, don't you know it's a pure blast being here again, with you and all the "family" at Hatchett Creek Trading Post!

We are always getting ready to live, but never living.
(Ralph Waldo Emerson)

Saturday—December 16, 2000
Trail Day—205/4
Trail Mile—3257/41
Location—Hatchett Creek Trading Post, Coleta, Alabama

And the party really doesn't get cranking till today! Okay *Nomad*, get your head back on, work yourself loose and get ready.

The day dawns cold again, but by noon it's warming nicely. *Griz* gets the grill up and glowing, and Junior comes out with his twenty-two to chase a couple of roosters from under the porch. He's got his eye on two in particular that invariably start their pathetic wheezing around three-thirty every morning. He manages to dust one pretty good, and that's it. The rooster freaks, the feathers go flying, and he's quickly two counties over. We're all leaning over the pickup bed, sipping cold ones, watching. Folks, this is more fun than big screen football!

Griz heads for the marinade vat, soon to return with a big sheet of pig parts. I watch as he dumps bottles of all kinds of stuff into the pot he'll use for basting. This is definitely going to be good pig, very good pig!

Barbecue chicken and pork is the planned fare. By afternoon *Griz* has the pig parts tanning nicely, but Junior is still chasing the chickens. So it looks like pork is gonna be it.

This party-turned-flyin'-machine touches down only briefly as "family" begins arriving early. A little refueling and it's off the ground again. By late afternoon it's become evident this day is going to be a serious darkin'-over day. Low, billowing clouds start moving through and the wind comes up, bringing more biting cold. Right about this time *Griz* wheels the cooker to the porch and everybody moves inside; everybody, that is, except Junior. He's finally nailed one of the roosters and is busy plucking it.

By nightfall the cold storm arrives, bringing snow. This isn't shaping well. Plans are for *Griz* to drive me back to Flagg Mountain just after first light tomorrow morning. The forecast is for cold and snow. The weatherman is dead on. I go for another helping of *Griz's* barbecued piggy, and then take a few minutes before turning in to talk with Jim Smothers, a reporter with *The Daily Home*, a Talladega newspaper.

I've had a grand time here at Hatchett Creek Trading Post, just the kind of break I've needed, but it's time to break camp and move on. Tomorrow, I'll continue ever south toward Montgomery.

Now and then it's good to pause in our pursuit of happiness
and just be happy.
(Guillaume Apollinaire)

Sunday—December 17, 2000
Trail Day—206/5
Trail Mile—3282/66
Location—CR-29 south of Titus, Alabama, to the home of Ed and
Emily Rutledge, Montgomery

I've been staying the nights in the loft here at Hatchett Creek Trading Post. This old place (loose boards on the gable ends, some missing) isn't well suited for sub-freezing weather, especially wind-driven, sub-freezing weather. At first light the wind comes up hard, moaning and whistling through. And at that instant does the old rooster that Junior managed to miss start his pathetic wheezing. I feel the gentle cold touch of snowflakes on my cheek and forehead and I sit up to open my eyes to a dazzling, twinkling wonderland of swirling snow. Here it seems is a microcosmic universe created by a gazillion points of pure light that ebb and flow, dancing through prismatic bars of shimmering brilliance formed by the light of dawn passing the cracks in the gable boards. I tug the drawstring on my Feathered Friends bag till only the squint of my eyes are exposed, to remain for the longest time totally still, totally captivated and hypnotized by the kaleidoscope of light and motion that is flashing and dancing full around.

I can hear *Griz* downstairs jiggling the grate on the old wood-burning cookstove. I'll give him a little time to get the kitchen warmed up. I no sooner roll out than my fingers start locking up, but I must collect my things, organize my pack, and prepare to go. As I stumble down the narrow, rickety loft stairs and open the old boards-of-a-door to the kitchen, *Griz* looks at me straight on, shaking his head. "How can you go out in this stuff in shorts and sneakers!" "*Griz*," I explain calmly, "I came out of Forillon, Cap Gaspé in seven feet of snowpack, just like this, and did fine." We both look out the window into the swirling fit. "Are we going?" he asks. Trying not to show my sadness, I respond, "Yes, *Griz*, we're going...it's time to go."

Tom is still under the quilts. Just as well, I hate goodbyes. It's just an absolutely agonizing time for me. Better just to slip out and be gone. *Griz* cranks the sagging, battered-but-trusty old Ford pickup, and we're sent bouncing and lurching onto the road. I'm consumed with sadness. Tom is not well and I'm thinking, "I may never see him again." Aww, this is awful. "Don't look back, don't look back *Nomad*. You'll return; you'll be back someday, and then you'll see your dear old friend again."

It has been snowing off and on all night, and the countryside is a wonderland of white. The wind buffets us as snow-snakes cross the road. The wheels spin and we take a little sashay to the side as we make the turn toward Stewartville. In just a while *Griz* slows to stop in front of a farmhouse.

"You remember Gerry?" *Griz* asks, "He came by for a few minutes the other day. He lives here. We've got time; let's go in." Don't know how I could have forgotten this kind and gentle man. I guess it's because I've met so many of the "family" these past few days. But I remember his glad and happy smile as soon as he answers *Griz's* knock. We're invited in to his comfortable, warm home to be greeted, and immediately seated, by his wife, Leslie. *Griz* had told me last evening that I would not go back on the mountain hungry, and was he ever right! Gerry had told him to bring me by for breakfast on our way. *Griz* had kept it a secret, and there were bright smiles on everyone's faces (me, too) when I finally caught on. Folks, you just haven't eaten biscuits and sausage gravy till you've been in the South. Thanks, Gerry and thanks, Leslie, for your thoughtfulness and for your generosity; have I got a fire in my furnace now! And *Griz* has packed a lunch for me: fried liver and pork and more woodstove-baked biscuits. I'll not run out of gas on this day.

The road winds up and around, then up and around some more as we climb Flagg Mountain. The hillsides all about are white with snow but the road is clear, and the old Ford chugs and bounces its way to the top. Here's a wide parking area, where the road passes to the other side, and *Griz* makes the turnaround to head back home.

I move in haste, not to linger. "So long, *Griz,*" my dear new friend. I wave as the old truck lurches off, and *Griz* is soon gone 'round the bend and down the mountainside. I'm once again alone, in the bitter cold, the only sound the biting wind. I hunch my shoulders and lean into it, thrusting my poles to the gravel.

The funk that began as I left Tom's door continues, for now I am leaving another great old friend, a friend that has been my constant companion these past six months. As I descend the last of these tranquil and majestic old mountains, I'm leaving the Appalachians behind. Down and down I go, into the lee and into the warmth of the southern sun. It feels so good against my face. As I descend, I'm thinking how these past 200 days and 3,000 miles have tested my mettle, and how, as a result, I've been forged into a stronger and better man. In a beautiful email recently from Laurie Potteiger, the now grand lady at ATC headquarters in Harpers Ferry, she talked about the "pioneering spirit." I've never thought of myself as a pioneer, but I suppose in a sense it is true. Hearkens now my memory to the beautiful words of Robert Frost in *The Road Not Taken*:

> *I'll be saying this with a sigh,*
> *Somewhere, ages and ages hence.*
> *Two roads diverged in a wood, and I,*
> *I took the one less traveled by*
> *And that has made all the difference.*

The gravel road leads to a paved road, which leads nearly straight south through rolling countryside. I'm leaving the Appalachians, my home. I'll so miss this dear old friend. There is little traffic, the wind has relented, and the day has turned pleasant. As I click along, right down the center of the northbound lane, a vehicle approaches then slows and pulls across to the far shoulder and stops. The driver gets out and crosses the road to greet me. Oh my, I recognize him immediately: it's Mack Hall, Ed Rutledge's friend from Montgomery, who had come to the mountain with Ed last Thursday. "This is right about where I expected to find you," he says, as we shake hands and exchange grand smiles. "Ed told me you'd be coming off the mountain today so I've come to spend it along with you, if that's okay—then take you on to Ed's; he and Emily are expecting you this evening." I can't believe this. Ed knew I would be spending the night, pulled off somewhere by the roadside. Mack continues beaming, pleased by how I'm taken by it all. I finally manage, "Sure Mack, sure, come along, but about this evening..." Interrupting me he exclaims, "Don't worry, Ed will bring you back to the very spot where you finish today, bright and early!"

And so, cheered now by the enthusiasm and kindness of this new friend, and as Mack drives ahead and walks back to hike along with me, do I find I now have an energetic bounce in my step and flare in my stride! The miles pass quickly. At sunset, by this little mom-n-pop store south of Titus, we call it a day, load up, and head for town.

In one of the most beautiful of Montgomery's new residential developments, to this grand and spacious new home built by Ed, Mack delivers me. Here Ed and Emily Rutledge greet me cordially, in the truest Southern tradition. I'm escorted straight away to their luxurious guest quarters where I relax, try to gain some composure, then shower in the privacy of my own bath. Emily has prepared a full-spread supper, and in the evening we dine in the finest fashion.

Mack, Ed, Emily, I'm absolutely taken by all of this, by such kindness and generosity. All I can say is thanks, thanks so much; this is Southern hospitality at its very finest!

Here in the forest I said good-by to my sheltering old friend
the Appalachian Mountains. I had not realized how protective
and secure they had been until I knew I was leaving.
(Peter Jenkins)

Monday—December 18, 2000
Trail Day—207/6
Trail Mile—3301/85
Location—US-231 Rest Area near Willow Springs, Alabama, to the
home of Ed and Emily Rutledge, Montgomery

Ed had shown an interest in hiking along, so I've invited him to come out with me today. We talked about it last night. "This is a roadwalk now Ed, we'll be on busy US-231 almost all day, you sure that's what you want to do?" I asked. "Sure, sure," he answered. "I need the exercise." So, after a fine breakfast prepared by Emily, Mack comes by to help us so Ed can leave a vehicle where we'll end the day, then to shuttle us on north to the little store in Titus. We've decided on a nineteen-mile hike, which will bring us to the rest area on US-231. We leave Ed's SUV here, to pile in Mack's car and head back to the little store. Bidding Mack farewell, we're on the trail by eight-thirty.

What a beautiful day, perfect for hiking, a cool breeze and warm sun. The road shoulder is fairly level and wide, no ruts, and the traffic is tolerable. Ed, though a bit my senior, is a strong, steady hiker, and I'm pleased that we are able to cruise along at nearly three miles per hour. By noon we have reached Wallsboro, the little town where Emily was born and raised. We find a picnic table by the road and pull off for lunch. By now the day has warmed nicely, and we're having a grand time of it. What a joy and pleasure to be hiking with someone again. Ed is great company, and we're sharing very enjoyable conversation.

In the afternoon, ahead of schedule, we decide to take a side trip into Wetumpka, an old town with much history, right on the Coosa River. Once out of Wetumpka, we're back on busy US-231 again. The traffic is very heavy, pushing the wind right at us. By evening, with both of us tiring, we decide to go for supper at Captain D's. Near sunset we arrive at the rest area and Ed's vehicle.

Roadwalks can actually be fun. This one certainly was—a grand time with a fine new friend! Folks, it's the people, the people that stir the heart, that bring the magic that has so charmed Odyssey 2000.

In the first place you can't see anything from a car;
you've got to get out of the goddamned contraption and walk...
(Edward Abbey)

Tuesday—December 19, 2000
Trail Day—208/7
Trail Mile—3322/107
Location—US-331, Wiley, Alabama, to the home of Ed and Emily
Rutledge, Montgomery

For more than the past two hundred days the trail has been my life. On such a long and extended journey, loneliness can become a constant companion, wearing, crushing—to the extent of affecting one both mentally and physically. But on this trek I've been so blessed. At critically important times I've been the fortunate sojourner—to have spent time with so many generous, caring people. My stopover here with the Rutledges is yet another example of the remarkable outpouring of kindness, generosity, and friendship that has been so lavished upon me. Toward the end of my trek o'er the Appalachian Mountains (and for weeks), this burden of loneliness wore heavy upon me. So to have been taken in by the Perry family, by Reverend Owen, by the Wades, by Tom's "family," and now by the Rutledges, it has been their love and their caring that have helped lift this terrible burden. Soon, before continuing this trek to Key West, I look forward with great anticipation to a much-needed rest, to go and to spend the upcoming holidays with dear family and friends in Florida and Missouri.

Emily has prepared another tank-stokin' breakfast, and Ed soon has me on my way back to the rest area on US-231. The morning is clear but cold; the only clouds a wide dark wall way to the north. Plans are made for Ed to come for me around sunset at some point south of Montgomery on US-331. These arrangements made, Ed is off to an appointment, and I'm off to my appointed task—hiking through Montgomery. On US-231, as the highway widens to six lanes the traffic comes heavy and hard, driving a cold, continuous blast straight at me. The sun, which brings some relief, its warmth so comforting upon by face, lasts for less than an hour, the dark wall of clouds now upon me. The harsh, cold wind has been steadily turning, now coming directly from the northwest, and the road to Montgomery now angles to the west, turning me directly into the traffic-aided blast. As the day darkens, the wind intensifies and the temperature continues to drop. I push on, but in a while I can take no more of it. Even with both pair of gloves my hands go numb, and I can no longer grip my poles. My face is becoming stiff and my lips feel like hard rubber. To my left is hurricane fence and open spaces to the horizon, so I cross the traffic to an old barricaded road that leads to the woods. Here, as the snow begins, by some low trees and brush I find shelter from the driving wind. I try eating an orange Ed had given me but I become frustrated trying to peel it and finally give up.

Though my hands and face have gone numb from the driving wind, I had managed while on the road to maintain my core temperature. As I sit huddled in the brush, from the inactivity I begin shivering and I can feel my temperature dropping. With much hesitancy, I return to the roadwalk. I've put my poncho on to help break the bitter wind, and I find to my relief that I'm managing much better.

The road angles back southwest and finally south to be sheltered by buildings on the west that break the wind, and I'm soon out of the worst of it. The feeling now returns to my face and hands. The snow, which began in flurries, comes harder now, and as I turn toward the Capitol I'm out of the traffic. No one is by the promenade or at the steps leading up and up to the Capitol. I have the whole grand place to myself. The road and grounds are turning white, the building ghostly gray in the midst of the swirling snow. As I look up to take in the whole impressive scene, the huge clock below the dome is hardly visible. I'm surprised to see that it's only twelve-fifteen. Oh my, I'm making good time today despite the unpleasant conditions.

Hiking on, I'm soon past the government buildings and the downtown business district. Turning south, I'm hiking through an old residential area, and by mid-afternoon I've passed the last of the strip businesses. At the bypass, I pull off to enter a convenience store, to get some coffee, warm my hands, and enjoy a little break from the cold. On US-331, heading ever south, the terrain opens and flattens. The wind (which had been less a problem along the streets of Montgomery) returns, kicking hard from the northwest in a no-nonsense, steady push. The traffic is moderate but the shoulder is soft and muddy, the result of current four-lane construction work. I must hike the edge of the road, lest I sink in the quagmire.

A mutt has been following me since the bypass, finally to adopt me, ranging back and forth across the road. Motorists slow, honk, then give me dirty looks as they pass. Mutt finally comes close enough for me to give her a good whack with my trekking poles a couple of times, but she thinks that's just in fun and romps on ahead, right back into the road. This goes on for the better part of four miles until the frustration of it is finally broken by the welcome arrival of Ed and Emily, who have come to fetch me. I climb in, muddy feet and all, to be whisked away to the warmth and comfort of their beautiful home.

Dear friends, you could not have a clue how incredibly happy and relieved I am to see you again! A warm, soft bed and friends, that's a slightly better choice than the cold, hard ground—and the mutt.

Press on till perfect peace is won; you'll never dream of how
you struggled o'er life's thorny road a hundred years from now.
(Mary A. Ford)

Wednesday—January 3, 2001
Trail Day—209/8
Trail Mile—3343/128
Location—US-331 north of Highland Home, Alabama, to the home
of Ed and Emily Rutledge, Montgomery

I return to the trail from a long, much needed rest, spending Christmas and New Years with family. Though a whirlwind trip, it was good, but I'm glad to be back.

It was almost midnight when my bus finally arrived in Montgomery yesterday, but Ed was right there waiting for me with his usual beaming smile. I should have gotten in at nine last evening, but my plane arrived late in Atlanta, yes Atlanta. I couldn't get a flight from Columbia, Missouri to Montgomery, my own fault, what with the last minute preparations. My friend Joanne Murrell at United National Travel in Florida did the best she could, considering. What an ordeal, though. I hate goodbyes, so the day got me off to a funk right away, what with having to bid farewell to sis and her family. Then the plane from St. Louis departed an hour late; the terminal was a zoo. That got me into Atlanta too late to catch the early evening bus to Montgomery. Zoo number two in Hartsfield—ditto for the MARTA ride to the bus station. Zoo doesn't describe the bus station, standing room only, no place to walk. I finally managed to get a ticket and catch the seven-fifteen bus, which didn't depart until nine, the time I should have been in Montgomery. Ahh, the whole ordeal was worth every hectic minute though, for I had a grand time with family and friends both in Florida and Missouri.

I'm more than ready to get back on the trail again, and here this morning Emily has prepared another big breakfast for me. As we're loading to go, I casually suggest to Ed that it would be great if he'd hike along with me again today. Oh yes, that's all the coaxing needed! He grabs his sticks and fanny pack. It's cold as Ed parks his SUV in the Snowdoun Baptist Church parking lot south of the bypass where he and Emily picked me up before Christmas two weeks ago. We're soon back on the trail, still a roadwalk. We head out with our gloves and head wraps on, but it isn't a bone-chilling cold, as I understand conditions have been here for the past two weeks.

It takes both of us a while to get the kinks out, what I've frequently referred to as "getting the old jitney up to normal operating temperature," but we're soon cruising along at a very respectable pace. It's a real pleasure having Ed along again. I don't have a clue why he'd choose to come out here on this busy federal highway and hike the shoulder with me. Perhaps hiking anywhere, anytime, with almost anyone is good enough for Ed. Beats me!

Today, so it seems, is roadkill day. It starts right out with two skunks...oooowee! The skunks are followed by three deer, an opossum, an armadillo, and finally a large hawk. The day warms nicely. Soon the gloves and head wrap come off and we have a grand time of it popping along, enjoying each other's company. Ed is a lot like me in many respects. I hate backtracking and apparently so does Ed. Backtracking is what he'll have to do at some point today unless he's able to reach Mack on his cell phone, and Mack is free to come for both of us this evening. So Ed tries off-and-on for Mack, finally connecting, and we're good to go straight through till Mack comes to get us at sunset.

The highway rolls up and down and round and about these low-lying hills that precede the Appalachians. The terrain reminds me much of the Ozark Highlands where I was raised. As we roll along, fond memories come back of days gone by. We stop a couple of times to rest, first at a gas station, then at Piney Woods Country Mart, a neat old mom-n-pop country store. Mack comes for us right on cue at sunset, to shuttle us back to Ed's vehicle. What a great hiking day with Ed, down busy US-331. Thanks, Mack; your help made it work!

I'll be the guest one more evening at the Rutledge home. They've continued taking me in, from many miles north of Montgomery to many miles south, where the drive back tomorrow morning will take Ed nearly an hour. And, of course, Emily has a great evening meal prepared for the hungry hikers on their return!

> *Those grand old Ozark Highlands,*
> *Fond memories...long ago.*
> *They tug upon my heartstrings,*
> *To strum them soft and low.*
> (N. Nomad)

Thursday—January 4, 2001
Trail Day—210/9
Trail Mile—3365/150
Location—US-29 at the St. Charles Motel, Luverne, Alabama.
Sue Patel, manager.

Another day of goodbyes, first to Emily as I rise from yet another grand breakfast she's gotten up early to prepare for me, then to Ed as he drops me off after the hour's drive back down US-331. It's definitely the people along the way, the people one chances to meet on a journey like this. They're the reason to go, their kindness, generosity and friendship bring *the joy and the blessings that come with the miles.* That's it; that's the payoff. Thanks Ed and Emily, I'll always remember the good you have brought into my life, the example you have set with your gentle, kind ways. I'll cherish your friendship—forever!

The hike today continues down busy US-331, but it is not the least unpleasant. At the little village of Highland Home, I find to my delight that the shoulder is paved, permitting me to move from elbow's reach of the fast-moving traffic. This benefit and good fortune stays the whole distance to Luverne, where I check into the St. Charles Motel. Right across the way is a Food Fair market where I decide to deli-it for supper with a hot meal carryout. I'm settled in my room by five-thirty.

For where many are riding, few will be able to walk.
Only those who feel rich can afford it...
(Walter Teller)

Friday—January 5, 2001
Trail Day—211/10
Trail Mile—3395/180
Location—US-29 at the Budget Inn, Heath/Andalusia, Alabama.
Neil Patel, proprietor.

I've decided to hammer the highway today, for over thirty miles, so I'm out and gone at first light. There's little traffic this early, and no wind. What a blessing, for it's bitterly cold from the hard freeze of the night. There's heavy frost everywhere, and the little ponds and streams all along are iced over, but the cold helps me hasten along. The sun soon comes, and the day begins warming nicely.

Just south of Brantley and on US-29, a southbound vehicle stops across the way, and the driver gets out and crosses to greet me. Here I meet Evan Carden, editor of *The Luverne Journal*. He's come out to interview me and get my story. He did a great write-up about Luke *Gnome* Denton last year as Luke passed through Luverne on his northbound ECT hike, and my dear friend Rick *Vagabond Rick* Guhsé suggested I stop in and see them, their office being right on the way. That I did the afternoon last, but Evan was out, so I'm surprised he's taken time this morning to drive the distance to find me. We have an enjoyable conversation about the ECT, the increasing hiker traffic thereon, and the need for a connector trail between Flagg Mountain and Conecuh National Forest. We also talk about *Gnome*, and our mutual friend, *Vagabond Rick*.

The hike is very long today, but there is much to occupy the time—first the interview, next a stop at Mama's in Dozier for lunch, and later the hike beside beautiful Lake Gantt. Oh, and a cold Bud with the guys and gals at the VFW south of Clearlake.

I manage to knock the thirty out by four-thirty and reach Heath/Andalusia and the Budget Motel before dark. Here I'm greeted kindly by Neil Patel, from whom I promptly yogi a hiker-trash deal, and I'm in for the evening. Pizza delivered and Mello Yello for supper.

Checking my email, I get great news from Marty Dominy, who's been in southern Alabama scouting potential trail corridor, and from Jay Hudson, who informs me of the ever-increasing number of folks interested in seeing a trail connecting Porter Gap, the Conecuh National Forest, and the Florida National Scenic Trail. This ECT is soon going to be a bona fide thru-trail, one of the most incredible and beautiful trails in the world.

Oh yes, a fine day for hiking, for enjoying life, for just being alive!

> *Very little is needed to make a happy life,*
> *it is all within yourself,*
> *in your way of thinking.*
> (Marcus Aurelius)

Saturday—January 6, 2001
Trail Day—212/11
Trail Mile—3418/203
Location—SR-137 at Blue Lake Grocery near Wing, Alabama, to the home of Leroy and Robin Zinkan

I've decided to go ahead and knock out the twenty-three miles down to Blue Lake Grocery today. *Vagabond Rick* had told me all about the kind, hiker-friendly owners, Jim and Eunice ("Mr. Jim" and "Miss Eunice") Grimes. Also nearby is Leroy and Robin Chaney Zinkan's place. Leroy befriended and shuttled *Vagabond Rick* around while he was up here last March scouting a route for the Alabama roadwalk, so I've been anxious to finally meet all these people. I called and talked with Leroy last evening, and he said to make sure and get back in touch with him from wherever I ended up today.

The hike through Andalusia is both pleasant and interesting. Here is a typical old Southern town, streets blocked out nice and neat, and in the center, a roundabout square. What a peaceful little city resting on the banks of the Conecuh River. Before the white man came, the Creek Indians inhabited this same spot. Later, Hernando de Soto passed through the region.

The streets leading to and from the old square have interesting and historic names. Hiking toward the square I'm on North Three Notch Street and from the square, South Three Notch. The names come from Andrew Jackson's passage through Andalusia, on his way to the Battle of New Orleans. The story goes, that as he passed, he marked his way by carving three notches in the trees along. These Three Notch Streets, having gained fame, are now part of Three Notch Trail.

Just off the square is the historic Central of Georgia Train Depot. It has been restored and now houses Three Notch Museum. I find enjoyment in these old places, so I decide to give it a look. Two old gentlemen welcome me as I enter, then follow me from room to room, not letting me out of their sight. Ha, an old relic, looking at a bunch of old relics, being watched by two old relics! Neat place, can't blame them for wanting to keep an eye on this old bum. I sign the guest register as I leave. Folks sure aren't beating the door down to Three Notch Museum. The last entry was dated December 8, 2000.

Traffic is running heavy and fast today on both US-29 and SR-137, the shoulders rutted and difficult to hike. I stay the road-edge white line as much as possible but end up off more than on. While on US-29 just before I reach SR-137, a lady driving a huge motorhome lets it get away, crossing the white line onto the rutted shoulder. She's coming right at me. I lunge toward the fence as she commences hauling it back on the road, lurching and swaying, right where I'd been hiking only seconds before. I've been on this roadwalk for over 200 miles now, and I'm very much ready for the woods again.

In the evening, after quite an eventful day, I reach Blue Lake Grocery. The Grimes work the store from 4:00 a.m. till 6:30 p.m., and they're both here today. Miss Eunice takes my order for a burger and fries. I make the mistake of suggesting to her that seventy-five cents worth of fries (their order price) won't do it. "Better double it up," I say. She responds casually, "You best wait and see first." Over the years, I've suffered frequent exacerbation of the common malady known as "foot-in-mouth-disease." Today it's out of remission full force. Oh yes, seventy-five cents worth of fries served up here by Miss Eunice is about all anybody could or would ever want to eat at one sitting; hold the double order of fries, Miss Eunice, thank you very much! You're right, *Vagabond Rick*, me and Mr. Jim and Miss Eunice hit it off first thing.

Living nearby are the Zinkans, Leroy, Robin Chaney, and children, Sam and Michelle. They befriended *Vagabond Rick* while he was here scouting trail in LA (lower Alabama is referred to by the locals as LA), and he had urged me to look them up on passing through. So I give them a ring. As I'm sitting at the counter awaiting Leroy's arrival, enjoying a pint of the local dairy's finest (passing up the outrageously overpriced freezer-burned national brand from New England—you know the one), who walks in but none other than Jay Hudson and Maggie Wade, my dear friends from Birmingham and Waldo. What a pleasant surprise seeing them both again! They're down scouting secondary and Forest Service roads that might be used to get hikers off the busy federal and state highways. Leroy soon comes and Mr. Jim lets us lounge at his counter. We have a grand time of it *bench hiking*, talking trail.

Leroy has cleared out a place for his family on a Conecuh National Forest outparcel, and quite a place it is. He's been coming up here for over two decades to hunt deer, and is now in the process of moving here permanently from Pensacola. He's brought in a large mobile home for he and his family, but the old hunting camp right next to it still stands, pickup campers, toilet and shower house, all still here. *Vagabond Rick* was the first fortunate benefactor of their kindness—now me. And Leroy says, "I want hikers to stop by here on their way through." Not to worry, Leroy. The hikers? They'll stop by, oh yes; they'll certainly stop by!

As I settle in for the night in the cozy little pickup camper kindly provided by these wonderful new friends, I'm thinking, "What a scary-turned-happy day this has been." God's hand rested on my shoulder today, nudging me quickly from harm's way. I could not feel it, but it was there. A little more magic to weave the spell of magic that is this remarkable Odyssey 2000–'01.

> *All the strength and force of man comes from his*
> *faith in things unseen.*
> (James Freeman Clarke)

Sunday—December 7, 2001
Trail Day—213/12
Trail Mile—3418/203
Location—Home of Leroy and Robin Zinkan near Wing,
Alabama

Those of you who've followed my journal entries for any length of time know how much I enjoy a campfire. Every evening there's an opportunity I have one going, first for cooking, then for warming, and then for just pure enjoyment. Seems there's an element in society that finds much relaxation and enjoyment sitting around a campfire. I'm of that ilk. So, too, are Leroy Zinkan, his wife, Robin Chaney, and their friends and hunting companions, Jim Garrett and Roy Kellogg. Arriving at Leroy's yesterday evening, being shown around,

I noticed a fire back in the woods. As I paused to look, Leroy commented, "We've got a campfire going almost every evening; come on over when you get settled in." Well, that was all the invitation I needed. Heading right there I was greeted by Jim and Roy. Leroy came soon with Robin to tell me soup was on and hand me a hot cup of coffee. We had a great time sharing each other's company, just sitting around the campfire, a mighty fine evening!

The old pickup camper Leroy put me in was very cozy. He'd brought in a little electric heater to keep the chill off, and I slept like a baby. This morning we're all treated to a deer-hunter (and thru-hiker) kind of breakfast by Leroy and Robin. These are such kind and generous people and this old hunt-camp-turned-homestead, such a pleasant and peaceful place. I've been invited to spend another day if I like. That's a no-brainer: I like! Anyway, I have a maildrop (my bounce box) waiting for me at Wing, just a short hike down the road. Today's Sunday; no need to hurry. I'll spend the day with all these great new friends, and my mail will be waiting for me in the morning. I'll have a chance to do some writing and help around with chores.

The Zinkans have two horses, one a beautiful Andalusian. What a fascinating and inspiring legend behind this remarkably handsome steed. I'll share the story with you—in Robin's words:

THE LEGEND OF ANDALUSIA

"Legend has it that a Spaniard, fearing for his life, made his magnificent white stallion a gift to the warriors' chief, Red Eagle (William Weatherford). The warriors, captivated by the horse, demanded to know his name and where he came from. The Spaniard carved the horse's name and his birthplace on a poplar tree: Destinado and Andalusia.

Destinado was taken to Red Eagle, who foresaw great things of the horse. Red Eagle rode Destinado into battle. It is said the horse saved his life when he gave warning of approaching soldiers sent by Andrew Jackson. Red Eagle was able to fight off the soldiers but unfortunately during the fight, Destinado was shot in the foreleg, shattering it. Red Eagle took him to the poplar tree carved with his name, and put him down. He then burned the carcass so that nothing would defile his body. The poplar tree stood where now the town square of Andalusia sits."

After 187 years an Andalusian stallion returns to Andalusia, Alabama. The stallion is Corron, a three-year old, and the proud owners are Leroy Zinkan and Robin Chaney. They're working to fulfill a dream, and that dream is to raise Andalusians, such stunningly beautiful animals that they've been described as "the only living work of art." And where will they raise them? Why right here in Andalusia, Alabama, which indeed may be named for the breed of horse the Spainard brought with him to the New World.

Oh yes, another wonderful evening by a great campfire, with great friends!

Beauty in things exists in the mind which contemplates them.
(David Hume)

Monday—January 8, 2000
Trail Day—214/13
Trail Mile—3434/219
Location—CR-37at the Alabama/Florida state line to Hurricane Lake Campground, Blackwater River State Forest, Florida

It's Monday morning and everyone is heading out: Leroy, Robin, children Sam and Michelle, Jim and Roy. Folks, I want you all to know what a great time I've had here at the farm Caballos de Andalusia. I'm certain I'll return to see all of you again. Thanks, dear friends!

I get a ride back to Blue Lake Grocery with Leroy. After bidding him, Mr. Jim, and Miss Eunice farewell, I'm out and on my way to Wing. The roadwalk is pleasant, the day cold but not terribly so, the wind gentle. I'm hiking through the last of the rolling hills and countryside of southern Alabama. The traffic is light and the road shoulders wide and flat.

I'm soon in Wing at the little post office. Jo Ellen Grissett is the new postmistress, and this is her first day on the job. In the back sorting mail is Earl Bailey, the mail carrier. They're the only postal employees at Wing. No line here this morning. The Wing post office is such a neat little place. With some cajoling I manage to get Jo Ellen and Earl outside for their picture in front of the little Wing ZIP code sign.

From Wing it's only a mile to the Alabama/Florida state line but I've a little over nine miles yet to go. The roundabout way is usually the way of the trail, and that's the way today. So I head west toward Bradley, a six-mile hike through secluded piney woods along a quiet country road.

In a while I'm in the little community of Bradley, at Elliott's Store. Here I meet Earl Bray, the kind old storekeeper. Getting to know Earl doesn't take long. The warmth of the old stove feels good, and Earl invites me to unload and rest. There's no pay phone here, but not to worry. "Go in the office. The phone's on the wall. Help yourself," says Earl, and so I go. I figure I'll need two or three days' provisions to get to Harold, the next convenience store, so I shop around, picking up a few things. "Let me know if I can help you," calls Earl from across the way. The place is remarkably well stocked, a little bit of everything from groceries to rat poison to "Vee" belts. Oh yes, and good local ice cream! On the faded old bulletin board are a bunch of faded old notes and cards: "Wyman's Poultry Service. Quality work to clean out chicken houses and spread litter. Professional sawdust hauling." He's got a pager if you really get in a bind!

Here's a dandy, "Jack Stokes, Old Hickory Medicine Company, quality medicines for 52 years."

Back at the checkout now (no lines here either), Earl and me, we have a good long talk. The last 75 years haven't always treated Earl so kind, but he's managed to make it. He made it through WWII, a decorated veteran of the European Theatre. Fought in the Battle of the Bulge. Drove trucks, called "frame movers," the big stuff, hauled field artillery and the ammo for them. Speaking softly of those bygone days comes a forlorn far-off glint in his eye, and a hint of a tear. God bless you, Earl Bray, it's the brave, the few remaining men and women from that war like you, who fought to keep this country free. What a joy talking with you! Thanks so much for your hospitality and gentle kindness, and thank you for this thing called freedom, which we all take so much for granted.

The day really wants to clear and become warm but it never quite makes it. Toward evening now, the wind comes up, not hard, but steady from the northwest. Earl drew a map showing me a much easier and shorter route to Hurricane Lake Campground along little-known Alabama backcountry byways and I'm headed off, map in hand down Middle Creek Road. As I continue south, and near the Florida line, I begin looking for a place to pull off for the night, but the road all along is posted on both sides. I continue on through dusk and into the last fading light of day.

It's now I see this figure, moving in the dark shadows of the trees. I become startled, for approaching is this hulk dressed in dark camo, face painted in disgusting swirled shades of brown and green. Closer and closer it comes, hunched forward, burdened with this huge, dark object strapped and shouldered, and at the ready, a large, scoped center-fire rifle. Near abreast now I hasten my already brisk pace, keeping a good distance. Suddenly I become gripped with fear, for to my absolute dismay does this apocalyptic figure slow and pull up right before me. I keep moving, oh yes, I keep moving! Just then do I hear this gentle voice greet me with a kind "hello!", and I meet Gary Booker. The warlike face paint turns out to be no more than a camo head sock, which he pulls down, revealing his bright, warm and smiling countenance. The grotesque contraption strapped to his back, his tree stand. And the gun? Well, it's deer season here in Alabama, and Gary is just now returning from an enjoyable evening of hunting his grandfather's old home place. Trying to gain some composure, I return the greeting and we linger and talk.

Gary offers me the use of his grandfather's place to set my camp for the night. He also offers to take me to Hurricane Lake Campground, yet some distance down the road but nearby where he lives. I choose this option as he remarks, "...and I'll be hunting here again at first light; you're welcome to ride back with me." We no more load and get rolling than Gary points out the state line. "You almost made it into Florida tonight," he exclaims.

There are no campers at Hurricane Lake Campground. The place is dark and I have it all to myself. I bid Gary goodbye as we make plans to get together in the morning just before dawn. I'm in Florida tonight, but I'll be in Florida for real tomorrow morning. What a long, long, time. But I have been patient for that day.

Old Man Winter apparently is not aware that I'm in the south, for he is here with me. For sure I'll need my sleeping bag liner tonight.

The great believers have been the unwearied waiters.
(Anonymous)

CHAPTER 4

THE FLORIDA NATIONAL SCENIC TRAIL (FT)

Tuesday—January 9, 2001
Trail Day—215/1
Trail Mile—3439/5
Location—Hurricane Lake Campground, Blackwater River State Forest, Florida

It's very cold this morning and my fingers begin quitting as I hasten to break camp. Gary comes at five-thirty, and we're on our way back to his grandfather's place just across the state line. I thank Gary for his help and kindness, then head ever south, crossing into Florida just before six. Two Canadian provinces and fifteen states behind me now; Florida, the last and longest yet remains.

A strange little road, this Charles Booker Road—can't decide whether it wants to be dirt or paved, so it alternates, first dirt for a few hundred yards, then blacktop, then dirt, then blacktop, and on and on, crossing little streams, then to meander up and down in a bewildering and unusual checkerboard way.

Dawn arrives clear, the sun soon follows, its job, to warm this day. I've a short hike back to Hurricane Lake Campground, and I arrive again at eight. I'll be meeting George Brinkman, Ed Walker, and Tom Daniel here later today. They're all members of the Western Gate Chapter, Florida Trail Association. They'll be assisting with maps, data, and other information to help me along toward the main east/west Florida Trail near Yellow River.

As I stop, does the cold come right up behind me. I quickly decide to climb back in my sleeping bag for a while, giving the sun a chance to warm things a bit.

Later in the morning, campground host Larry May stops by and we have a long chat. Then in the afternoon come George, Ed, and Tom. We talk about the trails I'll be hiking for the next few days: the Wiregrass Trail, the Jackson Red Ground Trail, and their pride and joy, the brand new Juniper Creek Trail.

These great new friends, each filled with contagious excitement for my hike, fill me with their enthusiasm! I have a feeling these next few days will be enjoyable and memorable times.

And now a word about this Western Gate Chapter, Florida Trail Association. I just don't believe you will ever find a more fired-up bunch of guys and gals. What an appropriate name, Western Gate, for indeed the trails they have and are building will soon serve as the "gate," the key link connecting the Florida National Scenic Trail to a glorious system of trails that, when combined, will form a continuous trail o'er near the breadth of the entire eastern North American continent, crossing in the remarkable span of it, sixteen states, two Canadian provinces (now five) and three (now three and one-half) time zones, for an incredible distance of nearly five thousand miles.

And that key? The key is the spur, a link if you will, connecting the Florida National Scenic Trail to trails now being built in Alabama and Georgia, to ultimately connect to that grand old trail, The Appalachian National Scenic Trail, then to The International Appalachian Trail in Canada and the Cliffs of Forillon at Cap Gaspé, Québec Province.

This spur, now almost complete to the Alabama state line, is a result of the foresight, inspiration, and dedication of members of Western Gate. And most recently, and again as a result of the urging by members of Western Gate, this link has been incorporated into and made part of the Florida National Scenic Trail. Thanks folks, thanks all—the great visionaries with Western Gate! Your labors are making possible the dream of those of us who envision such a grand scheme, a trail, perhaps to become known as the Eastern Continental Trail, stretching from the Caribbean Sea in the Gulf of Mexico, Key West, Florida, to the Atlantic Ocean, Gulf of St. Lawrence, Cap Gaspé, Québec.

On that dream (and on that trail) will I sleep soundly tonight.

There is nothing more powerful than an idea
whose time has come.
(Victor Hugo)

Wednesday—January 10, 2001
Trail Day—216/2
Trail Mile—3456/22
Location—Mile 16.4, Jackson Red Ground Trail, Blackwater River State Forest, Florida

I'm awakened this morning by two vehicles arriving at the lake. Folks from the Florida Fish and Wildlife Conservation Commission are down by the boat ramp taking water samples from Hurricane Lake. Soon comes another vehicle to stop by my campsite. It's Gary Booker. He's come to let me know how much he's enjoyed my website and to wish me well on the remainder of my hike through Florida.

It's another cold morning, but the sun is up and already warming the day nicely. I break camp and cross the earthen impoundment that forms Hurricane Lake, to begin my hike on Wiregrass Trail.

The hike today is off the roadway on beautifully cut and maintained treadway through Blackwater River State Forest. The trail undulates hither and yon and up and down across red, clay-based sandy domes inhabited by tall majestic stands of longleaf pine, carpeted beneath and all along by tufty-tough clusters of wiregrass. From dome to gently rising dome goes the trail, to descend down and through tightly woven thickets of turkey oak, to cross seeps and delightful little clear-flowing brooks. Blackwater River State Forest is the largest state forest in Florida and, when combined with the Conecuh National Forest in Alabama, the expanse forms the largest contiguous longleaf pine/wiregrass ecosystem in the world, a system that once covered over sixty million acres here in the southern coastal plain. Of this grand expanse of pine and grass, less than three million acres now remain. The good news is that, although reduced to two percent of its original size, this ecosystem still supports clusters of red-cockaded woodpeckers and bogs containing five different species of carnivorous pitcher plants. Also, the corner has been turned. Prescribed burns, essential to the balance within this ecosystem, are now part of the annual management program. Thousands of acres previously in slash pine plantations are now being converted back to the longleaf pine that has historically dominated Blackwater River State Forest's sandy soils.

The Wiregrass Trail soon connects to the Jackson Red Ground Trail, which continues through the rolling forestlands of pine and grass. My planned destination today was the second shelter just past Old Martin Road, but I arrive to find vehicles passing right next the shelter, and no water source. So I quickly decide to move along to another spot more remote where water is nearby. Within a mile the trail descends again to a clear little seep. Here I gather water, then to continue to a small clearing beneath the gently whispering pine where I pitch my little Nomad tent, get a fine cooking and warming fire going and settle in for the evening.

Sat off again, and continued traveling over
a magnificent pine forest,
the ridges low, but their bases extensive,
with proportionable plains.
The steady breezes gently and continually rising and falling,
fill the high lonesome forests with an awful reverential harmony,
inexpressibly sublime, and not to be enjoyed any where,
but in these native wild Indian regions.
(William Bartram)

Thursday—January 11, 2001
Trail Day—217/3
Trail Mile—3477/43
Location—SR-87 at Red Carpet Inn, Milton, Florida. Pete and Jo
Patel, proprietors.

Raindrops on my tent roust me just before six-thirty, and I hasten to break camp and be on my way before the sky opens. I no sooner get on the trail than I must duck under a pine to prevent getting totally soaked while donning my poncho. The remainder of Jackson Red Ground Trail follows mostly old open and grassy woods roads, the rain following along as I approach the end of it at Red Rock Road. Just across begins the Juniper Creek Trail.

I've been looking and looking with heightened anticipation to spot vegetation indigenous to the subtropics and the south. A few days ago, I came upon my first tupelo and bay, and today, here just a short distance south on the Juniper Creek Trail I see my first scrub palmetto. My anticipation continues, however, as I look forward with much excitement to seeing my first cabbage palm.

This Juniper Creek Trail is a beautiful trail, professionally designed and constructed. It meanders up and down and around the countless dune-like mounds and ridges, crossing many sandy washes with little spring-fed brooks that feed Juniper Creek. As the terrain undulates and changes, so too does the striking diversity of plants abruptly change. And so the trail goes. To the folks at Western Gate Chapter—certainly you know that Juniper Creek is a treasure chest of natural wonders! And the key to this treasure trove? The key is the trail you have constructed. It unlocks the beauty of this special place for all to see and enjoy. Thanks!

Exiting Juniper Creek Trail, I'm once again on the roadwalk, first crossing the bridge over Blackwater River then onto the tarmac into Harold. Nearing the little community, I begin looking for the American flag; that's the easiest way I've found to locate the post office. But alas, there is only one building along the highway, a canoe outpost/convenience store—no American flag anywhere. Entering the store, I inquire as to the location of the Harold post office. "No post office in Harold anymore; used to be right here in the store, but that was a long time ago," replied the lady behind the register. Oh my, now isn't this great! I'd looked up the ZIP code for Harold while in Wing; 32563, that was the number, and that's where I sent my bounce box, general delivery, Harold. "But I'm expecting a package; it was sent to Harold at 32563. Where the heck did it go?" I exclaim. "Beats me," says the lady, "Maybe Milton, maybe Holt. Beats me." Aww, this is just great. All my maps, data, and medications are in that box.

I leave the store in a funk-driven drear as the rain-driven drear of the day continues. I head west towards Key West, which is way to the east and south of here. There's much traffic on US-90, big trucks, and they're flying. I must turn and duck down to brace against their repeated flooding blasts. I manage to get away from it for a short distance by moving to the old brick road running along that once carried less frequent and much slower traffic between Pensacola to Jacksonville. At the blinker I finally turn south once again.

I was hoping to reach the main east/west intersect of the Florida Trail today at Range Road-211, but as I hike toward the I-10 interchange, the rainstorm starts throwing fits, passing in waves, bringing buckets of water. I'm soaked, cold, and tired as I reach the

Red Carpet Motel. So here I decide to call it a day. I yogi a fair hiker-trash deal out of Jo the proprietor, call for a pizza delivered, and settle in for the night.

If it weren't for bad luck, I'd have no luck at all...
(Hee Haw cast)

Friday—January 12, 2001
Trail Day—218/4
Trail Mile—3483/49
Location—Intersection of SR-87/Range Road-211, Eglin Air Force Base, to the home of George and Annette Brinkman, Gulf Breeze, Florida

I made a call last evening to George Brinkman, and arrangements were made for he and Tom Daniel to pick me up at noon today at the intersection of SR-87 and Range Road-211, just south of Yellow River.

The day begins overcast, but the rain, which had joined and accompanied me almost all of yesterday, has ended. I've a very short hike today, only six miles, so I linger in my room, working correspondence until nearly ten before venturing out to continue the roadwalk south. At Range Road-211 I'll reach the main east/west leg of the westernmost section of the FT that begins some forty-five miles to the west at Fort Pickens/Gulf Islands National Seashore. From Range Road-211 I'll be given a ride to Fort Pickens, and from there I'll begin my hike east, then south, on the main FT path.

Reaching Range Road-211, I have completed the hike o'er the spur connecting the main FT to the Conecuh NF in Alabama and ultimately to trails that will lead on north. This connector trail is becoming more and more important in the grand scheme of things, as has to do with a trail traversing the breadth of the entire eastern North American continent. Rick *Vagabond Rick* Guhsé has pointed up the importance of this trail eloquently in his outline titled *Flor-ida Trail Data*, so I'll let him explain:

"It is fitting that FNST certification be granted for this connec-tor trail to honor the vision and efforts of FTA's pioneers who long ago developed this trail, which has stood isolated from the rest of the FT for so long. A new day has dawned for the Jackson Red Ground Trail, which along with the Juniper Creek Trail to the south and the Wiregrass Trail to the north is the gateway into/exiting Florida."

I no sooner drop my pack and find a comfortable place to sit than George and Tom arrive. I load up and we head for Jackson Guard, headquarters for Eglin Air Force Base, located in Niceville. At Jackson Guard I'll request permits to enter and cross the reser-vation at Eglin.

Awaiting at Jackson Guard and coming from Fort Walton Beach to greet me is Lee *Lee I Joe* Parker. Lee is chairman of the new Choc-tawhatchee Western Gate subchapter of FTA. In a moment we're all welcomed by Justin Johnson and Steve Lawrence, both with the Department of Defense. Maps are brought out to plan my hike, and we soon have an itinerary worked up for the four days I'll be on the Eglin reservation. After watching a five-minute video indoctrinat-ing me on live ordnance (and how to leave them alone), I'm issued my permits by Nancy Reece and Paula Goldbaugh. Justin is the Fish and Wildlife Biologist with the Department of Defense and is responsible for natural resources management at Eglin. So, while I'm getting my permits, George, Tom, and Lee take the opportunity to discuss ongoing trail construction activities with Justin and Steve.

A gentleman has been waiting in the reception area and as I turn, permits in hand, George introduces me to Michael Stewart, reporter with the Fort Walton Beach *Daily News*. Michael has come to interview me, to hear about this grand scheme, a trail covering the breadth of the eastern North American continent, and about this remarkable adventure, Odyssey 2000-'01. He shows much interest and we spend a good while together. After the interview George drives me to a place where the FT crosses the road. Here waits Debi Houssermann, photographer with the *Daily News*. We hike down the trail a ways, and she takes many pictures. On the way back, George and Tom drive over some of the route I'll be taking from Pensacola Beach.

In the evening now, and at George's home in Gulf Breeze, I meet his wife, Annette. A fine evening meal awaits, and my bed is made. What a chock-full day; I'm very tired.

We are born wanderers,
followers of obscure trails,
or blazers of new ones.
(Royal Robbins)

Saturday—January 13, 2001
Trail Day—219/5
Trail Mile—3485/51
Location—Fort Pickens Road (CR-399), Gulf Islands National
Seashore, to the home of George and Annette Brinkman, Gulf Breeze,
Florida

George has planned for me to meet members of the Western Gate Chapter this morning at Fort Pickens, where we'll have the opportunity to do some hiking together. So after coffee and a light breakfast, George, Annette, and I head for the old fort.

I've been told about the beauty of Gulf Islands National Seashore, but I had not expected, nor had I prepared, to see anything quite so stunning and grand. The shimmering aquamarine waters that are the Straits of Florida (the Keys) have always had such a profound impact on me. The crystalline turquoise glow of those waters, lighting the sky with blinding brilliance and color, have always overloaded my senses, throwing them full-tilt.

Oh my, here we go again; it's full-tilt time once more! As we pass the entrance to Gulf Islands National Seashore and proceed toward Fort Pickens, looking to the Gulf I'm presented with a stunning, breathtaking kaleidoscope of color, a radiant brilliance I can't recall seeing before! The beach is pure white as if capped with snow, the surging surf the most iridescent beryl-gem aquamarine, with the cirrus-tufted sky radiating all in such a way as to complement and play the lustrous colors full about. Traveling on, the sea appears to rise as a dome, crowning the show, and seemingly we must climb to meet it, lest we become cast into its approaching flood.

Folks are awaiting our arrival at the fort. I meet Randy and Susan Creel, Tom Moody, and Susan Fishbaugh. Tom Daniel and Ed Walker have also come to spend the morning. With the National Park Service, here to welcome me, are David Ogden, Ann Folker, and Beckie Mims. I must answer many questions. In a while we all gather before the old fort for a group picture. It is a very happy time.

Standing now before the first Florida National Scenic Trail marker, I turn for one last glance to the west, for from this point will I journey no further west. We all gather together to walk the old approach road east past the crumbling batteries of WWI and WWII. We hike such a short distance, but I take much pleasure and enjoyment in the company of these new friends. Afterward, we all gather at Peg Leg Pete's Oyster Bar on Pensacola Beach, where I'm treated to lunch, compliments of the Creels. Thanks, dear folks from Western Gate, new friends all; your kindness has brought me much joy!

Back to the Brinkman's lovely home, their guest once again, I retreat to my room to work my daily journals. In the evening we dine at one of their favorite local spots. I've managed only two miles of hiking today, but that's not of concern. I'll reach Key West in good time; I don't need to hammer this trail anymore.

I believe the time today was spent wisely, certainly it was spent enjoyably, meeting new people and making new friends. It is the people. Ahh yes folks, indeed, it is the people!

Travel too fast and you miss all you are traveling for.
(Louis L'Amour)

Sunday—January 14, 2001
Trail Day—220/6
Trail Mile—3485/51
Location—Fort Pickens Road (CR-399), Gulf Islands National Sea-shore, to the home of Bob and Susan Fishbaugh, Gulf Breeze, Florida

I can smell the coffee brewing, so I'm up and to the kitchen. George and Annette are getting ready for church. As George comes to pour my second cup, the doorbell rings. It's Bob and Susan Fishbaugh. I met Susan at Fort Pickens yesterday, and they've invited me to spend the day with them; they're here to fetch me. Plans are to travel east to Grayton Beach, to meet their friends, Edward and Ginger Moore, and to hike some with them. Ginger is the past chair of Western Gate.

I've been out in the Florida Panhandle before, but never this far west on the Gulf beaches. Grayton Beach has the distinction of being one of the most beautiful of all of the Florida beaches. Now that we're driving along this white sand-washed bit of heaven, I can certainly see why.

The Moores have a beautiful beach home on a freshwater lake overlooking this grand storyland. We spend the day sharing each other's company, enjoying a hike, and enjoying their lovely place. In the evening and back now at the Fishbaughs I delight in being with these new friends and relish in the comforts that being trailside does not provide.

To travel hopefully is a better thing than to arrive.
(Robert Louis Stevenson)

Monday—January 15, 2001
Trail Day—221/7
Trail Mile—3496/62
Location—CR-399, Pensacola Beach, to the home of Bob and Susan
Fishbaugh, Gulf Breeze, Florida

The trail today will be like no other ever experienced, save those folks fortunate enough to know the Florida National Scenic Trail, the Trail of the Ancients, or this grand Eastern Continental Trail. For today does this pathway cross over to embrace the beckoning seashore along a majestic ribbon of surf-washed paradise extending all the way to Pensacola Beach.

If you've not had the occasion to enter and wander this realm of time suspended, where the only horizons are your tomorrows afore, your yesterdays behind, where the moment-to-moment earthly bindings are the mist of the sea blending the sand, surf, and sky—then you must certainly come. You must come taste the salt air, hear the elusive echo of the eons, pan the bending sea to infinity, all the while, staying firmly planted in the sand 'neath your feet. Here, drifting the winds of time, ebb and flow the eternal winging of sound and silence. In this spell, you will be lifted and carried along o'er ways never before seen or imagined, the pathways I know well. Some lead to magic mountain-filled skies, others pass across the mystic meadows of time.

Plans are to meet George Brinkman at Pegleg Pete's, have lunch, then hike together north through Pensacola Beach, then to end the day where the trail leaves the walkway to enter the dunes of the sound. This plan works well, and in the afternoon, right on cue, comes Susan to fetch us. Back at George's I bid farewell to yet more wonderful new friends.

It's a grand evening with the Fishbaughs—just like *home*.

Men live on the brink of mysteries and harmonies...
with their hand on the door latch...
(Ralph Waldo Emerson)

Tuesday—January 16, 2001
Trail Day—222/8
Trail Mile—3511/77
Location—CR-399, Navarre Beach, to the home of Gary and Millie
Buffington, Pensacola, Florida

All the folks that I've met, the members of this Western Gate Chapter, are so proud, so fired-up about the part they have and are continuing to play in this grand scheme, a trail the entire width and breadth of Florida—and indeed, a spur they're building that links nearly the breadth of the eastern North American continent. Susan Fishbaugh, a true-to-form member of Western Gate, is certainly enthusiastic. This morning, as we head into the dunes north of Pensacola Beach, her contagious excitement cannot be contained. The morning brings a cold, swirling mist, but this not-quite-perfect weather does not dampen Susan's enthusiasm, and I'm caught up in the magnetic energy of it.

The trail breaks over and back and across a waving sea of sand-swept dunes as we are guided by the familiar orange FT blazes painted on posts all along. And so the path meanders for over three miles, to the very edge of the sound, which presents its emerald-jewel spectacle even in the somber gloom of the day. This dream-spun hike soon ends back at the Gulf, where I bid yet another dear new friend farewell. Susan, to you and all at Western Gate, thanks!

Crossing the highway, the trail continues on the white sandy beach for better than seven miles, merging to a point on the surf-swept horizon. By late afternoon I arrive at the Holidome in Navarre Beach. Here I call Gary and Millie Buffington (*Bear Bag* and *Sweet Pea*, GAME 2000), who have invited me to spend time with them on my way through.

In a while Gary and Millie arrive with Catherine and Joyce, Gary's mother and aunt, and we're off to supper, then to spend a very enjoyable evening at their lovely home.

...no one is useless while they have a friend.
(Robert Louis Stevenson)

Wednesday—January 17, 2001
Trail Day—223/9
Trail Mile—3526/92
Location—Intersection of SR-87/Range Road-211, Eglin Air Force Base, to the home of Gary and Millie Buffington, Pensacola, Florida

At my urging, Gary has decided to hike out with me from the Holidome, and we're off on a cool, clear morning a little before nine. The FT leads out on the bike path, and at the intersection leading to Navarre we stop to talk with some folks out for their morning walk. In a few moments, my attention is drawn to a young man behind me, a hiker. I turn, and to my amazement, before me now stands *Spider*. This is astonishing! Our paths first crossed way north on the AT over five months, and 2,500 miles ago! We both started our hikes at Forillon; we're both bound for Key West.

We hike together for a while, enjoying each other's company. I feel such kindred ties with this quiet, gentle man. It has been unspoken, but we both understand that our journeys are a spiritual walk, though we are from different corners of the world. Our cultures and religions are so totally different, but yet, on this trail, we are the same. *Spider* soon turns east toward Niceville where he'll obtain his permits to enter Eglin and I continue north on SR-87. Goodbye *Spider*. I sense our paths will cross again.

Gary hikes along for another hour, then turns to return to the Holidome and his car. He'll come then to fetch me as I complete my hike today at Range Road-221, where tomorrow I'll continue on east through Eglin Air Force Base on the main through path of the FT.

In the evening, Millie prepares a special meal just for me. What a joy being with these dear friends again.

...all our journeys are sacred, and all our lives, adventures.
(Dan Millman)

Thursday—January 18, 2001
Trail Day—224/10
Trail Mile—3548/114
Location—Range Road 211, Gin Hole Campsite, Eglin Air Force Base, Florida

My bounce box has apparently gone to its final rest somewhere in postal purgatory. It's disappeared. This morning Gary puts out an APB in hopes of tracking it down. He spends the next hour and a half talking first to recorded messages, and finally, to (real, live) postal employees. But, no luck.

This puts us late getting back to Range Road 211 where *Lee I Joe* is waiting to hike some with me this morning. Here I bid farewell to Gary. Thanks, Gary and Millie, for your kindness and generosity, you've become such good friends!

Lee spends just a short time with me as I continue my journey toward Key West. We talk about this trail and the great people of Western Gate. But alas, too soon, he must turn and return to his work. It's my fault, getting started so late. Thanks for coming to hike with me, *Lee I Joe*!

Today the trail heads due east on a road of pure, red clay through Eglin Air Force Base. There is little traffic, much animal sign—tracks of deer, turkey, raccoon and armadillo. And bear scat, lots of bear scat.

I arrive at Gin Hole just before sunset, as the day turns cold and cloudy. I pitch on the banks of Yellow River, get a fine cooking and warming fire going, and settle in just as a thunderstorm arrives for the night. I'm (not so gently) rocked to sleep by an interesting and reverberating ensemble—the drums of *native* thunder echoing the drums of *alien* thunder from the bombs of Eglin.

If you hear a kind word spoken of some worthy soul you know,
It may fill his heart with sunshine if you only tell him so.
(Unknown)

Friday—February 2, 2001
Trail Day—239/25
Trail Mile—3810/376
Location—Town of St. Marks, Florida, to Shell Island Fish Camp.
Allen and Ruthie Hobbs, proprietors.

It's been two weeks since my last entry, most of those days a blur as I continue hiking pretty much due east—even though this trek is a north-south journey.

I remember hiking through a couple of new sections constructed on the Eglin reservation. The first began at SR-85 and ran some seven-plus miles to Jr. Walton Pond. The second picked up from Jr. Walton and continued on to SR-285, a distance of some nine miles. These trails crossed several creeks, many with low banks, where thickets of titi (please say *tie tie*!) grow. Between the unspoiled, spring-fed brooks I passed through well drained, crowned forests of longleaf pine and turkey oak. Pearl, Silver, and Honey Creeks are an ever-dwindling part of the North Florida wilds, where pristine waterways continue flowing even during seasons of drought. It was a joy being back in the woods again, thankful for those many blessings—the beauty and serenity only seen and felt from those new vantages. The Western Gate Chapter takes great pride in what they've accomplished, and well they should. Indeed, all involved, the USAF and the FTA, should be pleased with their labor and the fruits of their cooperative effort. I'm certainly proud to be a member of the Western Gate.

I spent a couple of days with Steve Webb and his FTA trail-building crew, mostly young folks with the Student Conservation Association (SCA). On the second day, the kids came out and hiked with me. It was a hoot. We climbed and crisscrossed tall, forested areas, each filled with pure stands of longleaf pine. Between, the trail dipped to ford numerous meandering spring-fed brooks protected by tight walls of titi. Up and down and on and on we went as the kids kept trading point. Toward the end of the day, the terrain turned very interesting as we entered the lowlands formed by Alaqua Creek. At the creek, the trail became submerged in a mass of tangle and roots as it followed the serpentine oxbow shoreline. Out to a narrow point it lead, the rushing creek closing on both sides. As the creek consumed the little point, I became suddenly gripped with the realization that somehow the trail had to cross that wide, deep-flowing creek. Sure enough, right at the very tip of land, a huge oak tree had fallen, its trunk on one bank and the upper branches touching the other. And there we crossed. Limbs had been trimmed from the tree, and the bark was discolored where folks had inched and shuffled their way. Somehow I managed to get across, the kids right behind. We were very tired after that thirty-one mile day, but it was a memorable, joyful time.

I met up with *Spider* again, and we hiked together for a while. But mostly, as usual, mine was a solitary time. Near Pine Log State Forest, our paths crossed with that of *Luke *Gnome* Denton. Luke had begun his northbound hike on the ECT from Key West on November 1st and was over 1,000 miles into his northbound trek. We spent a great time together, sharing the joy of our meeting and the excitement of our respective journeys. Later, hiking the Econfina Creek Trail, *Spider* and I spent an evening by the creek. There, I remember being serenaded by a *large* pack of coyotes.

The following weekend was an enjoyable time at the Ruck, an annual hiker gathering held in the Georgia Appalachian Mountains. *Lee I Joe* and his son *Trooper* had given me a ride. Many friends were present. I made a short, impromptu talk, and then showed off my pack and its contents—which didn't take long. I got to spend a few minutes with my dear friend and webmaster, Greg *Rockin' Roller* Smith, and he told me about *Backpacker* doing a great book review on *Ten Million Steps*. I really got my batteries charged!

I've gotten great service out of my New Balance 803 cross-trainer, low-cut shoes, six to seven hundred miles per pair. The ones I wore entering Bradwell Bay, a long swampy section, had nearly eight hundred miles on them. They'd sure taken a beating and were showing much wear, but they made it through just fine. I'm finding that low-cut cross-trainers, designed for off-road running, work quite well on the FT, what with much of the trail being submerged. In '98, during my northbound ECT hike, I wore an old pair of Vasque Sundowners, an above-the-ankle, canvas/vulcanized lightweight boot. They worked okay, but these NB 803s have served me much better. These shoes have a mesh vent above the toes, which lets water in, but which also evacuates and pumps water right back out. So after emerging from the numerous quags, I've found to my delight that the foot sloshing doesn't last nearly as long. With my lightweight GVP G-4 pack, my Leki trekking poles, and these great

NB 803s, I'm getting through the Florida swamps just fine.

The hike around and down along the Sopchoppy River was enjoyable, even in the rain. Jim *Restless Wandering* Davis, another FTA crew leader, and the guys and gals with his SCA team, have done a fantastic job with their bridge-building project. I counted thirteen bridges!

While hiking near Tallahassee, I was shuttled about and taken in by the Pardue family. Howard, his wife Carolyn, and their daughters Jackie and Amanda welcomed me. Carolyn loves to cook, and while I was a guest in their home, she prepared an absolute feast, attended by the Pardues and many of my friends. Howard works for the FTA, which has an office in Tallahassee. The office is manned by Howard and Kent Wimmer. While there, I had the opportunity to see first-hand the great work that's being done. Howard and Kent attend to much ongoing work, definitely a labor of love on their part. Their jobs are myriad, but primarily they're involved with FTA's ongoing land acquisition and trail certification programs. I recall wondering at the time if Jim Kern, founder of FTA and the FT, could have ever imagined how far his dream of the Florida Trail would come in only three short decades!

Today I entered the St. Marks National Wildlife Refuge to continue my journey east. Oh yes, I'm still hiking east. Although this odyssey is a southbound trek o'er near the breadth of the entire eastern North American continent, the TA, and now the ECT, have taken me not only south, but also west, clear into the Central Time Zone. It's hard to believe that at Fort Pickens, in the Florida Panhandle, I was closer to Beaumont, Texas than to Jacksonville, Florida! So, for nearly the last 400 miles I've been traveling almost due east, and this eastern jaunt will continue another 100-plus miles before I finally turn the corner to head south into the Florida peninsula.

The trail through St. Marks National Wildlife Refuge has led me on a journey across some of Florida's most beautiful and unspoiled lands, a secret known to few. Indeed, St. Marks is the crown jewel of the FT. The next few days will bring more delightful hiking. Slowly but surely the days are becoming longer, the temperatures warmer, and the winter less harsh. This is my payoff—from here to Key West I'll be hiking stunning and delightful treadway, and I'll be with many wonderful friends.

I'm headed for the little town of St. Marks. I reach Oyster Bay at Marsh Point, touching the very shores of the Gulf of Mexico. I've finally entered the natural environs of the sabal palmetto (cabbage) palm, showcased so well in the Cathedral of Palms. I've waited so long and hiked so far to reach them, and here they stand now, so majestic and proud, rustling their fronds in the gentle breeze as if to say, "Welcome! We're so glad you're here!" And, oh yes, am I so very glad to finally be in their company. What better place could this reunion have taken place than in the beautiful St. Marks!

In the cool of the evening, as the day wanes, I reach the quaint little "can't get there from here" village of St. Marks. The road and the trail dead end at the river, at Posey's Oyster Bar, and there I go for their famous shrimp basket. I linger, am greeted by many, and as I prepare to depart, I'm offered a ride to Shell Island Fish Camp some two miles west.

This has become such a long journey, but I have found much good, much peace.

And if my dreamings ne'er come true,
The brightest and the best,
But leave me lone my journey through,
I'll set my heart to rest.
(Martha Haskell Clark)

*Luke *Gnome* Denton and Candi Sonnefeld departed Key West, Florida on November 1, 2000. Candi left the trail in St. Marks, ending her hike. Luke continued on to the Cliffs of Forillon, Québec Province, a distance of some 4,800 miles.

Saturday—February 3, 2001
Trail Day—240/26
Trail Mile—3810/376
Location—Shell Island Fish Camp, St. Marks, Florida

At the fish camp store this morning I meet Kenneth Hobbs, Allen's cousin. He's been working here with Allen for years. Allen and Ruthie are on vacation, so Ken offers to shuttle me across the St. Marks River tomorrow morning. This St. Marks is way too wide, deep, and swift to try and ford or swim. Before reaching the river from the south in '98, I had considered garbage-bagging my pack and doggie-paddling it across, but once I stood, gawking from the banks of the river, better judgment kicked in and prevailed. So instead of swimming, I commenced hollering and hooting until a worker at Posey's across heard me and sent Allen to fetch me over.

I got in too late yesterday for the post office. So I head there first thing this morning. I was looking forward to treating my tired puppies to a new pair of cross-trainers, as the ones I'm wearing have over 800 miles stomped out of them and they're all tired out. But alas, the problem is I didn't give my sponsor, the kind and generous folks at New Balance, enough time to send out a new pair. So it'll be another 150 miles before my tootsies get a chance at some new tread. When the shoes come in here at St. Marks, Deborha (spelled correctly) will bounce them along to Live Oak.

Heading on toward downtown I stop in at Bo Lynn's Grocery to inquire about where I might get some sewing done. My pants and water bottle pouch are coming apart. My good friend Norma Jean fixed my shorts while I was back visiting my sister Salle Anne in Missouri; seems everything I've got is starting to fall apart. Perhaps I'll simply collapse and disintegrate into a dark little smudge-of-a-puddle at the monument in Key West! The kind storekeeper, Miss Joy, gives some thought to my inquiry, then disappears. In a moment she returns from the back, talking on a portable phone. "Just a minute, I'll find out," I hear her say, then she turns and asks, "You the hiker come all the way from Canada?" With puzzlement I reply, "Yes, I've hiked here from Canada." Returning the phone to her ear she says, "This is the man...okay I'll tell him, thanks!" Miss Joy's just gotten off the phone with her friend, Florence Clore. "Flo'll fix your pants," she says with a grin. "Let me show you how to get to her place."

Word sure travels fast here in St. Marks. At Posey's last, I'd gone right away for their incredible shrimp basket. I'd feasted on that in '98 and spent all day yesterday thinking about it. While at Posey's enjoying my shrimp, I struck up a conversation with Ted Pusey (yes, it too, is spelled correctly!), oyster shucker and bartender par excellence here at Posey's. Ted is responsible for making Posey's the most famous topless place around—for oysters, that is! Anyway, Ted gave me a ride out to the fish camp last night and on the way I told him about Odyssey 2000-'01. He right away told a friend of his, who told Flo, who just asked Miss Joy if that was me!

In the afternoon, I while away my time taking in the sights around St. Marks. Here is a remarkable history, much to do with the New World. At the confluence of the St. Marks and Wakulla Rivers is the jut of land where the first watercraft were built and launched by the white man from these shores. St. Marks was preceded only by the establishment of St. Augustine.

Early fortifications were built here at San Marcos de Apalache. The site's history began in 1528 with the arrival of Narváez, followed in 1539 by Hernando de Soto. I enjoy hiking the trail through the ruins and seeing these historic fortifications.

In the afternoon I head once more to Posey's. At this sitting, I go for the grouper basket, another great choice. I now recommend the weary ECT thru-hiker stay at least two days in St. Marks, the first to have the shrimp basket at Posey's and the second to have the grouper basket—oh yes, at Posey's! Note: Posey's has since been destroyed by a hurricane-driven storm surge and is no more.

In the evening, I'm picked up by Howard Pardue, to be whisked away once more to Tallahassee, this time to the lovely home of Linda *eArThworm* Patton. Many members of the Apalache Chapter, FTA are present to greet me, along with *Restless Wandering* and two of his Wakulla SCA crewmembers, Nathan and Lilah. What a great potluck get-together and what a grand evening talking gear and telling trail lies. It was a lighthearted time, filled with happiness and much fun. Thanks, Linda, and thanks, again, Howard!

Being an adventurer, full of wanderlust—it has its price. There are times of loneliness and doubt, even moments of despair, but it's worth it, every minute of it, to be ever on the go—to be free!

> *O may I go a-wandering until the day I die.*
> *O may I always laugh and sing beneath God's clear blue sky.*
> *Valderi, valdera, valderi, valdera ha, ha, ha, ha, ha,*
> *Valderi, valdera, my knapsack on my back.*
> (Antonia Ridge)

Sunday—February 4, 2001
Trail Day—241/27
Trail Mile—3831/397
Location—US-98 at St. Marks National Wildlife Refuge to USFS Wakulla Work Center, Apalachicola National Forest, Florida. Jim "Restless Wandering" Davis, SCA Crew Leader.

Allen's cousin, Kenneth Hobbs, has offered me a ride across the St. Marks River this morning. As I wait in the little store at Shell Island Fish Camp, talking to Liz the storekeep, and as Ken helps some customers get their boats out of dry storage and into the river, in comes *Spider*. I was hoping he'd make it. I'd sent his brother an email a few days ago letting him know my plans. So this is great; we'll get to hike together again!

Spider wants to hike on to the river, so I continue draining the coffeepot as he continues to Posey's Oyster Bar. The last boat Ken dropped in the water belongs to a fellow from Tallahassee, name's Ed. He comes in and stops by the table where I'm finishing my blueberry muffin, plus what's left of Liz's coffee. Ed's getting ready to head out on the St. Marks and offers me a ride, thus saving Ken the trip.

Ed loads me up and we're soon off to a perfect morning, cruising the no-wake zone down the St. Marks River toward Posey's. *Spider's* waiting right there at Posey's dock. We drift in, pick him up, and are quickly across the river, to where the FT continues as it heads toward the old ghost town of Port Leon, now part of the magnificent St. Marks National Wildlife Refuge.

The trail follows the old tramway from where a trestle once crossed the St. Marks. This trestle vanished, as did the little settlement of Port Leon (and all its inhabitants) during a hurricane that swept through over a hundred years ago. In Port Leon, we climb the rickety, rotting steps of the old fire tower to get a good look—at the tops of the towering pine! Meandering on, the trail follows the old tramway out into the marshes that fringe the bays and tidal basins of St. Marks. Here we see our first alligator. Then, within the next two miles, many, many more huge gators! Coming toward us we spot a solitary hiker, first on the far-sweeping and distant horizon that presents such a panorama all about, then closer and closer. Finally, closing the gap, we're greeted by *Restless Wandering*, with just as grand a sweeping smile! He's come out to meet us and to hike back through the remainder of this remarkable St. Marks with *Spider* and me.

Together we hike along, enjoying this perfect day, and the seemingly endless beauty of live oak and cabbage palm hammocks. Toward evening and nearing the eastern extent of the St. Marks Trail we see yet another hiker approaching. Tall, lanky, huge pack with articles and gadgets dangling: it's Joe *Wild Flamingo* Masters. "*Nimblewill Nomad*," he exclaims, huge smile now, as he drops his pack to greet us. What a joyful time, exchanging trail talk and wishing each other all good success. Joe is forty-seven days out of Key West, bound for the Cliffs of Forillon, some eight months and 3,800-odd miles away.

At the crew truck now, loading our packs, we all sigh that sort of sigh that proves the truth of it, a feeling of contentment that comes only from such a splendid and memorable day.

Jim heads up another of the FTA work crews, this one also made up of guys and gals from the SCA. They're busy building bridges along the Sopchoppy River and extending the trail northeastward up the Econfina River. They're headquartered and housed at the USFS Wakulla Work Center. That's where we're headed—soon to be unloaded and in for the night. The kids are all bubbly with excitement as *Spider* and I arrive.

Spaghetti is the order for the evening meal, and oh yes, ice cream, Breyers, the very best. What good fortune! *Spider* and I decide to stay over and be part of the work crew tomorrow.

Good luck is with the man who doesn't include it in his plan.

(Unknown)

Monday—February 5, 2001
Trail Day—242/28
Trail Mile—3831/397
Location—USFS Wakulla Work Center, Apalachicola National Forest, Florida

Spider and I have been invited to spend a day and do some work with Jim and the young folks with his Wakulla SCA crew. The job they're on today entails hauling building materials to two bridge sites along Sopchoppy Creek, an easy job, you'd think. However, as is often the case with this kind of work, the little gulches across which these bridges will span are pretty much inaccessible. So after a half-dozen pack trips each, all the two-bys, four-bys, cables, turnbuckles and anchors have finally been lugged to the sites. By this time it's well into the afternoon, so Jim lets us call it a day. No argument on my part. Jim's a big guy. When I saw him pick up only one board and head into the woods with it this morning, I knew right away that my work was cut out for me. I quickly found, as I suspected, that one board is plenty to tote for any distance more than half a mile, even for the big guys. With this kind of work, patience is a grand virtue. I have a new appreciation now for all that's involved in building this great Florida Trail!

In the evening, *Spider* and I are invited to join the crew as they attend the annual meeting of the Panhandle Chapter, FTA. After a hard day and the long journey to the Black Angus in Panama City, we all have quite an appetite. My prime rib, courtesy of Herbert Robertson of the Panhandle Chapter, really hits the spot!

A fine evening is enjoyed by all. I'm totally worn out by the time we get back to the work center. No problem sleeping this night...

> *Patience often gets the credit that belongs to fatigue.*
> (Franklin P. Jones)

Tuesday—February 6, 2001
Trail Day—243/29
Trail Mile—3847/413
Location—Aucilla River Rapids Campsite, Florida

In only two short days I've become such good friends with this great SCA crew. Goodbyes are always so tough it seems, for always, the time to say goodbye must come. So—so long Jim, Nathan, Lincoln, Lilah, Tia, and Mark. I'll miss you all, dear friends. Jim shuttles us back to the trail, and we're soon on our way east again.

I've been looking forward to this day for such a long time, for this is the day I'll finally hike the Aucilla River Rises and Sinks. I blue-blazed this section in '98. Had to, due to the flooding caused by El Niño. But today I'll get to see this amazing river, a river that disappears beneath the earth only to surface again, and then just as quickly, disappear once more!

And what a remarkable hike this is turning out to be. It's a beautiful clear, warm day, the sun playing hide-and-seek in and out of the grotto-like yawns that form the limestone sinks all along this amazing natural wonder. The trail winds up and down and around and through the many and varied limestone formations. Tell folks there are rocks along the trail in Florida, and they won't believe you. But believe me, there are rocks along the trail in Florida! In a while the river ends its disappearing act. As the terrain begins climbing, the river comes rushing and cascading toward us in riffles and rapids, creating a pleasant and joyful-sounding place to hike. We tarry for the longest time by one of these especially happy little tumbling waters. And so, it seems this is it for today. And what a better spot to call it a day. There's a great campsite right nearby with grassy tenting areas, complete with a large fire ring, plus abundant firewood all about. Here, *Spider* and I set up. A cooking fire is a snap and I soon have my rice bubbling and jumping.

Nature is always full of new surprises, which by now should certainly be no surprise. But the surprises today have proven to be amazingly fascinating and rewarding—what a great hiking day.

> *Some things have to be* **believed** *to be* **seen.**
> (Ralph Hodgson)

Wednesday—February 7, 2001
Trail Day—244/30
Trail Mile—3868/434
Location—US-19/US-27 to Gandy Motel, Perry, Florida

The peaceful and soothing sounds of the river rapids quickly worked their magic last night, sending me off to blissful, restful sleep. What great pleasure, not having to climb into my bag liner for a change, the night being warm enough to sleep without the need to bury my head in my bag hood.

The day dawns foggy but clear, the sun quickly burning off the early haze. We're off again along the upper reaches of the Aucilla, the trail passing through majestic stands of bald cypress, complete with vast areas of cypress knees, their little children in great numbers all about.

The trail turns now to emerge from the dark coolness formed by and within this mystifying and mysterious place, and we're off to the races across clear-cut private forest land, devoid of all trees. The day turns hot. There is no shade, no breeze. The trail continues along sandy stretches of logging roads that converge and emerge in web-like fashion.

Following along the (somewhat) blazed trail proves guesswork and uncertainty. By early afternoon we reach the Econfina River where we retreat to the shade for a brief lunch.

Back on the trail, we immediately take a wrong turn, the road leading us directly away. In a while we accept the folly of continuing and turn to retrace our steps. By late afternoon, and as the day finally turns cooler, we reach US-19/US-27, our destination for the day.

From here, plans are to hitchhike into Perry to find a motel for the night, but no one will stop for us (appearing as we likely do to passersby), a couple of bums. With evening approaching we begin walking the shoulder toward Perry, twelve miles to the southeast. In a couple of hours we arrive at the Perry rest area where we're able to call a taxi to take us on in. Never had to call a taxi before, but I'm glad to finally get to town, where the cabbie delivers us to the Gandy Motel. After a soothing shower and a little rest, I manage to hurt myself at the Golden Corral AYCE buffet. This has been a knock-out-the-miles day.

...you never know when something begins
where it's going to take you.
(Joan Blos)

Thursday—February 8, 2001
Trail Day—245/31
Trail Mile—3868/434
Location—Gandy Motel, Perry, Florida

Today will be a day of R&R. My face and arms are badly sunburned, and my feet really hurt. I did get my new NB 803s, in a funny round-about way. *Restless Wanderer* chased down a UPS driver and found out he had them! There's some break-in time, even for running shoes. So, I'll give my poor doggies a break today. It's catch-up for correspondence and journal entries—while *Spider* reads *The Hobbit*. It's good to be hiking and spending time with this dear friend again.

> *Some friends come and go like a season.*
> *Others are arranged in our lives for good reason.*
> (Sharita Gadison)

Friday—February 9, 2001
Trail Day—246/32
Trail Mile—3891/457
Location—Near intersection/culverts at Madison 5 and Blacklake 3, west of SR-53, Madison County, Florida

Spider and I head to Golden Corral for breakfast and on the way I have my thumb out. Now comes the taxi driver that brought us to town Wednesday. He stops, gives us a ride to US-19/US-27, and we're back on the trail a little after eight. This worked great; no breakfast, but that's okay.

The hike today is a roadwalk through timber company land belonging to Gilman/Foley. Pretty much the entire area has undergone recent harvest, new pine seedlings planted, so there's precious little shade—and less water. However, we do find water at the culverts at the Econfina River. But to our dismay, the river is not running, the water stagnant. A gator, sunning on the bank nearby flops in, churning up the already muddy soup. So much for this water source.

Spider and I hike together very comfortably at a pace a tad under four miles per hour. On these wide woods roads we travel along side by side, yakking and enjoying each other's company. Occasionally one of us will stop, the other continuing on, with the one dropping behind catching up usually within twenty minutes or so. Just after lunch today *Spider* pulls off, and I continue on. In twenty minutes I listen but he is not coming, so I stop, turn and look back down the long, straight road. I'm surprised to find he's nowhere in sight. I shrug it off, figure he'll be along in a while, and keep on trucking. By mid-afternoon, after making a couple of wrong turns, then returning, I'm thinking he's now ahead of me. I hike on to our planned destination for the evening, the culverts at the intersection of Madison 5 and Black Lake 3, but he is not here.

I'm able to tolerate heat very well, but some folks aren't. *Spider* is a veteran hiker, backpacker, and woodsman, so I know not to worry. This has been a very hot, very long day, so I finally conclude that he pulled off to rest a while and probably fell asleep.

Though there's not much out here, this has been an interesting day. I've seen gators, turtles, and many small birds, especially robins. I've heard ruff grouse for the first time since leaving the mountains, also the shrill squawk from (and have seen) my first pair of sandhill cranes. The spiders are out, and I've had to start brushing cobwebs. I've also suffered additional sunburn on my arms and face—and the trail goes on.

I pitch camp, get a small cooking fire going, fetch water, fix my porridge, then roll in for the night.

> *We shall never cease from exploration,*
> *and the end of all our exploring will be to arrive*
> *where we started,*
> *and know the place for the first time.*
> (T. S. Eliot)

Saturday—February 10, 2001
Trail Day—247/33
Trail Mile—3914/480
Location—US-90 at Suwannee River State Park, Ellaville, Florida,
to the home of Ron and Judy King, Live Oak

I'm filled with excitement, for this day I'll hike the Suwannee River for the first time, and I'll again see my dear friends of many years, Ron and Judy King. I called and talked with Ron when in Perry and made arrangements to meet him today around three where US-90 crosses the Suwannee River.

The forecast is for 30% chance of rain. Sure enough, the day dawns cloudy and the rain comes soon. It proves a great hiking day though, with the rain being gentle and the day cool. By noon I reach the banks of the Suwannee River. For the next three days, I'll be hiking along this historic and grand old river. And from first appearance, it's going to be a memorable, joy-filled hike. As I continue, the riverbank is nearly a bluff, with huge live oak, hickory, maple and gum all along, displaying such a proud, timeless presence. The oaks seem so tenacious, clinging precariously as they do to the sloping banks. The maple are beginning to bud, their crimson show so striking against the grays and browns of winter. Ahh yes, it is a joy to see spring approaching! Even with my poncho on I haven't broken a sweat, for the rain of the day is providing such a pleasant coolness.

In a while I can hear the far-off rumble of traffic from I-10, as the trail now takes me back north across this interstate, almost to Georgia. It has been nearly two months since I departed Georgia, but in less than two days I could be back there. Indeed, it is a very long way across the Florida Panhandle, as I've continually hiked east—and north.

The monotony of the interstate din continues as the trail crosses it, then turns to follow alongside for the longest distance. The winding path finally returns to the river, but I'm no sooner out of earshot from I-10 than I begin hearing the traffic din on US-90. My introduction to the Suwannee is not disappointing however, as

I know there will be many quiet and peaceful miles of trekking its banks during the following days.

Ronnie meets me at the highway with a glad handshake, a grand hug, and a cold frosty! We're soon off to his spacious and lovely home south of Live Oak, where Judy is there to greet me. Odyssey 2000-'01 is turning to be such an incredible journey. It's hard to believe I'm here again with these beautiful friends, all the way from Cap Gaspé. "Way down upon de Suwnee Ribber [is indeed] far, far away!"

Dere's wha my heart is turning, ebber,
Dere's wha de old folks stay.
(Stephen Collins Foster)

Sunday—February 11, 2001
Trail Day—248/34
Trail Mile—3929/495
Location—Y'all Mart/Adams Country Store on Adams Road,
Jasper, Florida to the home of Ron and Judy King, Live Oak

On the way in last evening to Ronnie's, we stopped in Live Oak for the essentials, pizza and beer, enough for the whole family. You see, Judy has four sisters—two in Michigan and two right here nearby in Live Oak. Over the years, I've also become great friends with these sweet ladies and their families. So last night we were together again—Dave and Erie, Bob and Shirley, Ron and Judy, and the old *Nomad*. Folks, the Suwannee is beautiful, the mystic old Appalachians are beautiful, the distant, forbidding lands of the Canadian tundra are indeed beautiful, but far and above all of these wonders of nature stand the people, the beautiful people! It's the people that make the journey, it's the people that make the odyssey, and it's the people that make the memories, the priceless, precious, everlasting memories.

After a restful night's sleep and a fine breakfast prepared by Judy, she and Ronnie shuttle me back to the trail. It's another overcast day, just the least bit cool—delightful for hiking. Today I'll journey through Suwannee River State Park past ancient hammocks of live oak, then to a roadwalk across the Alapaha River to again head toward the Suwannee at the entrance to the Holton Creek Wildlife Management Area.

The day passes quickly, and I'm soon at the little rustic, tin-roofed Y'all Mart/Adams Country Store. Shortly come Ronnie and Dave to fetch me. Back at Live Oak now, we head for the Colonel's and a huge bucket of his finger-lickin' finest. Then it's back to Ron and Judy's for another grand evening.

The life of a hiker can be great, don't you know. The life of this hiker is certainly great!

> *...take time for friendship.*
> *Friendship, after all, is what life is finally about.*
> (Nels J. S. Ferre)

Monday—February 12, 2001
Trail Day—249/35
Trail Mile—3945/511
Location—US-129 at the Suwannee River Bridge, Suwannee
Springs, Florida, to the home of Ron and Judy King, Live Oak

Ronnie has two black labs: Duper, nine, 140 pounds; and Clayton, three, 110 pounds. In Publix the other evening, as Ronnie saw me picking up chips, he just looked at me, smiled and said, "You don't need to buy chips." I didn't know what that meant, but when I got to his place I understood. Folks, this man has chips, bags and bags of chips—everywhere! Come to find, Ronnie's neighbor is a Wise distributor, and so it seems that when he gets home, completing his deliveries for the day, he unloads the outdated bags by his door, where Clayton promptly appears to delicately collect them and deliver them to Ronnie. "Doesn't your neighbor get upset with

Clayton?" I ask! "Naw," exclaims Ronnie, "He's glad to get rid of 'em." So here comes Clayton now, proud as can be, bright red bag of Krunchers Kettle-Cooked Mesquite gently clutched in his jaws. Oh yes, and later for an encore does he follow up with an orange bag of Smokin' Grill Burger 'n Fixin's...dated January 24th, not bad Clayton, not bad at all. Give him a dog biscuit, Ronnie!

Ronnie and Judy cart me back to Y'all Mart, and I'm off on yet another cool, overcast day. A short walk down a grassy woods road and I'm standing before one of Florida's remarkable natural wonders: crater-shaped Holton Spring. From this huge hole in the ground flow millions of gallons of water, creating a small river all its own that meanders for a great distance, the trail right beside, to eventually merge with the Suwannee.

Along the Suwannee, the trail follows beside the rim of near canyon-like formations, walls of striking white honeycombed limestone, eroded and pocked by relentless waters of the eon. And at each oxbow, dune-like mounds of blinding, pure-white sand. Ma Nature is so creative, so imaginative: how she forges her fortresses, patiently constructs her masterpieces, delicately places each speck of dust, each grain of sand, as she builds her sandcastles of time. What an inspiration, being with her—God's loving and gracious gift to me this day!

Plans are for Dave to fetch me from the trail where it passes under US-129, and at three, as I reach the underpass, he's waiting for me. From here it's back again to Ron and Judy's for yet another relaxing evening.

All are but parts of one stupendous whole
Whose body Nature is, and God the soul.
(Alexander Pope)

Tuesday—February 13, 2001
Trail Day—250/36
Trail Mile—3945/511
Location—Home of Ron and Judy King, Live Oak, Florida

Today will be a day of rest, my fourth night in the comfort of the King's home. I spend time in the morning on my journal entries and correspondence, then this afternoon we visit friends around.

What a great day of rest before heading into the Osceola National Forest and points south.

> **Dear Mr. Foster:*
> *Would you could have seen,*
> *How Nature kept her, blessed her*
> *With beauty, pure, serene.*
>
> *Dat grand ol' ribber Swanee,*
> *Dere's wha de old folks stay,*
> *And with dem folks I'll tarry,*
> *When come de judgment day.*
>
> *De world am sad and dreary,*
> *Eb'ry where I roam.*
> *But ever in my mem'ry,*
> *De old folks at home.*
>
> *Yes, down de whole creation,*
> *'cross rivers and loam.*
> *I searched to blamed tarnation...*
> *No Swanee, my home.*
> (N. Nomad)

*Variants and spelling are pure Foster demotic, taken from his original work, "Old Folks at Home." Stephen Collins Foster never saw the Suwannee River, nor did he ever visit Florida.

Wednesday—February 14, 2001
Trail Day—251/37
Trail Mile—3966/532
Location—Suwannee Motel, US-41, White Springs, Florida

Judy fixes me a tank-stokin' breakfast to send me on my way south, just as she did to send me on my way north in '98. I've had such a grand time once again with these dear friends, but alas, Dave has come to get me and shuttle me back to the trail. So, as is always the case, it's time to say goodbye. So long, Ronnie. So long, Judy. You have been so kind and so generous. Thanks, thanks so much!

The trail crosses US-129 a short distance north of Live Oak, and Dave soon has me there.

Dave and I have also been good friends for many years. He's Ronnie's brother-in-law, with Ron's wife Judy Jane and Dave's wife Erie Belle being sisters. Dave's retired now and has moved to Live Oak so the sisters can be together. Same for Bob and his wife, Shirley. They've also moved here after retirement. What an absolutely great bunch; my extended family, if you will. It's always fun time when the sisters are together, which makes for much joy for all. So now it's goodbye time again. So long, Dave. It's going to be tough keeping this day from kicking a funk on me.

I've got a twenty-one miler ahead, but I know it's going to be a grand hike, for today the trail follows entirely along the Suwannee River. It starts out overcast but soon burns off, the sun out, the morn warm and pleasant. I've sent my bag liner home, along with my heavy, insulated gloves and a few other items, so my pack is considerably lighter now, probably in the neighborhood of twelve pounds, including food and water. At mid-morning now I hear and see the first familiar "V" squadron of Canadian honkers headed north. Oh yes, definitely a good sign!

The trail I'm hiking now is all new to me. I was unable to hike any of the Suwannee in '98 because of flooding caused by El Niño. I was told then that if the river stood above 60 feet at the White

Springs Gauging Station, the trail would be underwater. When I passed through then the river was at 84 feet!

It's interesting how the trail along the Suwannee goes right through people's back yards, right between their houses and the river. Yesterday I had to climb over rope railings along a boardwalk that connected this fellow's house to his river deck! I've been told that the Suwannee is classified as a scenic waterway and, as such, is protected by public lands some distance back from its banks, thus providing the corridor for the trail—even where there's private land right next the river. Seems this might be the solution to solving the problem of roadwalking southern Alabama. For in southern Alabama are there the rivers Yellow and Conecuh, along which the trail might pass.

This day's hiking ends far too quickly, and I'm soon at the Stephen Foster State Folk Culture Center. To my delight, I've the place to myself, and Pat, the kind attendant, takes time to tell me about the Center and to show me around.

This FT/ECT passes some interesting places. This remarkable Center is certainly one of them. Stephen Collins Foster was a very interesting and very blessed and talented man, a pioneer if you will, for during his lifetime there existed no music business as we know it. Sound recording and radio were unheard of; no such thing as copyrights or royalties. At his death at age 37, he had 38 cents in his pocket, along with a scribbled note reading, "Dear friends and gentle hearts." Among his many famous compositions are two that have been adopted as state songs, "Old Folks at Home" by Florida, and "My Old Kentucky Home" by Kentucky.

In the evening I check into the Suwannee Motel then head over to the Country Café for their special, T-bone steak and baked potato.

What a blessing, this day!

> *Make new friends, but keep the old;*
> *Those are silver, these are gold.*
> (Joseph Parry)

Thursday—February 15, 2001
Trail Day—252/38
Trail Mile—3985/551
Location—FS-233, West Tower, Osceola National Forest, Florida

While I was snapping a shot of the beautiful plantation-style Culture Center yesterday evening, up pulled this passenger van towing a trailer loaded with canoes. "You that long distance hiker?" asked the driver. As I stuttered to respond, I was told that *Not To Worry*, my friend from way back on the AT last summer, had stopped recently at American Canoe Adventure here in White Springs and showed the owner my book, *Ten Million Steps*. "Recognized you right away from your picture on the cover," said Wendell Hannum, big smile on his face!

The Suwannee Motel is still run by Tom Salter. He remembered me from Odyssey '98, gave me the same great hiker-trash deal. After checking in, I hoofed it over to the outpost to chat some with Wendell, and met his brother George and his sister-in-law Judy. American Canoe Adventures is a great hiker-friendly spot. Wendell has a bulletin board on the wall with maps of the FT prominently displayed, along with notes posted from this year's FT/ECT thru-hiker class. White Springs is a great little trail town.

Today I complete the Suwannee. The weather's been kind, the hike a memorable time. There's a time-encapsulated, captivating magic about this place that can't be explained, but that can certainly be felt and experienced. It's baffling and quite remarkable that Stephen Collins Foster sensed, and in fact came under the spell of, this mystic old river—without ever having been here or having seen it.

The remainder of this day is mostly a roadwalk as I enter the Osceola National Forest. In the forest, at West Tower, there are picnic tables, running water, and camping is permitted. So this is it for today.

Two miles north of here I finally turned the corner. After weeks of hiking almost due east, I'm finally headed south again. It's hard to believe that I've traveled so far, over 500 miles, from Fort Pickens in the spellbinding Gulf Islands National Seashore, to finally arrive

here at West Tower. But the western extreme of the Florida Panhandle is, indeed, way out there, deep in another time zone. What
a remarkable amalgamation of trails, this grand ECT, the Eastern
Continental Trail. On the venerable old AT, I recall oft hearing
thru-hikers lament their less enjoyable experiences in dealing with
the "Virginia Blues," a funk-driven sort of mood that descends
like a fog after hiking for so many, many days and miles on the
trail through that longest AT state. But here on the FT/ECT, I've
already exceeded that great distance through Virginia, seemingly
all the while heading in the wrong direction, and I've still over 800
miles yet ahead of me, still in Florida, before reaching Key West!
Ponder this if you will: where else on earth is there such a grand,
extended trail, where it's possible for last year's southbounders to
meet last year's northbounders—and also this year's northbounders! On the AT last year I met my dear friend Jon *Class V* Leuschel,
then Chuck *Swamp Eagle* Wilson, both bound for Cap Gaspé, out
of Key West. And just this month I've met Luke *Gnome* Denton and
Joe *Wild Flamingo* Masters, bound for Cap Gaspé, out of Key West.
Oh yes, I'm still bound for Key West, out of Cap Gaspé. Of all the
thousands and thousands of hikers that shouldered a backpack and
headed out on an extended trek in the year 2000, only two, just two,
are still out here, still going! One of those intrepid is Sridhar *Spider*
Ramasami. *Spider* departed the Cliffs of Forillon on June 1, 2000,
on the ECT, where the Appalachian Mountains plunge to the sea
at Cap Gaspé, Québec, bound for Key West, where the trail meets
the Caribbean. We've hiked together off and on. He's only a day
or two behind me now, on the FT, still headed for Key West, still
southbound on the ECT. And the other intrepid? Oh yes, it's the
old *Nomad*, still headed for Key West, still southbound on the ECT.

> *Each warrior wants to leave the mark of his will,*
> *his signature, on the important acts he touches.*
> *This is not the voice of ego but of the human spirit...*
> (Pat Riley)

Friday—February 16, 2001
Trail Day—253/39
Trail Mile—4014/580
Location—Near CR-231 on the banks of Swift Creek, Lake Butler
WMA, Lake Butler, Florida

The hike today is through some of the most majestic piney woods yet: mature, expansive, far-ranging stands of longleaf, loblolly and slash pine, the understory lush and densely clustered with the evergreen broad-frond scrub palmetto. This section of the FT is under the capable care of Phil Niswander, Ranger, USFS, Osceola National Forest. I'm able to see Phil for a few moments at Olustee, where this weekend the Battle of Olustee is being reenacted. I'd planned on camping here this evening, but after seeing the mass of confusion and listening for just a short while to the annoying din, I decide to move on, right past the cattle pens, the orange-blazed FT leading right down the midway, craft and folk art booths on the left and food concession stands on the right! In '98 this whole place was under water, with not a soul about.

Today I cross I-10 and US-90 for the last time. Getting them behind me has taken a while. I met both way out in the Panhandle, first crossing them there, then again further east, and now for the third and last time, here near Olustee. Remaining, of the almost countless "I's," are I-4 and I-75, the latter with which I'll play similar tag before finally putting it behind me in Big Cypress.

Heading south from Olustee, I enter the Lake Butler Wildlife Management Area. The timberlands here are owned by Georgia Pacific, the lands managed by the Florida Fish and Wildlife Conservation Commission. It's a great cooperative effort, permitting Georgia Pacific to reap the bounty of their lands through timber harvesting and at the same time allowing public access under a professionally managed government agency.

Camping is not permitted on Georgia Pacific lands. I understand and respect that regulation, so I'm really hammering the trail now, hoping to make the nearly nineteen additional miles to the south trailhead. But with the sixteen miles already covered from West Tower, it just throws me too late into the day. Thirty-five miles is way too far, and I've run out of water, daylight—and energy. So reluctantly, I pull up and pitch on the banks of Swift Creek. Swift Creek is not swift this day, being as slow and nearly as dry as me, only a puddle. But what a joy it is to behold—and to have. Hundreds have pitched tonight at Olustee. Most, I'm sure, prefer the distraction and noise of their close encampments. Would they instead, have chosen the quiet presence of Nature and the peaceful solitude of such a place as this? Please forgive me, Georgia Pacific, but I could not stay there; so I ventured on. Know that you will not find the least trace of where I've camped this night.

Nature reaches out to us with open arms,
and bids us enjoy her beauty; but we dread her silence...
(Kahlil Gibran)

Saturday—February 17, 2001
Trail Day—254/40
Trail Mile—4037/603
Location—SR-100/US-301 at Starke, Florida, in a cabbage palm
thicket near Denny's

I've a short eight-mile hike into Lake Butler. I arrive there by eleven, filled with anticipation. Here, during my northbound hike in '98, a very kind man, name of John Hamill, befriended me, and I'm anxious to renew his acquaintance and to spend some time with him again. But alas, approaching the house where John lived, the door open, a woman running a vacuum there, I finally manage to get her attention and inquire about John. "Don't know any John Hamill, lived here more'n a year—don't know any John Hamill," is her reply as she goes back to her vacuuming. I thank the lady, turn back to the street and stumble in a funk across towards the IGA.

The water in Swift Creek was really stagnant, and I drank only the little I needed last night to keep myself reasonably hydrated, so I'm thirsty, real thirsty. A sub shop across the way gets my attention and I head there, thinking, "Bet they've got plenty of ice cold sweet tea." I immediately hasten my step. Yes indeedy, sweet tea! You know, the big plastic container that stands near ten inches tall...iced down, full-up, yup, good old made-in-the-South (not, "You can add the sugar") sweet tea! One big gulp keeps me from tripping further into a funk as I order a sub. Striking up a conversation with the lady, I inquire if she might know of a John Hamill, her establishment being near where he once lived. A fellow helping out overhears our conversation and as the kind lady directs me his way, he replies, "I'm cousins with John's boy Justin; my name's Chris." We shake hands. Now here's a great break! Doesn't take long though to see this isn't going to work, for John has moved to near Waldo, nowhere near where the trail passes.

I thank them both and return again to my roadwalk, as through here the FT follows SR-100. Seems it's truckin' time again. There's only a pricey bed and breakfast here in Lake Butler, so it's off to Starke, some fifteen miles to the southeast.

SR-100 is a busy, dangerous highway, not the ideal roadwalk. I've been here before, and it's not where I want to be. The whole thing starts out okay, what with a paved shoulder, but that quickly peters out at the New River Bridge. The eighteen-wheelers are really plowing their little tornadoes at me, and the other traffic isn't all that friendly—just as I remember it from the early eighties when I came through here the first time. Even little tornadoes get old fast, and fifteen miles can become a long haul, even to a long distance hiker. The sun's also been pounding on me today since I'm trekking nearly south now, but the sun and heat are welcome and I'm managing to strike a happy chord.

I arrive at Starke around three, have a Frosty (soft ice cream) at Wendy's, then go to Captain D's for supper. Later in the evening, to my dismay, I find that the motels all around are full up, what with this being "Daytona 500" weekend. So, looking around, I find a quiet little spot in the cabbage palms behind Denny's, roll out my pad and sleeping bag and call it a day.

Hiking the shoulders of SR-100 has knocked the starch clean out of me, tough, really tough—no scars, though. Thank you, Lord. Sleep comes soon.

> *Lord set me a path by the side of the road,*
> *Pray this be part of your plan.*
> *Then heap on the burden and pile on the load*
> *'n I'll trek it the best that I can.*
> (N. Nomad)

Sunday—February 18, 2001
Trail Day—255/41
Trail Mile—4037/603
Location—SR-100/US-301 at Starke, Florida, to the Budget Inn.
Mike Patel, proprietor.

The traffic, which starts rumbling and grinding on US-301 around seven-thirty, rousts me out, so I pack my bag and head across the back parking lot to Denny's for coffee. I slept with my hiking garb on last night, so I suppose I look just the least bit disheveled this morning. Anyway, seems as though this NASCAR bunch and folks hereabouts aren't used to seeing good old hiker-trash all decked out in shorts, gaiters and sporting a backpack. They apparently haven't seen this kind of "bum" before. It's a hoot watching their expressions and double-takes, a pure hoot!

While looking for a room last evening, I chanced to pass the Starke First United Methodist Church, the sanctuary not grand in size by any stretch. But its beauty and presentation, the impact that it had on me in a true, traditional sense struck me as being truly magnificent. To either side of the entry, which forms the base of the bell tower, are arched windows, the lower extent of each being filled with marble. To the left is inscribed the Lord's Prayer, and to the right, Psalm 23. On the little announcement sign I read, "God is good, all the time! Rev. Jerry Carris." I decided right then and there to attend their Sunday service, and here I am. Oh what a friendly, God-fearin' group of folks. Sure enough makes me feel at home, and that's a great feeling to a fellow who's been away from home.

After church I stop by Sonny's Real Pit Bar-B-Q for their AYCE chicken. I'm really proud, didn't hurt myself for a change! Over now to Budget Inn, I'm able to get a fine rate for two nights. My body and my feet are tired. I need the rest.

In the evening I call friends and family. I'm able to make plans for the next few hiking days. Rick *Vagabond Rick* Guhsé, Rich *Solar Bear* Evans and Sandra *Navigator* Friend will be providing maps and data to get me around the west side of Orlando on the new "Western Corridor." My southbound hike will be the first thru-hike around this way, so I'm truly excited. They'll be coming out to hike some with me. I also had the joy in talking with Bob *Sourdough Bob* and Rose *Ramblin' Rose* Goss in Paisley. I met them at the FT conference a year ago. I'll stay a day or so with them soon and will be getting maildrops there. Got emails recently from Jim *Thunder Chicken* Pitts and Tim *Long Distance Man* Anderson. They both want to hike some with me, so we've made plans to get together for a day in the Ocala National Forest.

This is my payoff, folks: great friends, great hiking. Life just couldn't be better. What joy!

The Lord is my shepherd; I shall not want.
He maketh me to lie down in green pastures:
He leadeth me beside the still waters.
He restoreth my soul:
(Psalms 23:1-3)

Monday—February 19, 2001
Trail Day—256/42
Trail Mile—4037/603
Location—Budget Inn, Starke, Florida

I'll not heed the call to go forth today. This is a day of rest.

> *A life akin to the mist on the wind,*
> *This the wanderlust's way.*
> *He'll roam about to his journey's end,*
> *A calling he must obey.*
> (N. Nomad)

Tuesday—February 20, 2001
Trail Day—257/43
Trail Mile—4057/623
Location—Sandhill Camping Area campsite #25 at Mike Roess Gold Head Branch State Park, Keystone Heights, Florida

I'm out and into another gorgeous, sky-blue day in Florida. Today I'll put the SR-100 roadwalk behind me. This is a treacherous path; there's something about the traffic on this highway. I know it isn't the people, but there's something bothersome and near-evil about this highway. I'll be very relieved when I reach Airport Road, the end of it.

At the intersection of SR-100 and CR-18 is Edward's Grocery. I crossed SR-100 here during Odyssey '98. Stopping in, I find that I have missed my dear friend *Ed Tric Talone. Ed, at the young age of thirty-ish has hiked over a thousand miles for each of those years, yes, over thirty thousand miles in his hiking career! We became friends in '98 when our paths crossed way out in the boonies in southern Alabama. Ed's hiking the ECT now. He left Key West around the middle of January, bound for Cap Gaspé, and we missed each other yesterday. I was holed up at the inn in Starke, and Ed passed just south of me on his way to the Florida Panhandle. Dang!

The trail now skirts around the south side of Keystone Airport, pretty much the same route I hiked in '98 when I got lost. The way the trail goes now is grand, passing by delightful little spring-fed brooks and crystal-clear pools, through the Florida National Guard property and into Gold Head Branch State Park.

I've much better luck with the **"Hike for Hope" folks. Our paths cross here on the trail in Camp Blanding. What a great bunch of kids, six in all: five guys and a gal, all inspired by my writings about the ECT during Odyssey '98. They're hiking out of Key West, all bound for Cap Gaspé. The mission during their odyssey is to focus attention on the dreadful problem of world hunger. We all drop our packs, find some shade and chat incessantly for the longest time. Oh, what a great bunch! There's Mike *Big Mike* Smith, age 21, from New Mexico; Dakota *Cow Doubter* LaCroix, age 27, from Vermont; Ray *Poppenstein Hauffenschlager* Ford, age 23, from Alaska; John *Jester* Gilette, age 24, from Connecticut; Jeff *Timmy* Smith, Mike's brother, age 18, from New Mexico; and Kim *Berly* Jackson, age 22, from Colorado. Godspeed my dear new friends. You've an incredible adventure before you!

I'm in early, so I while the time with ranger Don Musen before pitching for the evening. He puts me in a dandy spot, right under the miniature adolescent live oaks in the main campground. Don told me about an eagle he'd carved out of a stump that stands in the Park, so I take the short side-trip to give it a look. Very impressive, Don! Two, dark, angular knots form the eyes of the eagle. Now how did he do that?

> *Some come into our lives, then quickly go;*
> *Some find our hearts, to ever stay within.*
> *Either way, their presence strikes a glow*
> *...And we are never quite the same again.*
> (N. Nomad)

*Ed *Tric* Talone—As of 2020, Ed has hiked well over 50,000 miles.
**Hike for Hope*—departed Key West, Florida on January 1ˢᵗ, 2000.
All six successfully completed their ECT thru-hike, arriving at the
Cliffs of Forillon at Cap Gaspé on November 3ʳᵈ, 2000, 305 days,
3487 miles.

Wednesday—February 21, 2001
Trail Day—258/44
Trail Mile—4079/645
*Location—Trailside, Rice Creek Conservation Area near Old Starke
Road, Florida*

Another beautiful hiking day, cool and clear. The trail takes me
through the remarkable Etonia Ravine, the last of the truly northern-like areas I'll experience on my way ever south.

Late afternoon, I'm daydreaming along. Just before the gate
leading from Carraway Mail Route onto Old Starke Road, I gasp,
shudder and pull up in total disbelief. For before me, stretched
across the warm, sandy path, is a huge timber rattler, the biggest I've
ever seen; not long, as these fellows tend not to grow in great length,
but so remarkably huge—the meat end of a baseball bat, mostly.
Instantly and reflexively, he contorts from his sunning pose to his
rattling/striking pose. Up he comes like a cobra, head ten to twelve
inches off the ground. I back off, though I'm no closer than ten feet.

Folks, this is riveting. I've never experienced such a moment
of utter fear—ever. Try to get in this with me, will you? Do this:
put your arm on a table there; now bend your elbow, bringing your
forearm straight up. Okay, now flex your wrist at a ninety, make a
fist and turn it directly toward your face. That's the likes of this guy,
head size and all. Now add to this some menacing hissing and rattling, and back that up with the piercing gaze from two hollow slits
of cold, black, eyes—and you've got it. Wow, in the future when
folks ask me, "Aren't you afraid of snakes?" I'm going to give that

question considerable more thought! I finally manage to pass, get over the gate—and go. Whew, I'll remember this encounter for a while. There's sure a difference between the angels we know to be *Herald*, and that one we know as—*Satan*. I came close to meeting one or the other of them today. Got to make sure that when my judgment day finally comes—that I've properly prepared myself. Hopefully, I'll be in good stead to meet the *Herald* angels. Yes, Billy Graham, it is true; "...*this life is only a dressing room for eternity.*"

On Old Starke Road now, and past the depressing remains of an old, defunct dairy, I decide to head into Bud's Grocery, only a half-mile off the trail. Oh yes, good local (not the insanely over-priced New England brand) ice cream. I'm a happy hiker!

I pitch for the evening, trailside, west of Bud's, just north of Water Management Area lands.

> *So blessed be the day Your judgment comes due,*
> *And blessed be Thy mercy bestowed.*
> *Oh blessed be this journey, all praises to You...*
> *O'er this path by the side of the road.*
> (N. Nomad)

Thursday—February 22, 2001
Trail Day—259/45
Trail Mile—4102/668
Location—Rodman Campground east of Rodman Dam, Florida

Well, in '98—you're likely tired of hearing about '98! But anyway, in '98 I tried to get my good friend of many years, Jim *Thunder Chicken* Pitts, GAME '97, to come out and hike some with me in the Ocala National Forest. Circumstances were that it just didn't happen. So this year, time to try again, as tomorrow I enter the Ocala yet again. Also in '98, I hiked with Jim's good friend, and now my good friend, Tim *Long Distance Man* Anderson, GAME '98. Perhaps, just perhaps, tomorrow we'll finally get together.

It's another marvelous hiking day, partly cloudy and cool. Nothing much redeeming or memorable about the trail today, the treadway being mostly sandy roads and rutted two-track. But this is how the string of pearls that make up this remarkable Florida National Scenic Trail are hooked together.

By early afternoon I've walked the barge canal lock access road and am standing in front of the locked, chain-link barricade by the lockkeeper's building. Plans were to meet Jim and Tim here this evening, but this place looks like a fortification, gates and fences everywhere, and they shut the whole place down at five. The lockkeeper finally shows, opens the gate and lets me in.

While sitting and waiting I've been thinking, "What to do?" The decision I've made is to get over the locks and across the canal while the gettin's good. So I leave a note by the "Stop, do not enter," sign for Jim and Tim, and move on.

On the note, I leave instructions for my friends to meet me at the campground just up the canal at Rodman Lake. That's where I've decided to head for the evening. But alas, as I pick my site, get firewood, pitch, prepare my evening meal, and wait and wait; no Jim and Tim.

There are no bad days on the trail;
some are just better than others.
(N. Nomad)

Friday—February 23, 2001
Trail Day—260/46
Trail Mile—4118/684
Location—Ocala National Forest behind The 88 Store, Salt Springs, Florida

Today I enter the Ocala National Forest, and today, once again, I become saddened and disheartened, just as happened two years ago.

For, I have found that little has been done to halt the unauthorized use of the Florida National Scenic Trail. It's the off-road vehicle and horseback folks. Where once the trail was a blanket of pine needles and oak leaves, is there now only churned and bermed-up sand. This breaks my heart; it truly breaks my heart. I enjoy being in the woods on a quad-track, motorcycle or horse as much as anyone but not here; this is not the place. This bunch of yahoos in the Ocala are ruining it for all of us.

Once on Riverside Island, I manage to perk back up, for here is truly a beautiful setting, cathedral-like if you will. I must simply ignore the atrocity that is the treadway. Here stand magnificent monarchs, all in a glorious family, such a proud, majestic lot are they, so tall and straight. Here stand thousands and thousands of native longleaf southern pine. Oh, and what an understory, so open, so incredibly sweeping and far-reaching, not like any other place, such a strikingly beautiful home for the luxurious, colorful wiregrass and the shining-green scrub palmetto.

By two-thirty I'm at The 88 Store. For the last two days I've been following the dainty footprints of a fellow backpacker, and here at The 88 Store I meet Nancy *Magellan* Gowler, GAME '95. We talk trail at the bar for the longest time over BBQ and fries, washed down by a few cold ones. *Magellan's* headed for Alexander Springs.

Just as happy hour kicks in, in come *Thunder Chicken* and *Long Distance Man*. They'd camped near the locks last night, then all day today they hiked along a couple of hours behind me. Dang! I should have stayed at the locks yesterday instead of moving on. Like time, I just can't stand still.

Time is a circus, always packing up and moving away.
(Ben Hecht)

Saturday—February 24, 2001
Trail Day—261/47
Trail Mile—4139/705
Location—Hidden Pond, Ocala National Forest, Florida

What a great evening last. Patricia (same barkeep from '98) wheeled in another keg of Coors Light for our grand celebration. *Thunder Chicken* and *Long Distance Man* lingered, then after more sad good-byes, were able to get a ride back to the locks with Patricia. Around six, *Navigator* and *Solar Bear* came in. I'd met *Navigator* during Odyssey '98 at the ALDHA hiker Gathering, then ran into her and *Solar Bear* at the FTA Conference last year. We've since become great friends. I also made the acquaintance and became immediate friends with Jack Angle from Ohio and his good friend, Tim White, entertainer at The 88 Store. It was way past eleven before I rolled in.

Somehow I manage to get up and back into the store for coffee at eight this morning. *Solar Bear* is hiking with me today, and we're out and on our way before nine. We get a quick glimpse across Juniper Prairie, then it's on through the high-washed sandpine ridges to Hopkins Prairie. Here, time is spent meandering the deep coves and jutting peninsulas that form the "shoreline" of Hopkins Prairie.

The day heats up and we slow considerably, yet manage the twenty-one mile day quite easily by four-thirty. Arriving at Hidden Pond, we find *Magellan* already in. The respectable cooking fire, turned warming fire, chases the bugs and keeps the least bit of chill from the evening. It's a joy having company on the trail again. Ahh indeed, what are friends for!

> *Friendship is the only cement that will ever*
> *hold the world together.*
> (Woodrow Wilson)

Sunday—February 25, 2001
Trail Day—262/48
Trail Mile—4159/725
Location—CR-445, Ocala National Forest, to the home of Bob
"Sourdough Bob" and Rose "Ramblin' Rose" Goss, GAME '85,
Paisley, Florida

Hidden Pond was quiet, with only the occasional far-off sound of sandhill cranes; a cool, perfect night for sleeping under the stars!

Solar Bear and I hike the morning with *Magellan,* who gets off the trail at Alexander Springs. We continue on through the heart of the Ocala. Here the treadway is much less abused, the scenery grand. At three, hiking toward us we meet *Sourdough Bob* and *Navigator,* who've hiked in from the south. Oh, this is grand; now I'm hiking with three great friends! By four-thirty we arrive at SR-445 where their vehicles are parked. We all load up and head for *Sourdough Bob's,* where *Ramblin' Rose* has a fine home-cooked meal waiting. In the evening, *Navigator* and *Solar Bear* brief me on the maps and data they've prepared to help me along. At CR-445, my southbound hike will be interrupted, and tomorrow I'll head west to begin my (mainly) road excursion around metropolitan Orlando along the Western Trail Corridor, FT.

The only people who are worth being friends with
are the people who like you as you are.
(Charlotte Levy)

Monday—February 26, 2001
Trail Day—263/49
Trail Mile—4175/741
Location—FS-573, Ocala National Forest, to the home of Bob and
Rose Goss, Paisley, Florida

I had my own private room and bath at the Goss home, and a great night's sleep. The heat took it out of all of us yesterday and I became dehydrated. Sure glad I've asked Dr. Gary *Bearbag* Buffington, GAME '00, to send out some more of his thirst quencher. Gary is one of my kind sponsors and the innovator of Conquest, a drink mix designed to keep ultra-marathoners adequately and properly hydrated during their long and grueling runs. It really works. I know—I used it all last summer when the temperatures were unbearable.

I'm up at seven, enjoy a fine breakfast with Bob and Rose, then Bob shuttles me back to SR-445.

The hike today is entirely a roadwalk through Ocala's Big Scrub territory. All along are towering stands of sand pine bordered abruptly by neatly sectioned areas of clear-cut forest. The day turns very warm. There is no shade, only the occasional cloud to hide the sun. I manage to endure the heat better as I slog the Conquest, and recollect the many days my fingers wouldn't work due to the incessant cold.

I'll be staying the night once more with Bob and Rose, so Bob will come to fetch me from the trail a little before two.

I arrive at Doe Lake just a little before two, and Bob comes right away—with sandwiches from Rose and an ice-cold jug of water. Ahh folks, this is trail magic at its best!

Another great meal prepared by Rose, then it's off to my room to catch up on correspondence and journal entries. I'm not in debt to this day, nor it to me.

Happy the man, and happy he alone,
He who can call today his own;
He who, secure within, can say,
Tomorrow, do thy worst, for I have liv'd today.
(John Dryden)

Tuesday—February 27, 2001
Trail Day—264/50
Trail Mile—4195/761
Location—US-441/US-301, Belleview, Florida to the Vin-Mar
Motel

That time is here again; why must it come? More sad goodbyes—this time to dear friends, *Sourdough Bob* and *Ramblin' Rose* Goss. They've both shuttled me back to the trail this morning. What a blessing, though. I'm clean, well fed, rested and ready to go again. Just a few salty tears, the only problem to show. Thanks, *Sourdough Bob* and *Ramblin' Rose*. You've been so kind to this old hiker. Indeed, I'll remain in your debt!

More dear friends to help the old *Nomad* along, and what an incredible amount of time they've spent in scouting, hiking, and driving this fledgling Western Corridor of the FT—*Navigator* and *Solar Bear*. And that dear friend who's always been there to help me, no matter what, Rick *Vagabond Rick* Guhsé. It's so good to have such accurate, finely detailed maps and data to guide me along. *Solar Bear* and *Navigator* have even helped prepare my itinerary for the next two weeks. How thoughtful of them, and how helpful to me! Having a practical and workable plan is invaluable in calculating how much food to lug, and where each day will end. Most importantly, family and friends can keep tabs on me. Thanks *Solar Bear*, *Navigator*, and *Vagabond Rick*! Folks, I keep tellin' ya, it's the people, they're the reason, for from them and through them comes pure joy. And it's this joy that frames the pictures in my memory—happy, joyful pictures that will remain forever, never to fade with time.

The day begins, my last in the Ocala, on a bumpy sand-washed road with no traffic, but that soon changes. By eleven I'm in the thick of it, vehicles rushing everywhere as I pull into Duck's Dam Diner right next the Ocklawaha River. It's a neat old mom-n-pop place run by John and Debbie Duckworth. What a menu. I pick the catfish, slaw, biscuits, and fries. Oh, and do these kind folks know what real sweet tea is, tall, ice filled, brimming glassfuls of sweet tea—oh yes!

In the little berg of Ocklawaha now, I find the post office right next to the trail, where I head in to mail the remainder of my winter gear back home—my wool shirt and liner gloves. The trees are budding, the wild plum and dogwood blooming, and it's a pounding-hot eighty-degree day. I think winter is over!

Today is another total roadwalk, usually not a problem as I enjoy the diversion that comes with hiking the roads. But this SR-25 is a bear as it dishes out rutted shoulders beached up with sugar sand, which is lifted and propelled against me by the flying lines of traffic as they streak by. But in a while I heed all of it no-never-mind, for SR-25 also offers the jam-uppedest pub/tavern crawl I've ever seen—clear to Belleview! So after detouring through a couple of these by-the-by watering holes, the percussion and grind tend to settle down, and don't it seem the shoulders are becoming a tad smoother while the din of the traffic turns much less troublesome!

Last evening I received an email from a friend of a friend. That friend is again *Navigator*, and her friend is Kenneth Smith. I remember receiving an email from Ken quite a ways back, offering to assist me when down this way, and has he ever! I'm told that ahead I'll find jugs of water stashed along the trail in the Cross Florida Greenway where there's a long dry stretch, and he's provided "local" directions to the motel in Belleview, directions that get me in by three-thirty, saving me nearly two miles—a great benefit at the end of a hot, dirty, twenty mile roadwalk. Gee whiz, thanks Ken! The great Florida Trail folks have been out in force today.

It's amazing how much even little things,
like basic kindness and gestures of caring, can help...
(Paige Williams)

Wednesday—February 28, 2001
Trail Day—265/51
Trail Mile—4212/778
Location—Ross Prairie, Cross Florida Greenway, Ocala, Florida

From the motel I head up US-301 this morning to complete the remainder of the 38.5-mile roadwalk from the Ocala Trail to the trail through the Greenway (the planned and purchased route for the ill-fated Cross Florida Barge Canal). It's great to be away from the insane noise and confusion of the highway, to be back, finally, in the woods. I arrive at ten.

There's no water anywhere in the Greenway along the trail running through it for a distance of some fifteen miles, so Ken Smith has stashed water for me at two strategic locations. In the Greenway, the hike turns interesting and enjoyable. Interesting in that civilization is just outside the corridor, which is only a mile wide. Even though the trail's in the woods, noise from traffic and nearby industry carries easily to the trail. It's also interesting because of the stately live oak here. They're in rows (old but long-gone fence rows), not the century-old monarchs seen elsewhere along the FT, but oaks that provide shade that makes for pleasant hiking. Yes, this hike today is enjoyable! I find the two jugs of water that Ken's hid for me. I take a quart of water from the first and leave a quart in the second.

Today I'm hiking west. Even though I'm on a southbound trek, it seems I seldom hike for long in that direction. I'm used to that; thru-hikers get used to the trail flitting about like a butterfly, going the roundabout way. We're not supposed to be in a hurry. If we were, I guess we'd be at the airport.

Many miles have been added to this Western Corridor, apparently as a result of the FTA's desire to connect to the Ocala Trail. So whether one chooses to hike the Eastern or the Western Corridor, the Ocala is in! Thirty-eight miles is a long roadwalk, and most of it is not terribly pleasant, but that's the price the Western Corridor hiker pays in order to have the benefit of hiking the Ocala. And why hike the Ocala Trail? Indeed, why is it included in both thru-hike routes? As best I can figure, it's because the Ocala Trail is considered to be the "Crown Jewel" of the Florida National Scenic Trail.

The long roadwalk on the northern end of the Western Corridor, coupled with no progress for the hiker north or south, makes for a not-so-fun hike (since eliminated). I think it would be best for the Western Corridor to skip the Ocala entirely. I've hiked all over this Florida National Scenic Trail, and I don't see the Ocala Trail being the likes of a "Crown Jewel." In fact, I believe that asserting it to be such holds the FT up to the public in entirely the wrong light. If we must talk about certain segments of the FT in relation to jewels, then let's talk about an incredible natural treasure chest full of jewels—and gems and pearls if you will. As we open this chest (as we hike the FT) do we find a remarkable array of nature's bounty. There are the aquamarine waters of the Gulf; the National Seashore and dunes; the new and breathtaking Wiregrass and Juniper Creek Trails that lead to Alabama; the remarkable St. Marks that presents cathedral-like palm hammocks; the Aucilla and Suwannee Rivers with their mystical wonders, steeped in history and intrigue; the northern-like ravines of Etonia and Gold Head Branch; the longleaf pine groves and the islands and prairies of the Ocala; the majesty of the centuries old live oak hammocks of Kissimmee; the rookeries of exotic birds and the bromeliad-draped cypress of the Big Cypress National Preserve; (and hopefully soon) the spectacular wonders of the Keys! You pick one: which is the most beautiful of nature's wonders seen along the Florida National Scenic Trail? Well, if I've made you do no more than stop and think about it—is the Ocala really so much more spectacular than all the other remarkable wonders along the FT?

I finish the Greenway Trail around five at SR-200, find a quiet spot by Ross Prairie, and pitch for the evening.

> *...the beauty all around thee lying, offers up*
> *its low, perpetual hymn.*
> (Harriett W. Sewall)

Thursday—March 1, 2001
Trail Day—266/52
Trail Mile—4232/798
Location—Withlacoochee State Trail at Eden Road, Inverness, Florida, to Central Motel

Yesterday, before heading into the Greenway, I stopped at Publix for provisions. Just inside the door stood this huge Toledo Scales. I'd sent home the last of my winter gear recently, my pack once again pretty skimpy, so I'd been wondering how much it actually weighed. So over to the scales I went—plunk. The needle hardly budged, finally creeping up to nine pounds and change, slightly less than the weight I was carrying after shedding my winter gear on the AT last spring.

Would you like to know what I currently have with me (not counting food and water)? Okay, here goes:

GVP G-4 backpack with hip belt
Wanderlust Gear Nomad Lite tent
Feathered Friends Rock Wren bag
Thermarest 3/4 Guidelite pad
Wanderlust Gear poncho
Patagonia long sleeve capilene shirt
Nylon pants
Lightweight wool socks
Hiker Trash painter's cap

Water bottle belt pouch
1-liter pop bottle
20 oz. pop bottle (2)
Aluminum cook pot
Aluminum bowl
Cookware stuff sack
Nylon ditty bag/w: stainless steel spoon/pot holder, First-
     Aid Kit in Ziploc, meds in Ziploc, medicated powder in
     Ziploc, Conquest in Ziploc, small vial of bleach, butane
     lighter, Photon Micro-Light, clothesline, tooth brush,
     floss, comb, compass, extra slide film
Olympus Stylus Zoom 80 35mm/w 36x slide film
Sharp TM-20 PocketMail
Bread wrapper stuff sacks
Large garbage bag
Maps and data

On my person, in pocket, or otherwise not included in my pack
weight:

Nylon shorts
Short sleeve Capilene T
Homemade gaiters
Wool socks
New Balance 803 cross-trainers
Watch
Medicine pouch with touchstone/talisman
Gerber 400 lockback knife
Smith & Wesson Magnum 3G sunglasses by Olympic Optical
Halfeye readers
Plastic wallet with cards/cash/change
Cotton headband

Ponytail band
Panasonic microcassette recorder
Data sheet/map for the day
Leki Super Makalu trekking poles

It's another near-perfect day in (near) paradise. I'm up and out to a cool, foggy morn. Today I'm faced with a long roadwalk, twelve miles, along SR-200 to Hernando where I'll get on the paved Withlacoochee State Trail. The traffic is incredibly heavy and totally launched. Everybody's heading for work in Ocala, but the shoulder is paved and, although I'm only four feet from the deadly projectiles, everyone seems alert for such an early time. I'm making good progress into the constant tornadoes being churned up and hurled at me.

By nine I'm standing at the Withlacoochee River bridge, right next the famous Stumpknockers Restaurant, which doesn't open till four. Dang! Some other time, I guess.

As I pull up to look at this old, narrow bridge, comes raw fright—clean down to my nailless toes. Between the bridge crash rail and the road-edge white line there's one foot of pavement—both sides. That's all. I shudder as I watch two eighteen-wheelers buffet and sway as they pass dead center, with only inches between them *and* between their wheels and the crash rails. What to do? I begin with: "Calm down, calm down, there's a way, there's always a way. How about wading across? Aw, geez, this river is wide and deep. Not a good idea. Then how about bowing your head, saying a short prayer, then head 'er up and go!" And that's just what I do. And for over a full minute does not a vehicle pass in either direction, and I'm quickly across! Thank you, Lord. The path you're providing me is indeed wide and safe.

By eleven I'm at Hernando and the Withlacoochee State Trail. After lunch at the local mom-n-pop, I'm on my way south—yes, south! The bikeway is a cruise. It's actually a paved road, just no motorized vehicles, and by two I'm in Inverness, where I call it a day at Central Motel.

A fast, easy hiking day—almost.

> *A man there was, though some did count him mad.*
> *The more he cast away the more he had.*
> (John Bunyan)

Friday—March 2, 2001
Trail Day—267/53
Trail Mile—4251/817
Location—Hog Island Campground, Croom Tract, Withlacoochee State Forest, Nobleton, Florida

Another leisurely day of hiking the Withlacoochee State Trail. I'll be on it till Nobleton, where I head for Croom. Many have passed here before, but I'm content in its discovery. Partly cloudy turns out great, what with the occasional full sun putting a sizzle on the black tarmac.

I pop into the numerous watering holes along and still manage to reach Nobleton by two. Here I jump over to CR-476 for a road-walk across the Withlacoochee River and on into Hog Island.

Starting to get some ribbing from locals about my *ski poles*— "Ain't no snow down here old man." It's another easy, carefree hiking day!

> *There is no land discovered,*
> *That can't be found anew.*
> *So journey on intrepid,*
> *Into the hazy blue.*
> (N. Nomad)

Saturday—March 3, 2001
Trail Day—268/54
Trail Mile—4273/839
Location—Trailside of SR 50 at Richloam Tract, Withlacoochee State
Forest, Ridge Manor, Florida

I waited with great anticipation last evening after arriving at Hog Island Campground. Plans were: *Navigator* was to come in, camp the night, then hike out with me this morning. What joy to see her, and what joy, her surprise for me, for just after her arrival, and also to camp the evening, came Jon *Wanchor* Phipps and Joan *Bluetrail* Jarvis. All brought food and refreshments. Great friends, a memorable time!

Plans today are for *Wanchor* and *Bluetrail* to hike out with *Navigator* and me, then turn back after an hour or so. This is great, hiking with these friends, but the hour passes way too quickly.

The trail in Croom offers a gentle stroll through forests that roll from cypress dips to longleaf ridges. *Navigator* and I enjoy chatting as we pass by cypress domes, live oak hammocks and pine plantations.

The woods hike behind us now, we venture out on US-301. Here is not peace and quiet, but rather the clamor and crush of passing traffic, plus the blasting heat radiating from the tarmac. Before long we both start to wilt. Time to retreat to the shade, cool our heels, and try to stay hydrated. Back to the tarmac, back to the shade—we alternate often. At the intersection of US-301 and SR-50 we retreat once more to the cool of the Mobil Station/Food Mart.

Plans were for *Solar Bear* to meet us, but plans don't always work out, so I hike on to Richloam alone. Great hiking with you, *Navigator*; thanks for coming out! Along the way now on SR-50, and turning to read a billboard aimed at westbound traffic, I read, "Weeki Wachee Springs, 14 Miles." A few days ago I was less than two miles from the St. Johns River; now I'm almost to the Gulf again! I pitch by the trailhead. A huge half-moon keeps me company, and as its gentle, calming light reflects on me, I reflect on the joys of this day.

Abundance consists not so much in material possessions...
(John Sheldon)

Sunday—March 4, 2001
Trail Day—269/55
Trail Mile—4302/868
Location—Green Swamp East Tract Trailhead at Green Swamp
Wilderness Preserve, Rockridge Road, Lakeland, Florida

The forecast is for thunderstorms, but the day dawns without a cloud in the sky. The decision is to rack up some miles today, so I'm up and going by seven. A permit is required to camp in these upcoming Withlacoochee tracts. Problem is, I've not secured a permit, so unless I hike Richloam and both sections of Green Swamp, I'll be violating the regulations. My decision is to pound on through all three today, a distance just shy of thirty miles.

By nine I'm well on my way through Richloam. It's then I begin hearing thunder in the distance. In moments the wind picks up, the blue sky ahead turns pitch black, and the train comes shuddering and rumbling through. I manage to don my poncho and duck behind a large live oak to escape the initial onslaught. I stick tight, and in a short while the wind relents and the driving storm turns to moderate-but-steady rain. I'm in it now, but do manage good progress as the treadway has been remarkably well maintained, the blazing very dependable.

The rain doesn't dampen my enjoyment for this hike today as the trail now passes through the real Florida I know, huge cypress bays, grand live oak and cabbage palm hammocks, plus vast islands and rolling hills populated by groves of mature longleaf pine understoried with rusty wiregrass and shiny-green scrub palmetto.

The trail meanders old woods roads, tramways, and secret little winding paths through the forest. By six I've reached the game check station. Here there's a well and running water. What joy in the finding, as today I've had to make do with surface water taken from rain puddles.

This has been a long day. No fire or warm sustenance tonight. It's late, everything I possess is soaked, and I'm just too tired.

> *On the road to life there are many paths...*
> *some twist, some turn, some dip, some curve.*
> (Brenda Good)

Monday—March 5, 2001
Trail Day—270/56
Trail Mile—4321/887
Location—Deen Still Road/US-27, Davenport, Florida, to Super 8 Motel at US-27/I-4

The rain has passed and the day once again turns the brightest blue. The treadway that is the trail of the Western Corridor is behind me now, but my hike around is far from over. Before me lies an eighty-mile roadwalk, and not uncommon with roadwalks, the wind comes up and with it a bit of a nip, so I alternate my hands from the clutch of my trekking poles to the warm clutch of my pockets. The sun soon warms both the day and the wind, as the wind continues to whip steady at my back.

As each day is different, so is each day's accompanying hike. Folks find this hard to believe, but it is true. Yesterday I was in the quiet and peaceful calm of the forest, but today it's man's world of noise and confusion. No complaints. Though I certainly prefer the forest, I like it all—every single foot of this trek, every minute. Heaven-on-earth is what you make of it, and walking can be some of the best of it. Hey, if you've never put on a backpack, why not give it a try!

Navigator and *Solar Bear*, dear friends who have helped me with maps and data for this Western Corridor hike, have described cattle ranches, orange groves, cliffs of sandstone, a half-buried VW Beetle, and a cypress tree festooned with silk flowers as things to busy myself watching for along the road today. The cliffs are a stretch, the ranches and groves drift by, the half-buried VW is certainly a very odd and funny thing, but I miss the decorated cypress tree!

In the afternoon now the gusting wind begins launching me, and I'm literally lifted and propelled as I complete the two-mile blue blaze down US-27 to the motel.

> *I no longer leave society to visit the woods.*
> *Rather, I leave the woods to visit society.*
> (David Brill)

Tuesday—March 6, 2001
Trail Day—271/57
Trail Mile—4340/906
Location—Kissimmee Lakefront Park. Lakeview Drive, Kissimmee/ Lake Tohopekaliga, to home of Sandra "Navigator" Friend, Orlando, Florida

The wind has decided to stay, bringing a mild chill from the north, but the warming Florida sun is out dispensing its charm, and in just a short while the day comes around nicely. The wind persists though, pushing hard on my port freeboard, and I must take constant precaution not to get tacked out and into oncoming traffic.

I put another "I" behind me today. The numbers have slowly dwindled, all the way down to I-4. There's just one more "I" left, I-75. This one's turned out to be a tough nut. When I think it's behind me, back it comes. I've crossed it three times now on my journey south, and it will be there one more time, in Big Cypress. And there's a famous highway still remaining, one which has become my good friend over the years, US-1. We first crossed paths during this journey over eight months ago, right after I entered the US from Canada. And in fitting fashion I'll finish this southbound odyssey along its way, all the way to mile-marker zero in Key West. This ECT, it cuts such an incredible path as it crosses three (now three and one-half) time zones and pretty much the eastern North American continent (and much of its history).

The roadwalk today provides a full mix—the relentless bone-jarring barrage of commercial traffic along US-17/US-92, contrasted by the leisure stroll back in time along the old (not yellow but red) brick road to Tampa. These old bricks once paved the way for the grand old touring cars, and alongside, the telegraph poles and steam locomotives. As I close my eyes, quickly returns the nostalgia of that simpler day and time. As I journey along these old bricks, I hear the chug, and can even smell the sulfur as the smoke-belching old steam locomotives pass. Soon I reach a stone monument at the Polk County line. On it are engraved these words, "Citurs Country." Yup, that's what it says, "Citurs Country," right there for all to quander—since October 1930!

Roadwalk days usually pass quickly, as does this one. Nineteen miles, and by three I'm at the city park in Kissimmee, right next to Lake Tohopekaliga. Here, by the old caboose-turned-concession-stand, I relax and work my journal entries while awaiting *Navigator's* arrival, as tonight she has invited me to be her guest. Though a weekday, the park is full, kids swinging and romping the playground, their happy, cheerful voices bringing joy to my ear.

Every day's a fine day to be alive. This one's especially fine! *Navigator* comes for me a little after five.

> *There is no race to win and nothing to be proven,*
> *only dreams to be nurtured, a self to be expressed,*
> *and love to be shared.*
> (Donna Newman)

Wednesday—March 7, 2001
Trail Day—272/58
Trail Mile—4355/921
Location—Canoe Creek Campground, Canoe Creek Road, St.
Cloud, Florida. Tom Scheidt, proprietor.

We're up at six. The plan is to get the jump on the morning rush hour and get through Orlando before the crunch. This works great. We're away from the apartment by seven, and *Navigator* has me back on the trail before eight. Thanks, *Navigator* and *Solar Bear*, dear friends, for all your kindness and generosity, and for your help in getting me around this remarkable Western Corridor! You've both worked very hard to make my hike here a quality experience, and I appreciate it very much.

The hike through Kissimmee is very pleasant, as the trail follows the walkways and bike paths all around Lake Toho. There's a Wal-Mart, where I stop, and numerous convenience stores along the way today, which I also pop into. By two-thirty I'm at Canoe Creek Campground. I usually don't stop this early, but I've got fifteen miles knocked down already and I've been pounding hard these last few days, so in I go. At the campground office now I meet Tom Scheidt and his grandson, Matthew. Both make me feel welcome and right at home. So that's it for this hiking day; I'm staying!

As I sign in, Tom says, "Pitch anywhere you like; Matthew will show you around." So off we go, the youngster showing me about—right over to a neat spot, and I pick that spot, near the bathhouse, next the bingo hall. Matthew is fascinated. He watches with wide-eyed excitement and curiosity as I lay out my little Nomad tent. He then joins right in to help. "There, how's that!" he says. Folks, this is so humbling. So late in this life of mine have I found that I can become, and can truly be, an inspiration to others. It's a joy, seeing the spark of excitement in this young lad's eye—oh yes, it sheer joy!

The wind finally gave it up today, but the day remained cool, another near-perfect hiking day in sunny Florida!

Don't be embarrassed to become better at the end of your life than you were to begin with.
(Socrates)

Thursday—March 8, 2001
Trail Day—273/59
Trail Mile—4378/944
Location—Trailside at the south junction of the North and South Loops, Three Lakes WMA/Prairie Lakes Tract, Kenansville, Florida

Long, straight roads that disappear to a point on the horizon make for long roadwalks. There's something about the fact that passing motorists are going twenty times faster than me (they're doing sixty and I'm only managing three), and I'm able to see them flying along ahead of me for two or three minutes before they, too, disappear on the horizon. Problem is, the ground I've watched them cover in three minutes will take me the better part of an hour! But then again, at my pace there are lots more people to meet and many more things to see. Indeed, though I'm on the same road—mine is "The Road Less Traveled."

So today is a long, straight roadwalk, over seventeen miles, the last to complete the Western Corridor of the FT. As I reach the end now, the familiar orange blazes join me from the east. I'm glad I came this way. For even though it's involved a lot of roadwalking, the distance being eighty miles further and nearly all that difference being a roadwalk, I have been well rewarded for my time. Indeed it's been a memorable hike! Not passing this way, I would have missed the Big Scrub, the Greenway, Croom, Richloam, and the incomparable Green Swamp. And I couldn't claim to have done the "Big 360" around metro Orlando—and big it is at nearly 350 miles.

I had a premonition this morning—about water. In '98 water was everywhere; I couldn't get out of it. But this time around I fear there'll be trouble finding water. And sure enough, at Three Lakes Wildlife Management Area Campground, the hand pump is not working. Ditto for the pumps in Prairie Lakes. By late afternoon I'm able to find some respectable looking (only mildly light green) water in one of the sloughs—just a puddle with mud all around, the feral hogs having rooted it up. But pay no never mind. It's wet, and a quart of it slakes my thirst.

A hot, dry, sundrenched day, my face and arms sunburned again—soon to look and feel like so much leather. After twenty-three miles, I pull over under a majestic live oak and pitch for the evening. Winter is no more...

Now I see the secret of making the best person,
it is to grow in the open air and to eat and sleep with the earth.
(Walt Whitman)

Friday—March 9, 2001
Trail Day—274/60
Trail Mile—4399/965
Location—Trailside by trailhead of KICCO Wildlife Management
Area, River Ranch, Florida

I'm up and out by seven-thirty. As I shoulder my pack I take the last swig of water to down my Ecotrin and Osteo Bi-Flex. Reluctantly I steel myself for the possibility of there being no water for the next sixteen miles, nearly the entire hiking day. I've been told the Oasis store at SR-60/Kissimmee River is closed down, condemned by the state to provide roadway for the new bridge soon to be built over the river.

A short hike by a woods road, then through a live oak hammock, and the trail pitches me straight onto the prairie of Prairie Lakes. By nine the sun is hammering me hard. I stop to don my hiker-trash painter's hat and my long-sleeved Polypro shirt. This helps some, but by the time I reach Godwin Hammock and some merciful shade, I'm already very thirsty. I've been told there's water, supposedly, in a large hole dug near the hammock, but seeing it and heading there, my worst fears are realized: it is dry, with green plants growing in the bottom. This whole place was underwater my last pass through, even the hammock.

From the hammock, I'm back again on the shadeless prairie, finally to cross it, then to pass along a long, dug-up, shadeless fence-row followed by a two-mile walk down a shadeless, sand-washed road to SR-60. At the highway now, I've been without the benefit of water or shade for the last eleven miles, and here before me I am faced with the roughest five-mile roadwalk along the entire FT.

I can't remember ever being as thirsty as I am this moment. This is not fun. I try convincing myself, but not so easy am I convinced, that I've less than two more hours to go—less than two hours to reach the store west of the river, about a mile past Oasis.

As I cross the road, and turn to meet the onslaught, the heat from the pavement rises to greet me. The traffic on this highway runs hard and fast, mostly commercial, mostly eighteen-wheelers. The truckers try to give me some room, but there are rigs rolling just as hard and just as fast in the other direction. I try to fix my attention on the crushing traffic and not on my watch. Before me now is another road that disappears, lifting and bouncing to the horizon. I manage to keep moving, but time seems suspended. Oh Lord, please, if you'll lift 'em up I'll try to put 'em down. In a while I believe I see the bridge. Yes, it is the bridge. As I near, and look to the right down a narrow sand road, I see dwellings, all in a row. A pickup full of laborers turns in. It's a migrant camp. I, too, turn in. Many greet me, but none speak English. I clutch my throat, and then make the motion of drinking by lifting my hand to my mouth. A young man comes and takes my arm. He leads me to his door, and in a moment I have a quart of water in my hand. What a blessing; I gulp it down. Dear Lord, I promise I'll never, ever leave a glass of water sitting on the table before me again, never again!

Soon I'm over the bridge, and as I pass Oasis I look back. The door is open on the west side and a sign reads, "Yes, we're open!" Oh, what a blessing once again. I'll not need to walk the extra mile now to the next store. As I enter, the lady recognizes me, "You're that hiker from Canada, aren't you?" she says, "Been a feller in here looking for you, showed me the picture on your book, can't remember his name, said he'd be back by in a day or two." I nod as I head for the pop cooler, two quarts of Gatorade and a ready-made sub and I plunk myself down in one of the easy chairs by the door.

I rest here most the afternoon before heading out the remaining four miles to KICCO Wildlife Management Area Trailhead.

My philosophy: "There are no bad days on the trail; some just better than others." There have been better days.

...we grow strong or weak and at last some crisis shows
what we have become.
(Brooke Foss Westcott)

Saturday—March 10, 2001
Trail Day—275/61
Trail Mile—4418/984
Location—Fort Kissimmee Campground, Avon Park Air Force
Range, Florida

Well, I believe I've learned my lesson about the water situation. This trail is going to be dry until I finish this hike, and the only reliable way to be sure of having enough water at any given time is to carry it. So coming out of Oasis yesterday, I loaded both quart Gatorade bottles full of water. I also filled up a 20 ounce Mountain Dew bottle. Today I'll have water, no matter. And even if there's none at Ft. Kissimmee Campground, if the pumps there aren't working either, at least I can take water from the river.

I've hiked this trail before, but I recognize very little of it, for before, even the oak hammocks were submerged. This time the hike is an absolute joy! I remember this Kissimmee River section as being very special, a truly southern setting, with the magnificent live oak and cabbage palm hammocks.

I don't notice the heat being nearly as bad today and the hike along Ice Cream Slough, Rattlesnake Hammock, the ghost town of KICCO and on into Ft. Kissimmee goes by quickly. No rattlesnakes at Rattlesnake Hammock, but I did brush by a polite old diamondback just south of KICCO. And brush is the right word. My Leki trekking pole grazed his head as I passed. Only then did he coil to strike. We had a cordial conversation and I thanked him for his tolerance.

The first pump at Ft. Kissimmee is out, but I remember there being two. Sure enough, as luck would have it, the pump near the south campground boundary is working fine. This is it for today. I set a small fire for cooking, and then work my journal entries. Just as the cool of the evening descends, so do the mosquitoes, so into my spacious Nomad tent I go. What a fine hiking day, a reward for the day just passed.

> *...I know...the great rewards that await the lone wanderer...*
> (Chris Townsend)

Sunday—March 11, 2001
Trail Day—276/62
Trail Mile—4440/1006
Location—US-98 and CR-721 at Fort Basinger, to the home of
Doug and Pat McCoy, Okeechobee, Florida

The live oak hammocks south of Ft. Kissimmee are even more grand than I recall, one particularly so. Here are majestic trees, centuries old, perfectly aligned, limbs intertwined, yet their trunks a hundred feet apart, much the likes of a formal promenade, so striking and remarkable are they. I pass through their midst in silence, filled with wonder and awe.

Today I'll be hiking two new sections of trail in Boney Marsh Wildlife Management Area. The northern half has been relocated, the old treadway having been destroyed as a result of dike removal, part of the Kissimmee River floodplain restoration. The trail now weaves back and across the hundred-year flood line. And the southern half, which has been relocated to the hammocks near the hundred-year flood line, eliminates a nine-mile roadwalk.

I've been anxious to hike these new sections since hearing of them from *Vagabond Rick*. And I'm not disappointed, as the views of the Kissimmee River savanna are absolutely stunning. Plus, there's a hiker bridge that climbs nearly to the sky in order to clear a navigable canal. Yes, I'm having a great time here today!

Vagabond Rick has prepared a *Thru-Hiker Handbook* for the southern sections of the ECT. Doug and Pat McCoy are shown

there on his list of trail angels. They live in Okeechobee. A couple of days ago I dropped them a message hoping for a little trail magic, but then I ducked back in the woods and have been unable to check my email since. I'm hoping they'll come for me as I near the end of my hike today along US-98. Sure enough, just as I round the bend toward the Kissimmee River Bridge, up pulls Doug. What luck. This is great! We no sooner exchange greetings than I'm invited to be their guest this evening.

Oh yes, this has been one fine hiking day, shared mostly with Mother Nature. There, alone in her presence, I was struck by her spellbinding, awe-inspiring beauty—Florida, unspoiled. This odyssey is absolutely filled with the miracles and magic that only perseverance and patience can reveal; let it continue.

There are times when God asks nothing of His children
except silence, patience, and tears.
(Charles Seymour Robinson)

Monday—March 12, 2001
Trail Day—277/63
Trail Mile—4466/1032
Location—SR-78 at Okee-Tantie, to the home of Doug and Pat
McCoy, Okeechobee, Florida

Doug's route to work takes us right by where I resume my hike, how convenient! I'm back on the trail (roadwalk) by seven-thirty.

Problem to solve today: there's no good way for the FT south-bound thru-hiker to get from Ft. Basinger to Yates Marsh. The Kissimmee River is in the way. Northbounders can cross at the S65-D lock after knocking on the lockkeeper's door. She'll open the gate. Southbounders are out of luck. We could stand, holler, and yell from the far side of the lock all day, and she wouldn't hear us.

One alternative for the southbounder is to cross the river at the US-98 bridge, then walk around five miles to Yates. Another is to trespass on railroad property and cross at the trestle—not the best route, but the shortest and easiest for the southbounder. Oh yes, I do the trestle walk (again) just like in '98. Crossing takes only a minute and a half, but that short time seems an eternity. During this time warp I'm thinking about that extra, now seemingly short five miles, and the rest of my (possibly very short) life. Hey, look, I'm across and still in one piece—to beat the odds again! As I hike along the tracks, the next rail projectile (Amtrak) doesn't fly by for another half-hour.

Yates Marsh is a fun hike. I'm in the pasture right along with the cows. There's a mighty fine campsite here, complete with picnic table, fire ring, refreshingly cool, clear water from a piped well, plus an electric outlet. Lucky pasture residents we, eh! This whole place was underwater in '98 and I had to pitch by the watering trough, where the local four-legged folk stood sentry all night.

By late morning I'm at the S65-E lock and spillway where I pull up on the lee shady side of the lock control building, right next to the water faucet. Break time! Continuing, I'm on the levee now. The wind is really beginning to drive through, straight out of the south, and I must lean hard into it to make any progress. Here there is no shade, no escape from the hot blast and the sweltering sun, but I must not complain about the heat; it is far and away the better choice, compared to the freezing cold of last winter.

There are mobile homes to my right, and I can see the barricade ahead, the end of the Kissimmee River where it empties into Lake Okeechobee. Here is the Okee-Tantie Recreation Area and Lightsey's Restaurant. It's now just three so in I go for a late lunch. Plans are for Doug to come and fetch me and for me to stay another delightful night with him, Pat, and their children Heather and Brit. My waitress lets me sit on the porch, to wait and to work my journal ramblings. She continues bringing me more delicious sweet tea till Doug arrives.

For supper, Pat prepares a delicious steak dinner, complete with all the trimmings, rounded out with strawberry shortcake for dessert! Another fine evening with these great new trail angels—and another comfy night on their cushy Posturepedic!

Slowly but surely it's sinking in. I'm realizing this dream. It is true; this remarkable journey is coming to pass. In the beginning, the thought of hiking such a great distance seemed such an unreachable goal. It has been flowing though, and I'm flowing with it. It is truly becoming the dream of a lifetime!

Dreams come a size too big so that we can grow into them.
(Josie Bisset)

Tuesday—March 13, 2001
Trail Day—278/64
Trail Mile—4505/1071
Location—Pahokee Campground and Marina, Pahokee, Florida

We're up early. I have breakfast with Doug, and it's back to the trail. Doug, what a great time I've had with you, Pat, and the kids, Heather and Brit. Thanks, dear friends, for your thoughtfulness, your generosity and your kindness! The time spent with you will remain in my memory.

Hiking the Big O (the Hoover Dike around Lake Okeechobee) isn't my bag. There really are no bad days on the trail, but hiking the Big O tests it for me. Folks actually come out here and hike this circle-round every year and have a great time of it. It's just isn't my idea of fun. A couple of hours up here are more than enough for me. More power to y'all; I'll head for the Chic Chocs for my days in the sun!

So here I go, around the east side of the Big O. By one-ten I've beat out twenty miles of it into Chancey Bay. By the time I arrive, the wind is literally picking me up. Hiking into its constantly pushing wall becomes very tiring. At the bay, there's a lounge and a campground/trailer park. I was told the lounge was closed, and talking to the locals here, I find the campground is also closed.

Since the day is yet early, I decide to continue hammering on this dike walk. Looking behind me to the north I see where this relentless wind's been heading—toward a bank of ominous black clouds. Looks like the makings for an afternoon thunderstorm that will likely come chugging this way, the levee not being a very good place to be should a storm develop. So I take to the low ground, and a roadwalk down US-98/US-441 as I cross the Port Mayaca Bridge. US-98 has always been kind to me, and so it is today, the shoulders paved, the traffic light, and the motorists more than courteous.

At the bridge now, the roadwalk proceeding nicely (no impending storm), I decide to pound it on down to Canal Point. My data sheet shows it to be a distance of about six miles. There's a motel in Canal Point.

Here's where things start coming apart. It takes me well over two hours to hike the distance to Canal Point, and there's no motel. It's in Pahokee. So hike it on I go, down to the Grassy Waters Motel on the northern outskirts of Pahokee. Arriving, I find the place is indeed grassy—the driveway overgrown in grass and weeds. The place is closed, a permanent "no vacancy" sign in the door.

What the hey; it's totally dark now, so on toward Pahokee I trudge. In just moments I hear a loud racket as two juveniles come flying straight at me on a quad-track, lights out, barreling right down the shoulder. I take to the ditch to avoid being hit. Seeing me now, they spin around in a ripping grind, churning and throwing dirt in all directions. They come hell-bent, straight at me again, this time intentionally. Again I dive for the ditch as the passenger hurls a bottle. They turn again, zooming clear across the busy highway to spin around and come roaring straight back across the road at me. This time I stand my ground, jumping to the side only at the last second while taking a roundhouse swing with my trekking poles. I miss with the sticks, but the straps slap hell out of the kid on the back. Turning yet again as I shake my sticks at them, they decide they've had enough "fun." Heading back north on the shoulder, they're soon gone, the low-pitched drone of their engine fading into the night. Oh my, what an ordeal. This whole episode lasted little more than a minute. Thank you, Lord, thank you for seeing me safely through yet another one!

At the outskirts of Pahokee, thirty-nine miles for the day, two teens on bicycles come alongside. "We're ya going," says one. I give them my pitch. "You're heading into a bad neighborhood," says the other. "Well now," I'm thinking, "Like, I've been in a good neighborhood!" "Better let us go with you and show you a safe way," says the first. So, trusting their kindness, along we go. Soon, a policeman, the local night patrol, pulls to the shoulder to check me out. It's now I learn there's no place to stay in Pahokee.

We continue on, the two youths, and the old, tired and bedraggled *Nomad*. We soon reach one of the few local hangouts in Pahokee, Burger King. It's nine o'clock now, but the place is packed with rowdy kids, they're everywhere, in and out, order being maintained by Richard, Pahokee's chief of police. After a burger and fries, Richard instructs my new friends, Alan and Hector, to show me to the far end of Pahokee Campground, where he assures me I can safely pitch for the night.

Oh what a crazy day—a crazy thirty-nine mile day. As I pitch for the night, by the shores of the great lake, Okeechobee, I'm content in the feeling and in knowing that my faith in the goodness of man will remain unshaken. I have no scars, but I'm certainly the least bit wiser. Maybe there are no bad days on the trail, but there's no question, some sure turn out better than others.

> *God will not look us over for medals, degrees or diplomas,*
> *but for scars.*
> (Elbert Hubbard)

Wednesday—March 14, 2001
Trail Day—279/65
Trail Mile—4505/1071
Location—Pahokee Campground and Marina, Pahokee, Florida

With the wind off the lake, the waves lapping the shore, and near a forty mile hiking day, I wasn't long for this world once my head hit my makeshift pillow. My little Nomad tent has indeed become home. I drifted away to the Land of Nod, feeling safe and secure.

The fishing's been good recently and everybody's up early this morning, so I'm up early, too. With the crazy hike of yesterday, I'll be taking a day off. *Wanchor* won't be coming for me at Lake Harbor until tomorrow evening, when he'll fetch me from the trail and shuttle me to the FTA Annual Conference, where I've been invited to speak. Lake Harbor is only fifteen miles south of Pahokee by trail (levee) and I can easily knock that out tomorrow by one-thirty.

On my way back to Burger King for breakfast, I pass ancient and grand royal palms. They stand in a row all along the street, lining both sides. I'm in the subtropics now, no doubt about it. There are so many strange and exotic plants here. Yesterday I saw the first *Washingtonia* palm, the first Norfolk Island pine, the first coconut palm, and the first royal palm. There are so many more, but I do not know their names.

I spend the day in the library, catching up on correspondence and writing my journal. In the evening, Alan joins me for supper at Nana's, a little Mexican store up the street. After supper we head back to the lake where Hector has had good luck fishing. I enjoy the company of these two young friends before rolling in for another grand night on Pahokee Beach.

Faith is kept alive in us, and gathers strength,
more from practice than from speculation.
(Joseph Addison)

Thursday—March 15, 2001
Trail Day—280/66
Trail Mile—4521/1087
Location—Lake Harbor post office to the home of Joan Jarvis,
Oviedo, Florida

The fishermen are up again, so I'm up again. I manage to break camp and hit the levee by seven-fifteen. The wind is already kicking out of the south, and there's nothing up here to stop it. As I lean into it once more, I step out briskly with the pleasant assurance that this will be my last day hammering the Big O.

The wind finally succeeds in pushing me over the side at Paul Rardin Park, where I camel up on water and top off my 20 ounce

Mountain Dew bottle before heading back up and into it again. Entertainment today includes watching an old twin engine do touch-and-goes at Glades Airport, with the closing act being two officers, full dress, flak jackets, guns and all, being dragged along the canal bank by a huge bloodhound. I must have passed the guy whose trail they're tracking. Glad our trails didn't cross!

By one-thirty I'm at Lake Harbor. Problem is, I don't see any town. At John Stretch Park, I inquire as to the whereabouts of the town of Lake Harbor. With considerable amusement, the man emptying the trashcans points, "It's right over there," he says. I look but still see no buildings—nothing. I shrug. He continues, "Down that road right over there." I inquire further about a post office, restaurant, gas station. "Oh, there's a post office," he says, "but that's it. Lake Harbor's a real small place." Now that I take another look, I do believe I can see the flag flying over there a ways.

Heading down the side road, at the next crossroad I arrive at the Lake Harbor post office, the only building around. I enter and am greeted by Joy Hand-Pierce, the only postal employee around. We pass the time while waiting for Jon to come and fetch me, talking about my hike and about Joe *Wild Flamingo* Masters and Del Delahunty. According to Joy, they also stopped here at the Lake Harbor post office while passing through on their respective ECT northbound hikes.

As we're talking I inquire as to why the pop machine outside isn't working. Seeing that I'm thirsty, Joy says, "I've got something better than pop" as she heads to the back. In a few minutes she returns with a huge Styrofoam cup filled with ice, topped off with the last of her mother's mighty fine sweet tea—which serves to wash down the sandwich and chips she also hands me. What a joy meeting Joy! *Vagabond Rick*, here's another trail angel to add to your ECT *Thru-Hiker Handbook*!

At four, right on time, *Wanchor* arrives to help me on my way to the annual Florida Trail Association Meeting near Paisley in the Ocala National Forest. It's a long drive back to Oviedo to Joan's home, but well worth the ride. Joan has not only provided late lunch but has prepared a fine evening meal. Thanks, *Wanchor* and *Bluetrail*! In her comfy home for the night now, I try doing some writing but am just too tired. The crispy clean sheets feel so very good.

> *Dreams come true; without that possibility,*
> *nature would not incite us to have them.*
> (John Updike)

Friday—March 16, 2001
Trail Day—281/67
Trail Mile—4521/1087
Location—FTA Annual Conference, Camp Ocala, Ocala National Forest, Florida

Today I'll continue on to the annual FTA Conference in the Ocala National Forest. *Vagabond Rick* will be taking me. There's some time this morning, so Joan drops me by the library on her way to work. Here I plan do some writing. She isn't gone long, however, till she returns with another hiker. The writing can wait, for meeting and talking now with Bob Roscigo turns to quite an experience. Here's a very interesting man. Seems Bob is also on an odyssey. I think he's calling his a "tour." What's different and so remarkable about this man, however, is that he stays in the woods for upwards of seven weeks at a time and is currently carrying between 110 and 120 pounds on his back! He's down here hiking the Florida Trail. When Jon stops by later in the morning, he's just got to have a picture of Bob and me together. What contrasting hiking styles!

Jon delivers me to Travel Country Outdoors (TCO) in Altamonte Springs, where Rick is waiting. Here, I once again get to spend time with these great folks. TCO is a sponsor for Odyssey 2000-'01. They've provided me such great support, both in gear and in enthusiastic encouragement. To Mike Plante, TCO manager, and to all at TCO, thanks!

The ride from Altamonte Springs to the Ocala goes quickly as *Vagabond Rick* and I have many things to discuss. We're both fired up about these great new trails, the Trail of the Ancients and the ECT. Rick is also hiking them, but in sections. So far he's gotten from Key West to Andalusia, Alabama, and soon he'll return to the ECT to continue on to Springer Mountain, Georgia.

In the evening at the conference site, I talk with many dear friends again. Jon has provided me a fine room for the weekend and I soon head there. I have become so very tired the last two days. It seems I have no energy.

> *From the constant grind of this long old trail,*
> *Comes the grist to try a man's soul.*
> *But from the Lord's mill, grind the strength and the will,*
> *To carry me on to my goal.*
> (N. Nomad)

Saturday—March 17, 2001
Trail Day—282/68
Trail Mile—4521/1087
Location—FTA Annual Conference, Camp Ocala, Ocala National Forest, Florida

Sleep was fretful last, but I did manage to rest. This morning I attend a few presentations, then sit in on the annual Long Distance Hiker's Committee (LDH) meeting. Much is happening now with the Florida Trail, all good. Long distance hikers have begun moving into important positions of leadership within the FTA organization. For instance, Chuck *Swamp Eagle* Wilson, who has just successfully completed his TA/ECT northbound thru-hike, will be taking over the responsibilities of the LDH Committee, to continue the great momentum begun by LDH's Joan *Igloo* Hobson and *Vagabond Rick*. Joan is now VP of Trails.

Another example is the remarkable work coming out of the Tallahassee office. At the meeting conducted by Kent Wimmer and Howard Pardue, I learn of the great strides being made in identifying trail corridor, acquiring land, and certifying existing trail. Indeed, the Florida National Scenic Trail has come into its own as a long distance thru-trail. Jim Kern must indeed be very proud.

My energy level has left me again. By two I barely manage to return to my room before collapsing on the bed. I'm unable to rest, however, as I must make frequent and repeated trips to the toilet. I'd hoped to be able to sign and sell some books this afternoon, but I have neither the strength nor the resolve to get back out.

Thank goodness the evening schedule runs on and I'm not called upon to present my program until very late. This permits me the excuse for a shortened version. With the help of Jan *Dutch Treat* Benschop, who has set a number of my ditties to his beautiful music, I'm able to additionally shorten my time before the audience. Though it is late, and though the program is short, Jan and I are well received. I cannot remain as Jan closes the act. Thanks Jan, dear friend, and thank you, dear friends, FTA members all, for your kindness and understanding!

Live by faith until you have faith.
(Josh Billings)

Sunday—March 18, 2001
Trail Day—283/69
Trail Mile—4521/1087
Location—Home of Chuck and Betty Wilson, Naples, Florida

I managed to sleep a little better last night, but breakfast is the last thing on my mind this morning. Many friends come by my room to check on me before setting out on their journeys home. Gary *Bear Bag* Buffington, MD, has been keeping a close eye on me and has written a script for Flagyl (Metronidazole), the medication used for the treatment of *giardia lamblia*.

I'm still in my room, feeling little like going anywhere, when the cleanup crew shows at the door. Chuck and Betty Wilson have brought their luxurious motor home around. They've come for me, insisting I return with them to their home in Naples. It doesn't take much to convince me that I'm in no shape to return to Lake Harbor. With tears in my eyes, I manage little resistance to their offer. I finally get my pack together. It's raining as Chuck practically carries me to his motor home across the way. "You're in luck," he says, "Betty's got the bed all made up for you." Oh what an absolute blessing. I can remember Chuck stopping to fill Gary's prescription, and that's it. I know not how long it takes to reach Naples.

In the evening I'm feeling better. I manage to shower, and Betty fixes me a bowl of soup and a grilled cheese sandwich. I tell Chuck I want to return to the trail in the morning, but judging from his looks my plea doesn't sound too convincing. The Wilsons have such a beautiful, spacious home. I try to look around a little, but end up heading right back to my room.

Trail magic? More like trail miracle. Chuck and Betty, you're all about trail miracles!

Deborah, (Stewart-Kent, FTA President) I regret missing your always-inspiring conference closing ceremony; I just couldn't make it.

Never apologize for showing feelings.
When you do so, you apologize for truth.
(Benjamin Disraeli)

Monday—March 19, 2001
Trail Day—284/70
Trail Mile—4546/1112
Location—Levee along the L-2 Canal, Clewiston, Florida

It has rained off and on all night, continuing into the morning. But my decision is to go, so Chuck gets me loaded and we're off to Lake Harbor.

The rain has eased by the time we reach the post office. I introduce Chuck to Joy, the three of us chat a while, then I'm off again, heading ever south.

The hike today is along the Miami and L-2 Canals, not particularly exciting. The rain soon comes again, this time in the company of a generous supply of lightning. Thankfully, the show is all cloud-to-cloud, as there's no place to hide up here. Also thankfully, there is little wind as the rain comes heavy at times.

My energy level remains surprisingly high all through the afternoon, and by late evening, with another ominous black wall of clouds approaching, I hastily pitch for the night. I no sooner roll in than the storm comes through, the gusting wind driving torrents of rain. But I'm dry and away from it in my great little Nomad tent. Into each life some rain must fall. It's sure been falling in mine! Hopefully, it will soon end.

Into each life some rain must fall,
some days must be dark and dreary.
(Henry Wadsworth Longfellow)

Tuesday—March 20, 2001
Trail Day—285/71
Trail Mile—4570/1138
Location—Billie Swamp Safari, Big Cypress Reservation, Florida

The front passes through during the night, but it leaves a blanket of fog behind for the sun to burn away this morning. I'm now in the land of the sugar cane—and the sandhill crane. As the sun succeeds in lifting the haze, I have this remarkable view, which lifts and carries my gaze for miles in all directions, the anxious, raspy clangor of the crane carrying with it.

The rain has cleansed the air, making it crisp and clear, like ether. I'll bet anything the folks that work these cane fields are glad for that, because when it's so dry, as it has been, theirs is filthy, grimy work. I always thought the fields were burned after the harvest, but the burning actually occurs before. What a sooty, dusty mess! How they manage to extract such a pure white substance from the black scorch they haul to the refinery in their bouncing, rattling, grime-covered cane trucks is beyond me.

As the sun climbs, it comes with much humid heat. There is absolutely not a patch of shade up here on the levee, and I've managed to nearly deplete my water supply. I'm in luck, however, for as I hear a vehicle approaching from behind, I turn to see a pickup towing an airboat. It's the water management folks out to spend the day, and as they pass, down comes the driver's window. Now do I hear such kind and welcome words: "Could you use some water?" Oh yes, this'll work! Here I meet Jay. "I know what it's like to be out here without water," says Jay. And so you do my friend, and so you do. But I'm wondering, as I fill my pop bottles, drinking my fill in the process—I'm wondering if you realize, Jay, how truly thankful a person can be that receives such kindness!

On Snake Road, in the Seminole Indian Reservation, I'm offered many rides, just as I was while passing this way in '98. I've found the Seminole people to be kind and gentle folk. How paradoxical indeed, for were they not such brave and fierce warriors, the only nation to remain unconquered during the Indian wars!

In the evening, tired from the long, hot roadwalk, I arrive at Billie Swamp Safari. Here there are swamp buggy rides, airboat rides, and a zoo—literally, a zoo. For now is spring break, school's out, and I do believe every kid from Miami is right here. I manage though, after a very long exercise in patience, to get a chickee for the night (a small, elevated, thatch-covered Indian dwelling).

Heading to the bathhouse while deep in thought about these past few days, Chuck and Betty Wilson appear right before me with the grandest, broadest smiles I believe I've ever seen on any two individual's faces! "Everybody's asking about you, wondering if you're okay. So we've come over to check on you," exclaims Betty. I'm so completely taken; overjoyed is the word. Before I can respond, Chuck asks, "Can we buy you supper?" I finally manage, "Sure Chuck, sure dear friend, you can buy me supper." What an absolutely perfect day this has turned out to be!

It is only with the heart that one can see rightly.
(Antoine de Saint-Exupery)

Wednesday—March 21, 2001
Trail Day—286/72
Trail Mile—4598/1166
Location—13 Mile Camp, Big Cypress National Preserve, Florida

The man that thought he was invincible, the man that shot his mouth off to everybody about how he was immune to *giardia lamblia*, well, turns out the boob isn't so invincible after all. Yup, you've guessed it—the old *Nomad's* come down with the dreaded bug. Two hours after dinner last night, World War III erupted in my gut, rumblings, tremors, and outright explosions the likes of which I've never experienced before, a racket and commotion worse even than the crashing of tennis shoes in a drier! It all started around nine. The race was on after that, running to outrun the runs, and it lasted till around two this morning. From my chickee to the toilet is about a hundred yards. No receiver in the NFL could have stayed with me. Lordy, lordy, what an absolute nightmare. I started right then on the Flagyl.

This morning I'm not inside-out near as bad as I thought I'd be. In fact I'm rested and fairly ready to give the day a go. So it's over to Swampwater Café for breakfast, then to see the Florida panthers in their cage, then back to the trail. Plans today are to meet Chuck and Betty at the Alligator Alley Rest Area, where the trail crosses I-75. From there Chuck will hike the Big Cypress National Preserve with me, all the way to Loop Road, the present terminus of the FT.

The trail continues as a roadwalk through the lands of the Seminole, and near the end, passes beside a canal. In '98, along this canal, I saw some of the largest gators I've ever seen anywhere. I swear, I believe one monster had the girth of a 55-gallon drum flattened down. In my journal entry for that day in '98, I promised I'd bring my camera along next time, just to quiet you doubters. And so, this time I think I got him. Don't know though, I had trouble holding the camera steady (Yup, didn't turn out!).

Near the southern trail entrance to the lands of the Seminole, at I-75, there's a trail register for the northern section of Big Cypress National Preserve. Just as I'm signing out, along come Chuck and Betty. It's lunch time, and Betty's brought lunch and lots of cold pop in a cooler. The magic continues!

The last and final "I" is behind me now: I-75. This interstate highway has been the most persistent and stubborn of all, this being the fourth time our paths have crossed. But it's back there behind me for good now during the remainder of this odyssey.

It's a joy having company on the trail again. Chuck is a seasoned backpacker, having just completed the Key West/Everglades Roadwalk, the Florida Trail, the Alabama Roadwalk, the Alabama

Pinhoti Trail, the Georgia Pinhoti Trail, the Georgia section of the Benton MacKaye Trail, the Appalachian Trail and the International Appalachian Trail. Whew! Some hike, eh! Well, these trails and roadwalks that *Swamp Eagle* has just completed are the trails and roadwalks that form the Trail of the Ancients and the Eastern Continental Trail. The two of us have so many mutual friends we've made along these trails, so many magic and mystic places to talk about. And so, reminiscing the memory of those dear friends, those remarkable experiences, we share and spend yet another memorable day.

> *Walking is the best way to know a place, perhaps the only way.*
> (Chris Townsend)

Thursday—March 22, 2001
Trail Day—287/73
Trail Mile—4614/1182
Location—Near Oasis Ranger Station at US-41 (Tamiami Trail),
Big Cypress National Preserve, Florida

Friends have told me the Everglades are dry, but I couldn't comprehend that. Hard to believe, but true. Heading south from Alligator Alley yesterday, *Swamp Eagle* and I were in a little mud, down by a place I've dubbed the "lagoon," but then, only to our ankles. From there on south into Oasis Ranger Station at Tamiami Trail, the treadway remained dry.

At the trailhead register by US-41 this morning I find a card with a note from dear friend Smith *Old Ridge Runner* Edwards. It reads, "Check with the rangers inside, there's a package for you." So in I go. I hand the note to the ranger/receptionist; she heads to the back. In a moment she returns with this tall, narrow box covered with duct tape. I open it part way with much excitement. Oh yes, a bottle of Long Trail Ale! *Swamp Eagle* gets this silly little smirk on his face. Finally, it dawns on me—oh no, alcohol is forbidden while taking Flagyl! Gary warned me of this, and it's written in the precautions that accompany the medication. "Consuming alcohol while on this medication can cause severe stomach disorder." Aww great; now what? Consulting with *Swamp Eagle*, it turns out we'll be coming back through here, as he and Betty plan to come to Key West to celebrate with me, and from there, to bring me home with them. So back in the refrigerator the grand prize goes, to await another day. Dang it anyway—but thanks, *Old Ridge Runner*.

> *Never do today what you can put off till tomorrow.*
> (Anonymous)

Friday—March 23, 2001
Trail Day—288/74
Trail Mile—4637/1205
Location—Intersection Loop Road and US-41, Key West Roadwalk (KWR), to Everglades Tower Inn, Miccosukee Tamiami Trail Reservation, Florida

The trail today, south through the Big Cypress National Preserve, is like a highway, and I'm wondering how I could have possibly gotten so lost in '98. But that was indeed a different time and Big Cypress a different place. *Vagabond Rick* and Debbie Dalrymple have been here and have worked the treadway and the blazing for the last three miles. So we're able to cruise on in to Loop Road—and another congratulatory note—thanks, *Not To Worry*! We arrive here a little after eleven.

What an emotional time now, for here is where my son Jon dropped me off New Years Day in 1998. This is the place where Odyssey '98 began, and now, near where another miracle, Odyssey 2000-'01 will end. It's hard to believe I've hiked over nine thousand miles since that day, across near the breadth of the entire eastern North American continent—and back again. Many of us dream all our lives about far-off, mystic places, about grand adventures that lie beyond the horizon, that dwell on the other side, past the beckoning, luring arc of the sea. But few of us ever go. Why is it, why do we just dream? Is it fear; are we afraid to go? I don't know the answer, but I do know this: for those of us who couldn't stifle that instinctive, deep-down burning drive, for those of us who could not ignore the call of the wanderlust buried within our soul, we have been so very, very blessed in life. We made that decision, to chase our dreams—and we have gone!

I've only a short distance to Key West now, and I'm thinking as I move along, "What remarkably beautiful places I've seen; what wonderful life-long friendships I've made, and what times and adventures I've had." It's been another soul-searching journey with the Lord. And, *Ten Million Steps*, the book—what an amazing reception, and what recognition has come to me. What a truly humbling experience. It's been a long way from here to Canada and back again, both in distance and in time, like from a different world, another life.

Betty has come for Chuck, and I'm once again alone, on my way toward that final destination. It's in my sights now, the southernmost point on the eastern North American continent, the monument by the sea in Key West.

So stand ye true helmsmen, set wind to your sail,
Outbound on a journey anew,
And test your true mettle and fearing to fail,
And quit dreaming the doing...and do.
(N. Nomad)

CHAPTER 5

KEY WEST ROADWALK
(KWR)

Saturday—March 24, 2001
Trail Day—289/1
Trail Mile—4659/22
Location—Junction SR-997 (Krome Avenue) and US-41 (Tamiami Trail) at Dade Corners, Florida, trailside behind Exxon truckstop

Yesterday I completed my second thru-hike along the Florida National Scenic Trail, this time southbound. I've been told, and it's hard to believe, but this hike is a first. For, even though the FT has been in existence for over thirty-five years now, many folks having hiked it, no one apparently has thru-hiked it southbound. Guess that means I'm also the first to thru-hike the FT in both directions. Please forgive my boasting, but it's a neat distinction; I'll take it! Anyway, I remember what Walt Whitman said, *"If you done it, it ain't bragging."* Chuck *Swamp Eagle* Wilson, (chairman, FTA Long Distance Hiker's Committee), you'll need to send me another one of those really neat FT thru-hiker patches!

I'll be hiking roads beside the Everglades for the next few days o'er the KWR, as my hike along the beautiful trail through the Big Cypress is finished. Ahh, the Everglades, "River of Grass," as aptly named by Marjory Stoneman Douglas. What can one say about such a remarkably fascinating and mysteriously forbidding—but wonderful place! The grandeur of it is overwhelming, especially to one who takes the time to walk even a small part of it. Today, only one-fifth of the historic Everglades remains. The encroachment of man, our sheer numbers no doubt, will someday strike the death knell to its existence. But until that day there exists here such a unique ecological system, unique to the world. In our hemisphere's parks do the Everglades alone hold three internationally distinctive classifications: International Biosphere Reserve, World Heritage Site, and Wetland of International Significance. Yes, the Everglades remain a vast and uniquely special place—in the entire world.

I was again blessed to see the wood stork this hike, although its numbers have dwindled from over 6,000 as recently as 1960 to less than 500 today. Indeed, the numbers of wading birds nesting in colonies in the southern Everglades have declined 93% since 1930. Evidenced to me, to my dismay, I saw no rookeries of the magnificent snowy white egret. They were prevalent during my '98 hike. In my memory were the words of Amy Blackmarr, *Going to Ground*, "And the showy egret keeps watch from the east...where the small bass hide in the reeds." Oh, but I was blessed to see gallinule, great white egrets and blue heron, anhinga, osprey, black vultures, kite, ibis, a bald eagle, countless gators, deer, loggerheads, gar, Florida panthers (in captivity), and the remarkable and irrepressible sandhill crane.

Big Cypress refers not to the size of the trees that are here, but to the more than 2,000 square miles of wetlands that make up the western reaches of the Everglades. Here the FT passes through systems of dwarf pond cypress, hammocks of slash pine, cabbage palm and gumbo-limbo. There are wet prairies and sloughs, and occasional domes of the giant cypresses, the great bald cypress. Few of these monarchs have survived the lumbering era, but those that have embody antiquity, some as old as 600-700 years. Here among the black bear, panther, crayfish, bromeliads and orchids, there is a veritable paradise, where dwelt the ancestors of today's Miccosukee and

Seminole Nations. I have met them; I know them—for my spirit rose, and in a brief, fleeting moment of *silence*, and in that instant, my spirit was one with them. What a joy, my journey here once more. I must return someday. Indeed, my spirit *will* return.

I'm on US-41/Tamiami Trail, heading east all this day, far from that spiritual realm of silence—on the KWR.

> *God is the friend of silence.*
> *See how nature—trees, flowers, grass—grows in silence;*
> *see the stars, the moon and the sun, how they move in silence...*
> *We need silence to be able to touch souls.*
> (Mother Teresa)

Sunday—March 25, 2001
Trail Day—290/2
Trail Mile—4680/43
Location—Everglades International Hostel, 20 SW 2nd Avenue,
Florida City, Florida. Edwin Anderson and Owhnn, hostelkeepers.

I spent the night again, as in '98, behind the truckstop next to the chain-link fence, right under the microwave tower. I had a great night's sleep despite the continuous low-pitched, synchronous, rumbling hum of the idling diesels.

The hike today continues the roadwalk, this one down busy SR-997, another hot, clear day. I keep myself busy hugging the crash rail and picking up change, 54 cents in all. Along the way, I continue reminiscing my memorable and remarkable journeys through the Everglades, and the beauty of being with nature. This echoes within my mind, within my soul.

By early afternoon I reach Homestead, then Florida City. Here, on the southern outskirts of Florida City, which is also the eastern reaches of Everglades National Park, is the Everglades International Hostel, a classic (and classy) 1930s apartment house turned migrant tenement house, and more recently turned (totally renovated) international hostel. Owners Edwin Anderson and Owhnn (and Owhnn's daughter, Sotta) have done a remarkable job of transforming this rundown-but-quaint two-story building into a modern, comfortable hostel, now in its glory. It's here for the lucky sojourner who comes to spend a day, or a few, to enjoy. I'm here for at least two!

The clear realities of nature, seen with the inner eye of the spirit, reveal the ultimate echo of God.
(Ansel Adams)

Monday—March 26, 2001
Trail Day—291/3
Trail Mile—4680/43
Location—Everglades International Hostel, Florida City, Florida

What a great evening at the Everglades International Hostel. I met the owners, Edwin and Owhnn. Also residing here, I've found, is Andrew *Old Dude* Page GAME '99 & '00. *Old Dude* and me, we proceeded to have great fun "bench hiking." Oh yeah, many mutual friends to remember, many beautiful experiences to recall.

Today is a day of rest, working my journals and sending email to many dear friends. The last two days of confusion and chaos along the busy highway, they have sapped me. It is good to be here where I can rest. My old bones need the rest. I'll not worry; I'll rest—and sleep.

Blessed is the man who is too busy to worry during the daytime and too sleepy to worry at night.
(Anonymous)

Tuesday—March 27, 2001
Trail Day—292/4
Trail Mile—4701/64
Location—Junction US-1 and Card Sound Road, Key Largo, to
Everglades International Hostel, Florida City

While here at Everglades International Hostel, while lavishing myself with this much needed rest, I have come to know the good company of *Old Dude*. We've become friends. So it is that I've invited him to accompany me during the remainder of this odyssey, the hike on down through the Keys. Hoho! *Old Dude*, he just couldn't back away from this invitation. So, this morning we're off together—to Key West!

From Florida City to Key Largo is a long, rugged, utility-poles-pinned-to-the-horizon kind of hike. Even the locals that ply this desert-like landing strip have dubbed it "The Stretch." There's still treasure to be found down here in the Keys, though, so to occupy our time today, *Old Dude* and I, we set to finding some of it: 78 cents in all, three quarters, which trickle down to three pennies.

By early afternoon, in a much-welcome and cooling rain, as we're finally nearing the first road bend for the day, across pulls this pickup truck. In just a moment the driver comes over, a familiar figure from the summer past. Oh my, it's my good friend and AT hiking companion Travis *Shepherd* Hall, GAME '00—big guy, huge grin. "*Nomad*," he shouts, "That you, you still going, you still hiking?" After a grand, old-friend hug—"Yes *Shepherd*, yes, I'm still going, I'm still hiking." Well, what a wonderful day! We load right up and head for Hobo's Bar and Grill on Key Largo. It's party time folks; it's party time.

Late afternoon, *Shepherd* puts us back on the trail (road) as we make plans to meet in Key West. Then *Old Dude* and I stagger it on down to the Tiki Bar at Lake Surprise. Here *Old Dude* calls Owhnn, who soon comes to fetch us back to the Everglades Hostel in Florida City.

Well, what could have been a really tough day has certainly turned memorable. What with meeting *Shepherd*, the trip to Hobo's, and free beer, (compliments of Denise, one of the locals at Lake Surprise—great surprise!), hey, and then to cap it off, just about the best pasta I've ever wolfed down, prepared from scratch by Richard at Everglades International Hostel—oh yeah! Thanks Owhnn, for coming for us. Even though it seems that I'm so restless to just go, it's great to be back for another luxurious night's rest here at the Everglades International Hostel.

Oh, what is this tugging we feel in our heart,
That's calling so clear and so loud;
And what is this instinct that sets us apart,
From the masses, the rest of the crowd?

We might as well ask for the secret to time,
And solve then the mystery of space.
For man can find neither the riddle nor rhyme,
To puzzle the pieces in place.
(N. Nomad)

Wednesday—March 28, 2001
Trail Day—293/5
Trail Mile—4718/81
Location—US-1 bridge abutment catacomb, Tavernier Creek,
Tavernier, Florida

Owhnn gets us back to Key Largo plenty early. We're in good shape and on our way ever south (west) to that now-less-elusive southernmost point on the eastern North American continent, the monument at Key West.

Again comes the traffic of the Keys. And building, the heat of the tropics. But I'll not complain. I'm blessed to be here, so happy and blessed to be here. It's such a very far and great distance to walk, from the barren cold stretches of the north tundra to these tropical waters. I'll take much enjoyment and pleasure in these few, short, remaining days, the final days of Odyssey 2000-'01.

The treadway of this KWR is kind today, being mostly along the long bike paths that run the extent of Key Largo. Complimenting the normal daily routine of traipsing fifteen to twenty miles, I add the beneficial exercise of stooping to retrieve the few scattered remains, that long-sought treasure, the booty of the Keys, 10 cents, all pennies. There's no cooling afternoon shower, and the sun is outrunning us to the west, ever the victor, all the while glaring back as we slowly follow. Bidding us farewell, the sun embraces the radiant sea, lifting it above and before us, across and beyond the azure crescent that arcs the Straits of Florida. It presents the most striking appearance—as if the sea is advancing, soon to consume us in the flames of sunset—creating a convincing and mystifying illusion, rising, pulsing, and shimmering in its transparent hues of crimson, aqua, and white. It reaches, then lunges, then to finally crash defeated against the bastions of sand, to the horizon.

We savor the day by stopping at the great Mandalay Tiki Bar. Folks here are happy. Ahh, I too, am happy here!

But yet, how awfully great and sublime is the majestic scene...
The solemn sound of the beating surf strikes our ears;
the dashing of yon liquid mountains, like mighty giants,
in vain assail the skies; they're beaten back,
and fall prostrate upon the shores of the trembling island.
(William Bartram)

Thursday—March 29, 2001
Trail Day—294/6
Trail Mile—4737/100
Location—US-1 Gulfside, east of Channel Five Bridge, Craig Key,
Florida

A good wind-driven rain came late last night, but I remained snug
and dry under the Tavernier Creek bridge. You see, in between
the huge concrete I-beams that make these great bridge spans exist
many catacomb-like recesses where the beams rest upon their abut-
ments. It is on these narrow abutment ledges that one might roll
out—directly below the beam-end expansion joints. Some of these
joints are watertight, many are not. I've a knack for picking the dry-
when-raining recesses; *Old Dude* wasn't so lucky. Right after the
rain began I could hear him rustling about. Looking over I saw him,
headlamp flashing here, then there, as he retreated from the veritable river running directly through his camp. Oops, sorry *Old Dude*,
forgot to tell you about the expansion joints.

This morning we're out to another absolutely blue-perfect day,
and I'm immediately awestruck—again, by the perfect blue that sets
this breathtaking scene, a dazzling backdrop that lifts heavenward,
rising from the sea full around, a creation of magic known simply as,
"The Florida Keys."

Crossing Tavernier Creek, we immediately pull into this little
mom-n-pop stop for breakfast. Oh, is this grand! What a wonderful
payoff for having endured the countless frost-laden mornings of the
long winter past, mornings with no coffee, no warm meal to set me
on my way. And my fingers, they're working again. My shoelaces are
tied, my zippers zipped!

Lunch is at the beautiful rooftop Holiday Isle, where Karen
Wehner serves both as hostess and as waitress. What luck, she's
here today, just like in '98, a wonderful memory relived. I'm welcomed, and do I receive the long-lost-friend treatment from this
kind lady! *Old Dude* and me are served a grand lunch with a grand

view, compliments of Karen. Thanks, dear friend, for remembering. Thanks for your generosity and kindness once again. Indeed, I'll forever remain in your debt!

In the evening, with the relentless grind of oncoming traffic, not wanting to cross the long, high-span bridge leading to Fiesta Key, we pull off Gulfside. Here we pitch on a little grassy incline, as the setting sun blazes its golden path across the crystal blue Straits of Florida.

Folks, along this way, along this KWR, there are no blazes; there is no trail. But let me tell you this: Here in the Florida Keys, there's a hike the likes of which there is no equal. Indeed, it is hard to believe there could be such wonder, such magic—yet, should you come to this place, you would believe.

Belief consists of accepting the affirmations of the soul...
(Ralph Waldo Emerson)

Friday—March 30, 2001
Trail Day—295/7
Trail Mile—4758/121
Location—US-1 Marathon, Florida, to the home of David Kaplin and Maria Lester, Marathon Kayak, friends of Meg "Cowgirl" Letson

Old Dude and me, we've set ourselves a goal while here in the Keys— not an easy goal, but one we believe can be achieved. And that goal is to hit every tiki bar between Key Largo and Key West! Tuesday it was Lake Surprise Tiki Bar, Wednesday it was Mandalay Tiki Bar, and today the Holiday Inn/Outback Tiki Bar, followed shortly by the Lor-E-Lei Tiki Bar, both in Islamorada.

The hike we're on now is east to west, to Key West, and by mid-afternoon the tropical sun hits us straight on, the heat of it really working us over. And the traffic? Well, the traffic is crushing, continuously hooked up, nonstop. I subconsciously keep one eye on the traffic, one on the magic that makes the Keys. By late afternoon we reach Marathon. Here are friends of a friend. The friend—Meg *Cowgirl* Letson, a fellow hiker who befriended me while hiking the Pinhoti Trail through the Talladega National Forest in Alabama. And her friends—Maria Lester and David Kaplin, right here in Marathon at Marathon Kayak. "Stop and see them on your way through the Keys," I remember Meg saying, "I know they'll welcome you. I'll tell them you're coming!" And so she did, and so today, from the outskirts of Marathon, I call David. In just a short while, Maria pulls alongside. Down goes the window, up comes her beautiful smile. Ahh, indeed *Cowgirl*, your dear friends do welcome me!

In the evening, at David and Maria's lovely home right next to the crystal-jewel waters of the bay, I meet their son, Jason, and David's parents, Allan and Laura. What a grand time. David's friend Jim comes over, and David grills mahi mahi for *Old Dude* and me (and all here) as we celebrate the old *Nomad's* cracking the Keys fifty-mile marker.

I have had an inner peace all along in knowing that I would complete this odyssey. Now there is no doubt in my mind.

With confidence, you have won even before you have started.
(Marcus Garvey)

Saturday—March 31, 2001
Trail Day—296/8
Trail Mile—4761/124
Location—Home of David Kaplin and Maria Lester, Marathon, Florida

Seems it's a joy for the Kaplans all to have us with them. It sure is a joy for us!

I'm way ahead of schedule, that schedule being to reach Key West by next Wednesday afternoon, so at the invitation and urging of David and Maria, *Old Dude* and I remain another day. Their place has a beautiful setting, overlooking the bay, tucked just inside the point on a deep waterway, docks with tall-mast sailboats lining and marking its course. All is open, and the gentle, refreshing breeze coming across the placid turquoise waters that are the Keys—there is no air conditioning firm anywhere in the world that could possibly duplicate these conditions, that could make the air so refreshingly cool and sweet, in such a pleasing and perfect fashion.

I linger on the deck, watching the tide go out as I write. This is an inspiring place, bringing inspiration to the writer. I can see now why so many writers over the years have made the Keys their home.

Late afternoon, Allan shuttles me back to mile marker fifty where he drops me off. From here, I'll hike on west to Seven Mile Bridge. Plan is to run that gauntlet before first light tomorrow. David comes to fetch me back at four. Owhnn has come for *Old Dude* and they're off on their own.

In the evening, David, Maria, Allan, Laura and I enjoy pizza, a few tall frosties, and each other's company. What a wonderful day. Thanks folks!

I'm so blessed to have such help along the way, such caring folks about. And it is a blessing too, to be living to the fullest, each and every day—right on the edge.

The mill will never grind with the water that has passed.
(Sarah Doudney)

Sunday—April 1, 2001
Trail Day—297/9
Trail Mile—4791/154
Location—US-1 Sugarloaf Key, Florida, to the home of Phil and Ruth Weston

During the night a fierce storm drives through, dumping torrents of water, knocking out the power. But just before first light the storm passes, the wind turns calm. David and Maria get me loaded up and I'm soon back at the Seven Mile Bridge. Plans were to meet *Old Dude* here this morning, but the storm of the night has left things totally unsettled. He is not here. I bid farewell to David and Maria, shoulder my pack and head out in the dark, across the narrow concrete ribbon that is Seven Mile Bridge.

The plan is working; there is little traffic, and by first light I'm well on my way. Del Delahunty was hassled here as he headed north on his ECT hike earlier this year. A state trooper forced him into the patrol car then delivered him across. He promptly hitched right back to complete his jaunt o'er Seven Mile. Knowing this has concerned me. This morning, as the day brightens and the traffic increases, I try blocking the incident from my mind by picking up cast away treasure—coins tossed toward the sea by motorists in hopes of "good luck" on their long journey. By seven-thirty, less than a mile from shore, the first patrol car passes. But it continues on as do I, and soon I'm safely across. Thank you, Lord. This should be the last big hurdle!

The kind barkeep at Looe Key Tiki Bar tells me that Sunday is a bad time to be on US-1. That's sure true, for the traffic has been pretty much bumper-to-bumper in both directions. I'm making good progress however, so I give a call to Phil and Ruth Weston, my dear friends on Sugarloaf Key. I'm in luck; they're home, and they invite me to come on in. I hit it hard, and by five I've got the thirty miles knocked down.

What a blessing to be able to rest a couple of days as their guest. They have a beautiful home, they're beautiful people! Ahh yes, time now to reflect on all the beautiful people, and all the remarkable places along this journey, Odyssey 2000-'01. So now begins the time to look back, to remember, and to give thanks, especially to give thanks, for I have been granted another day.

The years of man are the looms of God,
let down by the place of the sun.
(Anson G. Chester)

Monday—April 2, 2001
Trail Day—298/10
Trail Mile—4791/154
Location—Home of Phil and Ruth Weston, Sugarloaf Key, Florida

As I rest here for the next two days, at the luxurious Weston home on Sugarloaf Key, I must take time to thank and give credit to all the great sponsors that have stood behind me and supported me all this journey. This has been such a remarkable hike, as to the enjoyment of it, the quality of it. Without these sponsors, such a grand and memorable experience would not have been possible.

I'll begin with my good friend, Larry Duffy. Larry's a member of the clan, the hiker-trash clan if you will, having hiked a good chunk of the AT off and on over the years. He's a professional photographer living in Dahlonega, the same little berg I call home. We knew each other long before Odyssey 2000-'01. Larry's responsible for the great shot that appears on the cover of my book *Ten Million Steps*. He lugged 25 pounds of camera gear up Blood Mountain, the highest point on the AT in Georgia, to spend nearly a whole day with me, taking roll after roll of pictures just to get that one great shot. Folks, tell me if the photo on the cover of *Ten Million Steps* isn't striking! Indeed, his time and talent, spent on my behalf, have gone far in making the book a hit. Thanks Larry, thanks so much!

I contribute the success of this journey, the quality of it, to three factors. All are benefits derived from sponsors. The first deals with my total pack weight. The second, with the fact that I was provided with trekking poles and taught how to use them properly. And third, that I had the good fortune of being provided Osteo Bi-Flex, a great natural product from Rexall-Sundown.

As to my total pack weight, comes into play the following: GVP Gear, Feathered Friends, Cascade Designs, and Wanderlust Gear.

GVP Gear is Glen Van Peski, owner of a small business in Carlsbad, California (now Gossamer Gear out of Austin, Texas). Glen has been a great supporter of Odyssey 2000-'01. He's the innovator and manufacturer of the ingenious G-4 lightweight backpack. He started me out with a standard one in Canada, then, at my request, made a custom take-off of his G-4, which has brought me all the way from Maine. Thanks, Glen. The G-4 is a mighty fine, tough, lightweight piece of gear!

Feathered Friends is a cutting-edge company dealing primarily in high-loft goose down, state-of-the-art sleeping bags. Aaron Leopold was of great assistance in providing me with their lightweight Rock Wren. I've carried it the whole way. Thanks, Aaron. Great company, jam-up quality product!

Cascade Designs is the manufacturer of Therm-a-Rest self-inflating mattresses. Karen Berger with GORP.com was instrumental in gaining this sponsorship for me. Some folks seem to do fine with the closed-cell foam pads, but I'm an old man and my bones are starting to scrape together pretty hard. Give me the Therm-a-Rest Guidelite, just a little over a pound. That'll work, and it has, without fail for this entire odyssey. Thanks, Cascade Designs, for a tough, durable product, and thanks, Karen, for securing this sponsor and their great product for me!

Wanderlust Gear, what a neat little company. Kurt Russell in Myrtle Beach, South Carolina, is the mastermind here. When I tell folks my dry pack weight (no food or water) is only 9½ pounds, their eyes roll right back! It isn't unusual to get a sort-of sneer, followed by a comment to the effect, "Well, we know your type, you're nothing but a masochist; you just crawl into the bushes at night, rolls up in the leaves, and let the bugs eat on you. You probably don't even carry a tarp." That's when I tell them that I go on the trail to have a good time, same as they do, and I recite the little quote attributed to Walter *Nessmuk* Sears. *Nessmuk* said, "I go to the woods to smooth it, not to rough it; I get it rough enough at home." So now, back to Kurt Russell and Wanderlust Gear. "Yup, you're right folks," I say, "I don't carry a tarp, I carry the luxurious Nomad tent." Hard to believe, but my 9½ pounds includes a tent! And this Nomad made by Kurt is not just a dink-of-a-glorified bivy sack like I carried (along with 30-35 other pounds) in '98. This Nomad is a tent in all respects—full pan, zippered no-seeum door, and a vestibule grand enough to cook under. You can sit up in the Nomad, change clothes, and even pack your pack, which incidentally, there's also room for inside. And get this: how much does your flimsy wet-when-raining, bugs-when-buggy tarp weigh? Well, my dry-when-raining, no-bugs-never Nomad tent tips in at just a little over a pound three. I've had the postmaster weigh it; that's all it weighs! My hiking sticks serve as the tent poles—neat, eh! I've carried the Nomad with me, beginning the first day in Canada. It's in my pack now, none-the-worse for wear. Kurt, yours is a remarkable product. Cool name, too, the Nomad. Thanks for your support, but most of all, thanks for your kindness and your friendship!

Tomorrow, we'll continue with the great sponsors of Odyssey 2000-'01. Right now, first things first. I'm being called to partake in a fine evening of dining with the Westons. Smooth it folks, smooth it!

If I've made it, it's half because I was game to take a wicked amount of punishment along the way, and half because there were an awful lot of people who cared enough to help me.
(Althea Gibson)

Tuesday—April 3, 2001
Trail Day—299/11
Trail Mile—4791/154
Location—Home of Phil and Ruth Weston, Sugarloaf Key, Florida

Sugarloaf Key, most-near paradise, and the Westons? The exact kind of people you'd expect to meet in paradise! They took me in and cared for me during Odyssey '98 and now they've taken me in again. Kind, generous folks, they. We've become good friends.

Tomorrow is a final day, a day that closes one of the final chapters in this old man's life. For tomorrow I'll live the last day of this odyssey, my southbound journey o'er such a grand and glorious trail, the ECT.

Today though, is another day of rest, a time for contemplation, a time to reflect, to remember, to count all the many blessings—a time to give thanks. So please permit me to continue, to finish giving thanks to all the great sponsors of Odyssey 2000-'01.

The second of the factors that brought such quality, such heightened joy to this hike, was accepting the fact that hiking sticks play an important and critical role in the whole equation. One might manage to backpack a distance of nearly 5,000 miles without them, but believe me, the quality of that hike, indeed the outcome of such a trek, would certainly be in doubt. Yes, I consider trekking poles essential. The usual claim I've heard is: the use of trekking poles gives a 20% improvement in hiking efficiency. I pooh-poohed that claim for years, before I picked up a pair and learned how to use them. I honestly believe now it's every bit of 20%, probably closer to 30%, in my opinion—and does the Lord only know how many times they've saved my butt! Consider, if you will, all of Nature's inhabitants who live in the woods (the squirrel, the rabbit, the deer, the moose, the bear, the caribou, everybody) they get around on all four. And man, smart old man, he's the only one out there tripping around on all two! Time now for Leki's great motto, their saying, "Two legs bad, four legs good!" Ahh, so true. I just love it! Hiking sticks folks, ya gotta have 'em—hiking sticks! Thanks, Chris Hall and Marty Callahan with Leki. Thanks for the great Leki Super Makalu trekkers! They're bent and battered and scarred, but they're going to make it. They're going to carry me through. Zero knee and foot trouble this trek. Great upper body strength too (as good as it's gonna get at 62). Thanks, *Pan*, and thanks Leki, we've done it together!

The third factor that contributed greatly to what became and has remained a basically injury and pain-free hike is my daily regimen, a combination of natural substances. These substances are produced by our bodies; however, their production decreases with age. For many, this may prove no problem, as strenuous activity also generally decreases with age. But for those of us who keep on hammering at it up into our sixties, we need help! What are these natural substances, and what part do they play in the healthy scheme of things? Well, the substances are glucosamine and chondroitin. And their critical function—the healing and reconstruction of joint and connective tissue. You guys and gals ever have any knee or foot trouble? Struck a nerve there, eh (no pun intended)! Rexall-Sundown Corporation, makers of Osteo Bi-Flex, provide a combination of the natural substances discussed above. Dear friends at Rexall-Sundown, I could not have accomplished this miracle without you! To you, Carol Walters: thanks for providing me this must supplement. And especially, thanks for your unwavering faith in me, faith that I would prove your trust. Thanks for believing that I would complete this incredible journey (no matter, and so be it) an old man of 62!

I first met Karen Berger at the ALDHA Gathering in Hanover in 1999. She gave a slide show, the feature presentation, and I had a brief part in the program that year. Karen's the resident expert on hiking and backpacking for the great website GORP.com. When the call went out for correspondents hiking the AT, I applied. Karen picked me up right away. Karen and GORP.com have assisted me in many ways—by securing gear for me, by supplying film and slide development, and by paying me handsomely for writing a few articles about my journey. Thanks, Karen, it's been great!

When one accepts money for what they do, especially as in sports—and I believe both hiking and backpacking can be considered a sport—then as a consequence one moves from the ranks of amateur to the ranks of professional. I don't mean to imply this places the individual in another league as to hiking ability. However, I do believe that accepting money and sponsorships creates for that individual certain responsibilities. There are commitments that must be met. I thought about this long and hard before actively pursuing the many great sponsors that have backed me this journey. Manufacturers don't want to support someone with their products, gear, and services, only to have that individual fail in his or her endeavor.

So where is this going? Well, it's going to the gut, to the crux of it. For does each of us not harbor doubt, do we not all have frailties as humans, indeed do we not each and all, fear failure! Ahh, and so now you know. Yes, the old *Nomad* feared failure, deeply feared failure. How can one contemplate a trek of nearly 5,000 miles and not suffer the fear of failing?

During Odyssey '98 my feet went flat; I literally walked them into the ground. After that hike, my dear friend Brian Holcomb, DPM, his surgical practice in Cumming, Georgia, cut and wired the bones in both my feet back together where they belong. The procedure was a total success, but I still had a serious problem foot-wise. I'd lost fourteen toenails during the '98 hike. All ten came off shortly after I emerged from the Florida swamps. Then when the nails on both great and second toes began regenerating, I lost all four of them again. They finally grew back, but in totally abnormal fashion. Thinking back, I knew there was no way I could tolerate the pain of losing them all again, and that attempting so would bring failure. So back to Doc Holcomb I went. "Take 'em off Doc," I said, "all of 'em, permanently, forever." I'll never forget the look of utter shock on his face! He finally managed, "Maybe the big ones, we'll take the big ones off." "No Brian," I said, "I want them all off." He just sat there looking, in befuddled amazement. Sensing my resolve, and with some urgency in his voice, he responded, "You're serious about this, aren't you."

And so folks, my toenails are gone, all of them, permanently, forever. It was the right decision, for the remarkably successful procedures that Brian performed on my feet have enabled me to strut with a spring in my step for another "Ten Million Steps!" Dr. Holcomb, it is through your great surgical skill that tomorrow the old *Nomad* will bow in prayer, to give thanks—for yet another unbelievable miracle. What a joy hiking with pain-free feet. And what a blessing, meeting my commitment to all my sponsors. Is that not what's expected of a true professional? Thanks, Brian, thanks so much!

Two great outfitters have given me their total support. They're Travel Country Outdoors in Altamonte Springs, Florida, and Appalachian Outfitters in Dahlonega, Georgia. These folks (TCO manager Mike Plante and AO owner Dana LaChance) know and love hiking and backpacking. From them came not only great gear but more importantly, genuine encouragement and well-wishes from folks who know what being out there on the trail for extended periods of time is all about. Thanks Mike, Dana, and staff!

You've heard a lot about my feet, but the story wouldn't be complete, nor would this odyssey have ever been such utter joy without— the shoes! So let me tell you about the great sponsors who've kept this old shank's mare shod! In Canada, Vasque got me going with two pair of their great Avanti cross trainers. Thanks, Vasque! In the states, New Balance picked me up and kept me skipping along with no less than five pairs of their great 803 cross trainer low-cuts, less than a pound each in my size! Thanks, Deirdre McDonnell, Amy Vreeland, and Kathy Shepard with New Balance. Two great companies, tough, durable, jam-up shoes, and fine folks. Thanks, all! An average of 700 miles per pair on low-cut running shoes. Not bad, eh!

When the weather got hot, first on the AT in the Mid-Atlantic States, then again here in Florida on the FT, a great thirst-quencher designed to keep ultra-marathoners going kept me going! The product is called Conquest. Its innovator is a fellow long distance backpacker and my great friend, Gary *Bear Bag* Buffington, MD. While all my hiking pals bailed during the heat of the day, the old *Nomad* chugged down the Conquest and kept right on chugging. Thanks, Gary, for your sponsorship and for your friendship. Oh, and thanks for curing my giardia!

And finally, the dear friend who created the remarkable *Nimblewill Nomad* website—Greg *Rockin' Roller* Smith (5/29/1962–

12/2/2002). Greg was a quadriplegic; he worked his keyboard with a stick in his mouth. Yet he diligently trekked along with me every inch of the way, vicariously of course, as he loaded my journal entries for each and every day since New Years Day, 1998—pecking away with a stick clenched between his teeth! Rest in God's pure Grace, my dear, kind friend!

I'll close today with this ditty written before his death and in his honor...

A LIFE OF GRACE
I have a friend who has been dealt
A monumental blow;
For he's not free like you and me,
He can't get up and go.

'twas on a dark and fateful morn,
He most-near met his maker.
They pried him from that gruesome scene
To meet the undertaker.

But God was not through with him,
...His days here on this earth,
And though he'll never walk again,
My friend has found true worth.

His life he lives full measure,
As good as it can get.
There's not a trace of lingering doubt,
Self-pity...or regret.

You'd think that he'd be bitter with
His quadriplegic life.
But like no man I've ever met,
He's learned to deal with strife.

His is a faith that's firm and strong,
A glow from deep within.
His countenance from ear to ear,
That old familiar grin.

So when the shuffle's dealt to me
A little out of whack,
I think of this courageous man,
To put me back on track.

Oh, what true inspiration,
A blessing...he's my friend,
For though his life was over
*...He **lives** his life again.*
(N. Nomad)

Wednesday—April 4, 2001
Trail Day—300/12
Trail Mile—4808/171
Location—US-1 Mile Marker 0, to the monument marking the
southernmost point of the eastern North American continent, Key
West, Florida

According to Percy Bysshe Shelley, "The soul's joy lies in doing."
Ahh yes dear friends, has this odyssey been such a joy in doing, from
its beginning at the Cliffs of Forillon where the Appalachian Mountains plunge to the sea at Cap Gaspé, Québec, to the Caribbean
Sea, where this magnificent Eastern Continental Trail ends at the
southernmost point on the eastern North American continent here
in Key West, Florida. Three hundred days, over 4,800 miles. What
a truly joyful adventure this has been, another amazing miracle in
this old man's life!

This morning Ruth and Phil get me up and cheer me on my way, this final day. At nine I'm back on US-1, mile marker 17, heading ever onward toward Key West. The morning sails by, as do the Keys of Saddlebunch, Shark, Rockland, Boca Chica, and Stock Island. I remember little of their passing. Somewhere around mile marker 12, Mark and Robert from WPBT-2 Miami pull off to greet me, and with them, Owhnn from Everglades International Hostel, Florida City. They boost me along with well wishes and a cold drink. Shortly follows Chuck, Betty, and Chuck's sister, Mae, from Naples, hooting and cheering.

It's another blue-perfect day in paradise as I turn the corner to arrive in Key West. Then it's onto Roosevelt, mile marker 2, then Truman, mile marker 1, then the crowd and the carnival that is Duval. Turning at Fleming now I soon reach mile marker 0, US-1, at Whitehead. What words are there to describe such emotion, such feeling of overwhelming joy! In moments, as I proceed down Whitehead, I can see the monument marking the southernmost point ahead. Now are there many dear friends shouting and waving. As I continue, here come Mae and Owhnn and *Sheltowee* and *Moonshine* and Frank and Ruth and Phil and Mark and Chuck and Betty and Robert and Les and Arlene and *Shaft* and *Meatball*. All congratulate me as I slump against the monument to thank the Lord for this amazing journey, Odyssey 2000-'01.

We've done it, Lord. We've done it. Thanks, dear friends, thank you one and all for being part of this remarkable adventure, the first southbound thru-hike o'er this network of trails that combine to create two magnificent trails—the Trail of the Ancients and this most grand and glorious of all trails, the trail of the 21st Century...

THE EASTERN CONTINENTAL TRAIL

A magic trail that wends its way
Along the mountain crest,
From high the cliffs of Cap Gaspé
On down to old Key West.

I set upon this path alone,
A journ to find true worth,
And as the way to me was shown,
Came peace, pure joy, rebirth.

For to me as I walked the land,
Sprang forth a boundless love.
From unclenched fist, the open hand
Revealed the turtledove.

The way of God is not the way...of man,
For it is true:
His path is sure a finer plan
He's set for me and you.

With laden pack all shouldered up,
I entered on this way,
As Nature's nectar from Her cup
Sustained me day-to-day.

O'er mountain high, through valley deep,
The trail continued on.
And as in dream-fil'd endless sleep,
The days have come and gone.

This path, as life, a burdened path
Fil'd full with strife and care,
The devil heaped a ton of wrath,
But God was there to spare...

My life, this trail, are trailing out,
The days turn short...I long.
But homing now, in gladness shout,
Fil'd full with joyful song.

The final step, I wend my way,
Ten million, more or less,
And I, naysayer, now must say
...to miracles confess.

I thank you Lord for all Your grace,
For all Your blessings, too.
This trail's indeed a holy place,
It's brought me home—to You.

KEY WEST ROADWALK (KWR)

Ahh!

A magic trail that wends its way
Along the mountain crest,
From high the cliffs of Cap Gaspé
...To end in old Key West.
(N. Nomad)

CHAPTER 6

THE NEWFOUNDLAND
APPALACHIAN TRAIL

Thursday—August 9, 2001
Trail Day—301/1
Trail Mile—4826/20
Location—Trailside, Wreckhouse, Newfoundland

Well, dear friends, the journey continues. And the reason it continues? Well, it's a story that won't take long to tell, but the trek—that will take a while. And just where am I? Newfoundland, folks. I'm in Newfoundland, Canada.

You see, for the past two years, after my Odyssey '98 trek, I've been going around telling folks how I've managed to hike the entire Appalachian Mountain range, from where the mountains begin near Flagg Mountain, Alabama, to where they plunge dramatically to the sea, to end (so I thought) at the spectacular Cliffs of Forillon, Cap Gaspé, Québec. During this grand exclaiming, and from time to time, friends would come to me and quite politely point out that, indeed, I had not hiked the entirety of the Appalachians, that there exist mountains in the Province of Newfoundland, Canada, that are considered part of the Appalachian Mountain range, quite a long range of mountains. Yes, it is true. In fact, these mountains are so long that they have been named the "Long Range Mountains!"

So now you know why I'm here! I'm here to finish what I'd started, and what I thought I'd finished. I'm here to hike the remainder of the Appalachian Mountains, at least as we know them to exist on the North American continent. So that's that story, and here now, day to day, follows the rest.

Last Sunday I bid farewell to family in Missouri. Two days and 1,700 miles later, I arrived in Portland, Maine, to board the ferry *Scotia Prince* for an eleven-hour crossing to Yarmouth, Nova Scotia. From there I hitched half a day to Halifax. Then from there, a six-hour bus ride to North Sydney. From North Sydney commenced another ferry ride on the *Caribou* across Cabot Strait to Channel-Port aux Basques, Newfoundland. I arrived here yesterday around seven in the morning—four days and two and one-half time zones away from where I started.

The beginning of the Long Range Mountains can be seen across the bay here at Channel-Port aux Basques. They're a remarkable upheaval of land, something to do with tectonic plates as I recall someone telling me. They're not incredibly tall mountains as we might know, rising to a little over 2000 feet, but they have been uplifted to stand abruptly next to the sea, quite a striking and imposing sight. And today I head into them.

First stop is at the Railway Heritage Centre to see the "Newfie Bullet," one of the original trains that ran the rails across Newfoundland as early as 1898. Here on that old railbed, the Wreckhouse Trail begins. This trail is part of the Newfoundland Trailway, which runs for 548 miles across the province to St. John's. It's part of a grand network of trails across Canada—the Trans Canada Trail, which runs from St. John's, Newfoundland, to Tuktoyaktuk, Northwest Territory, more than 16,000 kilometers, the longest continuous recreational trail in the world.

Over the next few days, I'll tell you more about this fascinating far-off north, about these magnificent mountains, and about the kind and generous people of Newfoundland (say *Nu*-fun-laaand).

I get started late heading north out of Channel-Port aux Basques on the Wreckhouse Trail. Toward evening, I stop to get directions at a little bungalow by Ragged Ass Road. Here I'm greeted by Wes and Carol Hann, who run a 4x4 tour service up Table Top Mountain. They immediately invite me in, for grand conversation—and for dinner. The magic continues!

At dusk, I arrive at Wreckhouse. Wreckhouse? Well, that's a very interesting story, a bit of the past, part of the history and heritage of this special part of North (far-north) America. I'll tell you that story tomorrow. For this evening, before rolling into my little Nomad, I'll content myself by just sitting here on the bluff at Wreckhouse, taking in the final blaze of light cast o'er the mountains as the sun paints its crimson ribbon across the watery arc of the Gulf of St. Lawrence.

> *The trails of the world be countless,*
> *And most of the trails are tried;*
> *You tread on the heels of the many,*
> *Till you come where the ways divide...*
> (Robert W. Service)

Friday—August 10, 2001
Trail Day—302/2
Trail Mile—4850/44
Location—Trailside school bus, Old Joe Brake's Farm, Newfoundland

Yesterday, a ways out of Port aux Basques, I got my not so casual introduction to the Long Range Mountains. Table Top Mountain it was, a climb of over five hundred meters in less than four kilometers. The pamphlet "Gateway to Nature" rates this climb as "difficult." And for my first day back on the trail after a three-month hiatus, the climb was indeed difficult. But from the summit I had command of the entire southern coastal peninsula of Newfoundland and a great extent of the Gulf of St. Lawrence, much as did the Allied forces during WWII. From here also can be seen the "Horizontal Wave Forest," where the forested hillsides show the effect of strong and baffling winds that have left barren streaks across the mountainside.

Along the trail yesterday were beautiful beaches stretching to the mist-spun horizon, at Grand Bay West and J. T. Cheeseman Provincial Park. Looking to the mountains, all along, are the amazing effects of time as it has formed the scenic Codroy Valley. Here are glacier-carved cirques and hanging valleys, present for tens of thousands of years. And the rivers, the spectacular rivers, they're world-renowned for Atlantic salmon, a fly fisherman's paradise. And birds, if you like bird watching! Well folks, right here's some of the finest bird watching found anywhere. Tucked away in this unspoiled corner of the world is the Grand Codroy River, designated as a "Wetlands of International Importance" under the Ramsar Agreement. Here are large flocks of Canada geese, great blue herons, and black ducks; and smaller numbers of pintail, green-winged teal, American widgeon and greater scaup. Along the beaches are nesting places for the piping plover, an endangered species. Only 5,000 of these birds are known to remain worldwide.

Oh, and Wreckhouse, now here's a truly fascinating story. Wreckhouse is a little spot that once existed along the old Canadian National Railway Line (now paved over into a parking lot). A fellow's house stood here, lashed down to the bedrock with cables! From a brochure about Wreckhouse, the story goes like this, "The Human Windgauge—Lauchie McDougall, 1896-1965. A trapper and farmer who lived at Wreckhouse, Newfoundland. He was contracted by the Railway to monitor the strong southeast winds in the area and to advise the Railway when it was safe to pass. He did so for over thirty years...[He] had a family of twelve children, all born at Wreckhouse." And why was his house tied down? And why did the Railway hire him? And what does the name "Wreckhouse" mean, anyway? Well folks, the wind gusts past Lauchie's house were so strong at times that train cars were literally blown completely off the tracks, to wreck at, oh yes, Wreckhouse!

The day is waning now. As I look for a place to pitch for the evening, I come upon this old school bus by the side of the trail, so down I go. On the rear emergency exit door is this little handwritten sign: "Everyone welcome!" So in I go, just as the rain comes in sheets. What a neat little place, complete with wood-burning stove, kitchen, dining area, and bunks. Folks you know the old *Nomad* is indeed a lucky (say blessed) feller!

The old bus is warm and dry, not a leak. I'll sleep just fine tonight. Thanks, dear unknown friend, for the use of your cozy storybook "cabin!" More tomorrow...ZZZZ.

> *Wind is air made tangible, air made destructive,*
> *air empowered as sculptor...*
> (Michael Burzynski)

Saturday—August 11, 2001
Trail Day—303/3
Trail Mile—4872/64
Location—Trailside, Barachois Brook, Newfoundland

As the trail continues along today and I leave the coastal Anguille Mountains behind, there are many streams to cross, some very wide, which lead from the Long Range Mountains to the St. Lawrence Sea. The old railroad trestles which span these rivers and brooks are interesting, especially in the crossing of them. The rails were taken up and hauled away years ago, leaving only the huge crossties teetering there. Some have shifted or are missing entirely, making wide gaps between. With each crossing I must look down, to concentrate and to maintain sure foot placement. This is not such an easy task, and I need stop at times to fight off the vertigo that seems to present itself when I'm in high places. But as I hesitate, I can look away and take in the sights up and down these old rocky brooks and across these ancient mountains, and in these short moments comes the presence of mind, and I'm again full with the joy and excitement of being here. There are no other sights like these that I can recall in my memory. As I journey on, I'm able to manage the crossings with assured confidence, no matter the breach or the height.

This hike is shaping to be very different than any I've taken before, both in challenge and reward. I had packed and lugged along much winter gear, having not a clue what to expect, but upon arriving in Port aux Basques it became immediately evident that winter gear was not what I needed. So into a box it went—and bounce it went, addressed to meself, to Corner Brook, a week or so on up the trail. Hard to believe, but my face, my arms and the back of my legs have become sunburned, and I must take measures now to prevent further exposure. Sure not what I expected!

On into evening and into St. Fintan's, I stop at a small grocery store for a few provisions before continuing on to Barachois Brook. Here I make camp, set a cooking and warming fire, then relax, completely content at my fireside, on the pebbled beach right next to the peaceful, clear, rushing waters of the Barachois. Happiness is many things to many people—here is my happiness.

He who needs only coarse food, water for drink, and as pillow his folded arms will find happiness without further search.
(Confucius)

Sunday—August 12, 2001
Trail Day—304/4
Trail Mile—4894/88
Location—Henrieta's Hospitality Home (B&B), St. George's,
Newfoundland. Ann Vincent, proprietor.

This day seems to be setting up for one of those grind-it-out days. Here I'm rolling through high open country, the old railbed lifting and rolling right along with it. At times I can see as far as two miles ahead, a sure test of patience and resolve.

Old railbeds are not my most favorite treadway, what with the inevitable loose goose-egg-sized rocks that sets one to more of a churning motion than a striding gait, surely not a desired hiking experience. But the scenery all along keeps my interest and the time passes quickly. Also keeping me alert and to the task are the passing ORVs, for I'm sharing this old railroad grade with them. Actually, they're sharing it with me, as they're many and I'm but one. It's blueberry time now, and the way to pick blueberries up here is to strap on your helmet, grab a bucket, jump on your quad-track and haul. Some of the guys and gals are just out for the mosey though, and they stop to chat. Others hurry on their way, dragging clouds of dust.

It's late evening as I reach St. George's, and I'm very tired. Here in this little village is a former Roman Catholic Convent that's been converted to a B&B, so there I head. Up a short grassy path to the door I go, to be greeted by Ann Vincent. And should I be surprised? Oh no, for from her brightly scrubbed, blushed and shining countenance, radiates that universal, ear to ear, grand Canadian smile! A refreshing shower and a gargantuan fish platter with fries (covered with gravy) down at Finny's little fish place, and this day chalks up as a mighty fine one indeed. I have done well.

*Who does his best shall have as a guest the
Master of life and light.*
(Henry Van Dyke)

Monday—August 13, 2001
Trail Day—305/5
Trail Mile—4907/101
Location—Dhoon Lodge, Black Duck Siding, Newfoundland.
George Pike, proprietor.

From my bedroom window at Henrieta's did I have such a grand view out and across St. George's Bay. And as the sun went down and the lights came up I could see the bright chain of white stretching all the way to the tip of Cape St. George, the Gulf of St. Lawrence.

Newfoundland, which includes Labrador, is a remarkably vast expanse of land, larger than almost all of New England. Yet the population here is just over half a million, smaller than any large New England city. And what is really interesting is the fact that most Newfoundlanders live along and by the coast, around the bays and harbors, like here in St. George's Bay. So once one ventures inland the least bit is the whole place pretty much nature's own! And inland I go today, toward a little village tagged with not such a catchy name, Black Duck Siding.

As I return to the trail, I'm immediately greeted by a grand, unobstructed view across the bay, to the city of Stephenville and the little town of Stephenville Crossing. At the head of the bay, where the old railbed crosses, stands this classic rusty old bridge, the kind that would have been shut down to any kind of use in the States years ago. But across goes the trail, the quad-tracks, and across goes me! Big gaps in the crossties again and the tide is coming in, the sea roaring between the piers in a flood. An old fellow sitting beside just fishing greets me, and we chat a while. "Doin' a little hikin', eh," says he. "Doin' a little fishin', eh," says I as he reels in a wad of seaweed. He responds with a sad-sack frown. I answer his frown with, "Looks like I'm havin' better luck," as I bid him farewell and continue on my way.

I've been told about this place just past Black Duck Siding, an old lodge built by Bowater Pulp and Paper Co. of England way back in 1941 (I was just a pup then!). It was used as their V.I.P. hunting and fishing headquarters; what with being bounded on the south and east by Harry's River, and there to be cradled by the Long Range Mountains. Sure sounded like my kind of place, so that's where I'm headed this evening.

After hiking right by the turn I was told to take and should have taken, and after directions from some berry pickers, I'm soon at the old Bowater retreat, now Dhoon Lodge, owned and managed by the Pike family, George and Odelle (got a picture of a big fish on their card). Typical Canadian greetings by George, Odelle, and their daughter Georgette. What a beautiful well-preserved old log lodge, the kind you read and dream about. I'm just in time for dinner—broiled salmon washed down with a couple longneck frosties. My oh my, is this ever roughing it! I'm having a grand, exciting time in Newfoundland.

When one is willing and eager, the gods join in.
(Aeschylus)

Tuesday—August 14, 2001
Trail Day—306/6
Trail Mile—4922/116
Location—Log Cabin Lodge, Spruce Brook, Newfoundland. George Pike, proprietor.

Up here in the great expanse of Newfoundland, especially toward the interior of the province, at night there's no light, no sound, just pitch-black silence. Under these conditions, sleep can be quite different. I sleep well under these conditions. Ah yes, what a great night's sleep at Dhoon Lodge!

This morning it's over to the main lodge great room for breakfast. Odelle is my waitress and she sets me a hiker's spread. With breakfast down now and seconds on coffee up, I take to looking the place over. Settings like these can't really be created, at least not that would appear authentic. They just kind of happen over the years. The old furniture ages and sags. Some of it gets broken and replaced. Pieces come and go, not with any grand scheme or plan. Pictures and stuff on the walls and things and objects standing around and in the corners just kind of end up there. The glow and the rich burnish, the patina if you will, the mark of time, just adds to the grandness. There always seems to be a centerpiece in these quaint old settings. Here, two are vying for that honor. One is a very well-endowed full life, bronze-skinned wooden Indian maiden, standing proud and smiling that seductive, high-cheekboned smile. The other hangs on the fireplace, above the mantel. It's a huge caribou trophy, looking out, trying to see past its wide-spaded antlers, eyes glazed in a blank stare as the TV weatherman below gives us the good news for the day, cool and partly cloudy, a perfect day for hiking.

George shuttles me the mile or so back to the trail, and by mid-morning I'm heading north again. My destination today will be about fifteen miles north by trail, to a place called Spruce Brook. Here, George Pike also runs a lodge, the Log Cabin Lodge. It isn't open now, and no one is there, but George said the power and water were on, and the water heater was even cranking. George offered the entire place to me for the evening. As you may recall, and as I've said before, "My mommy didn't raise no dummy!" I immediately accepted his kind offer.

As I hike along this morning, I'm thinking about the highest point on the island of Newfoundland. It's a mountain called Lewis Hill, standing at 815 meters and lying a fair distance to the west of here in the Lewis Mountains. George had told me about it, for he has been considering putting together a snowmobile guide service to take people there.

You'd think by now I'd be wore out climbing mountains. However, around noon, by the time I reach the little village of Gallants, I've made up my mind that I want to climb Lewis Hill. So from the little general store in Gallants I give George a call. He informs me that getting to the top of Lewis Hill might not be such an easy proposition. "You see," he says, "Most of the excursions in the past have been made in the winter by snowmobile, up the ice and snow-covered tributaries leading to the mountain. Lewis Hill lies in a very remote, inaccessible region." I press him, nevertheless, and plans are made for George to try and find a guide for me by Thursday, day-after-tomorrow. I'm to hike on to his lodge in Spruce Brook this evening, then continue on to Corner Brook tomorrow. There, if all goes well, I'll get a bus back to Black Duck Siding, and with the aid of a guide, I'll do the climb, hopefully, Thursday afternoon.

I arrive at Log Cabin Lodge in good order and find the key right where George had told me to look. Another neat old place, not quite standing straight up—but kept up. A fire in the old lodge woodstove sure feels good tonight. Thanks, George, for your kindness and hospitality. I have faith that a guide will be found, and that a way will be found to climb that mountain—see you tomorrow evening, George!

It isn't the mountain ahead that wears you out;
It's the grain of sand in your shoe.
(Robert W. Service)

Wednesday—August 15, 2001
Trail Day—307/7
Trail Mile—4948/142
Location—Log Cabin Lodge, Spruce Brook, Newfoundland. George Pike, proprietor.

A couple of days ago, in response to an earlier email I sent to friends telling them about the Long Range Mountains of Newfoundland,

I received a neat note back from *Spur*, a dear hiking friend. We met during Trailfest 2000 in Hot Springs, North Carolina. There, as fate would have it, we ended up sharing a room at Elmer Hall's Sunnybank Inn. That's where *Spur* got a good dose of what's since become known simply as "*Nomad's* poison!" I was in town at Elmer's invitation, to take part in the festivities, and *Spur* was passing through on his third AT thru-hike. While enjoying the time, it became quite apparent that *Spur's* current ramblings weren't doing much in the way of dousing that fire in his gut—that instinctive wanderlust-driven urge to go that suffers many of us. So over the course of the evening, after many questions, *Spur* pretty much set his mind that he'd keep right on going after he got to Katahdin, on over the Knife Edge, across Pamola, down into Roaring Brook and on north out of Baxter into those far-off, adventure-filled lands of Canada. And you know what, that's just what he did! And after reaching the Cliffs of Forillon at Cap Gaspé, Québec, some 700+ miles north of Katahdin by trail, *Spur* returned to Flagg Mountain Alabama, the symbolic southern beginning of the Appalachians, from there to complete his Trail of the Ancients hike back to Springer Mountain—to become at the time, only the fourth person known to have hiked the entire Appalachian Mountain range; so he thought! And so his neat email: "How many more miles have I gotta hike before I've finished this mountain range thing? And what new language do I have to learn now?" That's *Spur*, all right. He's just like me; he'll keep at it till it's over, till the hike is truly and finally done. There's no doubt in my mind.

And so, to answer his questions in part—and I guess it's time I tell you a little more about this remarkable island tucked away in the North Atlantic, this mystic, far-off place known as Newfoundland, where the Appalachian Mountains end, so far as we know them to exist on the North American continent, and where "The New World" as we know it, really began.

The history of the New World, at least as has to do with us folk that came late across the big pond, didn't begin with Columbus, nor with Cabot, nor with Cook, nor with de Soto, nor with Champlain, nor with any of the other early explorers that happened upon this place we know as North America. To learn of that history, we must return to a time long past, before the fifteenth century, to a time a thousand years ago—to the time of the Vikings, the Norse people. For it was the Norsemen that first set foot on North America, at a place called L'Anse aux Meadows, at the northern tip of the Great Northern Peninsula of Newfoundland. It is to that historic place north of me now that I journey, the end of the Appalachian Mountains—the beginning of the New World. Ahh, there will this remarkable odyssey finally end!

Log Cabin Lodge is a neat old place, much as were the old cabins I spoke about in the book *Ten Million Steps*. A place quiet and peaceful, old and rustic, leaning only the least bit, just as now lean so many of my kind old friends. Thanks, George and Odelle Pike, for your kindness!

I'm up and out to another long day of churning the rocks, 45 kilometers to the seaside village of Corner Brook. Along the trail I take many pictures of the Lewis Mountains, where stands the highest point on the island. Later in the day, further north, I take many pleasures, for on the horizon I can see the beginning of the Blow Me Down Range.

Many quad-tracks pass today. Two towing trailers slow, then stop, the fellows to chat some. "We saw you the other day when we were heading south to Port aux Basques; you're really covering some ground; how your feet holdin' up?" And so I meet Lew Stuckless and Harold Moore from Glenwood, over by Gander. They're knocking out 100-125 mile days through the rocks and dirt and are now on their way back home. Happy (but just a little dusty) smiles, both. Both are kind and gentle, as are almost all the people of Newfoundland. Lew invites me to stay the night as his guest should I pass by later toward St. John's.

In Corner Brook now I make the call to George Pike. Good news, the hike/bushwhack to Lewis Hill is on for tomorrow! So now my task: get to the bus station before the last bus goes through for the day. I make it with ten minutes to spare. At eight, George arrives at Stephenville to fetch me, and we're soon back at Dhoon Lodge.

I'm very tired. What a day. Before bed, George fills me in on tomorrow's activities. At five in the morning, two hunters George keeps on call to guide his clients on moose will come for me. We'll drive the hour-plus drive o'er the old logging roads to near the base of the mountain, there to get as close as possible. Then to begin the fourteen-mile, round-trip bushwhack, mostly through rock-filled gullies and ravines, over the tundra above treeline—to the summit of "Old Louie."

Oh, I hope and pray I can sleep tonight!

I think over again my small adventures, my fears...
(Inuit Song)

Thursday—August 16, 2001
Trail Day—308/8
Trail Mile—4962/156
Location—Log Cabin Lodge, Spruce Brook, Newfoundland. George Pike, proprietor.

It's still pitch black when the knock comes on my door. It's five to five (Newfie time) and I've been up for twenty minutes trying to get my pack organized and ready to go. As I open the door, I'm greeted by that ever-present wide beaming Canadian smile. It's Daniel MacDonald, one of the hunters George lined up to guide me up Lewis Hill. At the truck I meet Jackie Besaw, George's other friend. George is up too, to send us off with much encouragement into the dark of night.

We've been bouncing and lurching along for over an hour now, the dim light of dawn finally coming, and we've already seen eight moose. One, a big old fellow with a fine rack. Another forty-five minutes and we've gone as far as we can by vehicle, the mountain still seven miles away. Jackie parks the truck; we shoulder our packs and head toward Old Louie.

Jackie and Daniel are seasoned woodsmen, having guided for moose for many years. Both carry a GPS in hand and at the ready. We won't be able to track a beeline to the mountain, but the little satellite signal triangulations will keep us close. The first half-mile or so is over rutted quad-track trails, past ponds and islands of low bush and grass, leading to remote hunting cabins hidden in the spruce and fir. Cresting a hill, we get our first glimpse of the sheer mass of rock and barren tundra that is the fortification. Here again are boulders and imposing escarpments composed of that same strange and eerie camo brown color first seen in the Chic Chocs of Parc de la Gaspésie. I've never seen anything quite so strikingly rugged or imposing, anywhere in the Appalachians, nowhere but here. Jackie and Daniel have both seen this many times. No matter. We all stand and gape in mystified awe. Dan finally breaks the silence; "I told you we would see beautiful sights today!" What an understatement, my kind new friend. And the weather could not be better; a haze-free, blue-perfect day is in the making. From Lewis Hill we'll see past the sea to the edge of the world. This is going to be one incredible time.

This land is grand, expansive, wide open. Daniel and Jackie, binoculars in hand now, both pan the valleys and far ridges for moose. "De're over dere in da trees, we just can't see em," says Jackie. Descending now through the bush and the rocks, we arrive at the wide, boulder-strewn streambed that is the main tributary to Fox Island River. During rainy weather, crossing here would be out of the question, but today it's just a fun rock hop. I do manage to dunk one foot though. Across the river we begin our climb up one of the lunar landscaped ravines. The climb is steady, long and hard, through the drifted rocks and ice-rowed gravel.

At the upper extent of the ravine now, with a waterfall tumbling down, we must attack the wall of the uplifted tableland. Once gained there are now miles of tarns, packs and pockets of snow, and lava-like, bleached-gray rocky cliffs and lesser crags.

We stop to rest. The GPS certainly tells us where we are, but not how to get through this puzzle of water, ice and rock. So out come the good old topo maps, the contours to try and figure, to lead us along the best route. A way is chosen around the larger lake and up and back across the leading ridge behind. This works well, and we're soon through the maze to arrive at the final lift, the lower edge of the crown that is the broad and curving mound, Lewis Hill.

Beneath our feet is a meadow now, extending toward the summit where one could romp and tumble and play with abandon. Daniel exclaims with glee, "Sure wish I had this in my back yard!" I offer for his consideration, "Daniel, is this not your back yard?" Ahh yes, and yet again, from both Daniel and Jackie, that wide beaming Canadian smile!

The lovely, green meadow gives way to the rocks and boulders once more, they being the crown of it, and soon we three are proudly standing by the cairn that marks the top of Newfoundland. To our surprise, we have completed the climb well before noon. Now with much time to tarry, the warm sun being carried on the edge of a gentle breeze, we move off to the west a few paces to where the sea and all the shores and islands below come to view. Now can be seen the barren and splintered crags and peaks around, the tundra of the Blow Me Down Range, and the remarkable, uplifting lens of the sea, which curves and bends its way to the edge of the earth. There, the eye can't help but follow, to gaze and to ponder that final dancing bit of warp on the horizon, that leads perhaps to the brink of eternity.

The return trip tomorrow. Now, a little more about this remarkable land and the beautiful people of Newfoundland, in *Ode to Newfoundland*, as I proudly stand on the very tip top of this breathtaking and remarkable island in the sea:

When sunrays crown thy pine-clad hills,
And summer spreads her hand.
When silvern voices tune thy rills,
We love thee, smiling land.

When spreads thy cloak of shimmering white,
At winter's stern command.
Through shortened day and starlit night,
We love thee, frozen land.

When blinding storm gusts fret thy shore,
And wild waves lash thy strand.
Through spindrift swirl and tempest roar,
We love thee, windswept land.

As loved our fathers, so we love,
Where once they stood, we stand.
Their prayers we raise to heaven above,
God guard thee, Newfoundland...

God guard thee, God guard thee, God guard thee, Newfoundland.
(Sir Cavendish Boyle)

Friday—August 17, 2001
Trail Day—309/9
Trail Mile—4962/156
Location—Corner Brook Hotel, Corner Brook, Newfoundland,

While relaxing and taking in the wonders yesterday atop Lewis Hill, while Jackie and Daniel were busy spotting yet more moose grazing contentedly down below, I realized I no longer had my sunglasses. I'd taken them off to look at the topo maps way back in the rocks before the final approach to the mountain. As I fretted myself with this unpleasantness, Daniel casually remarked, "We'll stop and pick them up on the way back." "Daniel," I exclaimed, "That place is miles back. There are hundreds of piles of rocks; they all look alike. We'll never find that place again." Looking at me confidently, he simply said, "We'll find it."

Well folks, I guess you can see where this is going. Oh yes, put a GPS in the hands of someone trained to use it, especially an experienced mountain guide, and he can take you to the least of a smudge— anywhere. He needs only the coordinates; it's as simple as that.

Until yesterday, all I knew about the GPS was that it pretty much took the guesswork out of orienteering—if you knew how to use one. The way Daniel and Jackie guided me to Lewis Hill was simply by following a pointer on their respective GPS screens. The GPS knew where the mountain was from the coordinates they had entered. Signals traveling constantly back and forth from GPS to satellites triangulated our location, and from that information their screens constantly displayed the direction we needed to go, scrolling automatically as we went. Daniel's GPS was off about 100 feet from the actual summit marker, but he hadn't entered the coordinates to the finest detail.

What is so cool about this whole scheme is that once we had reached Lewis Hill, every inch of our exact path to get there had been recorded in the GPS's memory. Now I understand Daniel's smugness, his confidence about finding my sunglasses. We just followed the path on his GPS right back to them.

On the return trip, his GPS ever at the ready, along in the rocks that looked like countless other places in the rocks, Dan said, "Here's where we stopped to look at the topos. We walked over and sat down right there." So over he went (that's when I recognized the rock). Glancing casually, he bent down and picked up my sunglasses! I stood there in total disbelief. It was incredible! Well, Dan had great pleasure in handing me my lost and gone forever sunglasses. That grand, wide-beaming Canadian smile just gave him away. Thanks, Daniel. Incredible, absolutely incredible!

We got back to Dhoon Lodge well before dark to be enthusiastically greeted and congratulated by all the Pike family: George, Odelle, Georgette, Sis, Kari Ann, and Cory. It was truly an amazing day!

This morning I pack my pack and close the door to room #4 at Dhoon Lodge for the final time, and head over to the grand old great room for my final breakfast with these kind and gracious hosts. Odelle waits my table, and George cranks out the bacon and eggs for me. Daniel comes by, and in a while we walk together out to the road. Here we linger, reminiscing about our memorable time together as I await the bus that will haul me back to Corner Brook. Great guides always have such keen senses, "The bus is coming," says Daniel—five minutes before it arrives, screeching to a halt across the road.

A straight look in the eye and a good solid handshake, and I turn away. Dang, this is always the hard part. But we'll have the memories of our adventure, Daniel. We'll always have these beautiful memories, forever! Thanks, dear friends, the Pikes and Jackie and Daniel, thanks so much for all the joy you have brought my way. I'd really love to stay. Maybe someday I'll return, but I don't know. I doubt it. The wanderlust has got me, and it keeps driving me on.

I arrive late morning to check into the Corner Brook Hotel. Here I'll take a couple of days off and get rested up before tackling the next leg of this grand adventure, Gros Morne National Park, a UNESCO World Heritage Site, just up the trail.

...the fact that they do this year after year for
their entire lives is incredible.
They put out such effort to accomplish goals others
wouldn't begin to understand; they're part of a sub-culture
of guides and outfitters, those who take to the
mountains when the summer hikers...have fled.
(Jim Shockey)

Saturday—August 18, 2001
Trail Day—310/10
Trail Mile—4962/165
Location—Corner Brook Hotel, Corner Brook, Newfoundland

The forecast has been for rain, and it's here. Just as well; no problem burning another day. I need to take time for some writing anyway, so Corner Brook Hotel it is.

This is a neat town with much history, all the way back to Captain Cook. Cook surveyed the entire coast of Newfoundland for nearly five years around the mid-1700s. He named pretty much every place hereabouts, including Corner Brook, the Humber River, and of course, Cook's Brook.

The west coast of Newfoundland was slow to settle because of the disputes between the French and English. From the time of its "official" discovery by John Cabot in 1497, the French and British fought over the ownership of the island. Old records unearthed in Spain show that the Basques had plied the lucrative fishing grounds of the Grand Banks of Newfoundland long before Columbus or Cabot made their voyages. In 1583, Newfoundland became Britain's first colony, but it was not until 1949 that it became a province of Canada. The history of the province is one of continuous struggle. The French captured St. John's three different times, but each time it was retaken, rebuilt, and refortified by the British. Finally in 1904, the French agreed to relinquish their fishing rights along the western and northwestern shores of Newfoundland, and today less than three per cent of Newfoundland is French-speaking.

In the morning, I'll move on to Deer Lake, named for the great herds of caribou (deer) that moved about during the early years of settlement. There have never been any deer on the island of Newfoundland, nor are there any snakes, raccoons, skunks, or opossum.

Besides fishing, the main industries in Newfoundland are timber and mining. Here are there wide and endless forests to the horizon, with many varieties of trees, including fir, spruce, birch, pine, maple, alder, juniper, and aspen. On a placemat in one of the local restaurants I read about the importance of the various minerals and metals mined in Newfoundland, "Mining is a rich vein running through the lives of all Canadians...Imagine how different our lives would be without the cars, television sets, vitamins and medicines that come from minerals and metals extracted from the earth." It is true; we lament the gaping holes in the earth as we drive by in our metal cars, and we shrug with dismay at the clear-cut forests as we build our luxurious wooden houses. Who will be the first to do without these "necessities?"

Through all of this, the people of Newfoundland have endured, such a happy, proud, and joyful people. From "Receiving the World" celebration come these words, "The lamplight dances on the wall, the fiddler sets a feverish pace and we step out, bucklin' the floorboards, tryin' to keep up. We're arm-in-arm, swingin' wildly 'round the room, our lungs screamin' STOP!—but no one wants to. A time has broken out and she'll probably keep goin' till morning."

> *Q: How do you get a one-armed Newfie down from a tree?*
> *A: Why, just wave to him!*
> (Jokes from the Rock)

Sunday—August 19, 2001
Trail Day—311/11
Trail Mile—4994/197
Location—The Driftwood Inn, Deer Lake, Newfoundland

The rain continued throughout the night and this morning it remains steady, giving no sign of letting up. But no matter. "It's time to get out of Dodge," so around nine-ish, with pack up, I drop my room key off, then head down the steps and out the door for the thirty-two mile roadwalk to Deer Lake.

It's gonna be a long day, all of it a roadwalk on the Trans-Canada Highway (TCH). The old railbed I've been hiking for the past number of days used to go from Corner Brook to Deer Lake. I guess it still does, but it's now buried under the additional lanes that were built to widen the TCH, so it's roadwalk I go.

On the way out of town, I get a look at one of the old steam locomotives that, during the late 1800s and early 1900s, helped bring prosperity to places like Corner Brook and Deer Lake. Folks also alerted me to look for two other things during my travels today. One, the naturally occurring image of "The Old Man in the Mountain," and the other, "The Heritage Tree."

I guess almost every place where there are cliffs and rocky mountainsides, there's also a resident caretaker in the form of some kind of image in stone. In the States, at Franconia Notch, resides the famous chisel-faced old man. When viewed at the right angle he appears quite remarkable (since gone). But this old guy I'm looking up at now is another matter. No particular angle is needed to view him, nor does it take the least imagination for his image to appear. The bust of this old Newfoundlander is so striking and real, nearly the same as standing in awe at Mt. Rushmore. As I move along, his cold, piercing stare follows. Legend has it that he's standing guard, watching over pirate treasure buried on Shellbird Island just below him in the middle of the Humber River.

The Heritage Tree is a man-made wonder, but a wonder nonetheless. It's a 360-year-old cedar tree totem, standing 52 feet tall, with carvings representing over a thousand years of Newfoundland and Labrador history. Depicted are Cabot, Cook, the Vikings, the Maritime Archaic and Beothuck Indians, the Mamateek, the Shanadithit, the Dorset Eskimos, the whales, the lighthouses, the puffins, the icebergs, the moose, the railway, squid gigging, the Royal Canadian Mounted Police and the Newfoundland coat of arms, plus much more. It nearly reaches the sky, making quite a commanding presence.

The wind and rain keep pushing out of the north, and in a while I tire of pushing into its constant assault. So near Prynn's Brook, I pull off and head for a roadside pub. In a while, a cold longneck down and rested up, I reach for my pack. That's when this old fellow comes over, "Stick around a while," he says, "I'll buy you a beer." As we chat, I'm thinking I should know this guy, even with his face sagging and almost all his hair gone. "Where ya from?" he asks. When I tell him, "from the States, near Atlanta, Georgia," he comments, "Oh yeah, been there many times, used to do gigs all through there, into Alabama and Tennessee, all over." I finally ask, "What's your name mister, seems I should know you..." "Elvis," he says, "Elvis Presley." I can't believe it! Stuttering, I manage, "Man I loved your stuff, it was really good." With that he launches into a full-volume, spine-tingling rendition of Jailhouse Rock. Folks, those of you who've read some of my ramblings know I've got quite an imagination. But there's just no way I could have dreamed this one up! "So long Elvis, thanks for the beer—and the memories."

By late evening, I finally pass the powerhouse where huge pipes funnel water to the turbines below. This is Deer Lake. Ahead I see the hotel lights dancing in and out of the swirling rain. What a day. I'm soaked and tired. But a steak and baked potato, then a couple of longnecks, and everything comes around.

> *You can't depend on your eyes when your*
> *imagination is out of focus.*
> (Mark Twain)

Monday—August 20, 2001
Trail Day—312/12
Trail Mile—5012/215
Location—Old Lincoln Cabins, Wiltondale, Newfoundland

The rain continued again all night, and this morning the cloud ceiling is just shy of twenty feet. But I'm happy, as this hike is just shy of five thousand miles. I'll break the 5,000-mile mark today!

As I step out, the rain sets the puddles to dancing—sure looks like a repeat of yesterday. And it's another roadwalk, up the TCH to the entrance to Gros Morne National Park. On the way, I pass the Newfoundland Insectarium, so in I go. Neat place. I learn lots of good stuff—like there are over sixty species of butterflies in Newfoundland and Labrador, forty-seven of which are found here on the island. Also to be seen are hundreds of different moths. Looking at the specimens, I recognize many of the butterflies, such as the swallowtail, the monarch, the green comma, the painted lady, Peck's skipper and the common blue. Of the moths, the little virgin tiger moth is probably one of the most beautiful, so too, the white underwing. And one, due its striking resemblance, is called the hummingbird. It's really hard to choose a favorite.

I'm off the busy TCH, heading north now on NF-430. By mid-afternoon, the rain relents and the sun attempts an appearance. But the wind moves in, driving more mush. There are many ups and down, many lakes and hunting cabins, and I pass the time enjoying each as I pass. I'm heading deeper and deeper into the Long Range Mountains now.

The extended and sharp downhills have pretty much made ground meat of my soggy feet, and I'm very happy to see Old Lincoln Cabins down below. *I know the time will come when these long roadwalks will be gone and there will be a beautiful trail weaving its way through these Long Range Mountains.

*A trail of approximately 1,000 kilometers is presently
being planned in the Long Range Mountains of Newfoundland. It
would begin at Port aux Basques and pass through the
Lewis Hills (the highest point in insular Newfoundland),
Gros Morne National Park, and end at Belle Isle on the
tip of the Great Northern Peninsula...the terminus of
the Appalachian Mountain Chain in North America.
"Newfoundland Section of the Appalachian Trail" (Michael
A. Roy, Ph.D.)

Tuesday—August 21, 2001
Trail Day—313/13
Trail Mile—5032/235
Location—Gros Morne National Park to Woody Point Motel,
Woody Point, Newfoundland. Scott Sheppard and Nancy Crocker,
proprietors.

A chilly morning, but clear, and the rain appears to be gone for a while. With a stop at the entrance kiosk to Gros Morne National Park, I'm able to establish my itinerary for the coming days. At the next intersection, I'll turn west on NF-431 and head for the Tablelands and Green Gardens Trails along the southern shore of Bonne Bay.

At the intersection next to the Frontier Restaurant, I see a little homemade sign by a driveway that leads to a small cottage. "Knitted wool socks and mittens for sale." As my breakfast is being served, I inquire. "Oh, that's Mrs. Payne. I'll give her a call if you'd like," says the waitress. "Yes, please do!" I reply. So, after breakfast, up to Mrs. Payne's I go.

My mother made the last of my beautiful, hand-knitted socks before she passed away. They wore out over ten years ago, so here, ringing Mrs. Payne's doorbell, I'm filled with anticipation. In a moment comes this little old lady, and to my face comes this great big smile. For before me stands the perfect image that I'd formed and imagined in my mind's eye, the very looks of Mrs. Payne—short and petite, a rosy face, and just the least bit of a widow's hump. Her eyes bright and glowing, a perfect countenance. I'm invited in, to be seated before this enormous valise filled with beautifully hand-knitted socks and mittens, all shapes and sizes, unsorted by color, the likes from which to choose.

As I dig through the assortment, she tells me of her joy in making them. Even with her vision nearly gone at age 82, her work shows exquisite detail, near perfection. It's so remarkable! As I comment about her skill, she moves off to another room, soon to return with her darning needles in hand, a sock half-finished dangling there.

Her knotty, arthritic fingers begin flashing in a blur as she continues the conversation. She does not even look as the needles fly.

What a remarkable woman, so gentle and kind, and so blessed. As I watch, I'm reminded of the virtuoso who can sit before the grand piano, eyes fixed to the heavens, as fingers glide over the ivory keys, guided by some unseen power, setting our senses to the joy of it. Ahh, and you too, Mrs. Payne; you indeed are a virtuoso!

I choose three pair of knitted socks, each a different color. One gray for the days of rain, one blue for the blue of the skies today— and the last? The last a soft blush, as is the rosy blush in the smiling face of this sweet old woman.

By late afternoon nearing Woody Point, I get my first glimpse of the Tablelands, then of Gros Morne itself. These mountains do not stand at such great heights but they're spectacular. Now in view across Bonne Bay rises Gros Morne Mountain, the bay at sea level, Gros Morne at 806 meters. Oh yes, the scene is quite spectacular!

At Woody Point Motel I'm in luck; they've got a room. Here I meet Scott and Nancy who make me feel right at home. A warm soaking bath for my old, aching bones, a couple tall frosties for delight, accompanied by the finest supper of fresh pan-fried cod, and this racks up as one fine day!

Wouldn't life be lots more happy if we praised the good we see?
(Louis C. Shimon)

Wednesday—August 22, 2001
Trail Day—314/14
Trail Mile—5049/252
Location—Gros Morne National Park to Woody Point Motel, Woody Point, Newfoundland

I'm greeted to a morning of mist and low-hovering clouds. As I wait for Scott, who will deliver me to the far parking lot at Green

Gardens, *Gros Morne, I look the bay over for whale; for last evening as I tarried the time with Scott, we saw a minke whale breach as it made its way up Bonne Bay. Sure enough, this morning I see another, and yet another. There are two moving along, and with the quiet calm o'er the bay in the soft rain, I can hear their blowing plainly, much the same sound as the noisy snort of a startled buck when catching human scent.

Scott soon arrives and we're off. The plan is for him to drive me the twelve kilometers to the far trailhead at Green Gardens Trail, thus saving me that roadwalk both ways. From there I'll hike the Gardens, then walk the road to the Tablelands Trail and from there, the roadwalk back to Woody Point and Scott's fine motel, where I'll again spend the evening.

Scott bids me good hiking, and I'm off across this wonderland called Green Gardens. I'm filled with excitement, as so many people have described in such enthusiastic and glowing terms this place called Green Gardens, and what a reward it is!

I no sooner get started than I'm introduced to "tuckamore." This is a Newfoundlander term used to describe the stunted balsam fir and spruce that grow along the coast and in alpine areas. The trees never really get a chance to grow, as the frost and wind nip back their new buds and branches, producing an elfin-like forest similar to the krummholz found in the Alps. Here their windswept, stark, weathered profile and stout trunks indicate true tenacity. It is a sight to behold.

As I crest a barren hill and get my first look along the mist-laden coast this morning, I'm awe-struck by the jagged landscape before and below me. The last Ice Age carved much of this, and the wind, water and ice have been working it ever since. The trail passes along the seashore now, with towering stacks, volcanic cliffs, a grotto, and a secluded cove just back that hides a sparkling waterfall. Along the beach are scattered meadows full with wildflowers, the trail proceeding there.

Coming back inland and along the watershed for Wallace Brook, the trail climbs and descends through the rocks and tuckamore, and the protected coves of spruce and fir. Nearing the highway again, the trail crosses Wallace Brook on a long suspension bridge that delivers me back to the road. I'm once again set to another roadwalk, this one to the Tablelands.

The Tablelands, ahh, the Tablelands. Now here's an incredible place with an equally incredible history. For the Tablelands are composed of the very bowels of the earth, ancient rock pushed up from the ocean floor, making for a stark, scary, forbidding place indeed. At the Tablelands, earthly elements have come together to create great drama suited only for the grand theatres of Earth. Here rests ancient brown mantle rock disgorged by colossal collisions of drifting tectonic plates, creating landscapes so barren as to appear like the moon. Those were monumental forces, the result of the continents of North America and Euro-Africa slamming together. Gros Morne National Park was declared a World Heritage Site in part because of the weird rocks found here at the Tablelands.

What a hike, what a day. I'm in the Appalachians folks; these places I have described today are part of the long-reaching Long Range Appalachian Mountains! Another roadwalk, and by late afternoon I'm back at Woody Point, to spend another relaxing, fun-filled evening with Scott, Nancy and friends.

Gros Morne is the largest and most spectacular national park in eastern Canada—one of the best known parks... for its unexpected landscapes: massive cliffs, fjords, alpine tundra, white sand beaches, and the golden Tablelands plateau. Some park scenes have become icons for Newfoundland itself. The geology, plants, and wildlife have drawn naturalists and researchers for decades, and the human story of the coast stretches back over 4,500 years.
Gros Morne National Park, (Michael Burzynski)

Thursday—August 23, 2001
Trail Day—315/15
Trail Mile—5056/259
Location—Major's Hospitality Home Hostel, Rocky Harbor, New-
foundland. Jack and Violet Major, proprietors.

Today the old *Nomad* takes a ride, the third to cause interruption in the continuity of this journey, an odyssey that will span nearly the breadth of the entire eastern North American continent. The first break came in the crossing of the St. Marks River in Florida, the second, the crossing of the Gulf of St. Lawrence, from the Cliffs of Forillon at Cap Gaspé, Québec, to Channel-Port aux Basques, Newfoundland. And the one today will also be a water crossing, a shuttle ride of twenty minutes across Bonne Bay from Woody Point to Norris Point.

After a fine breakfast and plenty of coffee prepared by Scott and Nancy (and another sad goodbye), I'm off to the dock and the shuttle boat, *I'se Da B'ye.* What timing; the captain is starting the engines and the mate is casting the bowline even as I arrive.

It's another cool, cloudy day but the views are splendid as we ply the bay. Many photo ops, first of Woody Point Lighthouse, then of Bonne Bay, one of the most picturesque of all the mountain-embraced harbors of Newfoundland.

I'm soon into the roadwalk again, this a short one to Rocky Harbor. There I'll spend the day preparing for the ascent of Gros Morne tomorrow, weather permitting. Gros Morne is a formidable mountain rising abruptly from the sea to stand at 806 meters, only nine meters shy of Lewis Hill.

By early afternoon, as I near Rocky Harbor, a vehicle slows behind me. Down comes the window (it's drizzling again) and the lady calls out, "Need a ride? I'm going to Rocky Harbor." Declining the offer, I thank her just the same, telling her I'm a hiker and am bound for the hostel. With a smile she says, "I run the hostel. It's right on the way. Look for my car with the smashed front fender, and the two big flower pots out front." So on I trudge, soon to arrive at the smashed front fender and the two big flower pots—Major's Hospitality Home Hostel. I enter to be greeted by Violet, the sweet lady who offered me the ride. She shows me around. The place is her home, hers and Jack's. He's out hanging clothes on the line. Neat place. This is fine, mighty fine. And there's a local mom-n-pop café that serves fresh local seafood just across. Hiking can really be rough sometimes. Oh yes, *Nessmuk*, now ain't this roughing it!

> *Now shall I walk or shall I ride?*
> *"Ride," Pleasure said; "Walk," Joy replied.*
> (William Henry Davies)

Friday—August 24, 2001
Trail Day—316/16
Trail Mile—5056/259
Location—Major's Hospitality Home Hostel, Rocky Harbor, Newfoundland.

Summer days in Newfoundland can be unbelievably grand, the blue of the sky so blue as to provoke unusually attentive and hushed awareness. To this then add the pure white legions, domes, tufts, and rolling billowing pillows of cumulus and cirrus clouds backed against the horizon, as far as the eye can see. From across the craggy barrens and forested mountainsides to the edge of the sea, there is such glorious presentation as to create a spell, causing pause, followed by baffling, awestruck amazement.

Then again there are days, other kinds of days, as many or more days like today, with rain-laden clouds hovering and pressing their dark gray dismal and dreary gloom, swirling and engulfing, not only physically all about but mentally within, creating an unsettling presence of mind, a feeling such that days like this will never end.

So I'll not climb Gros Morne today, a mountain so named by the Basques to means "big" (gros), "dismal and gloomy" (morne). I'll, however, try to moderate the dismal, dreary gloom of this day by writing, studying at the library, and catching up on correspondence to family and friends.

> *When it's dismal and dreary, when you feel there's no hope,*
> *When your heart's filled with naught but regret.*
> *May your thoughts all be heady, your pack featherlight,*
> *And the trail six lanes wide when it's wet.*
> (N. Nomad)

Saturday—August 25, 2001
Trail Day—317/17
Trail Mile—5071/274
Location—Gros Morne Mountain to Major's Hospitality Home Hostel, Rocky Harbor, Newfoundland.

The forecast for today calls for cool and partly cloudy. What joy, awakening to the glow of the rising sun. This is the day to climb Gros Morne Mountain, a day of brightness, not of gloom. Ahh, patience is rewarded.

I have made many calls and have searched diligently over the last two days in hopes of finding a guide to lead me across the Long Range and North Rim traverses, from Gros Morne across the tundra and around Western Brook Pond, but I have had no luck. I dearly wish to do these traverses, but these are hikes the likes of which must not to be taken lightly. Although the highest mountain here rises just above 800 meters, the terrain is indescribably rugged and complex, with massive cliffs composed of some of the most ancient rock in the world, rising (or falling) 600 to 700 meters. Remember, this is where continents slammed together, where one ocean died and another was born. According to Michael Burzynski in his book

Gros Morne National Park: "This park has dangerous terrain, and weather conditions are changeable and sometimes extreme. Off-trail hiking in Gros Morne may be more difficult than anything you have ever experienced—a cross between the terrain of the Rockies and the Arctic with low clouds, high winds, sodden ground, impassable brush, large animals, false trails, biting flies, and driving rain thrown in for fun."

Hiking the traverses requires a permit, along with special instruction by a park ranger. All who attempt the traverse must carry a signal transmitting radio provided by the park. The distance is only sixty-two kilometers, less than forty miles, but park personnel recommend carrying food enough for at least seven days. Since I have been unable to find a qualified guide, I'll not tempt fate or try these traverses alone. I'll content myself with the ascent of the mountain today. The traverses must wait for another time.

Violet shuttles me the five miles to Gros Morne trailhead, and I'm on my way and into the climb by nine-thirty. Many people are out hiking today, and I enjoy their company. I meet Ted from Cleveland, who just recently climbed Springer Mountain, and Gavin from Toronto, a birder who points out the three most abundant and oft-seen birds. As we hike along together we discover the American pipit, the horned lark, and the rock ptarmigan.

Out of the trees and into the rocks, the climb becomes immediately precipitous and amazingly difficult. There are two routes to the mountain: one leading up, and one, around the other side, leading down. I see the reason now. One would certainly not want to go down the up route. Why? Because you would likely get where you wanted to go (down) much sooner than you wanted to get there! This mountain is no Katahdin, but the climb is every bit as difficult and challenging, perhaps even more so.

As I near the summit, the trail levels. The wind picks up and it turns very cold, but the sky remains clear, the day remarkably bright, totally haze-free. On top of the rock pile now, I get my first glimpse of the caribou that roam here, five animals, their images dancing on the horizon, a mirage on the vast rocky tundra. The views are breathtaking. I can see back across the Tablelands, the escarpment of their eerie brown brow most striking and prominent, commanding the heights of the distant heavens. To the east is Bonne Bay, where Woody Point can be clearly seen. To the northeast lies the sea and Rocky Harbor. And behind me? Behind me extends the great expanse of tundra, tarns and rifts and rolling mounds of boulders and rock, mountains and cliffs cloaked in tuckamore and bright green forests of spruce and fir. These are the Long Range Mountains, the Appalachians of Newfoundland, as far as the eye can see. Ahh yes, folks, the Appalachians do continue on beyond Katahdin. And here, standing before me are some of the most grand and glorious of them all!

The Appalachian Mountains
Don't end in northern Maine,
For as you tack a northeast course,
They reemerge again.
(N. Nomad)

Sunday—August 26, 2001
Trail Day—318/18
Trail Mile—5089/292
Location—Western Brook Pond to Major's Hospitality Home Hostel,
Rocky Harbor, Newfoundland.

Off the crest, around the mountain and on my way down yesterday, there were many more caribou along the way, twenty-eight in all. One old stag had a rack so huge he could hardly lift his head. I was able to approach him as he lay basking. When he stood, he presented a perfect profile against the sky.

Once back to the parking lot, I returned to Major's Hostel via a five-mile roadwalk along NF-340. Violet prepared a fine meal for me as we discussed how to work out another night's stay. Plans are for me to hike the eighteen miles north to Western Brook Pond, to await her arrival there to fetch me back to Rocky Harbor. Monday morning she'll drive me back to Western Brook Pond, where I'll take the first boat tour into the fjord. It's a great plan.

By nine this morning, after a stoking breakfast prepared by Violet, I'm out and on my way. In downtown Rocky Harbor and short of funds, I make my way to the ATM. Here I meet Peter Mylechreest from New Zealand, a direct descendent of the first Vikings converted to Christianity. He's very proud of "Old Blue," his '77 Dodge van named after the Chatham Island Black Robin, a species recently saved from extinction through a process called cross-fostering. From the immediate splatter of painted scenes on Old Blue, you might gather that Peter is a very interesting man. Indeed, this is true. We have a great chat. Cheerio, Peter!

I'm out to a clear but very windy day. Fortunately, the wind is to my back, and I teeter along, propelled by its gusts. The road follows the sea, and there are many vantages. One especially picturesque view is across the incoming breakers at Lobster Cove Head Lighthouse.

By early afternoon, I reach Sally Cove, beside which is the great Chip Shack. Here I stop for a medium order of fries to complement the fine sandwich prepared for me by Violet. While we're on the subject of fries, a word of caution. When anywhere in Canada, never, ever order a large serving of fries. "Medium" will be the very best even the most ravished hiker can handle, believe me!

By four, I've reached the parking lot at Western Brook Pond, just in time. Violet arrives to fetch me back to her lovely home in Rocky Harbor. In the evening, at the local fish market, Violet suggests we get the cod tongues for her to prepare for our evening meal. What a great suggestion! Never had cod tongues? Oh, are they ever good. You must try them sometime.

Tomorrow I'll be out and on my way again, leaving Rocky Harbor behind. Violet and Jack, it's great to spend another evening with you. You have both become dear friends. Thanks for all you've done for me. Thanks for your kindness!

> *From the red-rimmed star to the speck of sand,*
> *From the vast to the greatly small;*
> *For I know that the whole for good is planned,*
> *And I want to see it all.*
> (Robert W. Service)

Monday—August 27, 2001
Trail Day—319/19
Trail Mile—5101/304
Location—Bayview B&B/Shallow Bay Motel and Cabins, Cow Head, Newfoundland. Darel House, proprietor.

After a fine breakfast and much-too-much coffee, Violet shuttles me the eighteen miles back to the Western Brook Pond parking lot. Plans were to do the boat tour up Western Brook Pond fjord this morning, then hike on to Cow Head for the day, but plans have changed. It's blowing near a gale and raining steady, the boat tour cancelled. The magnificent Western Brook Pond fjord will have to wait for another time. With considerable reluctance and much sadness I bid farewell to yet another very good friend, then to don my poncho and turn into it, up the road to Cow Head. Goodbye, Violet Major, goodbye...

The hike today is a roadwalk north on NF-430, which leads beside the sea. There is scarcely little cover along, the wind and rain pushing relentlessly, thankfully from my port stern. The wind-driven onslaught continues the morning and into early afternoon as I gain the road to Cow Head. Thank goodness, I'm soon at Shallow Bay Motel, where I'm finally able to seek shelter and relief from the frightful deluge. Here I'm greeted quizzically by Darel House, proprietor. After the usual Q&A period, he directs the tired, wet, and bedraggled old *Nomad* to his beautifully restored B&B right next to the motel, very reasonable, right on the sea.

A shower, dry clothes and a warm meal—oh yes, that does it! There are no bad days on the trail. Aww, good grief, who am I trying to convince here?

> *There'll be days like this, son.*
> (Anne Eberhart)

Tuesday—August 28, 2001
Trail Day—320/20
Trail Mile—5101/304
Location—Bayview B&B, Cow Head, Newfoundland

Should the day clear, Darel has offered to drive me back to Western Brook Pond, then fetch me again after the boat tour and return me to his lovely place here on the sea. So I've decided to burn a day and sit this storm out. Great idea! The day starts coming around by late morning, and by noon I decide to avail myself of Darel's hospitality.

So many folks hereabouts have spoken of the raw beauty that is Western Brook Pond fjord. I'm convinced I must see this place. So here's my chance, and here we go! Darel delivers me to the parking lot and I'm off on the three-kilometer hike over a gentle gravel path to the boat dock at Western Brook Pond. Here I must wait to see if I might board, as I've made no reservations. Folks file by, and I sit. More folks file by, loading both boats. I estimate more than 100 people. Certainly there'll be no room for me. But just as the boats appear fully loaded, and more people arrive to board, I'm told that I can go!

The day is clearing still, the pond nearly flat, with only the slightest breeze. The captain welcomes us aboard as the taped presentation begins, a quite formal and impressive delivery by an old

sea-salted Newfoundlander. His voice is reminiscent of a powerfully solemn and striking voice, a style I remember from childhood, that of Orson Wells. The old salt begins, "Fellow Newfoundlanders and all here, greetings! If you have joined us for geological interests, you are in for a treat. Western Brook Pond offers many spectacular scenes of unique landforms, telling a story that had its beginning a billion years ago. The majesty of this geological epic awaits you. If you have joined us purely for a robust outing, to breathe our pure air, you too, will not be disappointed, for I'll wager me fish-brewis supper that you'll sleep soundly tonight."

The tour, which lasts over two and a half hours, is indeed a journey through time. The fjord is truly spectacular. You've heard the old adage, "A picture is worth a thousand words." Ahh, but there are no thousand words, or indeed a thousand thousand words to describe this timeless place. During the tour, I go through more than a roll of film, but these snaps will be the least snippet, a view into this remarkable place.

Late evening, Darel comes to retrieve me, to whisk me back to Shallow Bay at Cow Head, the ending of a perfect day, or so I believe. But as night descends I am treated to a grand supper, fresh cod, brought to my table in the table-packed Shallow Bay dining room by, oh yes, Darel, now my chauffeur-turned waiter. And this connoisseur's delight? Compliments of another new friend, Chip Bird, superintendent of Gros Morne National Park.

As I rise to depart, Darel asks, "Would you like to attend the theatre with me this evening?" I had looked at the plays highlighted in the lobby nearby and had considered attending this evening's performance, "Ed & Ed, Trapped," a spoof about Newfoundland fishermen and their times, playing at the Warehouse Theatre right next door. I immediately accept!

The play is a remarkable accounting of the continued hard times here, of the fishermen out of work, their loss of self-esteem, and the solemn awareness of a hopeless future that presents. It is, however, played out with much joy and comedic hilarity. I believe it was Steve Allen, one of the great comedians of my time that once said, to the effect, "For comedy to be truly funny, it must tell a story woven with an underlying thread of truth." Jeff Pitcher, you are a remarkable playwright/director! I went away from your splendid presentation with a sad yet joyful feeling. I thought I had come to know the people of your beautiful island, Newfoundland, but I did not know them. Now I know them!

Back in my room, with a feeling of melancholy, the thought of this remarkable day ending, I deign to recall broken dreams and other days of long ago. As I say my prayers and drift off to sleep, my spirit is lifted by the knowledge that the love of folks along the way will carry me. I constantly try looking toward tomorrow, not back—just like you told me to, Mother...

Out of the hinterwhere into the yon—
The land that the Lord's love rests upon,
Where one may rely on the friends he meets,
And the smiles that greet him along the streets,
Where the mother that left you years ago
Will lift the hands that were folded so,
And put them about you, with all the love
And tenderness you are dreaming of.
(James Whitcomb Riley)

Wednesday—August 29, 2001
Trail Day—321/21
Trail Mile—5127/330
Location—NF-340 at Daniel's Harbor, Newfoundland, to Mountain View Motel. Gloria Payne, manager.

Might I ruminate a few peculiarities (neat things) I've noticed about Newfoundland and its people since trekking across this fascinating island province?

Okay, well, one thing I've noticed—bathroom light switches up here are invariably located somewhere on a wall outside the bathroom. So should you enter a dark bathroom and close the door, you will certainly remain in a dark bathroom! In establishments frequented by us folks from the good old USofA, it is amusing to note the patina caused by our frequent fumbling for the switch, the finger marks on the bathroom wall just inside the door where the switch should be located. This is usually seen in restaurants and other public places. At such a lodging recently, I finally found the bathroom switch located in the bank of switches by the front door!

Another interesting observation concerns litter and graffiti. Indeed, the people of Newfoundland take great pride in their homeland, in their modest dwellings and in their personal possessions—a deep, underlying respect if you will. Therefore, litter and graffiti are virtually nonexistent. There are few "adopt-a-highway" signs here, which I've always thought made for annoying visual litter. There is scant trash to be found along their roadways, only a fraction of what's seen in the States. What little there is, like bottles, cans and other garbage that continues being hurled, I've sadly found generally comes from, and is in direct proportion to the number of vehicles bearing tags from the United States.

In the States, for the budget-minded individual, the most affordable lodging while traveling is usually the wayside motel, not the B&B. In Newfoundland, the opposite is true. Here a sojourn at one of the numerous local homes is assurance of comfortable lodging, a fine meal, and good company, all provided by the proud owner at very reasonable cost.

I'm out this morning to another delightful hiking day in Newfoundland, cool and with just the least breeze. Folks around have told me about the old Mailroute Trail that leads from Cow Head along the shore north toward Parson's Pond. So that's the route I seek. The way is pleasant, taking me beside Shallow Bay, then back to NF-340.

In Parson's Pond, at the post office, I retrieve my bounce box and lift the rest of my meds to place them in my pack along with three more rolls of slide film. I clip my fingernails, drop the nail clippers back in the box, then seal and send them (along with all my winter gear) to Anchor Point, a week or two on up the Great Northern Peninsula.

Heading ever north again, as I continue passing by Portland Creek Pond for the better part of the afternoon, I chuckle while thinking about yet another fascinating Newfie peculiarity—the way they identify landmarks. It is, however, understandable. For the land that is Newfoundland is so overwhelmingly vast as to dwarf what man's presence here might ever mean. Perhaps, as a result, those who live, work, and love this place pay their respect in an interesting and humbling way. Mountains, for example, which stand so majestically, with such power and might, are simply referred to as "hills." Land-locked waters, so grand and expansive, miles across and tens of miles long, that we'd refer to as nothing less than "lakes," are simply called "ponds." An old Newfie recently opined to me (to spoof it all the more) that waters deserving the title "lake" must occupy no less than that space possibly filled through a hole in one's boot!

By mid-afternoon, I've reached the Arches: interesting rock formations, the tidy work of eons of tides, now left to stand on eroded bowlegs by the restless sea. Here I relax, have lunch, and watch as families come and go. Even in the mist-driven wind, the children are set to scampering the jumble of rocks, having a great time.

By late evening I have accomplished my hike into Daniel's Harbor—in the rain, yet again. I declare, this weather seems no less than the devil's work.

> *It is the devil's masterstroke to get us to accuse him.*
> (George Meredith)

Thursday—August 30, 2001
Trail Day—322/22
Trail Mile—5127/330
Location—Corner Brook Hotel, Corner Brook, Newfoundland

While in Rocky Harbor, meeting with Superintendent Chip Bird and Land Use Specialist Jeff Anderson at Gros Morne National Park, it was recommended I contact Mike Roy, Ph.D. Dr. Roy is both the Executive Director of the Centre for Forest & Environmental Studies, and the Chair of the School of Natural Resources, College of the North Atlantic, Corner Brook, Newfoundland. Dr. Roy, I was told, and to my great pleasure did I find, is also the Founding Chair of the Appalachian Trail Foundation of Newfoundland, an organization charged with the responsibility of completing "... the 1,000-kilometer length of the entire proposed Newfoundland section of the Appalachian Trail," this quoted from a feature article in the October 3, 2000 issue of *The Western Star*.

From yet another *Western Star* feature, a front page article, comes the quote: "Roy has a vision of extending the Appalachian Trail by 1,000 kilometers through the corridor of the Long Range Mountains of Newfoundland. The trail would begin at Port aux Basques and pass through the Lewis Hills, the highest point in insular Newfoundland, Gros Morne National Park, and end at Belle Isle at the tip of the Great Northern Peninsula. When extended to Belle Isle, the terminus of the Appalachian Mountain chain in North America, the trail will have the distinction of being the longest continuous footpath in the world. In comparison, the Great Wall of China is about 3,500 kilometers in length, while this completed trail would be about 5,400 kilometers long. The proposed trail in Newfoundland would extend the trail system to the northern terminus of what I sincerely believe is the most exciting and diverse portion of this North American mountain range."

Oh, is this yet another modern-day Benton MacKaye? Perhaps, just perhaps, I would want to meet a man who dreams such a dream: the dream of a trail so grand and glorious, through all of these grand and glorious Appalachian Mountains!

So, as you might suspect, this afternoon at two, I'll interrupt this northbound hike to board a Viking Bus heading south, bound for Corner Brook, there to meet Dr. Mike Roy.

On the bus, bouncing over the frost-heaved highway, I'm thinking about the howling and wailing, the chaotic cries of alarm this will raise yet again back in the United States. I can hear it now, "Not *another* Appalachian Trail; this can't possibly be! Who are these people, anyway; who do they think they are, calling a trail in Newfoundland, an extension of *the* Appalachian Trail? That would require an act of Congress. Do they have an act of Congress?" Most assuredly will there come once more the wringing of hands, the gnashing of teeth, the finger pointing, and the name-calling. Remember when the International Appalachian Trail project was inaugurated, how those of self-appointed authority and so-called influence within the Appalachian Trail community sprang forth with their pathetic cries of "foul!" To follow were the maligning accusations and degrading insults directed at honorable men, men of great repute, one a direct descendent of Samuel de Champlain, Québec's most renowned and respected founder and countryman.

Late evening, arriving at Corner Brook, no sooner do I step from the bus am I greeted by Mike Roy—oh yes, with that glad and happy, full-beaming Canadian smile!

Neither evil tongues, rash judgments, nor the sneers of selfish men,
nor greetings where no kindness is...shall ever prevail against us.
(William Wordsworth)

Friday—August 31, 2001
Trail Day—323/23
Trail Mile—5127/330
Location—Mike Roy's mountain camp, Secret Valley, Newfoundland

Footpaths leading directly to the soul; we'll come to know them as Trail of the Ancients and the Eastern Continental Trail. Here exist (for a fair distance) trails not yet stifled or spoiled by the markings of man. Oh why-oh-why must we be constantly herded up, to blindly tramp *"...among the polished stone."* where (to stifle our wanderlust) are found gaudy, splattered paint blazes on tree after tree, where (to lead us ever so gently by the elbow) are found the meticulous line-drawn maps, where (not to leave a single stone unturned) we then pour over the painstakingly detailed topo maps for every little rise and dip, and finally: where (sadly) are found the rutted and beaten-down tracks, "pathways" to be blindly followed and tramped out by the faint of heart, by those legions who've set out in a so-called quest for *freedom*, legions that remain pitifully bound down by the burdens of life, and by the ridiculous burdens on their backs! Are we no more than lemming, being led along yet another well-beaten way? No we're not! Rather, there exists now, right this moment, other ways to pass. Indeed, there are ways for those of us who yearn for true *freedom*, who seek to escape the many narrow ruts that have been shaped by a few narrow minds. There *are* ways to journey forth o'er spirit-filled paths, toward peace, beauty, and truth. Today, I continue my journey along just such a spirit-filled path, as I venture ever forth o'er this remarkable TA/ECT.

I have been invited by Mike Roy to join him in discovering the secret of the ages, a secret known only to "The Old Man in the Mountain." Today we'll hike Mike's fifteen-kilometer preview, his pilot project for the Newfoundland Appalachian Trail—right over the crown of that old mountain gent whose cold granite stare has panned the Humber River, and has scanned across the Bay of Islands since time began.

A short quote from a recent email from Mike, and you'll understand my excitement about meeting this visionary and being invited to hike with him today. I'll lead you in. These trails, the Trail of the Ancients and the Eastern Continental Trail are evolving "... now and will continue to evolve into a true work of art: connecting two countries, sixteen states, three provinces [now five], hundreds of communities, millions of individuals, and a mountain range of grand natural and cultural history."

The forecast calls for rain today, but as Mike fetches me at seven-thirty, we're out to a cool, clear morning as we cross the Humber River just north of Corner Brook. We're immediately set to warming up the old jitneys, a climb up and around the escarpment that forms the main craggy edifice squaring the bay. The crown of the old fellow once gained, we are awarded a remarkable view, a vantage across all the eons, a brief glimpse into what Father Time has wrought and what Mother Nature has endured. Should you be one who loves the Appalachian Mountains as do I, perhaps from places visited, such as this place now, you would depart (as will I) with a confused feeling of humility and awe, a feeling totally different from any other ever recalled, ever! For here before me are revealed the grand and glorious works of God. Indeed the Appalachians go on, they go on, and upon the island of Newfoundland do they rise again to present in all their majestic might and splendor. Here Mother Nature stands steadfast with Father Time in such pure and innocent display, a profound show of silent dignity. These mountains, this instant, challenge me to muster a feeble attempt to see, as Benton MacKaye would say, "...to truly see that which we look upon," and to comprehend. Before me now rests the harvest Mother Nature has yielded, Her inner being—heaved, contorted and shoved about over a billion years—ground to so much fine dust by Father Time, His glaciers pressing and crushing Her shoulders. Yet has She prevailed; yet does Her mystery shine forth below and beyond, this very moment.

What a memorable day of hiking and fellowship. What joy to be with one of like mind, of kindred spirit. The day is too-soon spent as we wend our way past sun-blushed, high-held ponds, then families of white and yellow birch, spruce, fir, and juniper. O'er the backbone of these Newfoundland Appalachians we trek, embraced by their gentle demeanor and quiet dignity, to descend in the long shadows of the sun, down from the back of "The Old Man in the Mountain" to the Humber River, and home.

Thanks, Mike, thanks for sharing this special place, this precious time with me on this, your "Cradle Trail." From here will soon emerge the full-grown dream, a pathway through the cradles of Time and Nature's space, a path leading forth into these mysterious wonders, the Long Range Appalachian Mountains of Newfoundland.

He who understands Nature walks close with God.
(Edgar Cayce)

Saturday—September 1, 2001
Trail Day—324/24
Trail Mile—5127/330
Location—Home of Mike Roy, Corner Brook, Newfoundland

Today will be a day of learning about the Newfoundland Appalachian Trail initiative and about the many natural wonders that exist here in this special place, the northern reaches of the Appalachian Mountains. To my great joy and good fortune, I'll again spend the day with Mike Roy. We'll trek some less-used local trails as we share the common dream and enjoy each other's company.

Mike certainly knows these lands that are Newfoundland, from the canopy shading our heads above to all at our feet below, even the tiniest of plants that eke out an existence in what seems such a nervous way, wrestling as they do with the harsh and unforgiving elements of their near-Arctic environment.

Hiking along, we study the many trees and how to identify them. Mike has made a career of such skill, having gained his doctorate in Integrated Land Use/Forest Policy. All around us stand the ubiquitous fir and spruce, but how to tell the difference? "Pluck a needle from that tree," says Mike. "Roll it between your fingers. Oh, it won't roll? Well that needle's from a fir tree then. Now run your hand along one of the boughs, stroke it both ways. Feel its softness!" Now with exuberance, as if discovering these fascinating sensations for the first time himself, he exclaims, "'F' is for fir. Remember, the needle was (f)lat, it wouldn't roll, the bough was soft, thus we'd say the tree was (f)riendly! Now go to that one over there. Pluck a needle again and try to roll it, and stroke one of the boughs just like before. Does the needle roll? How do the branches feel?" Following his instruction, I reply, "Hey Mike, this needle rolls, this tree feels prickly and sharp." Smiling now, he replies, "Well, there you have it. 'S' is for spruce. The needles are (s)pindly or (s)quare-like, so they roll. And the feel of the bough as you stroke it is not friendly, but (s)harp." I'm into this now. "Wow, this is neat, Mike. I like this kind of instruction, I can remember these lessons. I'll always be able to tell the difference now between fir and spruce!"

In addition to these trees, I make my reacquaintance with white and yellow birch, pin cherry, choke cherry, mountain ash, red maple, larch (tamarack), white pine, and tuckamore.

One interesting flowering plant, one we know simply as bottlebrush, here it's called Canadian Burnett, and in France this same plant is known as *herbe à piser* (the herb that you piss on!). Other plants and shrubs along the way today are pearly everlasting, wild asparagus, cow parsnip, Joe Pye weed, goldenrod, crackerberry, white fringed orchid, pitcher plant, sundews, aster, cranberry, wild raisin, blueberry, dwarfbirch, mountain alder, bilberry, bearberry, rhodora, mountain heather, Labrador tea, laurel, and countless fens and bogs filled with reeds, mosses, sedges, and grass.

One section of trail today could well be known as the "Fern Trail," for along it we see eight different species of fern. They include: interrupted fern, wood fern, Swiss fern, oak fern, Long Beach fern, cinnamon fern, bracken fern, and the ostrich or fiddlehead fern. Oh my, I hope I don't get tested on all of this!

Returning to camp, we have a swim in the sun-warmed waters of the brook, then Mike prepares a grand supper before we head for his home in Corner Brook. Another great hike, another memorable day. Thanks, Mike! This has been a very enjoyable day, a day of learning.

Be not afraid of growing slowly, be afraid only of standing still.
(Chinese Proverb)

Sunday—September 2, 2001
Trail Day—325/25
Trail Mile—5127/330
Location—Major's Hospitality Home Hostel, Rocky Harbor,
Newfoundland

It's raining as Mike drives me back to Rocky Harbor. A somber day, but just as well, I suppose. Soon I'll be bidding another great new friend farewell, a friend with whom I have so much in common. When the trail-building gets going here, I've just got to return to Newfoundland again, to see my friend Mike Roy again, and to support him in his vision.

I've decided to stop in Rocky Harbor one more time instead of returning to Daniel's Harbor right away. Ever since I hiked out of here last Sunday I've been kicking myself for not making a more concerted effort toward finding a guide to lead me across the two traverses here at Gros Morne. So this time around I'm going to stick at Major's Hospitality Home Hostel until I've found a guide, and until these two traverses are done.

Mike soon has me back, where Violet greets me with surprise. In a few minutes, I'm settled in. So long, Mike, it's been great. The last two days of hiking have been a memorable time! The Newfoundland Appalachian Trail is going to be a very special pearl in the string of pearls that combine to make up these remarkable trails, the TA/ECT.

In the evening I call Frank Piercey again. Frank is a local guide. I reach him, but no luck. Frank's also a fisherman and he's going back to the sea. It's late now and I'm tired. I'll hit this effort another lick tomorrow.

> *Iron sharpeneth iron; so a man sharpeneth*
> *the countenance of his friend.*
> (Proverbs: 27-17)

Monday—September 3, 2001
Trail Day—326/26
Trail Mile—5127/330
Location—Major's Hospitality Home Hostel, Rocky Harbor,
Newfoundland

I'm back at it again this morning, undaunted. I'm going to cross the Gros Morne tundra, one way or the other, I will do the traverses!

First call (once more) is to Gros Morne Adventure Guides in Norris Point, just down the road. Sue Rendell, co-owner, answers and we have a long and enjoyable chat. Labor Day pretty much ends the season up here and things get a little unsettled, what with summer jobs winding down, so I strike out here again. Sue recommends, however, that I stop by Base Camp here in Rocky Harbor and talk to Kevin Vincent and Andrea Spracklin, the young folks that run Base Camp. Their little shop is mainly a kayak rental service with a smattering of outdoor and hiking gear. I'd stopped by there last week to find the place closed. It's time now to follow every lead, so out the door I go for the ten-minute walk downtown.

I'm in luck, the shop is open, and as I enter I'm greeted with that grand Canadian welcome. Here I meet Kevin Vincent, a certified guide. As I tell my story and explain my desire to employ his services, the kid literally lifts straight up with excitement. His face lights up, the whole place seems to light up! Well now, looks like I've got myself a guide—for both the North Rim and the Long Range traverses! Plans are to get permits tomorrow and head out early Wednesday morning. Whoohee! (That's the Canadian hoot.)

Persistence is to the character of man as carbon is to steel.
(Napoleon Hill)

Tuesday—September 4, 2001
Trail Day—327/27
Trail Mile—5127/330
Location—Major's Hospitality Home Hostel, Rocky Harbor,
Newfoundland

Lots to do today. A stop by the library for a while, then to the post office. Have to get food too, for at least four days. Then it's by Base Camp again for a meeting with Kevin to make final preparations for tomorrow. Plans are for Andrea to drop us off at the parking lot below Western Brook Pond around six-thirty tomorrow morning, where we'll begin our hike by climbing the North Rim of the fjord, from there to hike the rim onto the tundra and back south across the Long Range traverse to Gros Morne, a distance of some sixty-two kilometers (thirty-seven miles) by trail. Park rangers recommend taking four to five days for the Long Range traverse alone, eight to ten for both. We hope to do them in three, perhaps four days at the most.

I've pretty much become family here at Major's Hostel, having free run of the place. Violet's been cooking for me, and I've helped Jack some with the dishes and sweeping around. Today Violet works all afternoon, cooking up a tank-stokin' supper for me in preparation for tomorrow's hike: fried wild rabbit, potatoes and salt pork in onion gravy, corned beef and fresh greens, bread pudding, peas pudding, turnips, beets, and carrots—all from the garden. And oh yes, ice cream for dessert! My pack's loaded, my tank's loaded.

As I drift to sleep I'm thinking about what I've read in the Gros Morne literature concerning the North Rim traverse. "Particular care should be taken when walking near the edge of the Western Brook Pond gorge. In many places you can walk right up to the lip of a 610-meter [1900-foot] vertical drop. Winds in this area can be unpredictably strong and visibility is very poor during fog or heavy precipitation. The route [unmarked] travels over varied terrain and past numerous lakes and brooks. Travel can be confusing as a result and should not be attempted on days with poor visibility. Anything less than two kilometers creates unsafe travel conditions."

Folks, you just never tire of this whole wanderlust trekking thing...not never!

> *Then here's a hail to each flaring dawn!*
> *And here's a cheer to the night that's gone!*
> *And may I go a-roaming on*
> *Until the day I die.*
> (Robert W. Service)

Wednesday—September 5, 2001
Trail Day—328/28
Trail Mile—5139/342
Location—A fen in the tuckamore near Western Brook Pond fjord on the North Rim Traverse, Gros Morne National Park, Newfoundland

The forecast calls for a 90% chance of rain, but the day dawns mostly blue. The weather hereabouts, however, can change in a blink. In the States, we're used to seeing storms come in from the same direction most of the time. Here on the island of Newfoundland, storms slam in from every-which-a-way. Looking to the east this morning, on the horizon I see this ominous black wall, standing with dark mushroom domes and heads. Not a good sign.

Andrea drops us off at Western Brook Pond parking lot, and at six forty-five we're headed toward Snug Harbor, by the northwest shore on Western Brook Pond. Arriving, we're at the end of the groomed trail, to begin the unmarked traverse up and onto the North Rim of Western Brook Pond fjord, a climb from near sea level to over two thousand feet in less than two miles. By ten we're finishing the pull up through the tuckamore to reach the tundra above Western Brook Pond fjord. The sun climbs most of the way with us, only to bail out near the top as the mush sets in and the cold winds come. By noon the tuck and rain have joined forces to really work us over.

Of all the hiking I've done along these grand old Appalachian Mountains have I yet to see such stunning wildness. We're following the compass now (kicking the dial over 25 degrees for declination), eyes glued to the 1:50,000 topos bound in a Ziploc. Trails and tracks go everywhere, none made by man—up and down, through the rocks and the tuck, across the bogs, fens, and brooks. Once on the tundra, the boulder fields, tarns, eskers, scree moraines, cliffs and escarpments all look the same. Where we're going looks just like where we've been, and there we go! Am I ever glad to have a trained eye along that can read and understand this puzzling landscape!

Kevin refers to the compass only occasionally, usually from vantages offering a kilometer or two viewing distance, relying mostly on lesser topo features such as ponds and minor contour changes. His ability is uncanny, especially in working the maze of moose and caribou trails that meander helter-skelter with no rhyme or reason through the ever-present tuckamore. Stopping at intervals, he'll point to a spot on the topo, saying, "we're here now, a little east (or west, or north, or south) of the route the rangers have plotted, but this is the better way." Having not a clue where we are or where we're going, I respond with something like, "Okay, Kevin, great. Lead on!" And on we go through the rain and the rocks and the tuck—oh yes, and I had seriously considered trying these traverses by myself!

Our feet have been totally soaked since crossing a gravel bar down on the shores of Western Brook Pond. Now with the relentless rain and the tuck tugging at us, the soaking slowly works its way up through us and our packs. By late evening, after nearly twelve hours in the scramble of rocks and barbs of tuck, having covered no more than fourteen or fifteen miles—and hoping for a momentary break in the rain—we begin looking for a place in the lee to pitch for the evening.

Moving away, back from the driving wind and rain, over a little pop in the jumble of boulders I see him (my first sighting in over five thousand miles) a magnificent, mammoth black bear! Catching our scent, bounding away he goes, a perfect meld of graceful motion and muscular might, the raven-black glisten of his wintry coat rippling in waves like wind-bent meadow grass. In seconds he's gone. Kevin and I stand in silence and awe. After struggling and fighting all day to make our way, we've just witnessed a four-hundred pound ballerina dance straight across this stuff. Amazing!

The rain doesn't give, but we finally do. On a grassy slope tucked back in the tuckamore, we tuck in and call it a day.

> *And then he stepped on virgin land*
> *Not walked upon by any man*
> *And witnessed what no man had seen*
> *Silent, standing...still...serene.*
> (Bobby Bridger)

Thursday—September 6, 2001
Trail Day—329/29
Trail Mile—5151/354
Location—Major's Hospitality Home Hostel, Rocky Harbor, Newfoundland

It's nearly impossible to pitch in the rain without getting soaked. Kevin and I both dropped our packs, ripped them open and quickly dug for our tents, then worked feverishly to get them set. I beat him in; guess I've had more practice. Problem was, though, in such haste, I hadn't checked the ground where I pitched. I had problems all night with a big lump (say "rock") slap in the middle of the floor. And when I tried curling around it, searching for a comfortable sleeping position, something kept poking me in the butt. What a night. The rain remained vigilant, steady and hard. The drumming of it finally "rocked" me away to the Land of Nod.

We're faced with the same problem this morning, in reverse: breaking camp in the rain. We both hurry, but we both lose. Everything we have is soaked now, adding much additional pack weight. As I strike my tent, I see what had been poking me in the butt all night—the pointed tines from a huge moose rack shed last year, concealed in the grass. Somehow, in my haste to get out of the rain I missed seeing it.

First thing this morning we pass where we last saw the bear. Interesting, when I realize it's taken us fifteen minutes to cover the same ground the bear flew across in only seconds!

In a short while we come to the upper reaches of Western Brook Pond fjord. From here, the view down and directly into Western Brook Pond is something only pictures can try to tell. The sun makes a brief show, and Kevin takes a couple shots of me standing at the brink. The chill from inactivity doesn't take long to set in though, so we're quickly on our way again, in the cold wind and relentless rain.

To gain the far ridge across the gulch requires a cautious, slow, hand-over up for a short distance across a sheer rock face, the only way to the upper reaches of this glacier-shaved crown. The metal peg and ladder climbs up Katahdin and elsewhere along the AT pale in comparison to the challenge here. This is certainly not technical climbing, but groping for hand-holds and toe-holds, a hundred or so near-vertical feet above the sliding-board-like gulch floor—well, this is as close as I'll ever want to come to rock climbing!

As we leave Western Brook Pond fjord, we have completed the North Rim Traverse and are now beginning what is known as the Long Range Traverse. Few who come to hike here attempt both, at least not back-to-back. Rather, the choice is to come up the fjord by boat to the dock at the upper reaches of Western Brook Pond, and from there to ascend through the gulch to the point we've just passed, then from there to set out on one of the two traverses, either the North Rim or the Long Range. Three to four days are recommended for the North Rim hike, and officials at Gros Morne suggest taking four to five days to complete the Long Range Traverse.

Back in the tundra and moving along quite well, we take a wrong tack, one of few, but we're soon around and back on course again. As the rain continues, the caribou and moose ruts turn to bogs, the bogs to brooks, and the brooks to rivers. And the rivers? Well, the brooks-turned-rivers we must cross are negotiated with much hesitancy, caution, and deliberate concentration.

The Long Range traverse has had much more human traffic. There is much less tuck, and the ups, downs, and arounds through the gulches and moraines, ponds, and bogs are much less troublesome. Consequently, we're making much better time today. Visibility remains good despite the continuous rain, and the mushed-up clouds and fog tend to keep their distance, generally seeking higher ground.

The ruggedness, the cold harshness of this Arctic-like tundra, is incomparable, like nowhere else along the entire range of the Appalachians. Only here in Newfoundland do these mountains present at times in such a wild and uncomfortably forbidding way. Only in two other places have I ever felt so unwelcome, so separate and apart. Mountains are places I've come to love, places where warmth and love have always been returned. But not in these places—not on the camo-brown, barren flanks of Mont-Albert in the Chic Chocs of Parc de la Gaspésie, nor anywhere in all the western Rockies, and certainly not here on this cold, sodden tundra today.

As we continue tramping the rocks and splashing the bogs, and as the rain continues soaking us down, I'm thinking, "Do I really want to spend another rain-hammered night up here, everything cold and soaked, including me?" As we continue trudging, I begin a little mental calculating: "Let's see, it's one o'clock. In the past five hours we've managed around ten miles, the last of the sixteen-mile North Rim traverse, and some eight or nine of the twenty-one that make up the Long Range traverse. We've got seven hours of daylight left, with some thirteen or so miles remaining to reach the parking lot at Gros Morne." Inquiring of Kevin, I find that except for a little bumpy ride around Ten Mile Pond, the going will continue pretty much as it's been. So far today we've been slogging along at a two-plus mile per hour clip. So, all things considered, looks like we should be able to trudge this traverse on through and reach Gros Morne before dark.

In just a while Kevin stops to take a bearing and check his topos. As I move away to take a whiz, I wonder how to bring the idea up, how to suggest to Kevin that we hoof it on in, while in the process not wanting to raise anxiety or otherwise cause interruption to the great hike we're having.

As a conscientious guide would do, over the last two days Kevin's routinely inquired as to my condition, how I felt and how I was getting along. "Okay, that's it," I assure myself. "I'll show my interest and concern by raising the same questions, and at the same time find out if he's up to it." So before we set off again I step up, turn to him and ask, "How you holding up kid, your knees, your back, your feet, you doing okay?" Smiling, he replies, "Sure, I feel great, can't let this weather get ya!" "Okay," I'm thinkin', "That's good, here goes." Looking him square in the eye now, I begin. "Kevin, we can hike on for another three or four hours in this mush, pitch in the rain, change out of our wet clothes into our other wet clothes, climb into our wet tents with all our wet gear, have a cold trail food supper, then try staying warm in our wet sleeping bags. Orrrr, we can bang this on out today, get a hot shower, change into some warm dry clothes, pick up a pizza and a six of frosties, see our friends, then get a good night's sleep in a nice warm bed—Whaddayasay?" Startled, he stares back at me, totally blank. Recovering, with his face all screwed up, he exclaims, "We can't get in there today. That'll mean we do this whole thing in two days. It's too far; we'll never make it!" In the most reassuring voice I can muster, I explain, "It isn't too far, Kevin. We'll make it just fine before dark." With that I go over the time/rate/distance calculations, explaining the strategy. Satisfied now, he gives me a little smirky grin, turns, squares his shoulders, tugs his heavy, water-laden pack and he's off like a shot. Oh yes, hang on; here we go. Whoohee!

As we continue, the rain continues, but no matter, nothing is going to stop us. A sponge can hold only so much, and the bogs and our backs have soaked up their limit. The clouds persist, circling full around, but stay their distance. What a blessing seeing more moose and caribou in one day than most people ever see in a lifetime. And to cap it off comes the joy of gaining the last few pops to gawk with disbelief down into Ten Mile Pond fjord, for this view is as remarkable as the vantage from the rim of Western Brook Pond fjord.

Before descending from the traverse and on the last high ground, Kevin fires up his cell phone and calls Andrea to come fetch us (and to serve as delivery girl for food and refreshments). It was great to see plan two come together. Plan one was for a casual stroll across the tundra; plan two was to get off the tundra! Just as dusk settles to night, we emerge from the advancing shroud at Gros Morne parking lot, to be greeted by Andrea.

I've been on many a guided tour. This one was the first whirlwind, a certain test of will. Remaining happy and cheerful saved it for us. Kevin, it was a memorable time. Base Camp Outfitters in Rocky Harbor has a first rate guide!

It is easy enough to be pleasant,
When life flows by like a song.
But the man worthwhile is the one who can smile,
When everything goes dead wrong.
(Ella Wheeler Wilcox)

Friday—September 7 through Sunday—September 9, 2001
Location—Major's Hospitality Home Hostel, Rocky Harbor,
Newfoundland
Monday—September 10, 2001 through Friday—September 14, 2001
Trail Day—337/37
Trail Mile—5259/354
Location—From Rocky Harbor, Newfoundland, to grassy woods
road, NF-432

Bus service along the Great Northern Peninsula is a little sketchy to say the least. If you're not in the right place at the right time and going where the bus is going, you're liable to be sitting and waiting a while, quite a while. And so, there I sat at Major's Hospitality Home Hostel in Rocky Harbor, waiting for the bus to Daniel's Harbor.

Not a bad place to burn a few days though. Jack and Violet are my very good friends now, and I've become theirs. They'd opened up their entire place to me. Their home was my home. Violet is an accomplished seamstress and a great cook. While I waited, she made numerous repairs to my sagging pack, my clothing, and other gear. She also prepared numerous grand meals for me, including moose, rabbit, and many delectable confections. It was a joy to rest there a few more days.

But as the days wore on, Violet could tell that I was getting restless and fidgety, anxious to get going again. When Monday the 10th rolled around (no bus), after watching me pace the last long day, she off-handedly offered to drive me up to Daniel's Harbor. "Got family up there," she began, "haven't seen them in a long time." Continuing, nonchalantly: "Think I just might run up there today." She turned then, trying to make it appear that her decision had nothing to do with me. Quite casually then, she dropped the afterthought, "You wanna go along?" "Oh my, yes," I replied. We loaded up; I took the ride with Violet—and was back hammering the trail north by late morning.

Nearing dusk the following day, that fateful September 11th, I arrived at House's Cabins in River of Ponds, Newfoundland. After I signed the register, Susan, the cabin manager, turned the clipboard around, read my entry, then moved back abruptly, dropping her head. She turned as pale as a ghost. I'll never forget the expression on her face. Looking down and away, she tried concealing her distraught reaction. After the longest moment, finally forcing a look back, in the most urgent stutter, she managed, "You, you, you're from the United States?" Her voice was full with distress, completely broken. She was in tears. I thought, "What is going on here." Puzzled and confused, I responded, "Yes, I'm from the United States; I live in the South, in Georgia." Composing herself somewhat and managing to look straight at me with a hollow, blank stare, in a hushed monotone, nearly a whisper, she said, "You haven't heard, have you?" "I haven't heard what!" I exclaimed. I've never seen anyone act like this before, and I've been greeted in every conceivable way over the years, from the bum's rush, right on down. In a blurt it finally came, "The Towers, all the people in the Towers—the planes, the planes hit the Towers, all the people in the Towers, they're all dead!" I tried to calm her, "What towers, what planes, what are you talking about; tell me what has happened?"

A small black and white TV on the refrigerator in the little cabin where I sought rest played it out. From there I watched in shock and disbelief as the horror of the day unfolded. Telecasters reported the unbelievable, the unimaginable, the gruesome story that revealed the bitter reality of man's inhumanity to man. I sank into helpless, forlorn despair, a desperate feeling of loss and sadness.

As the days followed, and as I trekked on north, I stumbled more than hiked. I couldn't comprehend what had happened; I couldn't deal with it. It was such a nightmare. Even on the quiet, little-traveled roads of the Great Northern Peninsula of Newfoundland, my sticks clicking their mind-numbing, hypnotizing cadence, I couldn't lift my mind above it. Finally, in resignation, I accepted the fact that there would be little elation, little celebration at the closing of what should be a grand and glorious odyssey.

Yet was there a thankful and blessed soothing for both my anguish and woe, as the Lord would bless. What came to me, from time to time as I continued on, was the full-flowing love of the Canadian people. With their love came sincere and deeply shared human sadness. It poured forth to me constantly—the heartfelt grief and sorrow of the Canadian people.

Hiking along, as is life from day-to-day for the wandering vagabond, the physical activity and the rhythmic, narcotic-like spell that accompanies it tends to work its healing magic, and it becomes possible to clear away the mental static and clutter, the anguish and the sadness that can be so consuming. So, the defeat and loss I felt in my troubled heart and mind finally began to dim and fade. Once again I was able to experience the grand thoughts otherwise unattainable, thoughts that are free to those of us not otherwise bound and tethered. But as those thoughts came, and as I tried as best I could, I found it impossible to totally blot out the horror of these past days. So, for the entries to follow, and for the remainder of this journey, should these writings appear boringly mechanical, I beg your forgiveness.

As I journeyed north and met new folks along the way, I met the Maynards. Ahh, were the Maynards so very kind to me. new friends made at Torrent River Inn in Hawkes Bay. Thanks, folks, thanks for your caring, for your outpouring of love and kindness—to me and to my fellow countrymen!

Hiking north, I was told of a fisherman living in Eddies Cove West who might be able to guide me on a hike into Doctors Hills. So, at the road to Eddies I turned to inquire at the home of Bob McLean. There I met his wife Alma. Bob was out to sea for the day, but plans were made for him to come for me later at Castors River, where I'd be staying at Tucker's Cottages.

It was a very long day pounding the road, over thirty miles. I was tired, cold, and hungry. But a warm shower, a good meal at Viking 430 Restaurant right next, and I was set for the night.

I was filled with excitement and anticipation next morning as I readied my pack for the climb into Doctors Hills. I tried ignoring the mist, the homogenized mush, and the low-rolling clouds as I waited for Bob to arrive. He came, only to greet me with the bad news; the Doctors were totally socked in, we would not be able to climb. Dang, all the planning and preparation by Tom and Wallace Maynard and it's turned out a no-go. The day came around though, a great day for hiking, so I pointed her north and kept on truckin.' By late evening I'd logged another thirty, so I pulled off and pitched a short distance down and just next a grassy woods road, right in plain view from NF-432. Moose hunters were everywhere, not a good time to be stealthing in the woods! I was no sooner in than the rain began. A few tat-a-tats and I was gone.

Life lost, right bent,
Sorrow tossed, purpose sent,
Truth drives, love gives,
Joy thrives, glory lives.
(N. Nomad)

Saturday—September 15, 2001
Trail Day—338/38
Trail Mile—5279/483
Location—NF-432 at Tuckamore Lodge and Outfitters, Main Brook, Newfoundland. Barb Genge, proprietor.

The logging and chip trucks start rolling around six and I'm awake for good at seven. The steady cold rain persisted all night and shows no sign of backing off this morning, even as I lie patiently until near eight. It's another thirty miler to Main Brook and Tuckamore Lodge. If I'm going to reach there before dark I've got to roll out, take my soaking, strike camp, and get moving.

As I plod, I remain dumbstruck, the trauma of September 11th heavy on my mind as my pack with its sodden gear weighs heavy on my back. The old jitney isn't firing on all eight this morning, and as I stumble into the wind and over my trekking poles it takes forever to get cranking. I'm determined to make Tuckamore by nightfall though, and with this singular purpose I finally manage to straighten up and get going.

I'm in the middle reaches of the Great Northern Peninsula of Newfoundland now. There's nothing out here but wilderness, moose, more moose, and moose hunters. I manage to content myself with the bits of joy and happiness that seem to be resonating from the little full-rushing brooks as I pass them by, the rain still pounding. But they're probably just complaining. "Remember *Nomad*, there are no bad days on the trail, some just a little better than others." Okay, okay!

Tuckamore Lodge owner and outfitter Barb Genge, and Mary the lodge cook, both greet me with excitement and uplifting, cheerful Canadian smiles. They've been expecting me. "You weren't out in this last night, were you?" exclaims Barb. I reply, "Oh yes, last night, all this last week; sure glad to be here Barb, sure glad to be here!"

Mary settles me into a beautiful suite right next to the great room in the main lodge, then shows me their drying room for hanging my wet gear. She then hastens toward the kitchen to prepare the evening meal. I join Pete and Jack for supper, two moose hunters from Michigan. Enjoying the evening with Barb and the moose hunters brings the day around. It's good to shed some of the loneliness, and it's good to be out of the rain and the cold.

For weeks the clouds had raked the hills
And vexed the vales with raining,
And all the woods were sad with mist,
And all the brooks complaining.
(John Greenleaf Whittier)

Sunday—September 16, 2001
Trail Day—339/39
Trail Mile—5279/483
Location—Tuckamore Lodge and Outfitters, Main Brook,
Newfoundland

The rain continues today. What a blessing being out of it, to be with a wonderful new friend, Barb Genge, at Tuckamore Lodge and Outfitters. I first learned about Barb from Mike Roy. We had been talking over my itinerary and the route I'd be following to complete my trek across the Great Northern Peninsula. "How you getting to L'Anse aux Meadows?" I remember Mike asking. "I'll probably follow the coast up and around," I replied. "Oh no!" he said. "You'll miss Barb Genge and Tuckamore Lodge if you go that way. And you really need to meet Earl Pilgrim, too. Cut across to Main Brook— go that way."

And so I did, and what great advice! It's Sunday now, with no more than three days remaining to reach L'Anse aux Meadows. I'd asked Mike Roy to hike the last few kilometers with me and to travel along to Belle Isle, but he can't get away until next Friday. Barb has invited me to stay here at Tuckamore as long as I like, and she's already called Earl Pilgrim, who'll be coming up from Roddickton to visit with me tomorrow. It's quite rewarding to slow down and enjoy the last few days of an odyssey like this, to relax and reminisce the grand and memorable times. Ahh yes, Tuckamore is certainly the place to be right now!

So, let me tell you a little about this special place! Over the past fourteen years, Barb Genge has gained an international reputation as a leader in outfitting and eco/adventure tourism. Tuckamore Lodge has been recognized by *Outside Magazine* as one of the six best lodges for encountering and experiencing the outdoors in all of Canada! Indeed, from here, with the capable assistance of trained professionals (many who've attended courses created by Mike Roy), it is possible to hunt and fish and to hike and explore these remarkable wilds. I quote from one of the beautiful Tuckamore brochures: "The Tuckamore Experience—The island of Newfoundland is geographically the meeting place of two huge ocean currents, the cold Labrador Current and the warm waters of the Gulf Stream. This convergence has created an extremely rich and unique marine environment. Package trips include boating excursions to spot twenty-two species of whales and an annual parade of over 2000 towering icebergs. There are also bird-watching trips to view Atlantic puffins and common eiders at the nearby ecological reserve. For sea-kayaking enthusiast, there are miles of uncrowded bays and inlets waiting to be paddled. Camping trips to off-shore islands populated with hundreds of caribou are also available. Along the coast, there are trails through the tundra and forest, where hikers can spot moose, beaver and snowshoe hare. Newfoundland's lakes are a canoeing paradise, teeming with trout and Atlantic salmon where bald eagles nest, loons call and the northern lights play to an audience 240 nights a year." Oh my, can you see why I like it here!

Oops, gotta run, time for dinner. "Be right there, Barb!"

If your time is worth anything, travel by air.
If not, you might just as well walk.
(Will Rogers)

Monday—September 17, 2001
Trail Day—340/40
Trail Mile—5279/483
Location—Tuckamore Lodge and Outfitters, Main Brook,
Newfoundland

Four gentlemen from Indiana came in late last evening, all in the quest for black bear: Kevin, a schoolteacher; Rob, a veterinarian; John, a medical doctor; and Mike, a park's department supervisor.

They drove straight through, and including the ferry shuttle, had been on the go for forty-four hours straight. Also here are Fred and Una from Massachusetts. Fred is back again this year for another moose.

I'm sure not used to three squares a day. It's hard to believe that a group of folks might exist anywhere that could possibly out-eat us hiker-trash, but hunters returning from a day in the wilds can come in packing a pretty healthy appetite. I hung with them yesterday, breakfast, dinner and supper, but took a bye at breakfast this morning.

Late morning, while I'm relaxing in the lodge great room working a new ditty, in comes Earl Pilgrim. Mike had told me about this very interesting gentleman and that he probably knew more about the Long Range Mountains of Newfoundland than any other person. And quite well he should, having spent a good deal of his life and career in the backcountry. Earl's retired now after a distinguished career of service to the people of Canada, most recently in the Province of Newfoundland as wildlife protection officer. Earl has turned to writing now, and is the successful author of four Canadian best sellers. I have the pleasure today of being one of the first to see and receive a copy of his fifth published work, *The Captain and the Girl*, to be released this weekend.

Earl is indeed an interesting man, to say the least. From his latest book, and from a small section in the back entitled "About the Author," I quote: "Earl Baxter Pilgrim was born in St. Anthony, Newfoundland in 1939...He began his adult career in 1960 as an infantryman in the Canadian Army, serving with the Princess Patricia's Canadian Light Infantry. While there, he became involved in the sport of boxing, eventually becoming the Canadian Light Heavyweight Boxing Champion. Following a stint in the Forces, Pilgrim took a job as a forest ranger with the Newfoundland and Labrador Forestry Department. During this time, he came to recognize the plight of the big game population on Newfoundland's Great Northern Peninsula. After nine years as a forest warden, he became a wildlife protection officer with the Newfoundland Wildlife Service. For seventeen years, he has devoted his efforts to the growth and conservation of the big game population on the Great Northern Peninsula. Under his surveillance, the moose and caribou populations have grown and prospered at an astonishing rate. As a game warden and a local storyteller, he has gained the respect of conservationists and poachers alike. Among his many achievements are contributions as a conservationist for waterfowl. He has made a hobby of raising eider ducks, and it has been estimated that eighty percent of all nesting eiders in Newfoundland developed from his original twelve ducks."

Barb just beams as we share and enjoy the morning chatting. She and Earl have been the best of friends for many years. Earl acknowledged as much, having listed Barb as a contributor to his first book, *Will Anyone Search for Danny*, published in 1986. It was an honor meeting you, Earl. Thanks, Barb, for asking your good friend to stop by!

Near dark now, supper is being held, awaiting the hunters' return. And just as dusk is descending, Kevin comes in. "How'd it go?" I inquire. "No luck," he replies, "but I heard a shot. I think Rob got a bear." Sure enough, in just a short while, Rob, Mike, and John return. Rob shot a two-hundred pounder!

Just before bedtime I answer my email for today. Just received an order for another shipment of my book, *Ten Million Steps,* from the Appalachian Trail Conference Bookstore. This has been a great day!

> *Fair is the earth behind me,*
> *Vast is the sea before;*
> *Afar in the misty mirage*
> *Glistens another shore.*
> *Is it a realm enchanted?*
> *It cannot be more fair*
> *Than this nook of Nature's kingdom,*
> *With its spell of space and air.*
> (Mary Clemmer Ames)

Tuesday—September 18, 2001
Trail Day—341/41
Trail Mile—5279/483
Location—Tuckamore Lodge and Outfitters, Main Brook,
Newfoundland

Barb has invited me to spend another day relaxing here at her beautiful Tuckamore. This is a no-brainer; I accept! And relax I do, spending time writing and enjoying the company of guests and employees alike. Later in the day, I watch as guides skin and dress Rob's bear, then the thousand-pound bull moose that Fred shot. These are very large animals, and the process requires the help of boat winches and scalpel-sharp knives. An electric chainsaw is brought into play to split the moose into "sides." I estimate there's enough meat from the moose alone to feed a good-sized family for the better part of a year.

Barb is a great host, and she and her professional staff spare nothing in assuring their guests are both comfortable and well fed. I've made another great new friend in Barb Genge. Trekking on tomorrow will not be an easy task.

*I never suspected that I would have to learn **how** to live...*
(Dan Millman)

Wednesday—September 19, 2001
Trail Day—342/42
Trail Mile—5318/522
Location—NF-432, trailside near NF-430, north of Main Brook,
Newfoundland

Another tank-stokin' breakfast at the "banquet table" next to the great room here at Tuckamore, then it's time for sad goodbyes as I return to the road. I'm hiking the eastern extreme of the Great Northern Peninsula now, heading ever north along Seal Bay and beside the Northern Arm of Hare Bay. The day begins iffy, quickly turning to misty mush. Thankfully, the wind remains at my back and the traffic is light.

Upon entering the Great Northern Peninsula—and all along, especially since passing Daniel's Harbor—I've passed by fenced vegetable gardens, strung in profusion, helter-skelter, all along the road right-of-away. These meager plots have been hacked, mostly out of the rocks, by folks living in the remote little villages. They've planted potato, carrot, beet, turnip and other root crops, with some cabbage and lettuce mixed in. Inquiring of these "farmers" as I pass, I've found there's nothing the least formal about selecting these sites. Locals simply drive along, pick a suitable spot (that's using the term loosely), stop, get out, and start grubbing in the rocks! The fences, made from every conceivable material (but mostly of waste slabwood, site-cut spruce, rope, and trashed fishnet) are intended to keep the moose out. Most attempts, however, have met with little success, the stunted greenery well foraged, the crop rows pretty much stomped down. The growing season up here is pitifully short, and it drops off quickly just the least bit north, finally amounting to less than thirty days around Cook's Harbor and L'Anse aux Meadows. The garden plots have also diminished to few and far between, and the natural vegetation is becoming very sparse and stunted. Here the tundra quickly and steadily drops, seeking the sea, as I, too, seek the sea—the end of these long and magnificent Long Range Appalachian Mountains, and the end of this unbelievable odyssey.

Late evening, as the wind continues driving the cold rain, my legs and back begin complaining about the thirty-nine mile day, so I pull off. It's moose-hunting season, and the hunters are out in great numbers. A warden stopped to chat earlier today and warned that I be cautious. He especially urged that I keep a high profile. "Don't camp in the bushes," he said. So, finding a wide spot by the highway, I call it a day. Here I quickly pitch and roll in, as the incessant, cold, relentless rain begins yet another pounding. Oh Lord, I pray, and you know and have heard the grateful thanks within my heart for the beautiful, sun-drenched days past—and for this day, too.

....don't pray when it rains if you don't pray when the sun shines.
(Leroy *Satchel* Paige)

Thursday—September 20, 2001
Trail Day—343/43
Trail Mile—5322/526
Location—NF-430 at The North Atlantic Adventure Centre &
Wildberry Country Lodge, Pistolet Bay, Newfoundland. Lyndon
Hodge, proprietor.

The rain kept me company all night, and it has yet to tire of me this morning. Comes a break however: time to strike camp and get going. Moving along now, I take what little joy there is in finding the wind less troublesome. The hunters and me, we're both out and at it again today; we're both on the road. I'm in the mush though, and they're out of it, creeping along in their warm vehicles, peering intently through smeared, steamy windshields, wipers flapping. The moose are the smart ones. They're nowhere to be found, probably holed up way back in the scattered and stunted stands of spruce, fir, and juniper.

I'm pleasantly surprised when, in a short while, I come to Wild-berry Country Lodge and Restaurant; there's been no mention of it anywhere in the guides I've been reading. Hey, the place is open, so in I go! Behind the reception counter looking up, here's another of those glad and happy, broad-beaming Canadian smiles as Lyndon Hodge, proprietor and chief cook and bottle washer, greets me. His welcome: "I got hot coffee and fresh muffins, you like some!" I reply, "Oh yes, sure beats the crumbed-up pack of nature bars I'm planning on rationing myself later this morning." Lyndon invites me into the dining room, where right by is a comfy sitting area, complete with a warm, glowing fire. Here I peel off my wet poncho and drop my sodden pack.

The entire front wall of the expansive restaurant is filled with glass, making a large picture window. And as the shroud lifts and the sun tries making a play, the picture to be seen out and across the way is a range of *hills* known as the Whites. As I look, Lyn tells, with a faraway glint, of the remote, high-held ponds there—that are teeming with trout and salmon. "It's too far, though," he says, "to hike in, get in a good day's fishing and hike back out, so I'm building a cabin up there, already took most of the materials up by snowmobile last winter." He then follows with, "You wanna go see?" Well now, that's all the coaxing I need. I'm still a day ahead of schedule to meet Mike Roy tomorrow evening. That's when we'll hike the remaining distance together from Gunner's Cove to L'Anse aux Meadows. Anyway, Mike had suggested I try hiking the White Hills some if I got the chance, and here's my chance! "Great, Lyn, let's go," I reply. Comes that glad, wide-beaming smile again as he lifts straight up. "Been looking for a good excuse to make a run up there. Let me get my daypack and some goodies. Be right back!"

The sun has pushed the mush out, turning the day-dial to bright and warm, and with the Whites luring us from the distance, we're on our way. Crossing fens and bogs, and on fresh-cut trail that Lyn's been working, we talk of our mutual love and great respect for Nature's fine work, and for Lyn's good trailbuilding. Soon we're into the climb—and out of trail, as we work our way through and along the spongy, moss-covered forest floor. There are many blowdowns and rocks, and the going seems slow, but Lyn is a strong hiker, and I find much joy in having company for a change.

Up beside a resounding, happy brook we go, soon to emerge beside a wide, sparkling lake. Near the shore is a little tumbledown cabin where we stop for a rest. Lyn is a carpenter by trade. The beautiful Wildberry Country Lodge stands as a testimony to his skill and handiwork. In his eye now, I see that gleam of childlike excitement again as he tells of his dream to build a snug little cabin by the lakes high above.

Soon we're climbing again, and the going is becoming increasingly more difficult. We're nearing the tundra now, the spruce and fir gnarled and stunted, this, the ever-present tuckamore. "Just a little further," Lyn says, as we continue groping and lunging through the near-impenetrable maze of tuck. "This guy's gotta be lost," I'm thinking, "He doesn't have a clue." But just past what seems a no-way solid wall of tuck we break out of it, and in just moments we're standing among the barren rock. Here, by this happy little brook that's making its way, opens one of the most delightful high-held ponds—just like Lyn's been describing. "The fish are here?" I ask. "Oh yes!" Lyn beams, "They're here! Follow me; we'll take the brook down just a ways to where it tumbles through the boulders and rocks. There we'll be in the spruce again. Come, I'll show you where the cabin will go!"

Down we stumble, down through the ledges and rock-jammed drop-offs. Here, we're in moss-slick riffles and rapids, groping down and past cascading falls. "Hey Lyn, STOP," I shout, above the ever increasing crescendo of crashing water. "You're kidding me about the salmon, aren't you? There's no way they can climb up through this stuff!" I'm hollering at him now as we plunge down through the veritable wall of tuck. Stopping for a moment, he waits for me. Comes that gleam again as he looks me square on, "They're up there," he whispers, "oh yes, they're up there!"

We're back in the woods now, and just beside the frolicking brook I stare in amazement, for here before me, where I've had a devil of a time even moving about, is this huge pile of lumber! Beside the lumber there's a bathtub, a sink, a roll of black plastic pipe, boxes of nails, and a water tank! "Holy cripe," I exclaim, "How in God's name did you get this stuff up here!" "Snowmobiles and komatiks—they're neat contraptions," he says, calmly. Oh yes, and what is a komatik? Well, that's another story, for another time.

Just as the sun is setting, we slog the last bog, wend the last fen, and we're once again back at Lyndon Hodge's Wildberry Country

Lodge. In the evening, Lyn runs to fetch a few cold frosties, then prepares the finest steaks for our evening meal. Oh my, folks, what joy, another great new friend, another remarkable day on the trail!

"Hey Lyn, know what? I'm coming back some day. Oh yeah, I'm coming back. When you get that cabin built, I'm coming back—and you and me—we're a-goin' fishin'!"

> *Thank God! There is always a Land of Beyond*
> *For us who are true to the trail;*
> *A vision to seek, a beckoning peak,*
> *A farness that never will fail;*
>
> *A pride in our soul that mocks at a goal,*
> *A manhood that irks at a bond,*
> *And try how we will, unattainable still,*
> *Beyond it, our Land of Beyond!*
> (Robert W. Service)

Friday—September 21, 2001
Trail Day—344/44
Trail Mile—5346/550
Location—NF-430 at Valhalla Lodge B&B, Gunners Cove, Newfoundland. Bella Hodge, proprietor.

What a memorable evening at Wildberry Country Lodge. Other guests came in, and we all relaxed by the fire, each recounting and sharing the joys of the day. A few cold ones, the warmth of a glowing hearth, the warmth of glowing hearts—radiating. What more could one ask!

The day dawns with mush all about (again), but the whole scene brightens thanks to a warm fire and a tank-stokin' breakfast, set and prepared by Lyn. I'm finally out and on my way ever north by nine-thirty. Thanks, Lyn, for your generous hospitality. But especially, thanks for your friendship! Your kindness will remain in my memory.

As I trek along today, and as the wind and mush keep driving, those bittersweet melancholy emotions descend upon me once more, feelings that can only come when nearing the end of such an odyssey. It's a sort of funky jetsam that drifts, creating a clashing backwash of feelings, feelings of doubt and forlorn despair, and yet, at the same time, feelings of joy and elated fulfillment. "Lighten up, *Nomad*," I whisper. Like my old AT hiking buddy Kevin would surely say, "Been there, done that, got that T-shirt." Oh yeah, that's better.

Lyn Hodge is one of those guys with limitless energy, a hundred projects going at once. A while back he renovated an old house overlooking Gunner's Cove near L'Anse aux Meadows. His mother, Bella Hodge, operates it now as Valhalla, an impressive B&B, I'm told. That's where I'll stay tonight. I've made reservations there for both Mike and me. I'll meet Mike somewhere along the road today, hopefully near Valhalla, and from there we'll hoof it on to L'Anse aux Meadows.

Another plan comes together; what perfection! Mike drives up, stops to chat, then continues on, no more than half a mile south of Valhalla! I arrive there momentarily and check in. Then in just a while, we're off toward the northern tip of Newfoundland, where the Vikings landed over 1,000 years ago, where they established the first settlement on the North American continent, and where began what we now know as the "New World."

The hike goes quickly, as Mike and I talk about these glorious Appalachian Mountains, and his plans for a remarkably grand Newfoundland Appalachian Trail, a trail to pass along and across these breathtaking Long Range Appalachian Mountains of Newfoundland. We reach L'Anse aux Meadows in the fading light, as the rain comes yet again. At the sea now, I linger, to slowly walk the very paths the Norsemen once walked, where brave Vikings looked back toward their home far away. I've dreamed of this moment for

months. What inspiration, to stand here now, after nearly a year of trekking over 5,000 miles of this great continent of North America. It's time to reflect on this odyssey, on this grandeur before me— scenes from time, scenes that are unchanging, everlasting. I sense the presence of those brave adventurers, travelers from long ago. As I stand in silence, they approach, then fade away, to return to the mystic sea. But they're with me, just as sure as I'm here with them. We are kindred, adventurers all—displaced and separated only by time.

Ahh, but where does time go. Indeed, where has it gone; why must it be so fleeting? Mike's car is nearby. Too soon, we hasten and turn from the Meadows, from the sea, as the gloom of this day gives in to the storm-swirled shroud of night. We load, buckle our seatbelts, and like the Vikings that linger beyond that mystic veil, we too, fade into the mist of time—and are gone.

NEWFOUNDLAND

Back in the haunts where the shadows, long cast,
Chase the far away corners of time.
Search there through the annals of centuries past,
For a glimmer of reason or rhyme.

Brave Norsemen in long boats set out on the sea,
Sails furled to the rush and the roar.
Each one of them bent with a yearn to be free,
None daring a look to the shore.

Sailed forth those great warriors on uncharted wind,
Toward lands where the sun seldom sets,
Thence tacking to port for a southerly bend,
Set they all, nary one with regrets.

Pitched up o'er the depths in the frightening grips,
Through the tumult of violence and rage,
Came men steeled in armour aligning their ships,
Into fear, their foe to engage.

True venturers they to the ends of the earth,
Where certain, fierce dragons kept wait.
Truth-testing their mettle, their valor, their worth,
Their destiny sealing their fate.

Yet from fleeting shadows, did images form!
Through the brine-crested, shimmering hue,
And out of the gale and the teeth of the storm,
The sails of their ships came to view.

Time-shrouded in mystery...Vinland of old,
Thought only a scheme of the mind.
Defiantly stand, where Vikings so bold,
Carved marks in the land of the wine.

Oh hearken that time to have lived, to have sailed,
As only Leif Eiriksson knew.
A journ' throughout history that all thought had failed,
Set his flag, 'cross the surf-driven blue.

Came they to new-found-land? Not likely, we're told,
To lands set adrift in the sky.
Where glacier-torn mountains so ancient and old,
Might have captured their minds and their eye.

This place? L'Anse aux Meadows, here puzzled about,
Speak fragments of history's truth.
And so to a world fil'd with wonder and doubt,
Revealed!...America's youth.

So, come forth ye doubters to Vinland's glad days,
To these meadows on Newfoundland's shore,
And witness a-mingling the centuries' gray haze,
America's past...Evermore!

Ahh, yet comes another, his story to tell,
O'er hills set apart from the sea.
From lands of a nation where millions now dwell,
To these hallows, where man was set free.

So stand ye true helmsmen, set wind to your sail,
Outbound on a journey anew,
And test your true mettle and fearing to fail,
And quit dreaming the doing...and do!

(N. Nomad)

Saturday—September 22, 2001
Trail Day—345/45
Trail Mile—5346/550
Location—Home of Boyce and Joanne Roberts, Quirpon,
Newfoundland

Mike and I had been invited by the Roberts of Quirpon (rhymes with harpoon), to come directly to their home last evening, to stay as their guests until the weather cleared and Boyce could shuttle us by boat to Belle Isle, the northernmost of the Appalachian Mountains to rise above the Labrador Sea. Not wanting to impose, however, as they already had a house full of guests (twenty-eight, in fact, twenty-three international exchange students, along with five counselors), we chose instead to stay at the Valhalla B&B in Gunner's Cove.

We're headed their way this morning though, as Boyce has insisted we come by for breakfast. And what a grand gathering and affair it is. Boyce and Joanne obviously have prior experience with this sort of chaos, as heaping plates of eggs, toast, pancakes, bacon, sausage, ham, and fried bologna (a local favorite) come, as if conveyor-driven, from their little kitchen. It's a sight to behold, watching these kids from Germany, France, Belgium, Denmark, Sweden, Switzerland, Japan, Thailand, Argentina, Ecuador, Peru, Brazil, and Australia wolf down the grub, unable to keep pace with Boyce and Joanne as the platters of food keep rolling out!

On the Roberts' porch, before departing for a tour of L'Anse aux Meadows, all gather for a group shot, me included. I'm then asked to say a few words. What becomes immediately apparent is the fact that these students have been well-versed in proper decorum. All listen attentively, none shuffling the least, as I recite a few of my ditties and impart what some believe to be the least degree of wisdom. I'm humbled as many come down to have their picture taken with me!

The rain has set in for the day, and the marine forecast, monitored at regular intervals by Boyce, is not good. He reports, "The rain and wind, with low visibility, will continue through tonight, and tomorrow doesn't look any better. Bring your things in, looks like you'll be here for a while."

The students have headed for L'Anse aux Meadows. Mike and I decide to follow, as the interpretation center and the sod huts were closed when we arrived in the evening gloom last.

We're soon at the center, where there is much to see and learn about the Vikings who came here, establishing the first settlement in The New World, over a thousand years ago. From a brochure, *Welcome to L'Anse aux Meadows,* prepared by Parks Canada, I quote: "As a boy in Greenland, Leif Eiriksson grew up hearing stories about a mysterious land of bountiful forests that lay to the southwest. In about 1000 A.D., he and his crew of 35 sailed forth in a knarr, a freighter that could carry about 25 tonnes of cargo. By way of the northern coastlines, the expedition arrived at L'Anse aux Meadows on the tip of Newfoundland's Great Northern Peninsula...Upon their arrival, the Vikings established a base camp from where Leif and his companions proceeded to explore to the southern reaches of the Gulf of St. Lawrence. They found vast hardwood forests, grassy meadows, rivers and coastal waters teeming with fish, and wild grapes—thus the name, 'Vinland.' Life and work at L'Anse aux Meadows is evident from the eight buildings the Vikings constructed...with sod laid over wooden frameworks. Each hall housed 20 to 30 people and contained rooms, which served as living quarters...The halls were steep-roofed and high, allowing smoke to gather in the upper reaches before gradually seeping out through a hole in the roof. While the Vikings had the technology to build a working community, that was not their purpose...They spent their time repairing boats that were damaged on the long trip from Greenland, and to facilitate exploration, but the exploration stopped after only a few expeditions and the base was abandoned.

Little was [is] known about the Viking voyages to Vinland. When the Viking (Icelandic) Sagas were translated in the 19th century, archaeologists became enthused about a possible link between North America and Viking culture...L'Anse aux Meadows is, to date, the only authenticated Viking site in North America."

Later in the day, Mike and I visit the historic Grenfell House in St. Anthony. Grenfell is revered throughout all of Newfoundland, a national hero. He was the first physician to minister to the needs of the people along the Labrador (the coast and the lands of Labrador are simply referred to as "the Labrador"). Grenfell was born in England in 1865 and received his medical degree in 1886 at the age of 21. In 1892 he came to see for himself the deplorable conditions suffered by the fishermen along the Labrador, spending most of his remaining life administering to the medical needs of the people here, setting up missions and establishing hospitals that remain to this day. Of interest: Percival Baxter, a name all familiar with the Appalachian National Scenic Trail will recognize, was a great friend of Grenfell. Being a very wealthy man, a philanthropist, Baxter aided and supported the Grenfell Missions until his death in 1969.

Also of interest, it was about Grenfell, the fisherman and the Labrador, that Earl Pilgrim (whom I've met and spoken of previously) has written his latest book, *The Captain and the Girl*, destined to be yet another of Pilgrim's Canadian best-sellers, a powerful historic novel I highly recommend.

In the evening, back to the warm home and the equally warm hospitality of the Roberts we go. The forecast remains the same, "More rain, wind and fog," Boyce informs us, "So, it looks like you're here for at least another day." My (not so happy) reply, "Oh Boyce, I so hope we can go to Belle Isle soon." Patience, old man, patience!

I'm so fortunate to have met these dear new friends, Boyce and Joanne Roberts. Thanks, Wallace Maynard and Barb Genge, for introducing me to these gracious and generous people!

After a wonderful supper prepared by the Roberts, all head out for a little partying. I stay in to do some writing. For once, I make the right decision!

> *All human wisdom is contained in these two words,*
> *Wait and Hope.*
> (Alexandre Dumas)

Sunday—September 23, 2001
Trail Day—346/46
Trail Mile—5346/550
Location—Home of Boyce and Joanne Roberts, Quirpon,
Newfoundland

The day dawns. As I lift my head to squint one-eyed from the bedroom window, I gaze into the drifting shroud, a ghostly cloak of fog, laden with wind-driven rain. Trailing this gloom, as I arise, descends upon me again that irrepressible funk which at times seems to cause such difficulty. No one is yet stirring, just me. I try fixing my mind. Where am I? Why am I here? As I stumble down the stairs,

I'm greeted by the jaundice eye of the living room TV, and from there, in low-pitched monotone, the voice of a still-stunned newscaster announcing the latest victim count from the September 11th atrocity.

In the kitchen, standing before the coffeemaker, I try collecting my thoughts—coffee, COFFEE! I know better than to look in the cupboard directly above for the coffee and the filters. For some reason no one ever seems to put them there. Still half asleep, I rummage through all the other cupboards and drawers, to no avail. Finally I return to the cupboard just above, there to find the filters, but no coffee. I know there's coffee here somewhere; Joanne had made pots of it for supper last night. I search the cupboards again, then the refrigerator. No coffee. Dang. "Where's the coffee!" I mutter, as if Joanne were here listening. Finally, still not fully awake and in near desperation (I need my coffee fix this morning), I fling open the freezer door. Ahh, you almost tricked me, Joanne, but I've found it!

The coffee does little to chase the funk as I venture out to hunch around the dock, to get a better take on the approaching day. This weather's been around a while, and it shows no signs of leaving soon. "Dear Lord," I whisper in prayer, "Why this, why now? I'm so close to the end of these mountains, so near the completion of this journey. Please, Lord, don't withhold your Grace from me. Might I need more patience and understanding? Please teach me."

What has happened to that calm reassurance I've carried deep within, that faith-filled confidence, knowing that I've been venturing ever forth with God's blessing? What is happening? What are these pangs of fear and doubt now, these trembling emotions of forlorn sadness and despair? I must control myself. I must suppress these feelings. I must regain my composure, my faith—a faith I thought was unshakable.

I hearken back to that fateful time in the Chic Chocs, at the base of Mount Xalibu near the end of yet another journey, Odyssey '98. I vividly recall the next day, when I finally made the climb successfully, to rest atop Mont Jacques Cartier. There, in the warm rays of the sun, and in the warmth of God's hand as he comforted me, I wept, full with shame for having doubted, much as the fear and doubt consume me now.

> *Don't be pushed around by the fears in your mind.*
> *Be led by the dreams in your heart.*
> (Roy T. Bennet)

Monday—September 24, 2001
Trail Day—347/47
Trail Mile—5352/556
Location—Home of Mike, Michelle, Heather, and Jessica Roy,
Corner Brook, Newfoundland,

In a recent email from Dick Anderson, Founding Chair, IAT, I learned that Will Richard, board member and official photographer, IAT, was in Newfoundland making a presentation at Plum Point, only a short drive away. So arrangements were made, and we went yesterday to meet Will and shuttle him back here to Quirpon to await fair weather along with me and Mike, and Boyce and Joanne and friends, in hopes of making the crossing together to Belle Isle.

As Mike and I prepared to depart to fetch Will, Boyce came with the latest marine forecast. "Conditions are improving," he said with guarded optimism, "tomorrow might be the day!"

As we journeyed to Plum Point, however, the rain continued, coming hard at times. On the way back, Will and his friend Bill, who had come along, began wondering why they'd let me talk them into this whole ordeal. By late evening though, as the Roberts welcomed yet two more guests to their lovely home on the bay, the forecast for good weather seemed to be holding.

Looking out early morning, the wind is still driving the mist and clouds, but Boyce says the forecast is calling for improved conditions throughout the day. So the decision—GO! We'll journey to Belle Isle today!

I find it interesting that some folks who've lived in one particular locale nearly all their lives have never ventured to places nearby, places that have attracted others from far and wide. I found this true while living in Florida, near Kennedy Space Center and the beaches, and while living at the base of Springer Mountain, the beginning/terminus of the famous Appalachian National Scenic Trail. Many locals had never ventured to these nearby places of interest. And so I find this situation again today. I have urged Joanne to come along to historic Belle Isle, for she has never been there! As I plead and as she looks at Boyce tentatively, at his urging we all board, including Joanne, and we're off to Belle Isle.

As we clear the harbor, the sea begins chopping, heaving and rolling our little vessels, pitching us up and into the haze where we remain momentarily suspended before being slammed back again to the rolling sea. Boyce and his friends Alec, Shawn, and John are all filled with excitement. These men are fishermen, the salty blood of fishermen from centuries past flowing through their veins. But these men fish no more. The cod are gone, and as the cod have gone, so have their livelihoods gone, a way of life their forefathers knew, that they knew, and they're left to wrestle with the reality of unfulfilled dreams. So it is good for them to be back on the sea today, to have a purpose to go, to challenge the rolling waves again, though it be for another reason and for such a short time.

And so we head into the wall of gloom, Boyce following Alec's prompts, GPS ever at the ready. To our stern the other little boat jumps and dives. As the waves that are crashing against Quirpon Island become faint in the ever-engulfing mush, to our starboard I watch as an enormous spout of whitewater erupts from the sea. "Did you see that!" I point, shouting to Boyce above the hammering sound of the sea. "That's just the waves hitting the rocks off Quirpon Island," he shouts back. "No, no, over there, look over there." I shout again and point more emphatically. "There it is again," I exclaim. Everyone sees it now, an enormous humpback whale, breaching, leaping completely free. It's must be over a half-mile away, yet it appears so close. The whale dives, only to breach abruptly again and again, there to remain momentarily suspended before crashing to the waves once more, causing spectacular eruptions, as if from so many cascading cannonballs. As the whale moves away and as we continue on to Belle Isle, Boyce smiles and sighs, "I'm sure glad he's over there and we're over here!"

The land is gone, and we see nothing but the rolling and pitching sea for a full 360. We proceed slowly into the mist to lessen our leaping and slamming as we search the gray wall for approaching hulks, large ships that ply these waters. We remain at this task for what seems such a very long time. Finally, as the shroud lifts for a moment, the sharp eyes of the fishermen spot a far-off ghostly image, the towering gray cliffs of Belle Isle. But just as quickly they disappear again under the blanket of fog that rushes to conceal them.

Late morning, as the island comes steadily into view, the day really starts coming around. Ol' Sol is trying to make a show; there's blue sky above and the wind and sea are abating. The forecast was dead on! Our planned landfall is an inlet part way up the lee side of the island. Here in a small rocky cove, and with a little luck, Mike and I hope to leap ashore.

As we near Lark Island, where the small harbor is located, the day has turned perfect. The fog finally lifts and is gone, the angry sea with it. The task now is to negotiate the "tickle," a narrow run between the rocky backbone of Lark Island and the stark stone walls of Belle Isle. Here the current is tricky. As Boyce wheels about to brings us through, a large swell, raised by the funnel-like shallows of the tickle, lifts us to its face, to swiftly accelerate and propel us down and forward.

In the relative calm of the harbor, we turn to watch the other boat as it too is lifted and pitched along in the same manner. Shortly, our attention is drawn to the rocks that jut along Lark Island. Here are many gray seals, perhaps ten or more. I lose count as they plunge to the water. I've never seen these pinnipeds in their natural environment; this is so exciting! I grope for my camera, but they're way too fast.

Adding to the excitement today has been the abundance of life on and above the sea. Hardly a moment passed without Boyce pointing something out to us. We saw many gulls, hundreds of them, including herring, kittiwake, and noddy. Also on wing were many shearwater, gannet, razor-billed auk, dovekie, murre (turre), jaeger, and eider ducks. But the most fascinating of all the sea birds were the countless puffins. What amazing little creatures these, with their plump little bodies, short, stubby legs, webbed feet, and the strikingly bright rainbow-splashed colors of their unproportionately large bills and hilarious eyes. We saw them mostly on the water as they moved away, amazing little acrobats, raising up from the sea to run up and down and along the waves, web-feet churning like little propellers, to come to rest again a safe distance away.

Boyce turns the boat to the rocks now as he motions to a point just ahead. "I'll get as close as I can; you'll have to jump," he says. Oh my, I don't like this! Even here in the protection of this little bay, the swells are still passing, lifting the boat not-so-gently two to three feet. They're breaking around the little point right where Boyce is trying to maneuver. And the rocks? The rocks are covered with green, ice-slick algae. As I look, I'm confounded. Where the face of rock rises I look to the depths, there to see it just as quickly disappear.

Boyce is a master at the helm. He inches closer. My pack is shouldered, my trekking poles dangling. I'm standing in the bow, one foot on the gunwale. As another swell comes rolling through Boyce shouts, "Now!" But I'm paralyzed with fear and cannot move. He backs away, not the least put out with my hesitancy. As he waits for me to regain some composure, I'm thinking of the old Indian Proverb, *Call on God, but row away from the rocks.* "We'll try again," he says calmly as he inches back toward the rocks once more. This time I steel myself to the task. Just as the boat lifts, Boyce shouts, and I lunge! Thank God, I'm able to grasp dry rock just above the green sliding board and I clamber up as Mike jumps and climbs right behind me. Heaving sighs of relief we turn to see everyone waving and cheering! We've made it; we're safely on Belle Isle, here to begin the last leg of this remarkable odyssey, the conclusion of a journey o'er the entire Appalachian Mountain range, at least as I've been told it exists on the North American continent.

Climbing along and by a cut in the cliff wall, the steep ravine of which forms Lark Harbor, we stop to watch the boats below as they move away to the north. From here we will also move ever north, across the sea-encircled tundra of this sheer-walled summit formed by the last remaining mountain that stands to hold its head above the Labrador Sea—we'll head north toward the lighthouse at the far northern tip of Belle Isle.

The sky is completely blue, not the least wisp of haze. To the west, the lenticular sea bends off to the horizon, and to the north stand the rocks and rolling tundra of Belle Isle. Mike and I pause to take in the moment and to shed a layer as the day continues warming, the sun working its soothing magic.

I'm learning that there exist many forms of tundra. Here is like no other in Newfoundland, at least that I have seen. For here, where the growing days are a scant twenty or less, what an amazing diversity of plants there are, struggling in the most anxious way as they stunt out their meager existence. At our feet, growing no more than two to three inches in height, are crowberry, blueberry, bunchberry (crackerberry), squashberry, dwarf birch, Labrador tea, Caribou moss (reindeer lichen), ground juniper, and bog rosemary. There's even aged miniature spruce and fir less than four inches tall. And in the bogs and fens there are a variety of both grasses and sedges. Walking along, the experience is as if touching one's toes to lush carpet. For hundreds of yards, between the jumble of lichen-covered rock and boulders to our right and along the sheer precipices dropping five hundred feet to the sea to our left there weaves back and forth near-acres of such a tightly knit mat, clustered and interwoven in a delicate manner, displaying appealing shades of pale green, burgundy, and crimson. Ahh, dear folks, I'm standing a scant six miles from the end of this journey, after many thousands of miles of journey through these timeless mountains. Yet even here, even now, these ancient and mystic Appalachians continue to reveal their remarkable diversity, their indescribable beauty, and their precious secrets—to me.

Nearing Wreck Cove, our attention is drawn to what appears the silhouette of a man off in the distance by the cliffs. However, as we stop to look closer, there is no movement. After descending and then climbing back from the deeply cut ravine that forms Wreck Cove, we are able to see the object clearly, a large cross set directly at the brink. On a plaque near the base of the cross/headstone is this inscription:

PLACED IN LOVING MEMORY
OF A DEAR BROTHER, AND SON FRANK,
WHO WAS KILLED IN A SNOWMOBILE
ACCIDENT ON JANUARY 9, 1964 AT
THE AGE OF 20 YEARS & 10 MONTHS
SADLY MISSED & NEVER FORGOTTEN
ERECTED BY FAMILY
MOTHER ETTA, SISTERS MAXINE & PATRICIA,
BROTHERS CLYDE & ROLAND

Here in these mountains and by this sea, as kin are, Boyce and Frank Roberts were family. Boyce had told the story as to how Frank, while traveling in the snow during low visibility, missed a turn in the trail leading to the south lighthouse, drove his snowmobile over the cliff, and plunged to his death in the rocks below.

What a rugged, beautiful place, Wreck Cove, yet what a sad place. I find it hard to get a good picture without the cross. But ahh, isn't the cross now part of it, the young man whose life came to such an abrupt end here, part of it? On the gentle breeze there seems to drift, and I can hear now the faintest melodic whisper, notes of a heavenly requiem. I take the picture, with the cross.

We turn from the cliffs to journey more inland, away from the sea. Here we find the more familiar bogs and fens, but there are no caribou or moose trails anywhere about. It is as if we are the first to have ever passed this way. Soon we hear a familiar sound, the honk of Canada geese, and we are at Three Island Pond. Clouds are building to the southwest, but the day remains very mild. The geese glide and land, and we linger to enjoy the beauty and serenity of this watery sanctuary held high above the sea.

The time has passed so quickly, as does this trek today. Cresting a gentle rise are we presented with the finality of it, for here we're standing at the northern cliffs that face the Sea of Labrador and the North Atlantic, and just below us now, the lighthouse.

Reluctantly I turn to descend beside the cliffs, moving ever so slowly with labored, hesitant steps. I'm thinking of the millions of steps over the thousands of miles and hundreds of days, for these now are the final steps. My friend, Will, is waiting to get a few shots of this old man as he comes to grips with the reality of yet another miracle in his life. Mike pauses to let me hike on alone, sensing the moment and the shudder of emotions that are now engulfing me. I stop many times, to look, to try and comprehend. These mountains are timeless, near as everlasting as anything man might ever touch or ever hope to know. In terms of time, they may prove eternal; indeed, they may have no end. But in terms of space, there is an end. The lighthouse, the rocks below, and the waves breaking o'er a reef in the distant sea: here stand the last vestiges of these glorious cathedrals, the Appalachian Mountains of North America.

Near the lighthouse, Mike congratulates me. I'm greeted with much happiness and excitement by Will, Bill, Boyce, and Joanne, and their friends John, Alec, Adian, Shawn, and Trevor.

The wind has come up, and clouds are moving in. As we linger, I can sense Boyce's uneasiness. "We need to get going," he says. Ahh yes, we need to get going, for I'm out of mountains, and we are out of time. So ends this remarkable odyssey.

> *For afterwards a man finds pleasure in his pains,*
> *when he has suffered long and has wandered long.*
> (Homer, The Odyssey)

Sunday—September 30, 2000
Epilogue, Odyssey 2000-'01

On our return trip to Quirpon, as we passed the southern tip of Belle Isle, the wind began pushing the waves and we had to slow to reduce the incessant pitching and pounding. Along the way, two separate schools of dolphin stopped by, racing and cavorting along with us for the longest time. They came right up, breaching and diving, a choreographed weaving of water and air in perfect harmony and cadence. Their first performance was to our starboard. Then they disappeared only to emerge on our port for a repeat performance there. Before departing and leaving us to our way, each school finished their show by diving directly beneath us, to scoot forward as if so many launched torpedoes.

We again saw many more eider duck, gulls, and happy little puffins. This occupied us, keeping the return trip short and interesting. Back at the Roberts' dock, their daughter Jaime and two reporters, Chris and Angela Hodder, a husband-and-wife team from *Northern Pen* newspaper and NTV News, greeted us. Once in the warmth of their lovely home, we were treated to another fine meal prepared by Joanne. After the interviews and the joy of recounting the day, it was time to bid farewell, but oh so sadly, to all the dear friends in Quirpon.

Late in the evening, Mike and I returned Will and Bill to Plum Point. Then we continued on to arrive at Mike's home in Corner Brook just shortly before dawn. What an action-packed day, that last day on the trail in Newfoundland, the last of Odyssey 2000-'01. It was one incredible time, filled with excitement and emotion, leaving lasting memories to cherish forever.

For three wonderful days in Corner Brook, Mike and Michelle took me in. They wined, dined, and entertained me. There, I had the pleasure of meeting Michael's daughters, Jessica and Heather, and we shared and enjoyed much good time together. There was also another interview, this one with the newspaper *The Western Star*.

On that last evening with Mike and Michelle there occured such a grand fuss, a sendoff for the old *Nomad*—of the highest order! I was ushered away to the home of Glenn and Susan Spracklin, where a "Screechin' in Ceremony" took place, an affair of which the revelry and hilarity epitomizes the happy and joyful nature of the Newfoundland people. And the two happy and joyful Newfies who arranged these goings on and this grand celebration? Why none other than Kevin Vincent and Andrea Spracklin, of course! Kevin's the young guide who led me across the tundra of Gros Morne, and Andrea is his partner who watched the shop and then served as delivery girl, bringing us food and refreshments as we descended the mountain by Rocky Harbor.

Waiting to greet me at the Spracklin home, along with Andrea's parents, were Kevin's folks, Calvin and Betty Vincent, and more soon-to-be friends: Tony and Mary Buckle; Vicki Basha, Andrea's aunt; Heather Wilcox; Debbie O'Brien; and Janice Kendall. I was no sooner introduced to these folks than came the official "Screechin' in Delegation," Frank and Jamie Hepditch, a husband-and-wife team otherwise known around here—especially after the sun goes down—as *Uncle Garge* and *Nanny Hines*. They were carrying all kinds of paraphernalia, and they headed straight for me making the damnedest racket. *Garge* was decked out in typical fisherman's garb: yellow rubber slicker and slouch, and rubber boots. *Nanny* came on as the old hag; an act she'd polished to perfection, all painted up in gaudy red lipstick and rouge. She limped pitifully, hunched over an old cane complete with bulbous horn. This she honked, in between leaning over the cane and shifting hands on hips, then to stick her butt out—and her tongue out, as she looked over at me following each unsteady shuffle. A delightfully disgusting performance! This, while *Garge* shouted a garble of demands and instructions in Newfie rat-a-tat.

Out came a washtub, in went five gallons of saltwater from the bay, then in went me, decked out in rubber slicker, rubber boots and all, there to repeat the words to some solemn pledge. The initiation continued with the downing of a jigger of cod liver oil chased with a jigger of Newfoundland's golden elixir (rum) imported from Jamaica and bottled in St. John's, thereafter to be called...you guessed it, Newfoundland Screech! All this to prepare the poor old boob (me) for the final and most indignant of all the initiation formalities, the kissing of the cod; this being a huge smelly dead fish with its mouth gaping open and with whatever it is that makes fish fishy dripping from it. Still standing in the saltwater, another jigger of Screech down to get my courage up, I managed the dreadful deed, and the old *Nomad* was officially declared a "Newfie!" All then cheered and hailed another proud member of "The Royal Order of Screechers." What a blast!

Newfies indeed know how to have a good time, and they certainly know how to make folks feel welcome! Ahh, and therein lies the crux of it all.

Above all, *it's the people*. For all along the way, it was the people that made this amazing odyssey such a memorable experience, from Québec to Florida, and back again—all the way to Newfoundland.

Thanks, dear friends, one and all. Thanks so much!

WHY GO!

It's the people, the places,
The pain and the trials.
It's the joy and the blessings
That come with the miles.

It's a calling gone out
To a fortunate few.
To wander the fringes
Of God's hazy blue.

(N. Nomad)

Nimblewill Nomad

RESOURCES

Organizations that construct and maintain trails that link to form Trail of the Ancients (TA) and the Eastern Continental Trail (ECT):

International Appalachian Trail (IAT)
IAT-SIA.org
info@MaineIAT.org
atlasguides.com/international-appalachian-trail

Appalachian Trail (AT)
appalachiantrail.org
atlasguides.com/appalachian-trail

Benton MacKaye Trail (BMT)
bmta.org
bmta.org/thru-hikers-guide
atlasguides.com/benton-mackaye-trail

Pinhoti Trail (GPT&APT)
pinhoti.info
hikealabama.org
pinhotitrailalliance.org
atlasguides.com/pinhoti-trail

Alabama Roadwalk (ALR)
hikealabama.org

Florida Trail (FT)
floridahikes.com/florida-trail
floridahikes.com/the-florida-trail-guide
floridatrail.org/long-distance-resources
atlasguides.com/florida-trail

Key West Roadwalk (KWR)
floridahikes.com/eastern-continental-trail

Index

Index

Index

The Wanderlust will claim me at the finish for its own.
I'll turn my back on men and face the Pole.
Beyond the Arctic outposts I'll venture all alone;
Some Never-never Land will be my goal.
(Robert W. Service)

Made in the USA
Coppell, TX
25 August 2022

82106219R00371